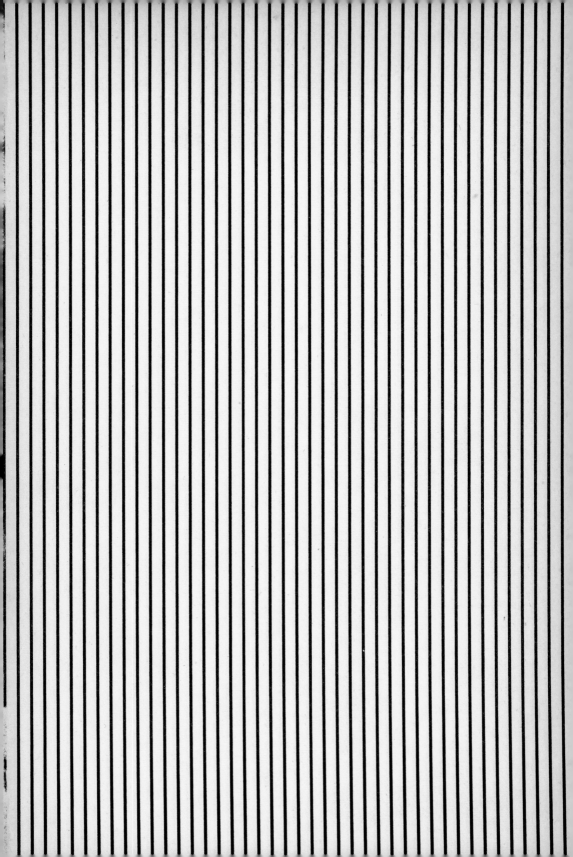

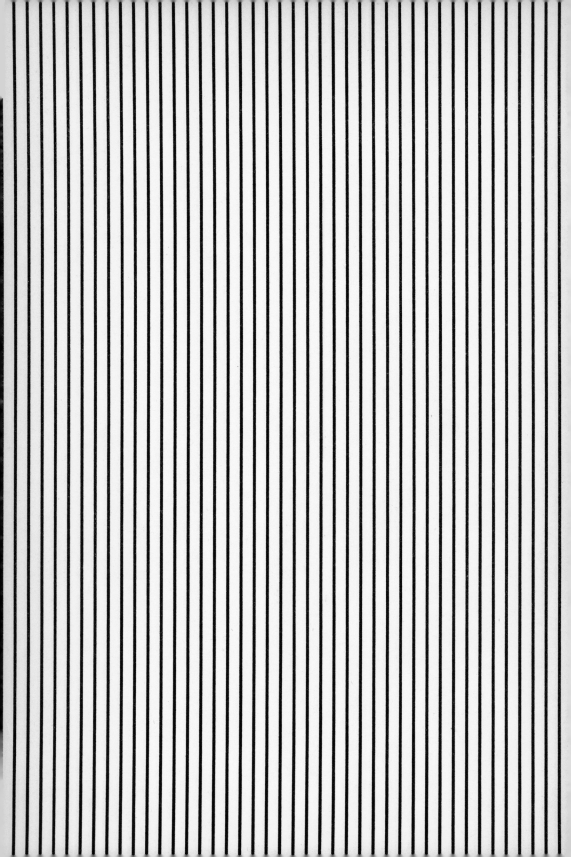

transition workshop

transition workshop

The Vanguard Press, Inc.

New York

edited by : *Eugene Jolas*

design: *Marshall Lee*

Manufactured in the United States of America by
H. Wolff, New York, N. Y.

contents

I.   paramyths:

2.   expansion of language:
_____

I. SONORISTS:

II. METAMORPHOSIS OF THE WORD:

3.   intercontinental poets:

4. spirit and language of night:
—————————————————

5. post-romantic documents:
—————————————————

● *transition workshop*

Eugene Jolas   *Transition: An Occidental Workshop*
   (1927-1938)

The aim of *Transition* between the wars was to forge a chain that would link together America and Europe. To me it was the realization of a youthful dream that had brightened my immigrant years before World War I: the vision of a linguistic and creative bridge between the countries of the Western World. I had spent most of those years in the crucible of New York, absorbing its universe of races and languages, and it had been my hope that my experience might one day help to span the Atlantic with a two-way flow of ideas between men of different races and tongues.

I started *Transition* in Paris, in April, 1927, with my friend, the American novelist, Elliot Paul, who remained associated with the review for two years, after which he returned to the United States. We agreed that the magazine should present an amalgam of Eur-American writing, and in the very first issue set the standard with the following table of contents: a sample from James Joyce's *Work in Progress* (later to be titled *Finnegans Wake*); an "elucidation" by Gertrude Stein; a translation of a story by the German expressionist, Carl Sternheim; a translation of work by the French novelist, Marcel Jouhandeau; narratives by three American writers, Kay Boyle, Robert Coates, and Ludwig Lewisohn; a translation of a story by the Swedish writer, Hjalmar Söderberg; translations of poems by André Gide, by the surrealists, Robert Desnos and Philippe Soupault, as also by the German expressionist poets, Else Lasker-Schueler and Georg Trakl. Early poems by such young American poets as Hart Crane, Bravig Imbs, R. Ellsworth Larsson, Archibald MacLeish, and Evan Shipman completed this list.

Almost immediately, *Transition* assumed the role of what it was to become later on; that is, a workshop of the intercontinental spirit, a proving ground of the new literature, a laboratory for poetic experiment. I had at the time, and I have still, an almost mystic concept of an ideal America, and I wanted to make of *Transition* a continuous manifestation of this concept. In a later essay (1929), entitled *Super-Occident,* I wrote: "I should like to imagine a Super-America which might be the idealistic intensification and sublimation of the Occident."

Our chief agent was Miss Sylvia Beach, owner of the famous Shakespeare & Company bookshop on the Rue de l'Odéon in Paris, publisher of *Ulysses,* and our good friend, who helped us through many difficulties. It was she who intervened with James Joyce in our favor when, as yet unknown to him, we envisaged the bold plan of printing serially the already famous Irish poet's new work. It was also in her hospitable little shop on the Left Bank of the Seine that we met many of the writers who later became contributors to *Transition*. Indeed, at the very outset, we were fortunate in obtaining the collaboration of writers who were representative of both continents, and their courtesy is still remembered with gratitude.

The reception by critics and readers was fervid, often violent, and the controversies raised continued for a full decade. The first of these controversies was due to the fact that the title was printed with a lower-case "t," for no other reason, really, than because Paul and I thought it might be fun to bait the critics with this innocent enough innovation; and we were right. Later, as we grew in stature, we reverted to the capital letter, but the change back was considered almost as irritating as had been the original little "t." There was no pleasing certain of the more captious of our critics.

The first issue appeared just two years before Wall Street "laid an egg," as *Variety* announced in its famous banner-line. Materially, therefore, the moment was not a propitious one. We managed to continue, however, with varying fortunes, and, faced with occasionally serious financial problems, were twice rescued by the generosity of friends and well-wishers. The last issue appeared in May, 1938. The by then inevitable approach of World War II made it no longer possible to concentrate on abstract laboratory problems, or to daydream about new forms in art and language. The totalitarian menace was looming on the international horizon, and I came more and more to feel that the writer could defend the spirit only by participating actively in the battle against the enemy. During its slightly more than ten years of existence, *Transition* had passed from an eclectic period, through a thoroughly exploratory one, into a final constructive period. The following writers, named in the chronological order of their association with the magazine, acted at one time as associate or advisory editors: Elliot Paul, Robert Sage, Matthew Josephson, Harry Crosby, Stuart Gilbert, Carl Einstein, James Johnson Sweeney. I should like to take this opportunity to express publicly my warm appreciation of their contribution towards making *Transition* possible.

Paris in the nineteen-twenties was a center of intellectual ferment, the undisputed capital of creation and experiment. *Transition* entered this moiling world with the avowed purpose of combining the various tendencies in art and literature into a single channel, which I once called "magic realism." All the narratives and poems we published bore this mark, and by retaining an antirealistic, antiphotographic bias in favor of the metamorphosis of reality we went on exciting voyages of discovery. We stressed work with a fantastic, dreamlike, apocalyptic trend and sought to give to expression a sense of the "marvelous." In fact, as *Transition* continued, we abolished the term "short story" in favor of the term "paramyth," because we considered that the narrative should be given a mythological prolongation. We also felt strongly that the notion of delimiting prose and poetry should be combated, for we regarded poetry as an existential entity.

In the beginning, Paul and I wrote resounding and, I fear, somewhat prolix editorials: "*transition* will attempt to present the quintessence of the modern spirit in evolution . . ." we announced in an early number. "We do not hold with the dogma that contemporary works of art cannot be evaluated. It is easier to judge a contemporary work because it arises from sources more readily and directly understandable. . . . We believe that although art and literature are, in many quarters, growing more definitely national in coloring and texture, their appeal is becoming distinctly international. . . . The reader is coming into his own." And again: "We need new words, new abstractions, new hieroglyphics, new symbols, new myths. . . ."

In looking back, however, it is probably no exaggeration to say that a new literary style resulted from this heightened esthetic awareness, a style that broke with the imagistic-objectivistic tradition in order to seek a symbolical form. This style, which derived from expressionist, dada, and surrealist experiments, flowed finally into the cosmological imagination of verticalism. Among its more daring American exponents should be mentioned Wayne Andrews, Hamilton Basso, Erskine Caldwell, Hart Crane, Kay Boyle, Morley Callaghan, Ernest Hemingway, Anais Nin, Katherine Anne Porter, Gertrude Stein, and William Carlos Williams. Among the Europeans, it gives me pleasure to recall that we translated the work of Franz Kafka well before the appearance of the Kafka "cult" [1]; that we were the first to translate Léon-Paul Fargue and St. John Perse,[2] and that the work of the surrealist group appeared in *Transition* when surrealism was as yet known only to a handful of *lettrés* in Paris.[3] Let us add that another of our most cherished aims—to bring about a sort of poetic *"Internationale"*—was

---

[1] The first time, in 1928.   [2] 1927.

[3] 1927. At this date, surrealism was still in what might be termed its heroic period. It had not yet discovered the Marxist ideology, nor had it shown esoteric or gnostic-mystic tendencies.

realized, and that we actually did publish the work of writers from some twenty countries.

Parallel with its efforts to extend the notion of reality was *Transition's* interest in language experimentation and, in this connection, we published the work of a number of British, French, Irish, and American writers who were conscious of the increasingly serious malady of language today. James Joyce and Gertrude Stein, of course, dominated the Anglo-Saxon experimenters, to whom were added such Europeans as Hans Arp, Robert Desnos, Léon-Paul Fargue, Kurt Schwitters, and many others. The sonorist iconoclasts appeared side by side with the pure neologists, and the attempts of yet a third group to find a "language of night" through dream writing were also numerous. In 1929, exasperated by the critical scorn and ridicule that greeted these innovations, *Transition* initiated a declaration of linguistic independence by publishing a manifesto entitled *Revolution of the Word,* which started a storm in the paper forests of two continents. Although this was undoubtedly the most controversial of the *Transition* manifestoes, there was another, written by the editor and signed by the following: Hans Arp, Samuel Beckett, Carl Einstein, Thomas McGreevey, and James Johnson Sweeney, which, under the title *Poetry is Vertical,* sought freedom from the purely materialistic conceptions then in vogue (1932), in order to find a nexus with cosmic and mystic forces. Numerous subsequently published documents—poems, stories and dream-texts—implemented this tendency, and certain attempts to find a language adequate for its expression were made, not without success.

Needless to say, however, our bellwether in the neologistic pilgrimage was James Joyce, substantial portions of whose new *Work in Progress* were published in *Transition* before it appeared in London and New York under its ultimate title of *Finnegans Wake.* For the sake of history, I should like to recall here that seventeen installments of the *Wake* were published in *Transition* between 1927 and 1938. The preparation of these installments was always exciting, for it entailed close cooperation with the author, who had to consult numerous notebooks, accumulated over the years, before he considered that any portion of the work was ready for publication. In addition to this already difficult task, he nearly always made last-minute neologistic additions which caused the French printers to tear their hair in desperation. Simultaneously with the work itself, *Transition* published the first exegetical essays on *Work in Progress,* which were later collected in book form by Sylvia Beach under the title of *Our Exagmination round his Factification for Incamination of a Work in Progress.*[1]

---

[1] Later republished by *Faber & Faber* (London) and *New Directions* (Norfolk, Connecticut).

It was from Paris, then, that *Transition* was edited during those confused years between the two great wars. A number of British, Irish, and
American writers were living there as "exiles"—an appellation I always
thought ludicrous—because they felt that the Seine capital offered the
essential background for creative work. In reply to one of the several
enquêtes organized by *Transition, Why do Americans live in France?,*
Gertrude Stein who, at that time (1928), was "dean" of exiles, wrote as
follows: "The United States is just now the oldest country in the
world, there always is an oldest country and she is it, it is she who is the
mother of the twentieth-century civilization. . . . America is now
early Victorian, very early Victorian, she is a rich and well-nourished
home, but not a place to work. Your parents' home is never a place to
work, it is a nice place to be brought up in. Later on there will be place
enough to get away from home in the United States, it is beginning,
then there will be creators who live at home . . ."

This paradoxical answer was only one of numerous extracts from
the work of Gertrude Stein published by *Transition.* Among the more
important of these were *Tender Buttons* (which had long been out of
print) and the first version [1] of *Four Saints in Three Acts* (later made
into an opera by Virgil Thompson).

Although for technical reasons [2] it is impossible to give pictorial rep-
resentation in this anthology to the very valuable contribution to *Transition* made by the painters, sculptors, and photographers of the epoch,
it should be recalled that certain of its covers were signed Picasso, Léger,
Miro, Kandinsky, Arp, Duchamp, Man Ray; that reproductions of the
work of these men appeared frequently in its pages, as did also the work
of such painters as Braque, de Chirico, Ernst, Gris, Grosz, Klee, Hélion,
Masson, Mondrian, Picabia, Tanguy, Rouault; of such sculptors as
Brancusi, Calder, Giacometti, Gabo, Moore, Nicholson; of such photographers as Abbott, Brugière, Powell, Man Ray, Sheeler; of such
architects as Moholy-Nagy, Le Corbusier, Nelson, S. Giedion.

The task of making this selection of representative material from
such a wide spate of contributions has been a particularly delicate one.
There were many others to be found in the twenty-seven numbers of
Transition which I should have liked to see included in such a miscellany, and only my agreement with the publisher to remain within
definite space limitations is responsible for their omission. It is my
sincere hope that this choice will, nevertheless, give a fair idea of what

---

[1] 1929.
[2] Most of the copper plates were seized by the Germans during their occupation of France,
and the photographs used were swallowed up in the disaster along with the other papers
that composed the *Transition* archives.

Transition tried to accomplish and—however short of the mark—what it did accomplish. The great period of transition through which humanity seems destined to pass so painfully into the as-yet-unforeseeable new era is surely not ended. I believe it is not impossible, however, that the review *Transition* may, for future generations, constitute an important record of certain of its earlier manifestations.

Stuart Gilbert *Transition Days*

The Archangel paused;

. . . .

Then, with transition sweet, new speech resumes.

(*Paradise Lost. Book XII.*)

Twenty years have gone by since a (for me) memorable afternoon when I had dropped in at that bookshop of happy memories for so many of us, "Shakespeare & Company" in the Rue de l'Odéon, and Miss Sylvia Beach handed me a small, green, red-lettered magazine, heartily commending it. Did space permit and had I the ability, I should like to indulge in a digression and try to reproduce something of the atmosphere of that unique bookshop, whence, from 1922 onwards, there issued yearly one or more editions of *Ulysses,* then unprocurable in America and England. Miss Beach's taste in books is as sure as it is boldly catholic, and amazing as was the diversity of the literature on shelves and tables *chez* "Shakespeare," you could count on certain qualities common to it all—adventurousness, originality, and challenge. My first glance at *Transition* showed me that here was a publication embodying these qualities, with the added advantage of being alive. Once published, a book is necessarily static; it has run its course and the binders have casketed its life (like that of a person who has had his day) between "boards." However living, perhaps immortal, it may be in one sense, it is never alive as a magazine—so long as it endures—can claim precariously to be.

On the opening page of *Transition* No. 1 I found:

> riverrun brings us back to Howth Castle & Environs. Sir Tristram, violer d'amores, fr'over the short sea, had passencore rearrived from North Armorica . . .

Memorable words indeed! That first installment of *Work in Progress* was not a landmark (nothing so terminal) but, rather, a dawn; and a stormy one, loud with a famous thunderclap in a dozen languages. Whenever I take up my *Finnegans Wake* (perhaps the only great literary work that is almost literally in motion everywhere, planetwise), and see the segment of its vast cycle which appears first in the printed book, my mind goes back to that spring afternoon in the Rue de l'Odéon.

One sometimes hears it said that *Work in Progress* "made" *Transition*—but, in some respects, the converse is equally true. The fact that James Joyce's work appeared by installments with a month's (later on, several months') breathing space, so to speak, between them, gave the reader time to study, digest, and assimilate it to some extent; whereas, confronted, out of the blue, by that portentous volume, *Finnegans Wake,* he might well have felt discouraged. Moreover, essays appeared from time to time in *Transition,* if not actually explaining Joyce's work (you cannot "explain" the *Wake* in the ordinary sense of the word "explain"), at least throwing light on facets of the huge, glittering, rotating fabric.

But the interest of that first number was not limited to one contributor, greatest though he was of living writers. Twenty-four names figured on the Table of Contents and the ensemble bore witness to a controlling mind, that of a daring and discerning *animateur,* a sort of Diaghilev of *avant-garde* literature (I use this inevitable epithet, which has cheapened with the years, reluctantly). That epoch of the twenties had an analogy to the buoyant nineties of the preceding century, and in some respects *Transition* was destined to be their *Yellow Book.* But it had an advantage over the Bodley Head publication in its greater independence and, above all, in the courage of its editor, Mr. Eugene Jolas. It reflected more truly and boldly the spirit of an age of transition, and was not hampered, like the *Yellow Book,* by the discretions of a publisher.

To understand how it all came about one needs, perhaps, to have been a youngster, or anyhow a youngish man, in that golden year of 1920; and—crowning boon—to have spent it in Paris. True, the fruits of victory were already showing signs of rot; but that was so much to the good. It confirmed the opinion of many intelligent survivors of the recent Crusade, who had escaped concussion by a hair's breadth, that the blessings of such martial exploits were somewhat overrated. They guessed—as Freud's forerunners, the Fathers of the Church, could have told them—that the true origin of that war had been an access of the death-instinct or, crudely speaking, Original Sin. And, like the Biblical children's, their teeth were set on edge.

Hence came the Dada movement, in some respects an outcome of what was then (naturally enough after four years' dosage of propaganda) regarded as these young men's bright, particular discovery—that of the futility of all doctrines and advertised ideals. The present writer had the privilege of being in Paris during that year of fleeting grace, 1920, and can remember the combined ferocity, hilarity, and pentecostal zeal of Dada meetings. Under farcical pretensions Dada followed a system of thought as plausible as Descartes', and its antithesis. *Non* cogito, ergo sum. In fact, Dadaism was quite the most *sympathique* of the many *isms* I have encountered during a long residence in Paris. Surréalisme, which grew out of Dada, was more doctrinary; perhaps its most important feature was the advocacy of a deliberate, total self-surrender of the artist to his subliminal self, and the practice of automatic writing.

As a matter of fact, the relation between automatism and the creative impulse had been fully discussed and interpreted by F. W. H. Myers many years before, in his great work on *Human Personality* (published in 1902). Freudian analysis is primarily therapeutic and, serviceable as it may be in that field, seems less applicable to the problems of esthetics, chief of which is that of expression. Thus, I would prefer the Myersian term "subliminal self" (i.e., the self *sub limine,* below the threshold of consciousness) to the more familiar "subconscious."

In the writer's creative impulse (the "subliminal uprush") problems of language play an important part. "Of all which we call genius," Myers writes, "or which we can ally with genius—of art, of love, of religious emotion—it is common to hear men say that they *transcend the scope of speech.* Nor have we any reason for regarding this as a mere sentimental expression. There is no *a priori* ground for supposing that language will have the power to express all the thoughts and emotions of man. It may indeed be maintained that the inevitable course of its development tends to exhibit more and more clearly its inherent limitations. 'Every language,' it has been said, 'begins as poetry and ends as algebra.' To use the terms employed in this work, every language begins as a subliminal uprush and ends as a supraliminal artifice." Through the successive issues of *Transition* (no "little magazine," incidentally, but a big one in every sense: importance, longevity, and indeed mere bulk) the interest in the problems of a language aspiring to transcend the norm of speech and to retrieve the poetic form of its beginning deepened and developed.

Perhaps the most dramatic moment in *Transition's* adventurous career was that when it launched the Revolution of the Word, in a famous manifesto (June, 1929) which, among other pronouncements, declared that "The creator has the right to disintegrate the primal matter of words"; "The writer expresses, he does not communicate"; "We are not concerned with the propagation of sociological ideas." The concluding article of faith struck the most defiant note of all: "The plain reader be damned!"—with Blake's aphorism appended: "Damn braces! Bless relaxes!"

One of the (to my mind) most admirable features of *Transition* was that, until its cessation on the eve of the war, it valiantly stood by this declaration of faith. In his brilliant description of life in Paris during the period 1926-1933 *(Paris Was Our Mistress),* Mr. Samuel Putnam mentions the "rumpus" created by this manifesto—which, of course, was far more than an expression of mere belligerency. Mr. Putnam and some friends issued a counterblast, "Direction," in which they pointed out (quite rightly) that precedents for the Revolution of the Word "were to be found in Aristotle's *Poetics,* Cicero's *De Oratore,* Horace's *Ars Poetica,* Castiglione's *Il Cortegiano,* and so on all the way down the line. Our basic protest, however, was against the overstress on form: 'We call for a return to content.' " There is, of course, no virtue whatever in mere newness, and the fact that the Revolution of the Word had been sponsored long ago by these great thinkers and writers was surely in its favor. The fundamental divergence lay in that last phrase, "a return to content," and, to my thinking, the significance of *Transition* (emphasized by Mr. Jolas in the subtitle: "An International Quarterly for Creative Experiment," and in sectional captions such as "Laboratory of the Mystic Logos") was that it championed the artist's right to express himself as an artist, without any claim to be the bearer of a message to the world or a caterer to plain readers. It seems odd that at a time when in the sister art of painting the picture that "tells a story" (like programme music) has fallen into disrepute, the artist in words should be expected to voice a message or serve up a slice of life, preferably *saignant.* Even in present-day France there are some in favor of what they call a *littérature engagée* (tendentious writing); though actually, experience suggests that the *homme de lettres* is usually far less qualified than, say, a factory hand, a businessman, or a grocer, to form any useful opinion on the material and social problems of his times. To these shoals *Transition,* ably navigated, gave a wide berth.

With the depression of the thirties a good many of the non-French writers living in Paris became, it seems, guiltily aware of being expatriate—the truth being, presumably, that they had struck root loosely in cosmopolis and when a sharp wind came it easily uprooted them and bore the weary wanderers back to their own native shores. Gallantly *Transition* rode out the storm. To the very end—the last of its twenty-seven numbers appeared in 'thirty-eight—it remained the *International* Workshop for Orphic Creation it had set out to be. Glancing through the list of contributors to the present collection, I find Americans, Englishmen, Irishmen, Canadians, Frenchmen, a Czech, Italians, a Welshman, Russians, Spaniards, a Guatemalan, a Peruvian, a Mexican, a Pole, a Rumanian, an Alsatian. For an "international workshop" of the kind, that Paris of the thirties was the obvious habitat—as it still is for the art that knows no frontiers. That international work *par excellence, Finnegans Wake,* was written wholly in Paris, where Joyce lived permanently from 1920 onwards, until the thirties ended in disaster. The same international—or interlingual—spirit permeated the contributions of Eugene Jolas; exemplified, for instance, in his *Intrialogue* (the "Intrialogue" is defined as an inner, trilingual converse of the mind), which begins:

"Chrismata?
Our ducts are full of heartling hours, denn unheimlich ist die
   asphaltnacht ohne Birken.
La nuit est devenue un masque-cuir.
Queer? Stop the hymnus!
And the Scala Paradisi?
L'avion anonyme part pour les cryptologues du sommeil."

The indignation provoked by the eleventh article of the Proclamation —"The writer expresses. He does not communicate"—was both extreme and exhilarating. The dictum (mischievously abrupt, we must admit) is explained in a booklet of much interest for the light it throws on the *Transition* movement: *The Language of Night* (*Transition* Series 1) by Eugene Jolas.

"To be sure, language used for purposes of documentation and exposition should use the signs that have a common denominator in the intelligence of the readers. There is, however, a state of mind that worries little or not at all if the masses understand its implications. It is in no way concerned with the problem of considering an audience. It is primarily interested in stating an aggregate of experiences that come from mysterious sources. It is a gratuitous state of mind. Words are treated instinctively as a fluid medium of vision."

There is really no reason why the imaginative writer should temper the wind to that unshorn lamb, the public. If he has trouble in getting himself published and if, when he succeeds in this, the response is poor—these are regrettable side-issues. The act of externalizing a creative impulse is its own reward. One of the great merits of *Transition* from start to finish was that it kept open house to creations of this type. A young author capable of remolding words and phrases into plastic form, of transforming the stuff of dreams into verbal sculpture, could count on a welcome in its columns. This is a far rarer gift than one might suppose. Though hundreds of typescripts must have come my way when I was acting as an advisory editor of *Transition,* and though many of the writers were obviously capable of striking word-effects, hardly any showed genuine emotion or felicity of expression. Too often the desire to be original at all costs had bemused the poet; the turbid masqueraded as the deep. But now and then a contribution reached us quickening that thrill of ecstasy or horror which only inspiration, an uprush from the self beneath the threshold, can evoke. It is significant that, as from the genial twenties we moved into the angry thirties, *Transition* turned, under the guidance of its editor, more and more towards mysticism; which has been analyzed into "a capacity to pierce through appearance to the underlying reality; a tendency to synthesis, to perception that all things are finally related to one another in a greater whole; a subordination—no more than that, emphatically not an abolition—of the intellectual side of human nature to the volitional; and finally an apprehension which is direct, not mediated or mediable through any intervening channel."

To express that direct apprehension new word-forms are often needed; not that words are lacking in the vast treasure-house of the English tongue, but that use and wont have blunted their edge, journalism and réclame have soiled them, they have been beslavered by the lips of public speakers. To give an example, during the last phase of the recent war British journalists hit on the word "shambles" as convenient for describing the effect produced by dropping explosive missiles from flying machines upon the heads and homes of people below. The associations of this word were apt enough, but soon it was overworked *ad nauseam;* indeed, letters of protest reached the newspapers. How much more telling was the Joycean coinage for a battlefield: "a bluddle-filth"!

Those *Transition* days linger with an unfaltering glow in the memories of all who shared in that great, perhaps Quixotic, enterprise, a venture almost on Elizabethan lines, when we watchers of the intercontinental skies saw now and again a new planet swim into our ken, and rejoiced greatly; when *Work in Progress* was still in progress, and, under the genial, clear-visioned leadership of its editor, *Transition* yearly advanced from strength to strength. The nucleus is dispersed, the "expatriates" have forsaken Paris—some of them for good, as it regrettably seems—but there remains, "so written to after times, as they should not let it die," this record of high, imaginative endeavor, a deflection of the trend of modern literature towards a visionary plane (whose keyword is of Mr. Jolas's coining: "Vertigral"), and a contemporary recognition, wider than in those combative days we dared to hope for, of the plastic element in language as a means of expression transcending the scope of mere communication and sufficient to itself.

Paris, 1949

1. paramyths

Eugene Jolas   *Paramyths*

The literature of the future will have no interest in competing with the possibilities for photographic and acoustic realism offered by the cinema, the radio, television, and similar mechanical inventions.

I believe, therefore, that the literature of the future will tend towards the presentation of the spirit inherent in the magic tale and poetry, towards the poet's exploration of heretofore hidden strata of the human personality. It will probably express the irruption of the supernatural, the phantastic, the eternal, into quotidian life.

This mantic night-world will need new forms for its expression. What is now known as the short story, the novel, the poem, etc., will give way to forms that are as yet unnamed.

I suggest the paramyth as the successor to the form known heretofore as the short story or *nouvelle*. I conceive it as a kind of epic wonder tale giving an organic synthesis of the individual and universal unconscious —the dream, the daydream, the mystic vision. In its final form it might be a phantasmagoric mixture of the poem in prose, the popular tale of folklore, the psychograph, the essay, the myth, the saga, the humoresque.

The language of the paramyth will be logomantic, a kind of music, a mirror of a four-dimensional universe.

transition 23

Wayne Andrews *The Evocative Treason of 449 Golden Doorknobs*

*dedicated to the perilous memory
of Don Luis de Gongora . . .*

Doomheavy, the innumerable headless heads of hair, billowing, evoked
a Portuguese embassy. They billowed to an eccentric rhythm, and the
walls of the rococo room began to palpitate like melted soap. Then
roses, petal-plucked, descended. "The atmosphere is very *before,*" said
April, and her forty-one flunkeys handed her their forty-one gardenias
bloated with black ink. Then April undid her hair, and petals grew on
petal-plucked roses.

April undid her hair (her languorous locks). All that music was very
Eastern.

Then April, who was beautiful enough to change St. Petersburg to
Leningrad, reclined on cotton sensuous enough to be forgetful. Her
eyes, soulless like empty cisterns, were as terrifying as clocks that would
never stop. Her breasts echoed a Japanese cascade, and in her sinuously
Directoire dress she yearned for an aubade.

But as stars were still painted that evening, an aubade would have
been unemotional. And as the Impersonal Past entered the room, the
heads of hair, crazy with fear, were like sea foam. Was it the Impersonal
Past who caused the mustache of Napoleon III, overladen with undue
rain, suddenly to appear on a red lacquer screen? And now little
animalets, half squirrel, half raven, raced over the imitation marble
floor that yielded to their pragmatic touch. There was fear in April:
she kissed the radium teeth of the Impersonal Past, who never grinned,
but only looked at his black watch. His hours raced: the animalets kept
an adorable tempo.

April then rinsed her hands in that "extraordinary" sea foam, April
then complained of the Impersonal Past, April then dismissed him,

30

gently; by lighting an unpleasant number of candles. The Impersonal Past departed, and the mustache of Napoleon III was only a display of undying affection for lighter sea dew and imperishable, and tragic, crinolines.

The entry, rather "solemn" to be sure, of 449 golden doorknobs cautioned a dreamheavy evening, and I listened to the inaudible words of April which thrilled the golden doorknobs into magic letters, so contemporary that one could no longer say
    "Evening has fallen"
without a betraying blush.

Meanwhile, the 449 golden doorknobs had arranged themselves before a worn but purple tapestry with appropriate years for the more human exclamation marks and other fragilities.

Although April's lips, a cool adagio, were as slow as the more penetrating pendulums of timepieces on less tragic planets, the doorknobs beat a warm allegro.

"My harmony at present is not tragic," pronounced April. "I only tie my son to energetic wolfhounds when I take him for a walk in these Northern parks. Those energetic wolfhounds, a most unsymbolic symbol, have drawn me to ignoble destinies. I have been complained of, and on that account the Impersonal Past pursued me. And then I told your watchmen of future gold in present banks that Peter was my son, which is true. And watchful men do allow the true when the quotation marks are not too flippant. So now I can take Peter, my four-year-old son, for countless walks in your ungentle parks, chained as he is to my comfortable wolfhounds. But that is not all my story, and as an ending, it is only worthy of newsprint.

"In these days when my living friends consider Jamaica an island, I love to recall one who cherished corpses there, and who made me know (and here the doorknobs shook before a suspicious rent in the tapestry) that a Palladian house with improved ruins is agreeable with centuried anguish.

"My Jamaican friend," and here April's Elizabethan years were moving, "cherished rare food in rare company; thus he re-created. Insufferably, he could only eat his baroque banquets with baroque barons. And thus he ate alone. He ate alone at his dining table with the wax and bloated figures of the Second Empire, who ate their wax food as crunchingly as rain falling on the charred wreckage of the Tuileries. True, these wax figures had been scorched, and some singers declined to sing to so meticulous a gathering. But I was fascinated by the ashlike and falling bits of the ceiling enamel which daintily sheltered the more obviously bald men, wax though they were.

"In those days the Jamaican moonlight never shone for fear of the somber peace of my torrential hair. But I knew that I could never be a swoonful singer without certain knowledge that Bismarck, that suit of armor filled with graveled sand, would never approach the desired tempest of our dreams. But as my Jamaican friend knew that
        'those ghosts of beauty wand'ring here reside,'
he sensed that Bismarck was as fated to them in Jamaica as in the clammy reality of a century. His watch, it is true, ran in mechanical time at the mere thought of Bismarck's arrival, and he realized his incomplete destiny. Still, he forbade English to be spoken, as he was aware that that uncarved and ponderous statue was most liquorish after its advantage when it spoke that language.

"But on afternoons when the cringing cypress shadows made my Jamaican friend forget the watery boots of the man after Sedan, my Jamaican friend understood that in a world in which the depth of cool pools was not mysterious, the spirit of the baroque would always be ill at ease. For the depth of cool dank cisterns on decaying autumn afternoons is the one solitary exception to the brown dullness of all that is actual. So he arranged a gentle island for me in the middle of a green lake, lit by purple sea lamps. Then he himself sat on the too downy shore beside an essentially sensually real statue of Eugénie. Then I sang.

"One dawn, when even an aubade as antique as an aria of Lully seemed contemptuously new to the fleet floating island and the immersed sea lamps, I was singing some of the unknown songs of Couperin in my then torturous soprano. But so frenzied was my Jamaican friend, so ready to swoon beside Eugénie, that he cried out (in English): 'Agonizing.'

"Suddenly. Then we both heard a crunching walk on the polite paths and allées that led to the estate. At first we thought it might have been one of his companions at the table, treading softly our soft sands at dawn. But it was not a walk, but a march. So we knew that it was not a spirit that was thus treading the uncrunched allée, but a Teutonic reality. Bismarck! Did any nightingale in any sonnet ever noon so real a word?

"And then what sea wrack wrecked our Jamaican dreams!

"Later that morning, when, by dint of American swimming, I at last reached the pathetic shore, I found that my Jamaican friend was already a scorched and bloated and wax figure, like his guests hungry only for wax food. Already the essentially sensually real statue of Eugénie had crumbled into the green lake, already the sea lamps had gone out, already my island had sunk beneath lakeless waves.

"And already, from the mansion, green and red flames dismayed the Jamaican sky."

And now the heads of hair clouded April from my sight. I only heard:

"Happy the man, whose wish and care
A few paternal acres bound,
Content to breathe his native air
In his own ground.
Whose herds with milk, whose fields with bread . . . ."

transition 23

Miguel Angel Asturias   *Legend of the Tattooed Girl*[1]

Master Almendro[2] has a pink beard. He is one of the priests whom white men used to touch, believing him to be made of gold, for he was so richly dressed. He knows the secret of healing plants, the vocabulary of the obsidian—the stone that talks—and can read the hieroglyphics of the constellations.

He is a tree that was born one day in the wood where it stands, without anybody having sown it, as if carried there by phantoms. The tree that walks. . . . The tree that counts four hundred days to the year by virtue of the moons it has seen; because it has seen many moons, like all trees, and was already old when it came from the Land of Abundance.

When the moon of the Owl-Fisher (which is the name of one of the twenty months of the year of four hundred days) was full, Master Almendro divided his soul among the different roads. Four were the roads, and they went in opposite directions towards the four uttermost ends of the sky. The black end: conjuror's night. The green end: spring storm. The red end: Guacamayo, or tropical ecstasy. The white end: promise of new lands. Four were the roads.

---

[1] *Leyendas de Guatemala:* Editiones Oriente (Madrid).   [2] Almond tree.

—Road, little Road! . . . said a white dove to the white Road, but the white Road did not listen. The dove wanted the road to give her the soul of the Master, which heals dreams. For doves and children suffer from this malady.

—Road, little Road! . . . said a red heart to the red Road, but the red Road did not listen. The heart wanted to distract the attention of the road, so that it should forget the soul of the Master. Hearts, like thieves, do not return forgotten things.

—Road, little Road! . . . said a green grapevine to the green Road, but the green Road did not listen. The grapevine hoped that with the Master's soul the road would reduce its debt of leaves and shadows.

—How many moons were the roads on the way?

—How many moons were the roads on the way?

The swiftest of them, the Black Road, to which nobody spoke on the way, stopped in the town. It crossed the square to the merchants' quarter where, in exchange for a moment of repose, it gave away the soul of the Master to the Merchant of Priceless Jewels.

It was the hour when white cats roam about from place to place. Admiration of rosebushes! The clouds were like washing hung on the line of the sky.

When the Master learned what the Black Road had done, he left his vegetal garments in a brook rising under the moon, and, blushing like an almond blossom, resumed human form and set out towards the town.

At the end of the first day he arrived in the valley as twilight began to fall, just at the hour when the herds come home. He talked with the shepherds, who replied to his questions in monosyllables, astonished, as before an apparition, by his green tunic and his pink beard.

On reaching the town he wended his way westward. Men and women were standing about the public fountains. The water sounded like kisses as it filled the jugs. And led on by the shadows, he found in the merchants' quarter the part of his soul which had been sold by the Black Road to the Merchant of Priceless Jewels. The Merchant kept it in the bottom of a crystal casket with golden locks.

Without losing time, he went up to the Merchant, who was smoking in a corner, and offered him a hundred measures of pearls for it.

The Merchant smiled at the Master's folly. A hundred measures of pearls? No, his jewels were without price.

The Master increased the offer, for merchants refuse until their demands are met. He would give emeralds the size of a grain of corn, hundreds of bushels of them, enough to form a lake of emeralds.

The Merchant smiled at the Master's folly. A lake of emeralds? No, his jewels were without price.

The Master would give him amulets, a doe's eyes to bring on rain, feathers against the storm, *mariguana* [1] to mix with his tobacco.

The Merchant refused.

He would give him enough precious stones to build a fairy-tale palace in the midst of the emerald lake!

The Merchant refused. His jewels were without price, and besides—why prolong the parley—he needed this little bit of soul, to exchange it in a slave-market for the most beautiful slave-girl of all.

So everything was of no avail. It was of no avail that the Master made handsome offers, or avowed his desire to recover his soul. Merchants are heartless.

A fine thread of smoke separated reality from dream, the black cats from the white cats, and the Merchant from the strange buyer who, as he left, shook his sandals on the threshold. Dust brings ill-luck.

After a year of four hundred days—according to the legend—the Merchant was traveling the roads of the Cordilleras. He was returning from distant lands, accompanied by the slave-girl bought with the soul of the Master, by the flower-bird, whose beak changed honeydrops into hyacinths, and by a suite of thirty attendants on horseback.

— You cannot picture, said the Merchant to the slave-girl, as he reined in his mount, what your life will be in the city! Your house will be a palace, all my servants will be at your orders, and I the least among them, if such is your demand.

— Down there, he continued, half of his face bathed in sunlight, everything will be yours. You are a jewel and I am the Merchant of Priceless Jewels. Your worth is that of a bit of soul I refused to exchange for a lake of emeralds! . . . . Together in a hammock, we shall see the sun set and the day break, doing nothing, only listening to the stories of a crafty old woman who knows my destiny. My destiny, she says, is in the fingers of a giant hand; and she may also discover yours, if you ask it.

The slave-girl contemplated the soft colors of the landscape, shading off into blues that the distance, in turn, made indistinguishable. The trees embroidered a whimsical design from a woman's blouse along the roadside. The birds gave the impression of flying in a state of sleep, without wings, in the tranquillity of the sky. And in the granite silence, the panting of the animals climbing uphill took on a human sound.

The slave-girl was naked. Her black hair, like a snake, fell in a single coil over her breasts and down to her knees. The Merchant was clad in gold, and from his shoulders hung a coat of goats' wool. Sick with malaria and love, to the chill of his body was added the trembling of

---

[1] A narcotic used by the American Indians.

his heart. And the thirty mounted attendants seemed in his eyes like the figures in a dream.

Suddenly, big isolated drops of rain sprinkled the road. Far off in the valley could be heard the cries of the shepherds, rounding up their herds through fear of the approaching storm. The horses hastened their pace in order to reach shelter, but there was not time enough. After the big drops, the wind began to lash the clouds, doing violence to the forests until it had reached the valley, which hastily donned its mantle of dripping mist. The first lightning flashes illuminated the landscape, like those of a mad photographer taking snapshots of the storm.

The horses fled like objects of terror, with reins broken, wild legs galloping, manes in the wind, and ears laid back. A false step on the part of his mount sent the Merchant rolling at the foot of a tree, which, struck by lightning at that very moment, seized him with its roots as a hand picks up a stone, and threw him into the abyss.

Meanwhile, Master Almendro, who had remained lost in the town, was walking the streets like a madman, frightening the children, collecting refuse, talking with donkeys and cattle and ownerless dogs, all of which, in his sight, together with man, formed a collection of sad-eyed animals.

— How many moons were the roads on the way? he asked the people from door to door. But they shut themselves in without answering, taken aback, as before an apparition, by his green tunic and his pink beard.

And after much time had passed, having questioned everybody, he stopped before the Merchant's door and asked the slave-girl, who alone had survived the storm:

— How many moons were the roads on the way?

The sun, poking its head from out the day's white shirt, effaced on the gold-and-silver-studded door the back of the Master and the brown face of her who was a little bit of his soul, the jewel he had not been able to purchase with a lake of emeralds.

— How many moons were the roads on the way?

Curled up under the lips of the slave-girl, the answer hardened there, like her teeth. The Master remained silent with the insistence of a mysterious stone. The moon of the Owl-Fisher was full. Silently, at the same moment, they bathed their faces with a mutual glance, like two lovers who have been parted and suddenly meet again.

The scene was disturbed by abusive noises. They were arrested, in the name of God and the King, he for being a sorcerer, she for being demented. They went to prison, between a double row of crosses and swords, the Master with his pink beard and his green tunic, and the slave-girl clothed in flesh so firm that it seemed to be made of gold.

Seven months later, they were condemned to be burned to death on the public square. On the eve of the execution the Master approached the slave-girl and with his thumbnail tattooed a little boat on her arm, saying as he did so:

— By virtue of this tattooing, Tatuana, you will be able to flee each time you find yourself in danger, as you will flee today. My will is that you be free, like my thought; draw this little boat on the wall, on the ground, in the air, wherever you will. Close your eyes, step into it, and go away. . . .

— Go, for my thought is stronger than a clay idol molded with *cebollin*.[1]

— For my thought is sweeter than the honey of the bees who feed on the *suquinay* [2] flower:

— For my thought is that which becomes invisible!

Without losing a moment, the Tattooed girl did what the Master had said: she drew the little boat, closed her eyes, and stepped into it. The little boat began to move, and the young girl was able to escape from prison and death.

And the following morning, which was the morning set for the execution, the *alguazils* found in the prison a withered tree on whose branches were two or three little almond blossoms, still pink. . . .

Translated from the Guatemalan
by Adam F. Flecker

transition 21

Hamilton Basso   *Rain on Aspidistra*

Gruelbubbling, the tightthroated protests not mine, the independent resentment of a laryngeal sphincter undaunted by their willimposing

---

1 The clay idols are mixed with *cebollin* leaves, which makes them harder.
2 Tree with heavily scented white flowers.

een which, accomplishing an escape from calcium strictures, wave merry tendrils of silver-splattered fire, a dankstill pool suspended beneath the spongy engineering of identical lungs.

> *segments of small-manymouthed-sucking detect*
> *the trickle of moisture in air-sacs while eyes*
> *truantlike return while he shakes his bald and*
> *gleaming and unfamiliar heed. Nicht wahr?*

I am suddenly in flight, heelleadenladen, sought by fiery silver-splatter and the weeping echoes of fear (the galvanized beard of St. Vincent de Paul), a grayslithery scurry into the mouthlike bubbles of restless discontent.

The sheer dark wall is eloquent and I detect familiar shapes and forms, young ambitions and determinations abandoned stillborn, caught flooted in the seashapened rook in all their young and helpless suffering.

I remember the vortices of young designs, the river of skulls and blood, all the slithering fish opening their thorny mouths to murmur patriotic songs.

Protest is futility, the Omnipotent Will is a shuttery succession of stars and bars *(Dixie, pianissimo, beyond the capitol hill)*. I sink peacefully into the dilkwarm sea.

Secret polyparian forms brush my face with kataplectic arms.

Secret polyphagous anemones lash my body with electric fire.

Secret polymorphous monsters lift me gently through the aperture that bears the mark of Satan's hoove, his gentle, wise, sensitive face peering like a companycurious child.

He is a gentleman and I like him. He has the look of a Southerner. He is a linguist and speaks ten languages. He speaks hissingly with an Alabama drawl.

"Even then I must have interpreters," he says.

"That's easy to understand," I say, "I can understand that."

He offers me a position but I decline.

"You must not misunderstand me," I say, "I am entirely in sympathy with what you are doing. I would like to help you in your inspired work. Despite the growth of atheism, which my good friend the Bishop of Blune denies, imagine that, imagine denying the growth of atheism, the man is a menace to society he *lives* to DENY, he denies that black aphids and red spiders have attacked my garden and that my favorite frog was startled by an iMACulate CONCEPTION the man is a chronier he is but what, what were we saying, it was about the bishop of bLUTE or was it the bIsHOP of Tulbe he baptized me didn't you know, upon my tender head the divine significance of his watery hand."

Here we are interrupted by a Blueridged Victoria (even to her liquid chin she resembles Our Late and Great and Glorious Queen) she darts out a flavforked tongue to demand if I, with the ignorance of the Young, expect His EXCELLENCY to remember even the birth of all his potential subjects much less their christenings, the very Idea. But his eXellenCy, who is a GENTLEMAN if nothing else, plants his hoove upon her soluble rump and she becomes an irate mauve shadow which, interrupting a ray of bass light directed upon a photo-electric cell, becomes a sampler, Done By Twinkle, age 2, GOD BLAST OUR HAPPY HOME.

"I have always admired that sentiment," he says, offering me his hydrostatic tail to spark a cigarette which I accept gratefully from an offering shade. "Now what were we saying before we were so rudely interrupted."

I hasten to explain but I am a ragged volume of Sidney's Aphorisms (pages 94-95 *et seq*). "It has been sayed that the abolition of duelling would multiply affronts and that the Messiah of the Gospel manifests this one and the Prophet of the Groan the other. From these vues it will be weadily ganted that mltry & nvl veterans esteem their vertues and be frndly wthot facieties."

> *This disturbs me for I am no militarist and my present incar-*
> *ceration cannot be reconciled with the fluid nature of my mind*
> *which slips across the rocks at Toxaway and drifts through*
> *the French Broad Valley splashing across the waterwheels*
> *resentful of the puny skill of man which captures my own*
> *swirling strength so that wishes may rise like Pandora's evils*
> *from wishing bibles of enormous ugliness.*

So I struggle to free myself and command an army of albino worms to organize an attack upon the hinges. They push slowly forward, like Halleck after Shilch, erecting parallels and mounting field pieces. The hinges are greatly brave, they have taken the sacred hinge oath, Death before DisHonor. The siege lasts for seventeen weeks and then the hinges retreat during the night taking away all their stores, ammunition, cannon, and supplies. It is a great hinge victory, but Jefferson Davis, weeping on Varina's shoulder, assumes command of the army which is immediately suffocated by Ben Butler's smell.

I am rejoicingly free but have lost all awareness of my former identity. I wander on the mountains, which I love, listening to the sound of the waterfalls. The sun sets, striking the rocks with bronze, and beyond the sun is the glacial purity of the sky. Little houstonias glow like star-splinters between the rocks of Carthaginian bronze. Somewhere a bird sings, dropping notes into the utter quiet and they resolve themselves into bright metaphors which fall into the rhododendrons with the sound of fragile bells. I pick them up and they are very beautiful and I put them by for a leaner time.

I climb the mountain, reaching the glacial coldness of the sky, little rocks are loosened and fall like nuggets of hail, but the path becomes the attic stairs of my old home and in the attic Jeb Stuart waits for his horse to be shod. He is brushing the plume of his hat and his sash brightens the attic like a golden comet.

"I am going to die tomorrow," he says.

"Tell me," I say, "what kind of person was Jefferson Davis?"

He laughs, and his booming laughter reaches the frozen ears of the piquets and they are inspired by his tremendous laughter and raid the Federal camp and bring in General Grant in his full-dress uniform. He smells of hides and his coat is unbuttoned and he is very drunk. The piquets take off his full-dress uniform and robe him in a faded wrapper and General Grant dances a minuet while Longstreet combs his beard and recalls amateur theatricals in Mexico.

> *She sat in the sun, a wrinkled crone, living in the utter purity of the mountain sky, with gnarled hands that were working before she was born, a spinner in the sun, adorning prosaic cloth with the poetry of stars and moons and Saturn's rings, of brilliant red and noble blue, descending, on the outer edges, to the Phoenician melancholy of inspired purple. She belongs to the mountains, to the clean reaches of the upper air, the bright core of her soul is rooted in the unyielding rock. She fills me with a sense of notbelonging. I am of the lowlands, of the swamps, of heavy nights and relentless rain and a hungry hound baying at the red moon across the undulations of the levee.*

The great river flows sullenly through the night, filling the darkness with an arrogant sound, sucking at the pilings of the wharves. The ferryboats quiver with their own exertions, ferrylights are yellow spangles spewn from grinning wheels. And within myself there are lights to be seen, hung like the Simutu lanterns at a garden fete, along the brittle ladder of my bones, and the sudden fury of volcanic fire leaping across my eyes, but here no lonely cry of river tugs nor the great Symbol, which is no symbol, since there can be nothing so terrific, so overwhelming, in our modern lives.

I creep humbly down to the willow trees and lie on my back by the river, the river voices an arrogant sound, and watch a clumsy formation of red clouds enter like Fifi's Trained Pony Troupe upon the three-ringed sky. The Catholic education of my apprenticeship emerges from the shapelessness of experience and achieves the definity of a dripping priest intoning the commemoration of the dead.

>   Memento etiam, Domine, famulorum, famularunque tuarum Violet and Ivy qui nos praecesserunt cum signo Fidei, et dormiunt in somno pacis.

He joins his hands and prays, rumguttingly, O Violet, O Ivy, outspreading his troutwhite puffy palms as he proceeds Christomnibusemper.

And now, while empty sound signifies thunder, the red clouds, pregnant with wine and blood, are ridden by all the Confederate Generals about the ring of stars, cavorting gaily with ribands of silver and blue until, outraged by the gutrumblingly graylord gray nothingness of his unctuous tone, they pour down the blessing of wine and good saints blood that beat with eventual understanding upon the taut canvas of my mind.

transition 22

Samuel Beckett   *Assumption*

He could have shouted and could not. The buffoon in the loft swung steadily on his stick and the organist sat dreaming with his hands in his pockets. He spoke little, and then almost huskily, with the low-voiced timidity of a man who shrinks from argument, who can reply confidently to Pawn to King's fourth, but whose faculties are frozen into bewildered suspension by Pawn to Rook's third, of the unhappy listener who will not face a clash with the vulgar, uncultivated, terribly clear and personal ideas of the unread intelligentsia. He indeed was not such a man, but his voice was of such a man; and occasionally, when he chanced to be interested in a discussion whose noisy violence would have been proof against most resonant interruption of the beautifully banal kind, he would exercise his remarkable faculty of whispering the turmoil down. This whispering down, like all explosive feats of the kind, was as the apogee of a Vimy Light's parabola, commanding undeserved attention because of its sudden brilliance. The actual imposition of silence by an agent that drifted off itself into silence a few tables away was merely the easy climax of a long series of subtle preparations: all but imperceptible twitches of impatience, smiles artistically suppressed, a swift affection of uninterested detachment, all finely produced and thrown into the heat of the conflict, so that the most fiercely oblivious combatant could not fail to be neatly and intolerably irritated. Then, when his work had been done and an angry lull was imminent, he whispered. As with all artists, this casting of an effect in the teeth of his audience was the least difficult part of his business; he had been working hard for the last half hour, and no one had seen him; that long chain of inspired gesture had been absorbed unconsciously by every being within the wide orbit of his control, and accepted as normal and spontaneous. To avoid the expansion of the commonplace is not enough; the highest art reduces significance in order to obtain that inexplicable bombshell, perfection. Before no supreme manifestation of Beauty do we proceed comfortably up a staircase of sensation, and sit down mildly on the topmost stair to digest our gratification: such is the pleasure of Prettiness. We are taken up bodily and pitched breathless on the peak of a sheer crag: which is the pain of Beauty. Just as the creative artist must be partly illusionist, our whispering prestidigitator was partly artist. A member of the Browning Society would say that he played on the souls of men as on an instrument; a unanimist, that he imposed his personality on a group. But we must be careful not to imply that the least apostolic fervor colored what was at its worst the purely utilitarian contrivance of a man who wished to gain himself a hearing, and at its best an amused experiment in applied psychology.

In the silence of his room he was afraid, afraid of that wild rebellious surge that aspired violently towards realization in sound. He felt its implacable, caged resentment, its longing to be released in one splendid, drunken scream and fused with the cosmic discord. Its struggle for divinity was as real as his own, and as futile. He wondered if the Power which, having denied him the conscious completion of the meanest mongrel, bade him forget his fine imperfection beside it in the gutter, ever trembled at the force of his revolt. Meanwhile, that flesh-locked sea of silence achieved a miserable consummation in driblets of sound, as each falling leaf saps the painful vigor of a tree in a cruelly windless autumn. The process was absurd, extravagantly absurd, like boiling an egg over a bonfire. But in his case it was not a willful extravagance; he felt compassion as well as fear; he dreaded lest his prisoner should escape, he longed that it might escape; it tore at his throat and he choked it back in dread and sorrow. Fear breeds fear: he began to have a horror of unexpected pain, of sleep, of anything that might remove the involuntary inhibition. He drugged himself that he might sleep heavily, silently; he scarcely left his room, scarcely spoke, thus denying even that rare transmutation to the rising tossing soundlessness that seemed now to rend his whole being with the violence of its effort. He felt he was losing, playing into the hands of the enemy by the very severity of his restrictions. By damming the stream of whispers he had raised the level of the flood, and he knew the day would come when it could no longer be denied. Still he was silent, in silence listening for the first murmur of the torrent that must destroy him. At this moment the Woman came to him. . . .

He was listening in the dusk when she came, listening so intently that he did not hear her enter. From the door she spoke to him, and he winced at the regularity of her clear, steady speech. It was the usual story, vulgarly told: admiration for his genius, sympathy with his suffering, only a woman could understand. . . . He clenched his hands in a fury against the enormous impertinence of women, their noisy, intrusive, curious enthusiasm, like the spontaneous expression of admiration bursting from American hearts before Michelangelo's tomb in Santa Croce. The voice droned on, wavered, stopped. He sketched a tired gesture of acceptation, and prepared to withdraw once more within that terrifying silent immobility. She turned on the light and advanced carelessly into the room. An irruption of demons would not have scattered his intentness so utterly. She sat down before him at the table, and leaned forward with her jaws in the cups of her hands. He looked at her venomously, and was struck in spite of himself by the extraordinary pallor of her lips, of which the lower protruded slightly and curled upwards contemptuously to compress the upper, resulting in a faintly undershot local sensuality which went strangely with the extreme cold purity stretching sadly from the low broad brow to the closed nostrils. He thought of George Meredith and recovered something of his calm. The eyes were so deeply set as to be almost cavernous; the light falling on the cheekbones threw them back into a misty shadow. In daylight they were strange, almost repulsive, deriving a pitiless penetration from the rim of white showing naturally above the green-flecked pupil. Now, as she leaned forward beneath the light, they were pools of obscurity. She wore a close-fitting hat of faded green felt: he thought he had never seen such charming shabbiness. . . . When at last she went away he felt that something had gone out from him, something he could not spare, but still less could grudge, something of the desire to live, something of the unreasonable tenacity with which he shrank from dissolution. So each evening, in contemplation and absorption of this woman, he lost a part of his essential animality: so that the water rose, terrifying him. Still he fought on all day, hopelessly, mechanically, only relaxing with twilight, to listen to her coming to loosen yet another stone in the clumsy dam set up and sustained by him, frightened and corruptible. Until at last, for the first time, he was unconditioned by the Satanic dimensional Trinity, he was released, achieved, the blue flower, Vega, GOD. . . . After a timeless parenthesis he found himself alone in his room, spent with ecstasy, torn by the bitter loathing of that which he had condemned to the humanity of silence. Thus each night he died and was God, each night revived and was torn, torn and battered with increasing grievousness, so that he hungered to be irretrievably engulfed in the light of eternity, one with the birdless cloudless colorless skies, in infinite fulfillment.

Then it happened. While the woman was contemplating the face that she had overlaid with death, she was swept aside by a great storm of sound, shaking the very house with its prolonged, triumphant vehemence, climbing in a dizzy, bubbling scale, until, dispersed, it fused into the breath of the forest and the throbbing cry of the sea.

They found her caressing his wild dead hair.

transition 16-17

Kay Boyle   *Theme*

There was one woman, a woman of habits, who would come down early in the day to the fire while the coals were still as black as iron. She had strong red hair that she would unloosen; and she would put her feet in the oven and sit watching the chestnuts cook in rows across the top of the stove. She would listen to the rats running about on their claws in the hallway and she would think of what a great master George Moore had been to her and that now there was no one. His books were put away among themselves on the shelf and she had said that when a man began to feed on the past it was time to leave off reading him. She was lonely but she would not go back to open his books or touch them even with her fingers. She would stay away from them and she would be afraid to read even the first ones again because of what had happened in her heart.

When the chestnuts were done she would crack them in her big teeth and draw the worms out with the point of a pin. She had a long face like a horse's face and she would sit eating the chestnuts slowly in her mouth with her long chin swinging back and forth under her face. And in her mind she would think of strong names and say them over to herself. They were names she called her son in her mind when he was a man and came home into the kitchen at night. He would come in and she would see him looking at her long face as she put out his soup for him. She knew she was ugly to him, with her great strong body and her bare arms out hard and white as salt; and in her heart she would be saying over the soft strong names to cradle his bones. She thought that if she had been a Russian mother she could have given him the words to make a wild music or a courage for him. But the Russians were humorless women, intense, tasteless women all of a piece.

In the morning she would walk about in the house with her back and shoulders drawn in small from the cold. She would set the rooms straight and then the feel of her blood moving in her would set her mind off again talking to her son. "Well, well . . ." she would see her voice like a bright coin between them. "Well, after all, what of the Russian writers. . . ." She would be leaning over the table in the kitchen to him so that her breasts hung down in points. She would be passing the bread over to him with her head on one side smiling. "I am an American woman so the Russians must always be strange old men to me. . . . Even the Cherry Orchard was only the other side of an old man's mind, and then only for a moment. . . ."

She would be talking in her mind with her son and then she would see her long teeth in the mirror bared with her thoughts. She would stand with the dirt rag in her hand and see her full eyeballs tied with veins and her heavy old flesh hanging down on her jaws. She would say "ah" to the mirror with her tongue out square like a beast's tongue. "Ah" and "Is that so?" she would say. It was like a dance around the room to her to escape the mirror. And after that she would have a fine scorn for everything. She would have a sneer for all the old things in the room. "Chekhov and his *femme!*" she would say over the table. "The old bitch and his *femme,* ha! I'd like to have seen them, the dear queer people. I'd like to have seen them when no one else was about. She with her white face hanging through her fingers and he with his foot in her mouth to stop her crying. . . ."

She would feel her own face long and heavy before her. She would be weary with the knowledge of her own heavy face hanging out before her. "God push my face up on me," she would say. "Push my face up till it is a round face with a crown of little ears about it." And her weariness went out over the table and fell on the backs of her hands. "I'm crying for you George Moore, George Moore," she would say. "Your storms would break the heart at the window, and every night your sorrow gnawed at my bones. . . ." She would hold the dirt rag up to hide from herself the shape of her mouth crying. And then she would think of her strong hands, and the long strong bands of her red hair. "You and your balderdash with Balderston! You and your Frank Harris coffee!" But she would never go over and touch his books with her scorn because her heart was too sore.

When her son came in she would be silent. All day she had been talking to him but now there was nothing to say between them. He said he would be going up to Chicago at the end of the month and she could only think of him sitting there while he said this looking at her dark old mouth and her hair. She thought it must be a sad thing for him to live with an old woman. Ah, but if he knew what there was in her blood, she thought, he would be afraid to be in the room with her. Her body was crouched there in her and if she would straighten up and cry out to him, she would give it to him like the back of her hand on his face. She set her knife and her fork carefully again at the sides of her plate, she turned her tongue in her mouth and touched the cloth of her dress with her long open palms. In her mind she said: "I am a fierce woman. I am a fierce woman who is not afraid of solitude. I am a black wind, boy. I am lean and gaunt and strong as the wind."

She opened her mouth and tears began to fall down her face and her voice was squeezed out of her throat to him.

"Ah, ah, I am an old woman," she said.

"No, no, you are not an old woman."

Her head shook back and forth in anguish and she said: "I am an old old woman, what shall I do with myself when you leave me?" In her heart she was sneering and she was saying: "I am a gaunt wind without fear, boy. I am a bleak wind that is strong alone."

She sat looking at her son and at his wrists thick like her own wrists and covered with blond hair. He was like her own flesh bared before her and she was thinking that a son should be always a shy bird at the heart. He should be a thin bird to hold in her fingers, with feathers to lay smooth, and a black mad beak to pierce her. He should have small bones that she would follow with her hands until love was a sharp taste in her mouth. She would be salt-strong flesh covering him. She would say: "You are soft and gentle as a fawn to me . . . you are soft, soft in my arms as I carry you out of fire . . ."

She went to a fortune-teller woman who would tell her in the cards what she wanted to know. The woman set out the cards, saying:

"Whether or not your son will come back to you . . . whether he'll come back to you, or whether he won't come back to you . . ." She got up angry and said that was not what she wanted to know. But there was something else to her anger. She left her long gloves on the woman's table and she was too angry to go back for them. "I'm a mother too," she had said. "I am a mother." The woman was a Slavic woman with a face smooth like a nut. But she had not found out what it was with her cards and her long sly looks that the other had come to be told.

One day she went up to Chicago after him. She wanted to be a Slavic mother, a dark slave mother to her son. She thought of the homage in her voice being a dark lullaby to him, she thought that he would come back to her and that she would carry books into the kitchen and read to him. She was thinking in anguish, "I can be many things to you. I can change into a soft skin for you." But when she talked to him of coming back she could see his mind between them seeing the kitchen and her face in the steam over the stove. She put her hands out across the table to him, thinking, "Ah, but there are other things I can be to you . . ."

"I'm an old woman," she said. She thought her hands were beating fiercely on her breasts but he saw them opened out hard before him. "I'm an old, old woman," she said to him, shaking her head in anguish. "Look at me, look at me. . . . Look at my poor old face and come back to me. . . ."

"You never wanted a son," he said to her. He saw her face ugly with crying.

"Yes, yes," she said. "Yes, I wanted a son."

transition   1

Whit Burnett   *The Night of the Gran Baile Mascara*

I am kept in this place as a prisoner. I have lost track of exactly how long I've been held here. But that does not very much matter. I am treated well and persons attend to my wants with courteous regularity and precision. What I fail to get is understanding. For the Spanish are a peculiar people; I doubt if they understand themselves, least of all me.

I am not a Spaniard, either, but was born in America. Though perhaps I am not wholly an American; maybe there is something other in me, something Russian, wilder, clearer. I do not know. But now and then, although I am still a young man, I have been able to see with a sharper clarity of vision than any others I have known, with a curious almost Fourth Dimensional eye. And I sometimes think that all the world is one great diseased mind, and only occasionally does an individual free himself from the compass of its illusions.

But this is aimless speculation. And not my story. For I want now to relate my experience, which has no duplicate in modern times.

It began in Toledo. Of that I'm quite sure. For, with my companion, an artist seeking picturesque spots for illustrative sketches, I had been in Spain not much longer than a week. From the French border, through Barcelona and Madrid, we had gone directly there, you see, seeking in the old towers and gates and castles bordering the Tajo some quickening of our feelings for all Spain. And the events I am to tell of occurred on the night of the *gran baile mascara,* for which the town, the day of our arrival, was garlanded, expectant, tense, and alive.

Yet, perched on the top of an eminence overlooking the muddy curling snake of the river that swirls about its base on three steep rocky sides, Toledo affected me oddly as we passed through its gates, and when I stepped from the conveyance that had brought us from the station, it was as if I had stepped into a kind of walled-up cage. But the sensation was very momentary and quickly dispelled in the noisy, moving bustle of the crowds in the old *plaza de Zocodover,* which was filling with its sauntering crowds of Spaniards who turn out to stroll and smile and amble along just before dusk each day.

As my friend, an Italian, was negotiating for rooms, I stood outside to watch the people: cadets in their bright infantry uniforms, *guardias civiles* in their dark blue capes trimmed with the blood-red dear to Spain; the old, shriveled men and women of other times and other generations; beshawled crones with sinewy faces and wide, swinging skirts; noisy, carnival-spirited boys with masks or blackened faces; blanket-carrying peasants; basket-laden matrons, and maids with great water-filled earthern *botijas*.

One old man—not, indeed, so very old—impressed me singularly. Dressed in a blanket cape of black, which he held around his chest with one bony hand, frayed of boot, and with a battered hat cocked over his left eye, he turned on me a fleeting, curious, bearded face, and passed on. His features were caught in a semi-levitous mood, his crooked brow and sharp brown eye and great descending bulbous nose all combined with a general air to make him seem strangely unreal and realistic at the same time.

My friend came out of the little hotel.

"*Complet*," he said. "Rooms all taken for the ball tonight." I hardly heard him.

"Just now," I said, "I have seen Menipo."

"Menipo?"

"Yes," I answered. "By Velasquez."

"Oh," he said, "Toledo is full of types. A person could spend a year here and never do them justice. You mean the old fellow, full length, in the panel that always seems to companion Velasquez' Aesop? Marvelous type!"

We went to another hotel. Also full. We were referred then to a smaller place, a *posada,* "for man and beast," and in a short time we had engaged two *habitaciones* in the Posada de la Sangre on the Calle de Cervantes, through the Arco de la Sangre off the public square, and almost in ·the shadow of the great murderous-spired fortress of the Alcazar.

Although by this time it was late twilight, there was still a fair amount of visibility and my friend, throwing down his bags in his room, left the *posada* at once with his portfolio under his arm, planning, as was his custom, to make a quick survey of the locality at once so that in the morning, with better light, he might go directly to his subject.

And I was left alone in the ancient inn.

From the Zocodover I could hear the blended noise of the crowds of Toledanos, whose gay spirits were quickening with the approach of night. Across the narrow *calle,* a light had appeared in a window, and inside I could see a Spanish woman sitting in a corner sewing on a huge white cloth, unmarked and immaculate as a shroud. Her face was full of character, lined and reminiscent of life. Her silent, steady needle-plying fascinated me, and I stood watching her from my darkened little room a long time before turning on my light (for this fourteenth century hostelry, remodeled since the days of Cervantes and his squire and serf, boasted at least this much of modern convenience).

Tired as I was from the railroad journey from Madrid, my mind was far from fatigued, and as I lay resting on the bed, scrutinizing my narrow little whitewashed room whose red flagstones, worn by generations, sloped weirdly to the door and to the balcony overlooking the patio, I was suddenly moved by a great desire to enter into the spirit and activity of the town while in Toledo, to know these people, or at least to be with and a part of them.

What better opportunity could have been made to my order, I

thought, than this very night, when all the town is masked and festive for the *gran baile mascara?*

I was stirred by the thought and, hurriedly washing and brushing up, I decided to purchase a costume at once and make ready for the ball, which was to be held, the announcements said, in the Teatro de las Rojas.

I tugged at the huge old-fashioned lock on my door, which yielded with irritating reluctance only after I had had to put in the tremendous key upside down and turn it backwards to disengage the latch.

I must describe briefly the Posada of the Blood of Christ, for it struck me so forcibly as a madhouse of architecture or, more exactly, as a sane house that, through the weary acquiring of years, had fallen into architectural senility and despair. Its rooms, all narrow and cell-like as my own, were built three stories high around an open-air court below, upon whose cobblestones were deployed the cluttery old carts and wagons of the guests, mostly peasants and out-of-townsmen. To the south, and off the main court, were the stables for the mules, the patient *burros* of Spain, and from these quarters came the strong and piercing smell of wet straw and manure.

Above me were the now clear stars, shining in a sky more deeply blue than the depths of a grottoed sea. A little light beside a water trough in the patio threw shadows behind the antique columns supporting the balcony and made a few old benches lifelike as recumbent sleepers. Standing at the north balcony of the court, I was surprised at the angles of the floor I stood on; it sloped almost precariously to the wobbly pillars, and I smiled at the thought that not even the strongest *vino de Jerez* such as we had had at a café before entering the *posada* could have induced such reckless equilibrium in my mind.

Here had Cervantes stayed in 16-something, and written his *Novelas Ejemplares,* centered in the square outside. Had he indeed, I wondered? Was this house then so sloped, so fallen in at the roof, so weak at the knees? Doubtless not. I stood musing, watching the walls around the patio, absorbing the unusual silence and black desertion of the place and staring at the opposite side of the balcony whose death-white surface was ribbed horizontally with the shadows of the upright balcony railing. . . .

"I could go," I thought, "as a matador. But everyone goes like that. And there are so many masked balls always in Spain. Something different, now. . . . A pirate? Old-fashioned. A clown? Pierrot? A peasant? . . . How unimaginative the mind is," I concluded, "in a new situation."

I shrugged my shoulders and walked along the western side of the balcony to the doorway leading to the ground floor. I will wait and see, I decided, what I can find at a costumer's.

At the last step but one, the curious revelatory idea that is essential in an understanding of my plight occurred to me.

"Go," said something deep inside me, "as Menipo!"

"I will," I said.

And, as if by some strange affiliation of will and chance, I walked straight to the water trough near the doorway leading into the stables and took down from a huge spike a great, dark-hued blanket coat that hung there, threw it round my shoulders, and pulled over my head some unknown owner's cold-banded hat.

I lacked now only a beard to be as Menipo.

I was exhilarated so disguised—suddenly, strangely let out of myself, in a manner none may understand except those who have experienced it.

As I stood at the entrance to the stables, which looked through the patio and out into the Calle de Cervantes, my mind was divided between the necessity of a beard for my disguise and with contemplation of the sudden activity in the street outside.

From the Gobierno Militar, passing up the narrow aislelike *calle, guardias civiles* in their great capes were moving in strange groups westward to the Arco de la Sangre that entered onto the Plaza. There was nothing so strange in their going there, but it seemed that either they too were affected by the *mascara* spirit, or that something was wrong with my eyesight, for these usually so precise and dignified police servants were beyond all dignity now and lurched and swung along with an abandon I had never seen before. Three or four, appearing at intervals, even made light of their stature, apparently ridiculing the very build that had assured them a government post in Spain, for they had bent their knees nearly to the ground and were waddling away, their legs hidden under their capes so that they appeared like absurd dwarfs beside the others.

I could not help laughing as I stood there, safely protected from conspicuousness by my own new trappings. I walked across the court to the outer doorway, and at that instant, from the Zocodover, came the sudden strains of band music, which drew more and more people through the channel of the street and thence through the arch and into the hidden crowds. Behind me passed some peasants from the interior of the *posada*; but I did not turn around. A second or two later I saw even the proprietor himself, with his apron around his middle, go up the street. I then looked behind me, and found myself almost dreadfully conscious of complete isolation.

But, as I stared into the shadows behind me, I discerned one significant dark shape. It was a man. He was emerging from the stables. Wrapped like myself in a blanket cape, he came with appalling slowness towards me, slowly but directly, inevitably, like a heavily looming mountain.

Fearful that he might bump into me, I decided to step out into the doorway. His slow, determined stride came on. There was no avoiding a collision. His face was down, hidden by the angle of his hat. A weighty oppressiveness settled on me. He was assuredly bound to walk right over me. I could not move.

With great effort I stepped, at last, to one side. But he did not pass. He lifted his head, and I saw the features of the man with the crooked brow and the great descending nose. It was Menipo!

"Buenos," I mumbled in greeting, and was for leaving.

He made no response.

Instead, he walked closer towards me until he was so near I felt his breath in my face. Then, muttering words or sounds I could not understand, he pushed me backwards, slowly, grossly, with his bent arm beneath his cape elbowing at my stomach.

Backwards I moved, unable, through surprise or something else, to offer any resistance. Further and further back I went, away from the door and into the shadows of the frightful court.

After a century of time, it seemed, I found my tongue and what few Spanish words I knew that I hoped would cover the situation.

"What do you want?" I cried. "Stop this!"

He laughed, mumbled, and then talked, in a disordered, broken, high-pitched voice that rasped and scratched my ears. The man, I was convinced, was mad.

Could I offer him money, I wondered.

I made out one word here and there. And then:

"Pasaporte!" he said.

It was now my turn to laugh, if I had had the courage. Pasaporte! Passport, indeed. He was like the multitudinous officials that board the trains in and out of Madrid, seemingly at random, to scrutinize the documents of the entrants. This was Spain. The man was an official? Possibly. But where his uniform? The Spanish are a funny people. . . . My mind began to lag in thoughts, my body to fail to function quickly as I continued to back and back like a tired horse.

He was no official. He was a madman, and my very life in danger. I should spring at his throat, I thought. I should kill him, lest he kill me. I looked sidewise, hopefully, into the street. Deserted as the court. I was helpless. I had no weapon. What lay behind his own great coat I could not tell.

Then, stumbling on a cobblestone, I fell backwards on the uneven flooring and struck my head an astounding blow on the ground.

Fortunately, however, I did not lose consciousness, for I remember that even in falling I had the presence of mind to cry for help.

And I added, too, "a madman, madman! *Loco, loco!*"

That I did not lose consciousness was apparent to me as soon as I fell, for looking up from the cold stones at the man above me, I could see at his elbow something I had not observed before. He was standing near the outer entrance to the court, beside a little wall shelf on which reposed an open ledger and beside it a bottle of ink and a couple of pens.

I remember, too, that this seemed unusual to me, almost as if the book were an American hotel register, and thus quite out of place in Spain where the guests must fill out little slips for the police instead of merely signing their names on the book.

Besides the ink bottle there were three other objects. A hammer. A hatchet. And a small, yellow wooden barrel I assumed to be filled with tacks.

I took these objects into my mind in a glance. As I did, my frightful torturer picked up the hammer and the hatchet. I saw the keen blade shining in the dim light, and I felt as one must feel who stands on the edge of his own death.

If I could divert this maniac's attention! How? My mind strove like a tugging animal.

"The tacks!" I screamed. "The tacks!"

He turned his bearded face to peer at the stand. Then he took from the tiny barrel one of the tacks. My plan was working! Renewed strength came into me, almost enough to enable me to lift my head. But not enough, it seemed. I sank back upon the stones, beside the smelly bristles of some dirty straw.

But his simple child's mind was occupied. I was glad. Perhaps he would spend time trying to drive these tacks, diverted from my case. And my cry for help would bring me aid. But when? Why did no one come? I listened, terrified, for some friendly sound in the street, some footfall in the house. But no sound came from the gloomy inn, none from the town but the misplaced music of the distant band in the Zocodover. These crazy Spaniards, with their *fêtes!*

He scrutinized the tack in his hand. He weighed it carefully and then pinched it in two fingers and lifted the hatchet in his right hand. Above the tack it poised an instant, and then descended.

No brittle metal sound came back. The tack bounced away and fell beside me, soundless, springing back weirdly into the air, and then was lost again on the ground where I lay.

The tacks were rubber!

I knew the tacks were rubber by no unusual faculty of mind. Who has not seen those insane products of the notion stores of America: ink blots made out of black celluloid to sell to juvenile minds for ten cents, cigars that explode when half smoked, imitation flies to pin on one's lapel and amuse one's friends? Rubber tacks!

Betrayed as I was by this heinous trick of fate, I sensed then the utter uselessness of living further. Why not capitulate? Why not for a tack's sake, as for a woman's, or a country's, or a people's, for art's sake, Menipo's, or for God's?

But it was strange withal, I mused, that they were really rubber tacks. Before I had reasoned out an action, I found I was on my feet beside the madman, absorbed with him in examination of these important objects.

He threw down the hatchet. It clattered on the stones. Then he tried to place a tack with the hammer.

The tack bounced away, and then, reaching again into the barrel, I saw him draw out of it half a dozen six-inch spikes, glistening with true steel. These were no rubber counterfeits. And then, ending all child's play at the shelf, he came at me, hammer in one hand, and these cruel, crucifixion nails glistening in the other.

"Now you," he said. *"Su cabeza! Su corazón!"*

I got that much. My head whirled with the pain of my fall and with the excitement and fear of my plight. He was going to drive these nails into my head, into my heart! I knew this as well as if he had said it a dozen times. From his eyes to mine danced a message of terror that drained me of my elements, of reason, caution, hope, and courage.

I crouched. I lay down. Flattened myself, as before, on my back. If I could worm away, I thought, from this towering oppressor! My hand touched the hatchet, and I hurled it with the crying speed of a cyclone.

It struck his head and the blood came. Rich and red as the Spanish flag, deep-hued as bull's blood on a black hide.

And then occurred what frightens me now, but did not then.

I had not killed Menipo. He reached for the hatchet, fallen again on the floor. But when he lifted his head, I saw then a great change in the maniac. Though blood was on his face and his hair and beard were tangled in a wildness, unearthly and mad, there was a new clarity in his eyes. He looked at the hatchet in his hands with wonder and then down at me.

Now, I thought, it is over. With calm precision he will slay me, hammering my head into the cobblestones. But I still have a voice. Ten seconds may save me.

"Loco, loco!" I shouted. "Help!"

And at that moment help arrived. I saw the white movement of the proprietor's apron as he turned the street corner to the doorway. But the madman had seen the movement, too. And on my chest I felt the hatchet fall. My fingers clutched it hopefully.

"Who called out?" roared the heavy-voiced proprietor. "Who is a madman here?"

Who indeed? I could not lift my head. Much time must certainly have passed with that great giant looming over me. I felt strangely relaxed, almost at home resting on the floor, like a worm, like a dog, smelling, with only half my consciousness, the ground, the chill stone, and straw.

I lacked a beard though, I recalled. That was it. If I had had the beard when starting out. . . . I clutched at the straw on the floor and tucked some under my chin. At a *mascara,* you know, it is the quaintness that attracts. And one must be imaginative.

I looked up.

"Who," cried the proprietor, "started all this? Who is crazy here?"

I could not answer him in words that he would know. My Spanish took queer turns and starts. I mumbled all the tongues I knew.

And then I heard a voice by the register shelf that was like the voice of myself, calm and well-poised as when I order dinner in a great place. And the voice was that of Menipo, the madman.

"There," he was saying, "is the madman. He is crazy—see him on the floor there, like a dog. I was passing by, on my way to the *gran baile mascara,* when the dog there sprang upon me with a hatchet. Look at my cheek here. Call a guard, and lock him safe in jail."

This is what I heard. Everyone heard it. Could I deny it?

I clutched at the proprietor's apron.

"Look," I said, "at my beard here. *I* am the real Menipo. How could I have hurt that thing? He is a picture by Velasquez. You are idiots. You are all mad!"

And so they are, though no one will see this but myself.

transition 18

Erskine Caldwell   *July*

Middleaged Ben Hackett with Cromwell and Julia was haying to beat hell when the thunderstorm broke on the eastridge. Ben knew it was coming, because all morning thunder rumbled up and down the river; but Ben didnt want it to come while most of his firstcrophay was cocked, and he didnt like it at all. Ben was hot and Ben was mad, but the rain cooled him down and took some of the anger out of him. Cromwell and Julia didnt like the heat, and now they didnt like the rain and thunder. Ben swore to them soothingly about the weather, and they stood all right.

When the storm was over, the hay was too wet to draw, and Ben had to pitch off his load because that too was wet. Swearing and sweating Ben unloaded, and drove Cromwell and Julia across the field and through the gap in the rock wall at the lane. In the lane Ben filled his pipe and perched himself on the hayrack. The sun was out, and it was hot again. But the hay was wet.

"If the weather knows all about making hay it ought to have to get it in itself, by Jesus," Ben told Cromwell and Julia.

Cromwell snorted some thistledown out his nose and Julia swished her horsehairs in Ben's face.

While he was getting his tobacco aglow the team stopt. Ben took five or six deep sucks without looking up.

"Get along there, Cromwell," he urged, puffing. "What's ailing you, Julia!"

The team moved forward a pace and again halted. Ben stood up balancing himself on the rack.

"By Jesus!" he grunted masking his face.

An automobile, unoccupied, blocked the narrow lane.

Ben climbed down, swearing to Cromwell and Julia. He walked around the automobile uncertainly, stopt, studying it, and walked around it again. No one was in sight. Going closer Ben laid his hand on the door taking from his teeth the pipe with his other hand.

"Damn a man who'd stand his auto abarring the lane," he pronounced, glancing around at Cromwell and Julia for confirmation. "I guess I'll have to push the thing out the way myself. By Jesus, if whoever left it here was here I'd tell him something he wouldnt forget soon!"

But Ben couldnt move the car. It creaked and squeaked when he pushed and when he pulled, but it wouldnt move. Knocking out his pipe and wiping his face Ben backed up to Cromwell and Julia grasping their bridles in his hands. He led his team around the automobile all right. When he got in the lane behind the car he stopt his horses and went back, looking at it and putting his hands on the doors and mudguards.

"By Jesus!" Ben exclaimed highpitched looking in the tonneau. He pulled out a creamsilk stocking and a pair of black patent leatherpumps.

He was too excited to say anything or to do anything with the stocking and shoes. He looked in the driver's seat, and there under the steeringwheel sat a gallonjug of cider almost empty. Ben pulled the cork to smell if it was hard. It was. He jabbed his thumb through the handlehole and threw the jug in his elbow. It was hardcider all right, but there was very little of it left.

"By Jesus," Ben smacked his lips, wiping them with his hand, "that's pretty good cider for a windfall!"

He replaced the jug under the steeringwheel. Before he screwed his finger out the handlehole his eyes discovered a garment lying on the floor beside it. He pulled out the garment and held it up before his eyes. It was a pair of lavendersilkdrawers. Ben stared openmouthed and wildeyed.

"By Jesus, Cromwell," he licked his mustache lip, "what do you know about that!"

Cromwell and the mare nibbled at the roadgrass unconcerned.

Ben handled the drawers a little more intimately. He turned them slowly around looking at all sides. Then he looked inside. Then he smelled them.

"By Jesus, Cromwell," he declared triumphantly, "this is a woman's thing, or else I'm a redheaded tadpole!"

Holding the drawers in his hands tenderly Ben climbed on the hayrack and drove down the lane into the road. They were nice and soft in his hands, and they smelled good, too.

He went down the road homeward thinking about the drawers. They made him want to do something but he didnt know what he could do. When he reached Fred Williams' place he drew up his team. Fred's wife was stooping over in the garden. Ben stuft the drawers in his pocket.

"Nice day, today, Mrs. Williams," he called unsteadily. "Where's Fred?"

"Fred's gone to town today," she answered looking around bent over her knees.

Ben's hand went in his pocket and felt the lavendersilkdrawers. Even in his pocket outofsight they made him feel like a new man trying himself out. He hitched the team to the horserack and went in the garden where Fred's wife was. She was picking peas for supper. Watching her pulling the long round pods and putting them in her apron Ben strode around her in circles putting his hand in the pocket where the lavendersilkdrawers were. Walking around her he spat behind him every other step. The woman didnt say much, and Ben said nothing at all. He was getting so now he could feel the drawers without even putting his hand in his pocket.

When he was behind her the next time Ben clutched her around her waist with his arms and held to her.

"Help!" she yelled at the top of her voice diving forward: "Help!"

When she jumpt forward both of them fell on the peavines tearing them and uprooting them. She yelled and fought but Ben was determined, and he held on to her waist with all his strength. They rolled in the dirt and on the peavines. Ben jerked the drawers out. He got one of her feet through one drawersleg but he couldnt get the other foot in. They rolled some more in the dirt tearing up the peavines. Ben was panting. But he couldnt get the lavendersilkdrawers on Fred's wife's other foot. He was determined to put the drawers on her. Presently she stopt struggling and Ben glanced around at her. She was sitting up looking down at him in the dirt. Both of them were brown with the garden soil, and Ben was sweating through his mask.

"Ben Hackett what are you trying to do?" she sputtered through the earth on her face.

Ben released her legs and looked up at her. He didnt say anything. She stood up and stept in the drawersleg and pulled them up under her dress. That was where he had been trying to put them all the time.

Ben got up dusting his clothes. He followed her across the garden into the frontyard.

"Wait here," she told him.

He waited, and when she came back she carried a basin of water and a towel.

"Wash the dirt off your face and hands, Ben Hackett," she directed standing over him wearing the lavendersilkdrawers.

Ben did as he was told. Then he slapt some more dirt out of his trousers.

When he finished cleaning himself Ben handed her the emptied basin and soiled towel.

"It was mighty nice of you to bring the towel and water," he thanked her.

"You are halfway fit to go home now," she approved.

transition 17

Morley Callaghan   *Last Spring They Came Over*

Alfred Bowles came to Canada from England and got a job on a Toronto paper. He was a young fellow with clear blue eyes and heavy pimples on the lower part of his face, the son of a Baptist minister whose family was too large for his salary. He got twenty dollars a week on the paper and said it was surprisingly good screw to start. For two fifty a week he got an attic room in a brick house painted brown on Mutual Street. He ate his meals in a quick lunch near the office. He bought a cane and a light gray fedora.

He wasn't a good reporter but was inoffensive and obliging. After he had been working two weeks the fellows took it for granted he would be fired in a little while and were nice to him, liking the way the most trifling occurrences surprised him. He was happy to carry his cane on his arm and wear the fedora at a jaunty angle, quite the reporter. He liked to explain that he was doing well. He wrote home about it.

When they put him doing night police he felt important, phoning the fire department, hospitals, and police stations trying to be efficient. He was getting along all right. It was disappointing when, after a week, the assistant city editor, Mr. H. J. Brownson, warned him to phone his home if anything important happened, and he would have another man cover it. But Bowles got to like hearing the weary, irritable voice of the assistant editor called from his bed at three o'clock in the morning. He liked to politely call Mr. Brownson as often and as late as possible, thinking it a bit of good fun.

Alfred wrote long letters to his brother and to his father, the Baptist minister, using a typewriter, carefully tapping the keys, occasionally laughing to himself. In a month's time he had written six letters describing the long city room, the fat belly of the city editor, and the bad words the night editor used when speaking of the Orangemen.

The night editor took a fancy to him because of the astounding puerility of his political opinions. Alfred was always willing to talk pompously of the British Empire policing the world, and about all Catholics being aliens, and the future of Ireland and Canada resting with the Orangemen. He flung his arms wide and talked in the hoarse voice of a bad actor, but no one would have thought of taking him seriously. He was merely having a dandy time. The night editor liked him because he was such a nice boy.

Then Alfred's brother came out from the old country and got a job on the same paper. Some of the men started talking about cheap cockney laborers crowding the good guys out of the jobs, but Harry Bowles was frankly glad to get the twenty a week. It never occurred to him that he had a funny idea of good money. With his first pay he bought a derby hat, a pair of spats, and a cane, but even though his face was clear and had a good color he never looked as nice as his younger brother because his heavy nose curved up at the end. The landlady on Mutual Street moved a double bed into Alfred's room and Harry slept with his brother.

The days passed with many good times together. At first it was awkward that Alfred should be working at night and his brother in the daytime, but Harry was pleased to come down to the office every night at eleven and they went down the street to the hotel that didn't bother about Prohibition. They drank a few glasses of good beer. It became a kind of rite that had to be performed carefully. Harry would put his left foot and Alfred his right foot on the rail, and leaning an elbow on the bar they would slowly survey the zigzag line of frothing glasses the length of the long bar. Men jostled them for a place at the foot rail.

And Alfred said, "Well, a bit of luck."

Harry, grinning and raising his glass, said, "Righto."

"It's the stuff that heals."

"Down she goes."

"It helps the night along."

"Fill them up again."

"Toodleoo."

Then they would walk out of the crowded barroom, vaguely pleased with themselves. Walking slowly and erectly along the street, they talked with assurance, a mutual respect for each other's opinion making it merely an exchange of information. They talked of the Englishman in Canada, comparing his lot with that of the Englishman in South Africa and India. They had never traveled, but to ask what they knew of strange lands would have made one feel uncomfortable; it was better to take it for granted that the Bowles boys knew all about the ends of the earth and had judged them carefully, for in their eyes was the light of faraway places. Once in a while, after walking a block or two, one of the brothers would say he would damn well like to see India and the other would say it would be simply topping.

After work and on Sundays they took a look at the places they had heard about in the city. One Sunday they got up in good time and took the boat to Niagara. Their father had written asking if they had seen the Falls and would they send some souvenirs. That day they had as nice a time as a man would want to have. Standing near the pipe rail a little way from the hotel that overlooks the Falls, they watched the water line just before the drop, smooth as a long strip of beveled glass, and Harry compared it favorably with a cataract in the Himalayas and a giant waterfall in Africa, just above the Congo. They took a car along the gorge and, getting off near the whirlpool, picked out a little hollow near a big rock at the top of the embankment where the grass was lush and green. They stretched themselves out with hats tilted over their eyes for sunshades. The river whirled below. They talked about the funny ways of Mr. Brownson and his short fat legs and about the crazy women who fainted at the lifted hand of the faith healer who was in the city for the week. They liked the distant rumble of the Falls. They agreed to try and save a lot of money and go west to the Pacific in a year's time. They never mentioned trying to get a raise in pay.

Afterwards they each wrote home about the trip, sending the souvenirs.

Neither one was doing well on the paper. Harry wasn't much good because he hated writing the plain copy and it was hard for him to be strictly accurate. He liked telling a good tale but it never occurred to him that he was deliberately lying. He imagined a thing and straightway felt it to be true. But it never occurred to Alfred to depart from the truth. He was accurate but lazy, never knowing when he was really working. He was taken off night police and for two weeks helped a man do courts at the City Hall. He got to know the boys at the press gallery, who smiled at his naive sincerity and thought him a decent chap without making up their minds about him. Every noonhour Harry came to the press gallery and the brothers, sitting at typewriters, wrote long letters all about the country and the people, anything interesting, and after exchanging letters, tilted back in their swivel chairs, laughing out loud. Heaven only knows who got the letters in the long run. Neither one when in the press gallery seemed to write anything for the paper.

Some of the men tried kidding Alfred, teasing him about women, asking if he found the girls in this country to his liking; but he seemed to enjoy it more than they did. Seriously he explained that he had never met a girl in this country but they looked very nice. Once Alfred and Bun Brophy, a red-headed fellow with a sharp tongue who did City Hall for the paper, were alone in the gallery. Brophy had in his hands a big picture of five girls in masquerade costumes. Without explaining that he loved one of the girls Brophy asked Bowles which of the lot was the prettiest.

"You want me to settle that," said Alfred, grinning and waving his pipe. He very deliberately selected a demure little girl with a shy smile.

Brophy was disappointed. "Don't you think this one is pretty? A colorful, bold-looking girl."

"Well, she's all right in her way, but she's too vivacious. I'll take this one. I like them kittenish," Alfred said.

Brophy wanted to start an argument but Alfred said it was neither here nor there. He really didn't like women.

"You mean to say you never step out?" Brophy said.

"I've never seemed to mix with them," he said, adding that the whole business didn't matter because he liked boys much better.

The men in the press room heard about it and some suggested nasty things to Alfred. It was hard to tease him when he wouldn't be serious. Sometimes they asked if he took Harry out walking in the evenings. Brophy called them the heavy lovers. The brothers didn't mind because they thought the fellows were having a little fun.

In the fall, Harry was fired. The editor in a nice note said that he was satisfied Mr. H. W. Bowles could not adapt himself to their methods. But everybody wondered why he hadn't been fired sooner. He was no good on the paper.

The brothers smiled, shrugged their shoulders, and went on living together. Alfred still had his job. Every noonhour in the City Hall press room they were together, writing letters.

Time passed and the weather got cold. Alfred's heavy coat came from the old country and he gave his vest and a thin sweater to Harry, who had only a light spring coat. As the weather got colder Harry buttoned his coat higher up on his throat and even though he looked cold, he was neat as a pin with his derby and cane.

Then Alfred lost his job. The editor, disgusted, called him a fool. For the first time since coming over last spring he felt hurt, something inside him was hurt, and he told his brother about it, wanting to know why people acted in such a way. He said he had been doing night police. On the way over to No. 7 station very late Thursday night he had met two men from other papers. They told him about a big fire earlier in the evening just about the time when Alfred was accustomed to going to the hotel to have a drink with his brother. They were willing to give all the details and Alfred thankfully shook hands with them and hurried back to the office to write the story. Next morning the assistant editor phoned Alfred and asked how it was the morning papers missed the story. Alfred tried to explain but Mr. Brownson said he was a damn fool for not phoning the police and making sure instead of trying to make the paper look like a pack of fools printing a fake story. The fellows who had kidded him said that too. Alfred kept asking his brother why the fellows had to do it. He seemed to be losing a good feeling for people.

Still the brothers appeared at noontime in the press room. They didn't write so many letters. They were agreeable, cheerful, on good terms with everybody. Bun Brophy every day asked how they were doing and if they felt at home there. Harry would stand for a while watching the checker game always in progress, knowing that if he stood staring intently at the black and red squares, watching every deliberate move, he would be asked to sit in when it was necessary for one of the players to make the rounds in the hall. Once Brophy gave Harry his place and walked over to the window where Alfred stood watching the fleet of automobiles arranged in a square in the courtyard. The police wagon with a load of drunks was backing towards the cells.

"Say, Alfie, I often wonder how you guys manage," he said.

"Oh, first rate."

"Well, you ought to be in a bad way by now."

"Oh no, we have solved the problem," said Alfred in a grand way, grinning, as if talking about the British Empire.

He was eager to tell how they did it. There was a store in their block where a package of tobacco could be got for five cents; they did their own cooking and were able to live on five dollars a week.

"What about coming over and having tea with us sometime?" Alfred said. He was decidedly on his uppers but he asked Brophy to visit them and have tea.

Brophy, abashed, suggested the three of them go over to the cafe and have a little toast. Harry talked volubly on the way over and while having coffee. He was really a better talker than his brother. They sat in an armchair lunch, gripped the handles of their thick mugs, and talked about religion. The brothers were sons of a Baptist minister but never thought of going to church. It seemed that Brophy had traveled a lot during wartime and afterwards in Asia Minor and India. He was telling about a great golden temple of the Sikhs at Amritsar and Harry listened carefully, asking many questions. Then they talked about newspapers until Harry started talking about the east, slowly feeling his way. All of a sudden he told about standing on a height of land near Amritsar, looking down at a temple. It couldn't have been so but he would have it that Brophy and he had seen the same temple and he described the country in the words Brophy had used. When he talked that way you actually believed that he had seen the temple.

Alfred liked listening to his brother but he said finally: "Religion is a funny business. I tell you it's a funny business." And for the time being no one would have thought of talking seriously about religion. Alfred had a casual way of making a cherished belief or opinion seem unimportant, a way of dismissing even the bright yarns of his brother.

After that afternoon in the cafe Brophy never saw Harry. Alfred came often to the City Hall but never mentioned his brother. Someone said maybe Harry had a job but Alfred laughed and said no such luck in this country, explaining casually that Harry had a bit of a cold and was resting up. In the passing days Alfred came only once in a while to the City Hall, writing his letter without enthusiasm.

The press men would have tried to help the brothers if they had heard Harry was sick. They were entirely ignorant of the matter. On a Friday afternoon at three thirty Alfred came into the gallery and, smiling apologetically, told Brophy that his brother was dead; the funeral was to be in three quarters of an hour; would he mind coming; it was pneumonia, he added. Brophy, looking hard at Alfred, put on his hat and coat and they went out.

It was a poor funeral. The hearse went on before along the way to the Anglican cemetery that overlooks the ravine. One old cab followed behind. There had been a heavy fall of snow in the morning and the slush on the pavement was thick. Alfred and Brophy sat in the old cab, silent. Alfred was leaning forward, his chin resting on his hands, the cane acting as a support, and the heavy pimples stood out on the lower part of his white face. Brophy was uncomfortable and chilly but he mopped his shining forehead with a big handkerchief. The window was open and the air was cold and damp.

Alfred politely asked how Mrs. Brophy was doing. Then he asked about Mr. Brownson.

"Oh, he's fine," Brophy said. He wanted to close the window but it would have been necessary to move Alfred so he sat huddled in the corner, shivering.

Alfred asked suddenly if funerals didn't leave a bad taste in the mouth and Brophy, surprised, started talking absently about that golden temple of the Sikhs in India. Alfred appeared interested until they got to the cemetery. He said suddenly he would have to take a look at the temple one fine day.

They buried Harry Bowles in a grave in the paupers' section on a slippery slope of the hill. The earth was hard and chunky and it thumped down on the coffin case. It snowed a little near the end.

On the way along the narrow, slippery footpath up the hill, Alfred thanked Brophy for being thoughtful enough to come to the funeral. There was little to say. They shook hands and went different ways.

After a day or two Alfred again appeared in the press room. He watched the checker game, congratulated the winner, and then wrote home. The men were sympathetic and said it was too bad about his brother. And he smiled cheerfully and said they were good fellows. In a little while he seemed to have convinced them that nothing important had really happened.

His last cent must have gone to the undertaker for he was particular about paying bills, but he seemed to get along all right. Occasionally he did a little work for the paper, a story from a night assignment when the editor thought the staff was being overworked.

One afternoon at two thirty in the press gallery Brophy saw the last of Alfred, who was sucking his pipe, his feet up on a desk, wanting to be amused. Brophy asked if anything had turned up. In a playful resigned tone, his eye on the big clock, Alfred said he had until three to join the Flying Corps. They wouldn't take him, he said, unless he let them know by three.

Brophy said, "How will you like that?"

"I don't fancy it."

"But you're going, though?"

"Well, I'm not sure. Something else may come along." It was a quarter to three and he was sitting there waiting for a job to turn up before three.

No one saw him after that, but he didn't join the Flying Corps. Someone in the gallery said that wherever he went he probably wrote home as soon as he got there.

René Crevel   *Mr. Knife, Miss Fork*

A little girl is asking: "What is death?" but without allowing time for an answer she forestalls any by saying:

"And please don't try to make me believe it is the same as being asleep. People who are having a good time are never sleepy, and you swear to me that everybody dies. Tell me, do you really think it's fair yourself that even if you don't think about death it just comes along anyway and mixes itself up with you?"

The mother is of a family that never touches a drop to drink except water, that suspects the aftereffects of pepper, banishes Worcestershire Sauce from its table, as well as pickles and even mustard; holds forth a bit too willingly on the question of social hygiene; and justifies the high industry of its masculine members and the helpless virtue of its feminine element by the indisputable arguments of positivism. Upon the threshold of her thirtieth year, this mother is already resigned to the dreariest and most objective sort of reasoning.

"When you are grown up, my darling," she states, "experience will teach you that there are people whom one has nothing to do with, and to whom one is more or less a well-wisher, but they will nevertheless do all they can to make you miserable."

"Yes, I see. I know death is something like Cousin Cynthia. Everybody did nothing but talk about her all the time before we knew her. She was very pretty, with red hair and a green dress, and her eyes were gray like clouds. And her smell. Do you remember how good she smelled? She was born in a country where there is never any summer. But she has seen everything. She speaks French, English, German, Italian, and even Spanish. She brought such nice presents and grandma said 'Cynthia will be our ray of sunshine.' We loved her so much even before she came that we put her in the most beautiful bedroom of all. She could have stayed there all her life, but one day Cynthia wasn't there any more. She went away without saying anything, just like a robber. And she was a robber, too, because she took Papa with her. You remember the other evening in the parlor after dinner when you were crying on grandpa's shoulder you said Cynthia was a whore? Is death a whore too?"

Silence on the part of the mother. But even though lips are pressed together and closed as tight as lips can close, childish curiosity does not so easily give in. A look is thrust straight into the woman's eyes, as if simply by pressing there it could force the secret out of their muteness, while the little voice insists:

"What is death, what is a whore?"

Still no answer, but already that burrowing mole, anxiety, had begun to hollow its tunnels through the obstinate silence of the mother. For some months past she had never ceased asking herself if the hour had not come in which to begin the child's sexual education.

Deprived by atavism of the pagan possibilities of joy, and deprived by nature of an imagination strong enough to uproot the memory of her domestic failure, this blond-headed woman, prematurely abandoned as she was, did not seek to put a romantic structure upon the life that her fly-by-night husband had certainly made light of. As naturally as she had given nine months of her life so that her body might bring forth another body, so did she determine to devote the months and the years that were to come to the spiritual formation of the fruit of her womb. Moreover, her frank and materialistic father, a bearded neurologist, asked nothing better than to aid her with the great gifts of his mind.

On this particular day he is unfortunately out of town. True, quite recently, when his daughter questioned him upon the matter of an early sexual education, he gave his opinion, but one so inserted with ideas as had never even occurred to our Maintenon in her bedchamber, that the mother could make nothing of it at all. But how could she ask the great man to repeat himself, he whose indulgence for all human beings was measured out with such disconcerting precision? His titles, his assurance, and his world renown intimidated those of his own flesh and blood quite as much as they flattered them.

This uncertainty still prevails in the mind of the mother. But once more the little girl asks: "What is death, what is a whore?" and the one to whom the query is put needs no one to tell her that it is better to postpone a bit longer the perilous care of explaining the mysteries of procreation. In the meantime, the thing is not to be thrown into confusion by this audacious curiosity. The mother herself at her daughter's age would never have had the temerity to ask such questions, and, moreover, would never have imagined them possible. Hunger for knowledge or thirst for experiment, however imperious they might be in the family, were certainly not sufficient explanation of this insistence. On the other hand, how could a spirit that even in its extreme youth readily accepted facts attempt a comparison between death and the word whore? The word had escaped in a moment of anger from a mouth which was nevertheless incapable of using milder terms in description of a cousin with red hair who had emerged from the fogs of her native land with the sole intention of carrying off from the most patient of wives a husband whom solid virtue could no longer hold.

In fact, here we are. It is the faithless one that fires the child's preposterous imagination. A strange race, that race of little girls whose fathers have departed from the shores of wisdom for the sake of a creature with hair of flame. The father's conduct is eloquent proof of the fact that he has neither principles nor method, nor has he morals. The one thing to be seen is if the little girl herself responds to the vagabond frivolity of one, or to the austere submission of the other of her generators. That she had in this case seized of her own accord upon the role to be played by a woman soiled by the disunion of her parents bears witness to her possessing a remarkable sense of intuition, no less than a precocity of a rather inferior quality. Impossible not to deplore her leanings toward the bizarre. For the comparison attempted between death and the fatal cousin from England is not the only symptom of her bent, and the astonished mother now remembers a whole series of men painted blue, of houses made violet with orange shingles, of red fields, all messed out of the paints of the child's first box of water colors. It is useless to point out that there is a white race, a yellow, a black, and a red race, but not a blue one; useless to say that houses are made of stone or brick and therefore white or rose colored, or even that grass that grows in the fields is green. A child reconstructs the world according to his own caprices, preferring above all the fabulous animals, making fun of the swans in the Bois de Boulogne, laughing in the faces of the bears in the Jardin des Plantes, despising lions, camels, and elephants, and deigning to throw a glance at the rhinoceros only because of the horn that is planted there on him where you would never expect to find one. And how many questions are asked concerning the gnu that the cook used to chase away at dusk last autumn in the country!

But at this moment the apocalyptic beast is death, and with eyes big enough to swallow whole houses, the little girl insists: "What is death, what is a whore?"

A young woman thus alone might quail before the persistence of childish questioning and let slip from the reserve that is after all hardly suited to her years a betrayal of her treacherous cousin. But understanding that the innocence of her young questioner is her safest ally, she responds:

"The lesson is over, darling."

"But you haven't answered me."

"Run along and play. Tell your nurse to give you your tea."

The child sees the hopelessness of persisting. She will go as she is told, but not to ask for bread and butter. She takes a knife and a fork and, hiding away in a corner of her own room, she begins to talk very softly to herself.

"The knife is Papa. The white part that cuts is his shirt, and the black part you hold in your hand is his trousers. If the white part that cuts was the same thing as the black part, I could pretend he was in his pajamas, but I can't do that.

"The fork is Cynthia. Beautiful Cynthia, the English lady. This is Cynthia's hair, the things that stick into the food that you want to take off your plate. She has a pretty neck. Papa is very happy. He is smiling at her. He is speaking to her.

" 'You know, Cynthia, I love you. I'm in love with you. Whenever we pass each other in the halls I am always absolutely mad to kiss you. You are so lovely, with your red hair and your green dress. I want my little girl to look like you when she grows up. Handsome young men would come to call on her and she would marry the one who played tennis the best. My wife knew a lot of things. She was just as well-educated as you, but you couldn't have much of a good time with her. Now us, when we're together we laugh, we sing. Now we're going to take a trip. Every night we'll sleep in a new room, but there will always be two little twin beds right close to each other, and we will talk for a long time before we go to sleep. We'll stay in bed very late in the morning. We'll eat in dining cars and, so that nobody will recognize us, I'll call you Miss Fork and you'll call me Mr. Knife, and we'll be taken for Spanish people on a wedding trip. We'll go to very gay places where there'll be red flowers the same color as your hair, and in shops I'll buy you beautiful dresses with necks cut very low. In very hot countries we'll drink lemonade so cold and prickly that it will make us sneeze. Before we go to bed at the North Pole we'll put so much rum in our tea that we'll laugh ourselves to sleep. We'll go up all the Eiffel towers, and if we ever meet any tigers, I'll give you my arm and then you won't be afraid. We'll buy a trained seal and he'll play with a ball on his nose and amuse us when we are old. We'll send hummingbirds and rhinoceros horns to my little girl. We'll write to her on beautiful postcards, because I'm sure she is going to be very bored with her mother. She gives her a lesson in arithmetic every day and so we must be nice to her because we're so happy together. I love you so much. You are not at all like other women. You are so beautiful. You are like death, Cynthia, you are a whore like death, Cynthia, my darling, my little whore!' "

At lunch several weeks later the child is seated between her grand-father and her grandmother. She asks why there is no one seated at the fourth place that is laid at the table, which is usually her mother's place.

"Your mother was not feeling well this morning, but she is coming right down."

And in fact a few minutes later the doors open and in comes the young woman, her eyes red in her ashen face. She sits there sniffling, unable to swallow a mouthful. The grandmother shrugs her shoulders, following the rhythm of contempt which has served as metronome to her entire existence. The grandfather, with his beard more majestic than ever, his fork in one hand and his knife in the other like scepters betokening Justice and Authority, seeks the phrase which will encom-pass the situation. Meanwhile, the child cannot help thinking:

"I only hope he won't see that the knife is Papa and the fork is Cynthia. They certainly would have a bad quarter of an hour, poor things. . . ."

But the child has hardly had time to formulate this to herself when, laying aside the signs of his domestic power, the paterfamilias begins to speak in the beautiful grave voice that gives such a troubling aspect of depth to the slightest diagnosis or remark that he may make at the Academy of Medicine.

"Your husband, a gangrened limb. Nothing to be done to save it. Sooner or later you will have to resort to amputation. If not . . . if not . . ."

A single gesture of his hands opens the field wide to the most terrible suppositions.

"And to go further: the wisdom of nations is sound when it declares 'birds of a feather fly together.' The red-headed creature is not through with her prey so soon. It is without doubt our own fault that we drew Cynthia into our midst, but if it had not been that one, he would have gone off with another. . . ."

Hearing her unavoidable ill fortune thus set forth, the abandoned woman let her emotion perish under her beefsteak and potatoes. A great clearing away takes place. She chews up her sorrow with her meat, and down with the gurgles of despair goes a meal well watered by tears. Meanwhile, the patriarch-neurologist continues:

"I know, I know you are emotional. You take after your dear mother. And I am the first to admit that a happening of this kind is enough to simply bowl you over. The scandal of it isn't restricted to one capital. A London paper is now publishing the photographs of the runaways and already announcing their marriage, even though your divorce hasn't been granted yet."

The grandmother has not seen the paper in question and asks that it be fetched for her. So the child is sent off to find the English weekly, on the first page of which, printed between the photograph of a Whitechapel satyr a few minutes before hanging, and a bride, medieval to excess, coming out of Westminster on the arm of a young, immaculate, and smiling lord, is pictured Cynthia. A Cynthia dripping with pearls, and in spite of the poor quality of the paper and the ink which reproduce her, so perfect that her brow, her cheeks, her shoulders, and her arms seem to be glowing with a sunlight of joy, her very skin and her garments shining as if a rainbow were breaking in triple cascades of brilliance over her. One wrist is so heavily weighted with bracelets that the hand, like a drenched bird in the April sunlight, rests momentarily upon the arm of her chair, while the other, barren of rings, bathes in the foam of pearls which cascades from the silky summit of her bosom to the frail plateau that the dress of a seated woman spreads from knee to knee. In a little rectangle cut in the miracle of her skirt is the head of the young father who has allowed himself to be bewitched. Below this, three lines to say that he is the son-in-law of the celebrated European neurologist, to explain the adventure, and to give a few names.

But the child knows they are waiting for her and that she cannot remain hours in contemplation before the picture. In one final moment she concentrates the whole intensity of her gaze upon Cynthia's face, and then closes her eyes tightly so that a new image will not efface from the dark of her memory the marvelous impression that the photograph of Cynthia has fixed there.

She gropes her way back to the dining room where the family, immediately engrossed in a contemplation of the picture, fails to notice that the child's eyes are closed. She is thus unable to see her grandmother lift her lorgnette and study the evidence before her as gravely as the bacteriologist member of the family studies germs under his microscope, but she can at least hear the judgment as her grandmother pronounces it.

"Better were my poor sister dead than to see her jade of a daughter photographed half naked in her yards of false pearls. And have you noticed the dress Cynthia has on? You'd think she was decked out for a tropical sun instead of for the fogs of England. The last country, as my dear brother-in-law (the unfortunate father of this creature) used to say, where a certain notion of dignity was still to be found. At any rate, our young slut won't die of the heat, with her three rags tied around her hips. And to think we received and entertained such a Messalina. When I think of my sister! So upright, so well balanced. She was very young when she left us to marry a colleague of our father's in London. But even so, she conducted herself as admirably abroad as she had in France, and never for a moment failed to live up to the letter of our traditions. Of course, my brother-in-law, in spite of the difference in race, was really one of our own sort. I can see him now, immaculate, economical (a little farther in that direction even and he might have been called a bit mean), and I ask myself how in the world he and his wife, with their kind, good hearts, could ever have had such a daughter. The stupidity of men! When I consider, dear child, the family life we offered your husband. We are not the kind to go in for a lot of high jinks, but even people of note have never seemed bored in our company, and the other evening, in offering a toast at a banquet, some colleague or other of your father's went so far as to praise his dry wit."

"Tra-la-la-la-la-la-la," sings the little girl to herself, waiting to open her eyes until she is quite sure the family has risen from the table and left the room. And then the fruit she is eating looks so dull on its colorless plate that she dreams awhile of the joy of eating an ice, seated upon a red plush-covered bench between Cynthia and her father. There would be flowers strewn on the cloth, and an orchestra mingling its notes and chords with the happiness that is too great for words. In order that the dream linger with her, she picks up a knife and a fork, and with these symbols in her hands she whispers:

"You know, Papa and Cynthia, if Grandma says bad things about you it's only because she's absolutely raging. She'd love to have bracelets and necklaces for herself, and she knows perfectly well that she's not pretty with her old wrinkled skin and her ugly black dresses and her fur piece that smells like a wet dog and her funny old hat sitting on top of her head. I don't pay any attention to her when she scolds me, but you can be sure that the day I'm grown up I won't stay home and play cards or do my scales after dinner. I'll put on a new dress every night, and red flowers on my shoulder. I'll have gold slippers and a pink feather fan as big as I am. Then I can be an actress. I wouldn't like to play in tragedies, but I'll sing songs that don't mean anything, and I'll laugh, and I'll dance the way the American did this summer at the Casino at Vichy. They'll bring me bunches of flowers the way they did to the American, and I'll come back on the stage six or seven times. When I go out the stage door, all the young men will try to make me get in their cars with them, and I'll always pick out a red car because it's prettier in the country and if you go very fast you can kill chickens or even sheep on the road and they won't leave any mark. When Cynthia came Grandma wasn't jealous yet, and she kept saying all the time 'my sister's daughter will be our ray of sunshine.' That's really the truth, too. Cynthia's hair is so beautiful that you'd think you'd burn your fingers if you dared to touch it. And her bosom smells so good and lifts itself up high as though she had closed two little birds in the front of her dress. Papa must be very proud to live with such a beautiful lady with such pretty color on her cheeks. A man can't be happy if he goes out with a woman who looks sick. But Grandpa and Grandma and Mama will never understand why Papa is so happy with Cynthia. Today he is wearing white flannel trousers because this is a knife with an ivory handle. They're at the seashore. Cynthia is in a bathing suit, and the wind is blowing her hair straight up. It looks exactly like real fire. The tablecloth is the Atlantic Ocean. Cynthia is climbing up on a rock. Papa wants to follow her but he is slipping all over on account of the seaweed. Thank the good Lord, Cynthia catches hold of him and saves him from falling in the water. Papa thanks her, and kisses her hand, not on the ends of her fingers, but on the inside where it is always so soft. Then he says:

" 'Cynthia, you have just saved my life. You are so light and slender, but even when you climb a rock in the middle of the ocean you are quite at home. If I didn't know who you were and if I saw your picture beside the picture of some murderer in the paper, I'd hardly be able to wait to read all about you. I wouldn't even look at the story about the murderer, because there's something so wonderful about you. . . . !'

"This is the way they go on talking, up on their rock. They hold each other very tight because it is in the evening and it's cold. All of a sudden the night falls down on them. A great big bird comes and sits on Cynthia's head. He likes her hair better even than his own nest."

A winter and a springtime pass.

Every night through the mist of dreams shines the name of Cynthia. Not a meal passes without a storm of abuse falling upon the head of the adventuress, the creature with red hair. Again and again the bearded professor volunteers the statement that work is the best remedy for a melancholic obsession, so that finally the abandoned woman asks that she be allowed to aid him in his researches. So that now, when there are guests for dinner, the neurologist speaks of his daughter as "my collaborator," or as "my most devoted pupil," or something in that line.

As for the fugitive father on whom the whole painful affair hinges, the child has seen him but once, when he was obliged to come to Paris for the divorce proceedings. She had intended to ask him a thousand questions about Cynthia, about her pearls and her dresses, about their trip and their happiness. But the monologues she invents by day and the dreams she dreams at night are made up of such high and such peremptory phantoms that she cannot bear the thought of their comparison with the possible realities. So, guided by this scornful wisdom, she breathes not a word of all that hour after hour has been a delicious torture to her, thus condemning herself to remorse for never having shown her confidence in the pale young man whom she continues to call father, but who must now ring the doorbell of an apartment whose key he once carried in his pocket.

A winter and a springtime pass. Cynthia, remaining a flaming idol in the memory, by turns brightens a gray sky or warms the azure mildness of the minutes, as if, with water colors, painting a blue sky between two showers. After these miracles, a child would be only the more nauseated by the pious preachings through which the family voices its hate.

Cynthia, red-headed goddess, from your fingertips spring arrows of light, but once they have flown they only heighten the sorrow of the days that follow, each one exactly like the other. Boredom, that foster child of pride, a little girl is dreaming that she herself will never be taken in by the acts and the gestures, by the whole collection of fables on which grown people live. She imagines mornings in which no lies are spoken, afternoons as unadorned, weeks without a single stupidity taking place. Who, then, would dare refuse her in exchange the severe right to criticize a woman who never stops bewailing her luck and complaining of a man whom she will never set eye on again? And the bearded and spectacled professor keeps on repeating that salvation lies in labor, as if he had to keep saying it over and over to convince himself it is true. And that old woman rants on because another woman was preferred to her daughter. The child comes finally to believe that grown people, who have the right to go out at any time of the day or night, have nothing or no one to interest them except Cynthia and a son-in-law, on whom they have perversely set the limits of bad breeding and of fickleness.

A winter and a springtime pass. The hour strikes for the lighting of lamps, but instead of getting up to switch on the electricity, a little girl watches the night falling about her and blotting out the boundaries of her childhood's rooms. Unpeopled dreams, songs without words come alive in the obscurity that has swept away all sordidness and opened a door upon unfathomable depths. Syllables, heard only by the one who utters them as she sits with her hands on her knees, her voice lowered, murmuring sounds unweighted by any meaning, akin to the sounds of the wind, until an invisible triumph has been won over the creatures that surround her. It is this conquest that flings in ecstasy an aura of transparent birds victorious over the fury of the seas, over the cries of the creatures themselves, to the very threshold of the Shakespearian forest wherein Cynthia, at the height of her triumphs, is bestowing enchantment on all about her. Presently wearying of the dull idiom of mankind, Cynthia disappears into the realms of complete mystery, vanishing to the refrain of a page boy singing:

"With a hey and a ho and a hey nonino."

A hey and a ho and a hey nonino, just that and no more than a line from *As You Like It* do Cynthia and her pearls and her plumes and her miracles weigh in the evening's reverie. But, alas, at dinner one must resign oneself to the stupidly, the uselessly exact language of man. Above their heads, emerging from the soup tureen like Venus from the sea, and quite as worthy of being the daughter of an ordinary soup as was the most beautiful of goddesses of being the daughter of the elusive seafoam, the hanging lamp throws its ridiculous dancing shadow upon them, and from the skirts of this *ballerine* falls a waywardly green light.

But because far, far away on the open plains of a night where no domestic fire burns, where no face brings to the dinner table the burden of its age, of its weariness, of its rancors; because far, very far, without attacking things or creatures, the wind goes on its own way, singing to live, living to sing, fearing nothing and no one, because of this, a child refuses to be absorbed by small talk, by small things, by small people. She closes her eyes, and as she swallows the soup without tasting it, she hears at each throb of her heart's beating the invincible murmur:

"With a hey and a ho and a hey nonino."

Translated from the French
by Kay Boyle

transition 18

Léon-Paul Fargue   *The Drug*

> *In this land of enchantments, I viewed everything with*
> *a sort of disquietude. Of all that I saw in the city, nothing*
> *seemed to be quite as my eyes beheld it. It seemed to me*
> *that, due to the infernal power of certain incantations,*
> *everything must have undergone a metamorphosis.*
>
> *(Apuleius)*

> *If the Sun and Moon should doubt,*
> *They'd immediately go out.*
>
> *(William Blake)*

I had suspected it a long while. I was sure of it. I had even said it in
two or three conversations. If I had spoken, I had not seen in their eyes
that they had heard me. I did not think about the thing, it thought me;
I did not act, it acted me. I had grown unable to rise above things or
examine my motives, could no longer come to a decision, or pull myself
together. Negotiate a matter of business? And with whom was I negotiating? Just exactly whom did I have opposite me? Whence came those
dull voices? Whence did their assurances reach me? Whence those odd
words, sluggish as slow-spreading mushrooms? No more confidence
in the given word, no more confidence in anybody. In the streets I
moved about with great circumspection, full of preambles and repent-
ance, offended by the houses whichever way I turned, afraid of glass,
maneuvering with a hunter's cunning, sharply interrogated by the
night air, slipping like flotsam between the portholes of the shops, wasting away in the cafés, fagged out, shriveled up, chewing on brass,
tortured by a badly put question, pinned down for a long while to one
spot by a sort of crevice in the earth, a gap that tapered off, irritatingly
white. I believed Pascal, who always felt there was an abyss on his left.
Was it that I only saw the statement of the problem? I remembered
certain glowing, concealed periods of my childhood, full of clamor, of
moist beams and tears of pleasure, of states of anger or silence, when our
family doctor discerned slight disturbances which he said might be
charged to my precocious activity, aggravated by vivid impressions
which I took care not to betray, and which riddled me with bitter
kisses for the sake of some relentless wonder such as sea shells in a shop

window, the atlas in a natural history dictionary, a miniature ship in the Navy museum, or some absurdly high-priced toy that I could never possess. I never experienced more harshly the sense of the impossible, unless it was in certain moments of rising fever, when I labored like a machine to make an indeterminate but considerable mass fit into an imperceptible opening, like a cathedral into the eye of a needle; or when we were riding the hobbyhorses and the order would come for us all to commit suicide with our lances, under penalty of death, before the merry-go-round, which had already begun to slow down, came to a complete stop. All this in front of my mother, who was contending with a long animal in order to reach me, then lost all form like a cloud, and could no longer save me.

In any case, life was becoming unbearable. The atmosphere was co-agulating. Some days I would rise suddenly while eating, and be aware that I was standing, or lying down, or running through crowds at the wrong time and in the wrong garb, with all my mental compartments exposed. Naturally, impossible to sleep. I could no longer do anything that was right. I had put my affairs in order. I hurried like a carter overtaken by night. I struggled like a sick person who is putting up a game fight but from a little lower down, with a little more waste motion, and who breathes a little more heavily than he did the day before. Things were too slow in taking form, both horizontally and vertically. I must either win or crack up. How it happened, I no longer have an idea. The scholar abandons the problem he is working on when the pencil slips, when the mind, nibbling away, falls asleep. One morning, after a refreshing sleep, he is wakened by the solution. His choice is made. I shook the tree so hard that the rotten fruit fell to the ground. The suspect, smoked out, started to make a clean breast of it. The question was so tautly stretched that it hummed. Finally the warning came. I rose and left, as we hasten to play when luck seems with us. The statement of the problem telescoped with its solution. Everything became clear. I had only to follow. I went down. I followed one of them.

Why that one rather than another? What was there about him which gave me the hint? Nothing that I can remember. He was tall, well-dressed, with a straightforward walk. It was easy not to lose him. He mapped out his plans, his pauses, his entrances, his exits in the corridors of the ant hill. He was doing his day's work like any other passer-by. He played his role of cheese-giving animal. I saw him plunge into the head waiters and dimly-lighted windows of a luxurious hotel. I waited for him, just as a precaution. He stayed there nearly two hours, and that is what caused me the most trouble. At last, here he is, come to life again. He drags me along like a tug, by an invisible rope. Anxiously, he walks round and round in a public square until I begin to think he has missed a rendezvous. No? Off again. Tobacco shop, then three other small shops. Neighborhoods quite unlike each other. The Halles, the Rue Saint-Denis, the Boulevard de la Chapelle. I am going through all the places I love. In remote streets, on sidetrackings, we skirt by hedge-rows of architectural whores, built in a style which is disappearing, running along like shunting locomotives, or lighting up from the portholes of an occasional 'tween-decks. No fooling, my eye on my man! His feints are easy to see through. The day is getting on, and our feet are growing tough. Is he going to make a tour around the world? He passed the Olympia, which has an exit on the Rue Caumartin. He entered the two-exit houses numbered 18 Rue Pigalle and 56 Faubourg Saint-Honoré. He left them by the right door, the skunk! Still, I began to open my eyes, for I felt the rope slacken.

He crossed the Rue Royale. It was at that moment that I lost him in the crush of a traffic jam. I thought I saw him take a cab which got mixed up in a platoon of vehicles that had started up again. I jumped into a cab myself, but, just here, I was no longer sure and, as a measure of precaution, gave orders to follow after. This pursuit led me so far that I began to be seized with doubt, opposed by an inner ringing. . . . We were at the Buttes Chaumont. The cab presumed to be his slowed up. I urged my chauffeur ahead. We passed it. It was empty.

Darkness was coming on. Nothing more to be done. Having paid the taxi fare, I went back by the Rue Bolivar, shaking bunches of mis-calculations, when I saw my man coming towards me on foot, walking with long strides, and his head completely, obstinately turned back-wards, as though it were unscrewed. I avoided him and retraced my steps. I felt the onward rush of events, and could hear my heart beating. I took up the chase again, but followed him on the opposite pavement, on account of his head. Without appearing to have noticed me, he started up the Rue des Mignottes, then the Rue des Solitaires, and here is what happened.

His gait became jerky, then wavy. His head was bordered with a strange piping, and the edges of his body, then the middle, began to brighten up, making visible through transparency, and as though through smoked glass, the entire scaffolding, with all the perches, all that he had in his pockets, everything he had eaten, like a contractile sack, then the coronet in a vivid blue coloring (he must have been treated with potassium methylate), then the passers-by, who were be-coming fewer, then the houses, then the sky. Suddenly he stopped, I had time only to draw back, the pavement darkened around his feet, as though wet by the circular spatter from a spit, he became diaph-anous, and sank into the earth like a bag of silent glass. There was a low chirping sound, the pavement raised two or three large blisters, and with a rather loud smacking noise everything was back in place; I had won.

Since then I have not given up the chase. What day was it that I went home? So, so many, who aren't real! The greater part aren't real! It happens in so many different ways! There are those who smolder gently, like solfataric vapors, or leave the ground like a skeleton rigging, or rise almost invisibly, like a balloon a child has released. A woman appears, with straight hair and skirts turned up like a candle-drip. I don't know if other people see them, but I do. Others plunge into a porous wall, where they are absorbed as though by a blotter. One day, I saw two of them plunge at the same spot into the wall of a factory. Night hemmed us in. Their double contour became legible like invisible ink, and remained luminous a long while on the stone. Where were they? I could not leave this palimpsest wall. One of them seemed to want to come up again. I fled. There are some who spring up on the spot almost under your feet, like a phantom of dust from a hot-air register, armed from head to toe, with canes and brief cases. And then there are the exchanges, repurchases, losing numbers, replacements, permutations, prescriptions, substitutions, volunteers—ah, all sorts of combinations and resources, a monstrous activity, lost in the excitement, a silent ferryboat, a quiet going and coming between life and death. The reasons of the dead and those of the living balance. Love and death fought their first matches in the sea. They coil about and hunt each other out among the rock. How far does their fencing go? The serried text of the herd overawes you. Spindles of smoke, acrobats walking on a ball, suspicious-looking boats steered back into a cove; obese prowlers, hammerhead sharks from the rocky sea, lacerating themselves against the shoals in the streets, falling apart by degrees, greasy meshes against the sky. A sort of hollow tom-tom of voices, stuffed clubs in a dance of death, migration of mourning letters, dispersed order, campaign service in geodetic quarters, for asides filled with numbers, the couplings of garrulous worms, gluttonous cockroaches, sticky, sonorous barter surrounding the houses like dark, dirty foam. It is a matter of sorting out the misleading resemblances, the memories from the visiting demons, the supers from the ghosts, from faces prematurely arrived from limbo, from cheaters, hypocrites, the precociously reincarnated, fugitives from death, the temporarily formulated criminal thought swollen like a steaming muzzle, the clothes-thieving astral body. Somebody frisked your overcoat in a café? No use to look, it's none other. What a task! Only unyielding patience permits you to dominate it. If you place one sea louse on the sands between a thousand sea lice, and don't take your eyes off it, you bewitch it. The others leave with a general shudder, pulverized by fear, while he remains on the spot, with his enormous eye.

Suppose you do the same to any country insect. Your glance weighs on him. You can see him turn over on his back, cut the air with his nippers, throw back the shutters of his wing case with a quick gesture, uncover a little motor which makes you want to pray, and then, when you release him, melt into the sky with a word of sadness. I have caught men in the same way as these little fellows. And then I saw, indeed I did see, that there were some odd fish among them. One day I met my friend three times. Twice in his eyes, it was not he. The third time, he spoke to me. I took fright and slipped away into the crowd. The baker's wife at the crossroads was deceived for two years by the flightiest of lovers who came over just to see her. We must be able to distinguish persons. I will teach you a lot about following them. I have stumbled on lots of them like that, who only walked around for an hour in their hats and clothes, and I kept my eye on them till the moment when they sank cravenly into the ground. There are many sources of supply and lanes of escape, there are many divine ruses, uncomprehended snares, mysterious fly-catching plants, opercula which can be opened, points at which we sink into quicksand, larynxes in the stone, dark sequestrations, executions without judgment. Sometimes I hear a strange tinkle in the crowd. I distinguish, above the noise of the wheels, a muffled rebuke which comes from somewhere in space. Someone says: It's going to storm. Towards noon, the senses become inflamed. In the early evening the air freshens, the revolving stone has ceased to toss up jetsam, flies fly away from silent leather bands, the light undresses in the windows, and I remember that peace was good. Then it is I uncork my solitude crammed with difficultly acquired knowledge, and I inhale it in the darkness.

One day we are set upon by the divine spirit. It has enough of stumbling against its matter. It is we who are the matter, the spirit that becomes indurated. It is tired of feeling these heavy incombustible flies in its flame; it is irritated to feel in its belly, in the very finest of its blood vessels, these saline bubbles, these calculous concretions, these dirty splinters, these miserly straws, these sad reservations, these fungus-covered sinuses, this restless, unbearable question that we are. So it throws us a life belt, hands us a drug, poisons us, chews us like cud, and digests us. Catalytic reabsorption, spiritual precipitate, immediate chemical dissociation, anything you want. . . . At whatever point we pass, on whatever highway of space and in whatever metamorphosis, for centuries and centuries, we shall have the honor of bartering with this inconceivable spirit. Occasionally it shrinks the world—during an incalculable time. For one moment it does away with time, space, and matter, to the point of making us all invisible. But does anybody notice it? For the world remains in scale. You, perhaps, who do not adapt yourself quickly, with your manias, your dullnesses, your own peculiar plasticity, your interminable intuitions. Shh! May nothing of the dialectician infect your flair for God. Sometimes I cling to his yardarms, and fly over myself in pursuit of him in the fourth, which is the radiant, dimension. However, I was just a simple man, and should have liked to remain in my own little niche, anthology coxcomb, subtle insect of genius, friendship, or love. Too late. I can be an artist no longer. I can remain quiet no longer. Like a train in the night, I hear behind me echoing cries which are gaining on me. If I want to keep my distance, I must myself pursue something, I must track down one of these black dancers who do so much harm and who have been caught in the act of not being men! I follow them, preyed upon by their thought, dissolved by it as by a corrosive, by indifference, or ecstasy. They no longer respond to the plasmagnetic Eternal. They no longer hear God tell them they exist. So they doubt in themselves and collapse. They die of an attack of skepticism, as one dies of septicemia. Discriminative sensibility to God. But I want to know how it happens!

Ah! I am an active occidental phantom! This relief, which I ask so often of myself, what would I do with it? I must be brewing something, I must keep busy, give chase to men, the bus, or to God. Smite the buttocks of the earth with your leather flail, run along in your own little jog-trotting way, Babonin. Sakyamuni can do nothing for you, you will suffer!

Translated from the French by Maria Jolas

transition 8

Ernest Hemingway   *Hills Like White Elephants*

The hills across the valley of the Ebro were long and white. On this side there was no shade and no trees and the station was between two lines of rails in the sun. Close against the side of the station there was the warm shadow of the building and a curtain made of strings of bamboo beads hung across the open door into the bar to keep out the flies. The American and the girl with him sat at a table in the shade outside the building. It was very hot and the Express from Barcelona would come in forty minutes. It stopped at this junction for two minutes and went on to Madrid.

"What should we drink?" the girl asked. She had taken off her hat and put it on the table.

"It's pretty hot," the man said.

"Let's drink beer."

"Dos cervezas," the man said into the curtain.

"Big ones?" a woman asked from the doorway.

"Yes. Two big ones."

The woman brought two glasses of beer and two felt pads. She put the felt pads and the beer glasses on the table and looked at the man and the girl. The girl was looking off at the line of hills. They were white in the sun and the country was brown and dry.

"They look like white elephants," she said.

"I've never seen one," the man drank his beer.

"No you wouldn't have."

"I might have," the man said. "Just because you say I wouldn't have doesn't prove anything."

The girl looked at the bead curtain. "They've painted something on it," she said. "What does it say?"

"Anis del Toro. It's a drink."

"Could we try it?"

The man called "Listen" through the curtain. The woman came out from the bar.

"Four reales."

"We want two Anis del Toro."

"With water?"

"Do you want it with water?"

"I don't know," the girl said. "Is it good with water?"

"It's all right."

"You want them with water?" asked the woman.

"Yes, with water."

"It tastes like licorice," the girl said.

"That's the way with everything."

"Yes," said the girl. "Everything tastes of licorice. Especially all the things you've waited so long for, like absinthe."

"Oh cut it out."

"You started it," the girl said. "I was being amused. I was having a fine time."

"All right. I was trying. I said the mountains looked like white elephants. Wasn't that bright?"

"That was bright."

"I wanted to try this new drink. That's all we do, isn't it? Look at things and try new drinks."

"I guess so."

The girl looked across at the hills.

"They're lovely hills," she said. "They don't really look like white elephants. I just meant the coloring of their skin through the trees."

"Should we have another drink?"

"All right."

The warm wind blew the bead curtain against the table.

"The beer's nice and cool," the man said.

"It's lovely," the girl said.

"It's really an awfully simple operation," the man said. "It's not really an operation at all."

The girl looked at the ground the table legs rested on.

"I know you won't mind it, Jig. It's really not anything. It's just to let the air in."

The girl did not say anything.

"I'll go with you and I'll stay with you all the time. They just let the air in and then it's all perfectly natural."

"Then what will we do afterwards?"

"We'll be fine afterwards. Just like we were before."

"What makes you think so?"

"That's the only thing that bothers us. It's the only thing that's made us unhappy."

The girl looked at the bead curtain, put her hand out, and took hold of two of the strings of beads.

"And you think then we'll be all right and be happy."

"I know we will. You don't have to be afraid. I've known lots of people that have done it."

"So have I," said the girl. "And afterwards they were all so happy."

"Well," the man said, "if you don't want to you don't have to. I wouldn't have you do it if you didn't want to. But I know it's perfectly simple."

"And you really want to?"

"I think it's the best thing to do. But I don't want you to do it if you don't really want to."

"And if I do it you'll be happy and things will be like they were and you'll love me?"

"I love you now. You know I love you."

"I know. But if I do it then it will be nice again if I say things are like white elephants and you'll like it?"

"I'll love it. I love it now but I just can't think about it. You know how I get when I worry."

"If I do it you won't ever worry?"

"I won't worry about that because it's perfectly simple."

"Then I'll do it. Because I don't care about me."

"What do you mean?"

"I don't care about me."

"Well I care about you."

"Oh yes. But I don't care about me. And I'll do it and then everything will be fine."

"I don't want you to do it if you feel that way."

The girl stood up and walked to the end of the station. Across on the other side were fields of grain and trees along the banks of the Ebro. Far away beyond the river were mountains. The shadow of a cloud moved across the field of grain and she saw the river through the trees.

"And we could have all this," she said. "And we could have everything and every day we make it more impossible."

"What did you say?"

"I said we could have everything."

"We can have everything."

"No we can't."

"We can have the whole world."

"No we can't."

"We can go everywhere."

"No we can't. It isn't ours any more."

"It's ours."

"No it isn't. And once they take it away you never get it back."

"But they haven't taken it away."

"We'll wait and see.'

"Come on back in the shade," he said. "You mustn't feel that way."

"I don't feel any way," the girl said. "I just know things."

"I don't want you to do anything that you don't want to do."

"Nor that isn't good for me," she said. "I know. Could we have another beer?"

"All right. But you've got to realize—"

"I realize," the girl said. "Can't we maybe stop talking?"

They sat down at the table and the girl looked across at the hills on the dry side of the valley and the man looked at her and at the table.

"You've got to realize," he said, "that I don't want you to do it if you don't want to. I'm perfectly willing to go through with it if it means anything to you."

"Doesn't it mean anything to you? We could get along."

"Of course it does. But I don't want anybody but you. I don't want anyone else. And I know it's perfectly simple."

"Yes you know it's perfectly simple."

"It's all right for you to say that but I do know it."

"Would you do something for me now?"

"I'd do anything for you."

"Would you please please please please please please please stop talking?"

He did not say anything but looked at the bags against the wall of the station. There were labels on them from all the hotels where they had stopped.

"But I don't want you to," he said, "I don't care anything about it."

"I'll scream," the girl said.

The woman come out through the curtain with two glasses of beer and put them down on the damp felt pads. "The train comes in five minutes," she said.

"What did she say?" asked the girl.

"That the train is coming in five minutes."

The girl smiled brightly at the woman to thank her.

"I'd better take the bags over to the other side of the station," the man said. She smiled at him.

"All right. Then come back and we'll finish the beer."

He picked up the two heavy bags and carried them around the station to the other tracks. He looked up the tracks but could not see the train. Coming back he walked through the barroom where people waiting for the train were drinking. He drank an Anis at the bar and looked at the people. They were all waiting reasonably for the train. He went out through the bead curtain. She was sitting at the table and smiled at him.

"Do you feel better?" he asked.

"I feel fine," she said. "There's nothing wrong with me. I feel fine."

transition 5

Eugene Jolas   *Carrousel*

The old-world house has the accents of a folk song. The swallows chant sonnets under the eaves, the children follow rondos around the arc lamp, a blue haze spirals with fables. The gray-haired woman calls from an oil-lamp-swaling room.

I listen into the town. The voices that once were familiar to me tangle into a confusion of syllables. Ten years ago I sought the clemencies of an alien harbor, but steel gnawed my nerves, and the red phantom danced before me in cities where my homesickness became the echo of a desire. Whoever has not felt that ache, when the nocturnal streets in the foreign land swarm with molluscs, succubi, and vertigo, and when the silhouette of a word comes from midnight solitudes, does not know the intolerance of despair. Night hangs with tears. Muted violins play in the brain, and a funeral bell clangs across caresses.

The spring I had dreamed of is now in the veins of my home town. The priest wanders through the main street, girls and boys stand in a paralysis of sunset, the cinema plays Charlot, the girl I once loved smiles at me. And father and mother? They are old and talk about death and the departing sap. They ask questions and wait in long silences. They remember my letters, and wonder why cities brought misery, why my eyes look into space, as if waiting for something they cannot guess.

I wander through the house like a somnambulist. Nothing has changed. The rooms look the same, the crucifix hangs at the same angle on the wall of the kitchen, the garret has the same dusty calendars, the same smell of fruits. What is this unrest in me? The lamplight flows harshly over the faces of my family. I sink into a mythology. My brothers are strangers, and their voices seem to come from ravines in dark forests.

I walk through the streets and eyes come towards me with hostile vision. The alleyways that knew my laughter stare hallucinated into blueness. A merry-go-round plays on the market place. The same tunes I remember from vanished days creak through the air, while the shrill cries of the children accompany the rhythms. The public school nearby stands with yawning windows. The bell hangs rusty over a window sill. I remember its ringing across the years, when it was prophetic of conflagrations, crashing of planets, mud-colored dawns.

Sinister steps pursue me, as I walk in the delirium of the evening. The sunset throws its dying aura around the ivied castle ruin. The parish house sinks into a hypnosis. What am I looking for? Always I carry with me the memory of nightmares. O insanity of the lingering Angelus! Shadows glide through the furrows of the fields, and the lights begin to glimmer in the valley houses. The organ of the merry-go-round chants from the acetylene-sprinkled market place below.

The teacher droned, but the boy mused over Pizarro's adventures. Sometimes he looked up into the steel eyes of the pedagogue, and his meditations continued over geographies. He thought of the table at home strewn with pamphlets which his father had ordered from overseas. They were studying plans to emigrate. The children talked about the new countries, where the earth would be kind to them, and where their hunger-drugged spirits would smile in the sun.

The boy had a longing for huge savannas. The red man wanders on mysterious missions. The yucca plant waves in the moon. Coyotes rove in the prairie-solitude. White men love Indian girls and Arcadias. Blockhouses hold the sorcery of strange adventures. Trappers live lonely beneath the stars. O virgin forests that shake with mysteries! No one enters you without being wounded by your green darkness.

Pampas grass rustles silvery in the wind. Vira Cocha is humbled, and his gold shimmers before greedy eyes. Haciendas lie sleepily in the afternoon, and something greens in our minds, balsam of illusions. The calendars swoon in dust. O tropical nights, when the apes chatter legends and the flamingos flutter in the palms, when the stream swirls through flower-nights, and the Indians think of the anesthesia of forgotten sagas!

We will be ecstatic with going to luminous twilights. Always our feet will carry dust and dew and our minds will drink in the last moonbeam behind mysterious hills. We will live hidden from darkling eyes, and the peace of the loam will flow over us.

The teacher droned. The carrousel started outside. The boy was far away. Out of the air there whipped the ferule lacerating his back.

This is the Walpurgis night, I said. The sky is a vertiginous scrawl. Cling-clang of iron overhead. The last sparrow sleeps in the park. My muscles remember pavements and burdens. Vermin have tarried over me. I am the only one in a universe of sounds. The knees of young girls brush against me. My trance is a mechanical flute.

Trip hammers shrill. Planes of violence soar. Metallic facts circle. O cinema of chaos! O anguish of wheels, hungers, convolutions! All day long I work in a prison gray with dust. Skyscrapers collapse in my wishes. Basements are tunnels, where hideous animals creep through darkness. There is an invasion of comedies, but my hero stands in a tragic pose.

My fever drowns in the thunder. The police station near my tenement house yawns. I speak past the static globes, go up to my room, fumble treacherous thoughts. I write home: Dear Parents—New York is magnificent, but I am very lonely for you. My pen stops. Something shakes in me like tears.

I put out the gaslight. The darkness is a healing hand over my forehead. My youth storming to adventures lies tired and faint, and a requiem whines tonight. I listen to the wail of children. I stare out of the window at the walls of the teeming tenement opposite. A man and a woman, nude, embrace each other in a lighted room below.

I am a beast at bay. The city crushes me. I am afraid to move. Someone brews poison in a room nearby. Eyes smile ironically. Men spy on me. My voice lies in a narcotic slumber. My wishes suffer. I walk out into the night. A young girl leans out of a window. I speak to her. She calls into the shadows behind her. I flee down the street. It is midnight and my steps still sound on the asphalt.

With me always is the phantom of my fears. Everything in me collapses with a shriek of horror. Voices shrill into my ears words about trackless nights, hallucinations, tyrannies, suicide.

I cannot stay long. Riding to the stars, letting myself whir into huge spaces, deflecting into dialogues on shifting continents, it all ends in censorship, spider webs, tombs. O peace of my house! My memories splinter against the syllables of prophets. The evening cries its folk songs, its forest winds, its music of blood.

Why does the terror of city twilights come back when the nightingale sings again, and nerves slacken in the tranquillity of the beams of the attic? Apple blossoms shake in the valley wind, and my heart listens to the coming fruit, when the last of the lonely has found a companion, and music trickles into the organ of the sorrows. I cannot find the way out of the labyrinth, where my thoughts stumble over phantoms.

The merry-go-round creaked, steamed, whistled, sank into the rhythms of a moldering epoch. Boys raced out of the schoolrooms nearby, and hallooed into the blueness of the dusk. I stood held by the bruises of the ecstatic evening. Something led from these steps into the bleeding of my stigmas. I watched the children stream out, followed by their teacher, who slowly crossed the square. He stopped, stared at me, called me by name. I turned around, and looked into eyes I knew, eyes that had harrowed my days and nights, eyes that had hurled faggots of hatred into me long ago.

I looked, then walked away, listening into the dusk. The silhouette of the pedagogue hunched itself against the whirling hobbyhorses, near where the children were clustered. The evening was a bacchantic glow around the gables, and a crucifixion shook the hills. A blasphemy flamed from my mind. It grew wings above the roofs, fluttered over oceans and continents, and crackled convulsively over charred bones into nothingness.

transition 9

James Joyce   *A Muster from Work in Progress*

No Concern of the Guinnesses?

Now, concerning the genesis of Harold or Humphrey Chimpden's occupational agnomen and discarding once for all those theories from older sources which would link him back with such pivotal ancestors as the Glues, the Gravys, the Northeasts, the Ankers and the Earwickers of Sidlesham in the hundred of manhood or proclaim him offsprout of vikings who had founded wapentake and seddled hem in Herrick or Eric, the best authenticated version has it that it was this way. We are told how in the beginning it came to pass that like cabbaging Cincinnatus the grand old gardener was saving daylight under his redwoodtree one sultry sabbath afternoon in prefall paradise peace by following his plough for rootles in the rere garden of ye olde marine hotel when royalty was announced by runner to have been pleased to have halted itself on the highroad along which a leisureloving dogfox had cast followed, also at walking pace, by a lady pack of cocker spaniels. Forgetful of all save his vassal's plain fealty to the ethnarch Humphrey or Harold stayed not to yoke or saddle but stumbled out hotface as he was (his sweatful bandanna loose from his pocketcoat) hasting to the forecourts of his public in topee, surcingle, plus fours and bulldog boots ruddled with red marl, jingling his turnpike keys and bearing aloft amid the fixed pikes of the hunting party a high perch atop of which a flowerpot was fixed earthside hoist with care. On his majesty, who was, or often feigned to be, noticeably longsighted from green youth and had been meaning to inquire what, in effect, had caused yon causeway to be thus potholed, asking substitutionally to be put wise as to whether paternoster and silver doctors were not now more fancied bait for lobstertrapping honest blunt Haromphreyld answered in no uncertain tones very similarly with a fearless forehead: Naw, yer maggers, aw war jist a cotchin on thon bluggy earwuggers. Our sailor king, who was draining a gugglet of obvious adamale, upon this, ceasing to swallow, smiled most heartily beneath his walrus moustaches and indulging that none too genial humor which William the Conk on the spindle side had inherited with the hereditary whitelock and some shortfingeredness from his greataunt Sophy, turned towards two of his retinue of gallow-glasses, Michael, etheling lord of Leix in Offaly and the jubilee mayor of Drogheda, Elcock, (the two scatterguns being Michael M. Manning, protosyndic of Waterford and an Italian excellency named Ginbilei according to a later version cited by the learned scholarch Canavan of Canmakenoise) and remarked dilsydulsily: Holybones, how our red brother of Pouringrainia would audibly fume did he know that we have for trusty bailiwick a turnpiker who is by turns a pikebailer no seldomer than an earwigger! Comes the question are these the facts as recorded in both or either of the collateral andrewpomurphyc narratives. We shall perhaps not so soon see. The great fact emerges that after that historic date all holographs so far exhumed initialed by Haromphrey bear the sigla H.C.E. and while he was only and long and always good Dook Umphrey for the hungerlean spalpeens of Lucalizod and Chimbers to his cronies it was equally certainly a pleasant turn of the populace which gave him as sense of those normative letters the nickname Here Comes Everybody. An imposing everybody he always indeed looked, constantly the same as and equal to himself and magnificently well worthy of any and all such universalisation, every time he continually surveyed from good start to happy finish the truly catholic assemblage gathered together in the house of satin from their assbawlveldts and oxgangs unanimously to clapplaud Mr. Wallenstein Washington Semperkelly's immergreen tourers in the problem passion play of the millentury *A Royal Divorce* with ambitious interval band selections from *The Bo' Girl* and *The Lily* on all gala command nights from his viceregal booth where, a veritable Napoleon the Nth, this folksforefather all of the time sat having the entirety of his house about him, with the invariable broadstretched kerchief cooling his whole neck, nape and shoulderblades and in a wardrobe panelled tuxedo completely thrown back from a shirt well entitled a swallowall, on every point far outstarching the laundered clawhammers and marble-topped highboys of the pit stalls and early ampitheater. A baser meaning has been read into these characters the literal sense of which decency can safely scarcely hint. It has been blurtingly bruited by certain wisecracks that he suffered from a vile disease. To such a suggestion the one selfrespecting answer is to affirm that there are certain statements which ought not to be, and one should like to be able to add, ought not to be allowed to be made. Nor have his detractors, who, an imperfectly warmblooded race, apparently conceive him as a great white caterpillar capable of any and every enormity in the calendar recorded to the discredit of the Juke and Kellikek families, mended their case by insinuating that, alternately, he lay at one time under the ludicrous imputation of annoying Welsh fusiliers in the people's park. To anyone who knew and loved the christlikeness of the big cleanminded giant H. C. Earwicker throughout his long existence the mere suggestion of him as a lustsleuth nosing for trouble in a boobytrap rings particularly preposterous. Truth, beard on prophet, compels one to add that there is said to have olim been (pfuit! pfuit!) some case of the kind implicating, it is interdum believed, a quidam abhout that time stambuling haround Dumbaling with his tarrk record who has remained topantically anonymos but (let us hue him Abdullah Gamellaxarksky) was, it is stated, posted at Mallon's, at the instance of watch warriors of the vigilance committee and years afterwards, cries one even greater, Ibid, a commender of the frightful, seemingly tropped head (pfiat! pfiat!) waiting turn for thatt chopp pah kabbakks alicubi off Hawkins Street. Slander, let it lie its flattest, has never been able to convict our good and great and no ordinary Southron Earwicker, as a pious author called him, of any graver impropriety than that, advanced by some woodwards or regarders, who did not dare deny that they had, chin Ted, chin Tam, chinchin Taffyd, that day consumed their soul of the corn, of having behaved in an ungentlemanly manner opposite a pair of dainty maidservants in the swoolth of the rushy hollow whither, or so the two gown and pinners pleaded, dame nature in all innocency had spontaneously and about the same hour of the eventide sent them both but whose published combinations of silkinlaine testimonies are, where not dubiously pure, visibly divergent, as warpt from wept, on minor points touching the intimate nature of this, a first offence in vert or venison which was admittedly an incautious but, at its wildest, a partial exposure with such attentuating circumstances (garthen gaddeth green hwere sokeman hrideth girling) as an abnormal Saint Swithin's summer and a ripe occasion to provoke it.

A Mole

This wastohavebeen underground heaven, first in the west, our mister-bilder openly damned and blasted by means of a hydromine, system Sowan and Belting, exploded from a reinvented bombingpost up ahoy of eleven and thirty wingrests *(circiter)* to sternbooard out of his aerial thorpeto, Auton Dynamon, contacted with the expectant minefield by tins of improved ammonia lashed to her shieldplated gunwale, and fused into tripupcables, slipping through tholes and playing down from the conning tower into the ground battery fuseboxes, all differing as clocks from keys since nobody appeared to have the same time of beard, some saying by their Oorlog it was Sygstryggs to nine, more holding with the Ryan wacht it was Dane to pfife. He afterwards carefully lined the ferroconcrete result with rotproof bricks and mortar, fassed to fossed, so encouraging additional useful councils public such as the Breeders' Union, the Guild of Merchants of the Staple *et,* a. u. c., to present unto him over and above that a stone slab with the usual Mac Pelah address of velediction: We have done with you, Heer Here-whippit, skidoo! Show coffins, winding sheets, goodbuy bierchepes cinerary urns, liealoud blasses, snuffchests, poteentubbs and for that matter any kind of funeral bric au brac would naturally follow, halas, in the ordinary course, enabling that roundtheworlder to live all safeathomely the presenile days of his life of opulence, ancient ere decrepitude, whaling away the whole of the while, lethelulled between explosion and reexplosion from grosskopp to megapod, embalmed, of grand age, rich in death anticipated.

Peaches

Take an old geeser who calls on his skirt. Note his sleek hair, so elegant, *tableau vivant.* He vows her to be his own honeylamb, swears they will be papa pals, by Sam, and share good times way down west in a guaranteed happy lovenest when May moon she shines and they twit twinkle all the night, combing the comet's tail up right and shooting popguns at the stars. For dear old grumpapar, he's gone on the razzle-dar, through gazing and crazing and blazing at the stars. She wants her wardrobe to hear from above by return with cash so as she can buy her Peter Robinson trousseau and cut a dash with Arty, Bert or possibly Charley Chance (who knows?) so tolloll Mr. Hunker you're too dada for me to dance (so off she goes!) and that's how half the gels in town has got their botom drars while grumpapar he's trying to hitch his braces on to his trars. But old grum he's not so clean dippy between sweet you and yum (not on your life, boy! not in those trousers! not by a large jugful!) for someplace on the sly old grum has his gel number two (bravevow, our Grum!) and he would like to canoodle her too some part of the time for he is downright fond of his number one but O he's fair mashed on peaches number two so that if he could only canoodle the two all three would feel genuinely happy, it's as simple as A.B.C., the two mixers, we mean, with their cherrybum chappy (for he is simply shamming dippy) if they all were afloat in a dreamlifeboat, hugging two by two in his zoo-doo-you-doo, a tofftoff for thee, missymissy for me and howcameyou-e'enso for Farber, in his tippy, upindown dippy, tiptoptippy canoodle, can you?

Be Sage and Choose

There is some thing-more. All I can tell you is this, my sorellies. It's prayers in layers all the thumping time begor in the suburrs of the heavenly gardens, once we shall have passed through to our snug eternal reward (the scorchhouse). Shunt us! shunt us! shunt us! If you want to be felixed come and be parked. Sacred ease There! The seanad and pobbel queue's remainder. No petty family squabbles Up There, nor homemade hurricanes in our Cohortyard, no cupahurling nor apuckalips nor no nothing. With the Byrns which is far better and eve for ever your idle be. Iereny allover irelands. Hogmanny di'yegut? Hogmanny di'yesmellygut? And hogmanny di'yesmellyspatterygut? You take Joe Hanny's tip for it. Postmartem is the goods. With Jollification a good second. Toborrow and toburrow and tobarrow! That's our crass, hairy, and evergrim life! We may come, touch and go, from atoms and ifs but we're presurely destined to be odd's without ends. Here we moult in moy Kain and flop on the seemy side living sure of hardly a doorstep for a stopgap, with Whogoesthere and a live sandbag round the corner. But upmeyant you sprout all your abel and woof your wings dead certain however of neuthing whatever to aye forever while Hyam Hyam's in the chair. Ah, sure, pleasantries aside, in the tail of the cow what a humpty daum earth looks our miseryme heretoday as compared beside the Hereweareagain Gaieties of the Afterpiece when the Royal Revolver of these real globoes lets regally fire of his *mio colpo* for the chrisman's pandemon to give over and the Harlequinade to begin properly SPQueaRking Mark Time's Finist Joke. Putting Allspace in a Notshall.

On the Death of Mrs. Sanders (Pippip)

To the Very Honourable The Memory of Disgrace the Most Noble, Sometime Sweepyard at the Service of the Writer. The just defunct Mrs. Sanders who (the Loyd insure her!) I was shift and shuft too. She was the niceliest person of a wellteached nonparty woman that I ever acquired her letters, used to babies and tottydean verbish this is her entertermentdags for she shuk the bottle and tuk the medascene all times a day. She was well under ninety poor late Mrs. and had tastes of the poetics, me having stood the pilgarlick a fresh at sea when the moon also was standing in a corner of sweet Standerson my ski. P. L. M. Mevrouw von Andersan was her who gave me a mutton-brooch, stakkers for her begfirst party. Honour thy farmer and my litters. This, my tears, is my last will intesticle wrote off in the strutforit about their absent female assauciations which I, or perhaps any other person, have the honour to had upon their polite sophykussens in the real presence of devouted Mrs. Grumby when her skin was exposed to the air. O what must the grief of my mund be for two little ptpt coolies worth twenty thousand quad herewitdnessed with both's maddlemass wishes to Pepette for next match from their dearly beloved Roggers, M.D.D.O.D. May doubling drop of drooght! Writing.

The River and the Mountain Converse

O foenix culprit! Ex nickylow malo comes mickelmassed bonum. Hill, rill, ones in company, billeted, less be proud of. Breast high and bestrid! Only for that these will not breathe upon Norronesen or Irenean the secrest of their soorcelossness. Quarry silex, Homfrie Noanswa! Undy gentian festyknees, Livia Noanswa? Wolkencap is on him, frowned; audiurient he would evesdrip, were it mous at hand, were it dinn of bottles in the far ear. Murk, his vales are darkling. With lipth she lithpeth to him all to time of thuch on thuch and thow on thow. Hairfluke, if he could bad twig her! Impalpabunt, he abhears.

Vikingfather Sleeps

Liverpoor? Sot a bit of it! His braynes coolt parritch, his pelt nassy, his heart's adrone, his bluidstreams acrawl, his puff but a piff, his extremeties extremely so. Fingless. Pawnbroke, Chilblaimemds and Baldowl. Humph is in his doge. Words weigh no no more to him than raindrips to Rethfernhim. Which we all like. Rain. When we sleep. Drops. But wait until our sleeping. Drain. Sdops.

"Muster" was prepared and occasionally revised by the author from fragments published in Transition *numbers 1, 2, 3, 4, 12, 13, for inclusion in* Transition Stories *(New York: McKee, 1929).*

Franz Kafka   *The Sentence*

It was before noon on a Sunday in a most lovely spring. George
Bendemann, a young businessman, was sitting in his room on the first
floor of one of those low, lightly built houses strung in a row along the
river, and differing from one another in height and color only. He
had just finished a letter to a friend of his youth who was now abroad
and, after dawdling over sealing it, was sitting with his elbow on his
desk, gazing out of the window at the river, the bridge, and the hills
on the opposite bank, with their delicate green.

He was thinking about a friend of his who, discontented with his
slow advancement at home, had decided to emigrate to Russia many
years before. This friend now ran a business in St. Petersburg, which,
although it had begun under excellent auspices, had for some time
been facing difficulties, to judge by the complaints made during his
less and less frequent visits. Thus he was working himself to death
abroad, without profit. His strange, full beard hid his face only scantily
—a face that had been familiar since childhood—and his yellow complexion seemed to denote a progressive illness. According to him, he
had no real connection with the colony of his own countrymen, and
hardly any social contact with native Russian families. He had, therefore, definitely adjusted himself to a bachelor existence.

What could one write to such a man, who had obviously gone to
seed, and whom, although one could feel sorry for him, one could not
help? Should he perhaps be advised to come home, to begin life over
again here, to pick up all the old ties and simply to have confidence in
the help of his friends? But that would amount to telling him at the
same time (and the more delicately it was said, the more it would hurt)
that so far his efforts had failed, that he should therefore abandon them,
and return to let himself be stared at as one who had come back to
stay—that he was somewhat childish, and would just have to follow
in the tracks of the successful friends who had remained at home. But
was it by any means certain that all the trouble this would make for
him would bear fruit? Perhaps nobody would even succeed in getting
him to come—he himself having said that he could no longer understand conditions at home—in which case, despite everything, he would

still be a stranger in a strange land, embittered by the advice given him, and separated even further from his friends. But suppose he should follow the advice and then go to pieces here, suppose he should be unable to adjust himself, either with his friends or without them; would it not be better for him if he stayed abroad, as he was? For could one, under such circumstances, assume that he actually would be able to make his way?

For these reasons, if one were really desirous of remaining in correspondence with him, one could not write him certain details that could be explained to the most distant acquaintance. The friend had not been back home for three years, a fact he explained most unconvincingly by the uncertainty of political conditions in Russia, which did not permit a small businessman even a brief absence, while a hundred thousand Russians were traveling peacefully around the world.

But in the course of these three years a great many things had changed for George. To be sure, his friend had heard of the death of George's mother, which had occurred about two years earlier, and since which George had lived with his old father; the friend had expressed his sympathy in a letter of such coldness that it seemed to be explainable only by the fact that he simply could not grasp such an occurrence in the outside world. Since then, George had plunged into his business with greatly increased energy. Perhaps his father had prevented real activity on his part while his mother was alive, by insisting upon asserting his own views. Perhaps, too, his father had grown more reticent since his mother's death, although he was still active in the business; perhaps—and this seemed more probable—a few felicitous accidents had played a much more important role; at any rate, business had flourished these past two years most unexpectedly. They had had to double the staff, the profits were five times more than formerly, and further improvement seemed likely.

But his friend had no idea of all this. In the old days, the last time perhaps in that letter of condolence, he had tried to persuade George to emigrate to Russia, and had expatiated on the prospects that existed for George's business in St. Petersburg. His friend's earnings were small compared with the present expansion of George's business. But George was not inclined to write his friend about his commercial successes, and now, after all that had gone before, to do so would really have looked strange.

Thus George limited himself to writing his friend about unimportant happenings, such as accumulate in the memory while one muses about them on a quiet Sunday. He had no other desire than to leave undisturbed the impression of his home town which his friend had retained during this long interval, and which was surely to his liking. Then

it so happened that in three letters, following one another at long
intervals, George had told his friend of the engagement of a certain
man to a girl, both of them equally unknown, and the friend, entirely
contrary to George's intentions, had begun to grow interested in this
unusual event.

But George preferred writing him about such things rather than
admit that he himself had become engaged a month ago to Miss
Frieda Brandenfeld, a girl from a well-to-do family. He often discussed
his friend with her as well as the rather special relationship they maintained by correspondence. "I suppose he won't come to our wedding,
then," she had said, "and yet, I have a right to know all your friends."

"I don't want to disturb him," George had replied. "Don't misunderstand me, he probably would come, at least I think so. But he would
feel forced to do it and would be hurt; he might even envy me, and
then he would have to go back alone, certainly dissatisfied and incapable
of throwing off his feeling of dissatisfaction. Alone—do you know
what that means?"

"Yes, but might he not hear of our wedding through some other
source?"

"That, of course, I can't prevent, but it is improbable, considering how
he lives."

"If you have such friends, George, you should never have become
engaged."

"Well, we're both responsible for that; but I would not want things
otherwise, even now."

Then, when, breathing heavily under his kisses, she had objected,
saying, "It really hurts me," he had decided he would have to write his
friend everything.

"I am like that," he said to himself, "and he will have to take me as
I am; I can't make another human being out of myself, even though I
might be better fitted for friendship."

And, in fact, he had announced his engagement in the long letter he
had written to his friend that Sunday afternoon, in the following words:
"The best news I have saved for the last. I have become engaged to Miss
Frieda Brandenfeld, a girl from a well-to-do family which settled here
long after your departure, and which you probably will not know for
that reason. I hope to have an opportunity to tell you more about my
fiancée; today, however, I shall only say that I am very happy and that
the only change in our relationship is that you will have, instead of a
very ordinary friend, a really happy one. And then you will have in my
fiancée, who wishes me to send her regards, and who will herself write
you soon, a sincere friend, a fact which is not without importance for
a bachelor. I know many things prevent you from visiting us. But don't

you think that our wedding might offer the right opportunity to throw all objections overboard? However that may be, please act without taking us into consideration, just as you see fit."

With this letter in his hand, George sat at his desk a long time, his face turned towards the window. Smiling absent-mindedly, he hardly answered a passing acquaintance who greeted him from the street.

At last he put the letter in his pocket and, crossing the room, went through a little hallway into his father's room, where he had not been for months. There was never any real necessity for his going there, for he saw his father during business hours every day. They ate lunch together in a boardinghouse, although they had dinner separately. Then both sat for a little while in the common living room, each with his newspaper, unless George went to see a friend, which happened most frequently, or, as he now did, visited his fiancée.

George was astonished to see how dark his father's room was this sunny forenoon. Strange, that the high wall rising beyond the small courtyard should cast such shadow. His father was sitting at the window in a corner decorated with diverse souvenirs of his mother. He was reading the newspaper held sideways in front of his eyes, by which operation he attempted to compensate for his feeble eyesight. On the table there were the remains of breakfast, of which he evidently had eaten very little.

"Ah, George," said his father, who rose to meet him. His heavy bathrobe came open as he walked, and flapped about him. "My father is still a giant," thought George to himself.

"It's really unbearably dark in here," George said out loud.

"Yes, it really is dark," his father replied.

"Did you close the window?"

"I prefer it like this."

"It's quite warm outside," said George, as if adding an epilogue. He sat down.

His father took the breakfast dishes away and set them on a box.

"I simply wanted to tell you," George continued, while observing absent-mindedly the motions of the old man, "that I finally did announce my engagement to St. Petersburg." He took the letter from his pocket, then let it wander back again.

"To St. Petersburg?" asked the father.

"Well, to my friend," George said, trying to meet his father's eyes. "In business he's entirely different," he thought to himself. "It's funny how he sits there, his arms crossed over his broad chest . . ."

"Yes, to your friend," his father said emphatically.

"You know, father, I first intended not to tell him about my engagement. Simply out of consideration for him. He is a difficult man. I said to myself, he may learn of my engagement from other sources, although that is hardly probable, considering his solitary life—I cannot prevent it anyway—but he should not learn it through me."

"And now you have changed your mind again?" his father asked. He laid the large newspaper on the window sill, then on it he laid his glasses, which he covered with his hand.

"Yes, I thought it over again. If he is a good friend, I said to myself, my happy engagement will be a source of happiness to him. And therefore I no longer hesitated to send him the announcement. But before mailing the letter, I wanted to tell you about it."

"George," his father said, opening wide his toothless mouth, "now listen! You have come to me with this affair to talk it over. That is undoubtedly to your credit. But it is nothing, less than nothing, if you do not tell me the whole truth. I do not want to stir up things that do not belong here. Since the death of your dear mother, a number of disagreeable things have happened. Many things elude me in business, perhaps no attempt is made to hide them from me—nor do I want to assume that they are being hidden from me—for I am no longer very strong, and my memory is failing. I no longer have control over many things. That is due first of all to the slowing up of nature's functioning, and secondly the death of your mother has affected me much more than it has you. But since we happen to be discussing this letter, I must beg of you, George, not to deceive me. It is a small matter, not worth wasting one's breath on, so don't deceive me. Have you really a friend in St. Petersburg?"

George rose, embarrassed. "Let's leave my friends alone. A thousand friends cannot replace my father. Do you know what I think? You do not take enough care of yourself. But old age takes its toll. You are indispensable to me in business, you know that well enough; but if the business should endanger your health, I should prefer closing it to-morrow. This can't go on. We shall have to organize your life quite differently. Something absolutely fundamental. You sit here in the darkness, when you could have a nice light in the living room. At break-fast you simply nibble at your food, instead of really nourishing yourself. You sit here with the windows closed, when the air would be so good for you. No, Father! I am going to get the doctor, and we are going to follow his advice. We shall exchange rooms—you must take the front room, and I will stay here. It will not alter anything for you, everything will be moved over there. But we'll do that in due time. Meanwhile, you might lie down now a bit, for you need absolute rest. I'll help you undress, you'll see I can do it. Or perhaps you would prefer moving to the front room at once. Then, for the time being, you might lie down on my bed. That's a good idea."

George was standing beside his father, who let his head, with its scraggly white hair, sink onto his chest.

"George," his father said softly, without emotion.

George knelt down beside him; he saw the overlarge pupils in his father's tired face staring at him out of the corners of his eyes.

"You have no friend in St. Petersburg. You have always been a practical joker, even with me. Why should you have a friend there, of all places? I don't believe it."

"Think for a minute, father," said George, lifting his father from the armchair and taking off his bathrobe. The old man seemed very weak. "It's almost three years ago that my friend was here for a visit. I can still remember that you did not care much for him. At least on two occasions I denied him before you, although he was sitting with me in my room, for I could easily understand your aversion to him. My friend has certain peculiarities. But at other times you got along with him very well. I was so proud then that you should listen to him; you nodded and asked questions. If you think about it, you will surely remember this. He told incredible stories about the Russian Revolution; for instance, how during a business trip in Kiev he saw a riot and a priest on a balcony who cut a wide crucifix of blood in the palm of his hand, then raised his hand in an appeal to the crowd. I remember you yourself repeating this story from time to time."

By now George had succeeded in getting his father to sit down again and he began to take off his drawers and socks. At the sight of the not particularly clean underclothes, he blamed himself for having neglected his father. It certainly should have been his duty to watch over his father's laundry. He had not yet talked with his fiancée about his father's future, but it had been tacitly assumed that his father would remain in the old home. Now he decided once and for all to take his father with him into his future household. It might even be that such care could come too late.

He carried his father in his arms to the bed. A fearful feeling came over him, as he noticed that during the few steps to the bed his father was playing with the watch chain on his chest. In fact, he could not lay him directly on the bed because he clung so firmly to the watch chain.

But hardly was he in bed, when everything seemed all right. He himself drew up the covers, and the gaze he turned on George was not unfriendly.

"Of course you remember him, father, don't you?" asked George, nodding encouragingly towards his father.

"Am I covered up now?" the old man asked, as if he did not know whether or not his feet were sufficiently covered.

"So you're beginning to like it in bed already?" said George, drawing the cover more closely about him.

"Am I well covered up?" his father asked once more, seeming to await a reply most attentively.

"Just be quiet, you're well covered."

"No!" his father cried, hurling the answer after the question. He threw off the cover with such force that it came unfolded, and he stood for a moment erect in bed. One hand was pressed lightly against the ceiling. "You wanted to cover me up, I know you, my lad, but I'm not covered up yet. And even if it is all the strength I have left, it's enough for you, too much for you. Of course, I know your friend. He would have been a son after my own heart. So it's for that reason that you have been deceiving him all these years. Why otherwise? Don't you think I wept over him? That's why you lock yourself in your office; nobody must disturb you, the boss is busy—just so you can write your deceiving letters to Russia. But fortunately nobody warned the father to find out about his son. You thought just now you had got the best of me, so that you could tumble down on me without my stirring. And so my Honorable Son has decided to get married!"

George looked up at the terrifying picture of his father. The friend in St. Petersburg, whom his father suddenly seemed to know so well, captivated his imagination as never before. He saw him lost in the immensities of Russia. He saw him at the door of the empty business, which had been looted. He saw him standing amid the debris of the shelves, the ruined merchandise, the falling gas fixtures. Why had he gone so far away?

"Look at me!" his father shouted, and almost without thinking, George ran towards the bed. Suddenly he stopped short.

"Because she raised her skirts," his father was saying in a flutelike voice. "Because she raised her skirts, the trollop," and in order to picture it, he raised his own shirt so high that the scar from his war days could be seen on his upper thigh. "Because she raised her skirts this way and that way, and this way. That's why you went to her, and in order to satisfy yourself with her without being disturbed, you have dishonored your mother's memory, betrayed your friend, and put your father to bed so he cannot move. But he can still move, or can't he?"

And he stood up straight—hurled his legs into the air. He was luminous with cunning.

George was standing in one corner, as far away from his father as possible. Some time ago he had decided to observe everything very accurately, so that he might not be taken by surprise either from behind or from above. Now he remembered again his long-forgotten decision, then forgot it again, as one draws a fine thread through the eye of a needle.

"But nevertheless your friend is not betrayed," his father cried, and his index finger bobbing to and fro affirmed it. "I have been watching out for his interests here."

"You're joking." George was unable to refrain from saying this, but recognized his mistake and bit his tongue, although too late. In considerable pain, his eyes took on a staring expression.

"Yes, of course, I am joking! A joke! Excellent word! What other consolation did an old widowed father have? Look—and during the moment of your reply be still my living son. What was there left for me, in my back room, persecuted by unfaithful employees, and old to my very bones? While my son was racing jubilantly through the world, concluding business affairs which I had prepared, standing on his head with joy, and avoiding his father with the enigmatic face of a man of honor. Don't you think I loved you? I, from whom you came?"

"Now he is going to bend forward," thought George. "Suppose he should fall and crack his skull." These words hissed through his brain.

His father bent forward, but did not fall. Since George, contrary to his expectation, did not come nearer, he rose up again.

"Stay where you are, I don't need you! You think you still have the strength to come here and you hold back merely because you are so minded. But you are mistaken. I am still much the stronger. Alone, perhaps I might have had to retreat, but your mother has now given me her strength; I know all about your friend; the list of your customers is in my pocket."

"There are pockets even in his shirt," said George, thinking this would bring his father to his senses. But he thought this only for a moment, for he quickly forgot things.

"Just stick to your fiancée and be condescending to me. I will separate her from you, and you will never know how."

George made a grimace, as if he did not believe it. His father merely nodded towards George's corner, affirming the truth of his statement.

"You really amused me when you asked me if you should write your friend about your engagement. He knows everything, you fool, he knows everything already. I wrote him, because you forgot to take my writing materials away from me. That's why he has not been back for years, he knows everything a hundred times better than you yourself. Your letters he crushes, unread, in his left hand, while holding mine in his right hand, the better to read them."

Enthusiastically he swung his arm over his head. "He knows everything a thousand times better," he shouted.

"Ten thousand times," said George, in an attempt to sneer at his father, but the words had a deadly serious sound, even in his mouth.

"For years I have been waiting for you to come with this question. Do you think that anything else interests me? Do you think that I am reading newspapers? There," and he threw the page of a paper, which somehow had been carried to the bed, in George's direction, an old newspaper with a name with which George was unfamiliar.

"How long it took you to become mature! Your mother had to die, she could not experience that day of joy; your friend is wasting away in his Russia, three years ago he was as yellow as death; and I, just see how things are with me. Haven't you eyes to see?"

"So you were spying on me?" said George.

Pitifully his father said: "You probably wanted to say that sooner? Now it's not the thing to say."

Then louder: "Now you know what was going on outside yourself. Before, you only knew about yourself. You really were an innocent child, but in reality, diabolical! Listen to me: for I hereby condemn you to die by drowning."

George felt himself being chased out of the room; in his ears rang the thud with which his father had crashed onto the bed. On the stairs, down the steps of which he raced as over an oblique plane, he stumbled against the charwoman who was on her way upstairs to clean the bedrooms, after the night. "Good Lord," she called, and covered her face with her apron. But he was already gone. He ran out of the doorway, and something drove him across the streetcar tracks to the water. He held on to the parapet, like a hungry man to his food. Then, being an excellent athlete, he swung over it. Clutching the railing with failing hands, he saw an omnibus which he decided would serve to cover the sound of his fall. He cried softly: "Dear parents! Yes, I have always loved you," and let himself sink down.

At that moment the traffic over the bridge was very heavy.

Translated from the German by Eugene Jolas

transition 11

Anais Nin   *The House of Incest*
(fragment)

My first vision of earth was water veiled. I am of the race of men and women who see all things through this curtain of sea and my eyes are the color of water.

I looked with chameleon eyes upon the changing face of the world, looked with anonymous vision upon my uncompleted self.

I remember my first birth in water. All round me a sulphurous transparency and my bones move as if made of rubber. I sway and float, stand on boneless toes listening for distant sounds, sounds beyond the reach of human ears, see things beyond the reach of human eyes. Born full of memories of the bells of the Atlantide. Always listening for last sounds and searching for last colors, standing forever on the threshold like one troubled with memories, and walking with a swimming stride. I cut the air with wide-slicing fins and swim through wall-less rooms. Ejected from a paradise of soundlessness, cathedrals wavering at the passage of a body, like soundless music.

This Atlantide could only be found again at night, by the route of the dream. As soon as sleep covered the rigid new city, the rigidity of the new world, the heaviest portals slid open, on smooth-oiled gong, and one entered the voicelessness of the dream. The terror and joy of murders accomplished in silence, in the silence of slidings and brushings. The blanket of water lying over all things stifling the voice. Only a monster brought me up on the surface by accident.

Lost in the colors of the Atlantide, the colors running into one another without frontiers. Fishes made of velvet, of organdie with lace fangs, made of spangled taffeta, of silks and feathers and whiskers, with lacquered flanks and rock-crystal eyes, fishes of withered leather with gooseberry eyes, eyes like the white of egg. Flowers palpitating on stalks like sea harts. None of them feeling their own weight, the sea horse moving like a feather . . .

It was like yawning. I loved the ease and the blindness and the suave voyages on the water bearing one through obstacles. The water was there to bear one like a giant bosom, there was always the water to rest on, and the water transmitted the lives and the loves, the words and the thoughts.

Far beneath the level of storms I slept. I moved within color and music like inside a sea diamond. There were no currents of thoughts, only the caress of flow and desire mingling, touching, traveling, withdrawing, wandering—the endless bottoms of peace.

I do not remember being cold there, nor warm. No pain of cold and heat. The temperature of sleep, feverless and chill-less. I do not remember being hungry. Food seeped through invisible pores. I do not remember weeping.

I felt only the caress of moving—moving into the body of another, absorbed and lost within the flesh of another, lulled by the rhythm of water, the slow palpitation of the senses, the movement of silk.

Loving without knowingness, moving without effort, in the soft current of water and desire, breathing in an ecstasy of dissolution.

I awoke at dawn, thrown up on a rock, the skeleton of a ship choked in its own sails.

I am floating again. All the facts and all the words, all images, all presages are sweeping over me, mocking each other. The dream! The dream! The dream rings through me like a giant copper bell when I wish to betray it. It brushes by me with bat wings when I open human eyes and seek to live dreamlessly. When human pain has struck me fiercely. When anger has corroded me, I rise, I always rise after the crucifixion, and I am in terror of my ascensions. THE FISSURE IN REALITY. The divine departure. I fall. I fall into darkness after the collision with pain, and after pain the divine departure.

Oh, the weight, the tremendous weight of my head pulled up by the clouds and swinging in space, the body like a wisp of straw, the clouds dragging my hair like a scarf caught in a chariot wheel, the body dangling, colliding with the lantern stars, the clouds dragging me over the world.

I cannot stop, or descend.

I hear the unfurling of water, of skies, and curtains. Hear the shiver of leaves, the breathing of the air, the wailing of the unborn, the pressure of the wind.

I hear the movements of the stars and planets, the slight rust creak when they shift their position. The silken passage of radiations, the breath of circles turning.

I hear the passing of mysteries and the breathing of monsters. Overtones only, or undertones. Collision with reality blurs my vision and submerges me into the dream. I feel the distance like a wound. It unrolls itself before me like the rug before the steps of a cathedral for a wedding or a burial. It is unrolled like a crimson bride between the others and me, but I cannot walk on it without a feeling of uneasiness, as one has at ceremonies. The ceremony of walking along the unrolled carpet into the cathedral where the functions unravel to which I am a stranger. I neither marry nor die. And the distance between the crowd, between the others and me, grows wider.

Distance. I never walked over the carpet into the ceremonies. Into the fullness of the crowd life, into the authentic music and the odor of men. I never attended the wedding or the burial. Everything for me took place either in the belfry where I was alone with the deafening sound of bells calling in iron voices. Or in the cellar where I nibbled at the candles and the incense stored away with the mice.

I cannot be certain of any event or place, only of my solitude. Tell me what the stars are saying about me. Does Saturn have eyes made of onions which weep all the time? Has Mercury chicken feathers on his heels, and does Mars wear a gas mask? Gemini, the evolved twins, do they evolve all the time, turning on a spit, Gemini *à la broche*?

There is a fissure in my vision and madness will always rush through. Lean over me, at the bedside of my madness, and let me stand without crutches.

I am an insane woman for whom houses wink and open their bellies. Significance stares at me from everywhere, like a gigantic underlying ghostliness. Significance emerges out of dank alleys and somber faces, leans out of the windows of strange houses. I am constantly reconstructing a pattern of something forever lost and which I cannot forget. I catch the odors of the past on street corners and I am aware of the men who will be born tomorrow. Behind windows there are either enemies or worshippers. Never neutrality or passivity. Always intention and premeditation. Even stones have for me druidical expressions.

I walk ahead of myself in perpetual expectancy of miracles.

I am enmeshed in my lies, and I want absolution. I cannot tell the truth because I have felt the heads of men in my womb. The truth would be death-dealing, and I prefer fairy tales. I am wrapped in lies which do not penetrate my soul. As if the lies I tell were like costumes. The shell of mystery can break and grow again overnight. But the moment I step into the cavern of my lies I drop into darkness. I see a face which stares at me like the glance of a cross-eyed man.

I remember the cold on Jupiter freezing ammonia, and out of ammonia crystals came the angels. Bands of ammonia and methane encircling Uranus. I remember the tornadoes of inflammable ethane on Saturn. I remember on Mars a vegetation like the susock grasses of Peru and Patagonia, an ocherous red, a rusty ore vegetation, mosses, and lichens. Iron-bearing red clays and red sandstone. Light there had a sound, and sunlight was an orchestra.

transition 27

Elliot Paul *Enharmonics*

Because you have remained so long within the dim borders of my life, moving on as I have moved, and like a mirage detached not only from the reality you reflect but even more mysteriously from the surroundings into which my capricious atmosphere has projected your appearance, I offer you a shimmering death such as none has experienced before. The loam remains unbroken.

Instead, you shall wear the soft brown muslin which veiled the edge of the precipice, and you shall continue the gesture which cautioned me, but not decisively—that unforgettable movement that stirred the timid flow of reminiscences over your half-averted face. This is your destination. Darkness has ceased stalking by the windows. No more shrill dawns shall be ripped from the edge of the sky.

Did you ever live? I cannot say.

Did I create you? There are shadows, but the furtive beasts slink from cover to cover, and the birds have muffled wings and eyes that gleam at night. Hordes of instincts drive my creatures elsewhere, leaving only footprints and broken twigs.

(What cursed eavesdropper prompts me to answer yes? Once again to falsify my universe by halving it with a positive assumption?)

I create nothing! Let that be written down. And forgive me for mentioning the jungle. It is only a public park, where the wind blows old papers into fence corners, and my name is written upon none of them.

Am I really giving you death as a present, carefully wrapped? Am I killing you? That is certain.

(Again the tormentor.) Some day I shall pass beneath a familiar balcony. I have not destroyed the cuckoo clocks, nor torn the lace from all handkerchiefs, nor obliterated all the labial syllables. Could I face my own reflection in an urn of bright blood, and, if so, have I seen myself thus?

To have used the word "certain" is humiliating. To believe in destruction is as futile as the myth of creation. Killing, like all else, has become intimately and intricately involved with science. One must have all the disgusting virtues in order to destroy. Patience, above everything. Perseverance. Industry. Poise. One must take care of one's health and think clear thoughts if one aspires to kill.

Silence, dyspeptic swine! Your calculations are at the mercy of my temper . . . But why must all deeds be violent? And, again, to what purpose should impulse be tamed?

Forgive me, my dear. This was to have been between you and me. Already intruders have broken in. Perhaps if I repeat that I love you, they will have the decency to retire. I am disposing of you, not of myself, so clownishly I shall begin to say many things and end by mumbling of my love, my itch, my shameful subterfuge, my gold fishes and forcible feeding, my concert so poorly attended.

I have asked pardon for everything else, now I shall do so for having raised my voice.

Still I cannot reach the real depths of absurdity, any more than I am able to rise to the heights of clarity. Nothing would be more comforting than to regret, with even a semblance of sincerity, a single act the resultant of forces playing upon my wretched instrument has given me the momentary illusion of having committed. My authentic sorrows are all spineless, since they grow out of things which never have happened.

I have had three dimensions in which to meander, the colors of the spectrum to tinge my variety, all stinks from garlic to tuberoses, generous graduations of hot and cold, nicely measured rattlings in both my ear drums.

More frankly, I have the feeling of your hair between my fingers, the drooping of your hands in sleep, the swift eager curve of your arm leaping once from the pillow to my shoulder, the moist pressure of your lips, your armpits, moments of tenderness in your eyes. That should have been enough.

In a world of confusion, the palest experience alone should be poignant. Actually, that is the case. At times I am almost convinced that our only dignity lies in insurrection, in deliberate refusal to supply predicates for predestined subjects, to dot the "i's" in manuscripts copied by automatons.

I wanted you to answer unasked questions, to precede me through the doorway where all the jaded were gathered to greet us, to clasp a hand that waved from behind the black velvet curtain of a cabinet. The penalty is that I must survive you.

Years have not broken the deadlock, the stable balance of emotions, ethics, caution, courage, results, and nonsense. Why, knowing all this, do I shudder with faint nausea at the mention of virginity, or at the sight of wilted poppies? The lost secrets of the weavers have perished.

You were most tender when I needed you most, and most affectionate when you were quite untroubled, and was it this that paralyzed me? Or did I seek the reverse, to have you cling when I was the stronger? I never said so, nor thought so, but I am not proud. Where can I find the bleached bones of an explanation?

I was in a long narrow corridor where the walls and all the articles contained in it were made of a curious substance like wax but more fragrant, and upon the floor was a flower, made of the same cool substance, yet, unlike everything else, absolutely without an odor of any kind. The sensation produced by covering my nostrils with this flower was the rarest I have ever experienced, for the absence of odor, in a scented gallery—the only complete escape from mingled perfumes—seemed to clear my mind of all previous impressions of that character and to afford me the illusion of having been born again. But here I met the defeat which has always seemed to me to be the point in the curve of my life at which my destiny hung suspended in the air an instant, then yielded reluctantly to gravity. I knew that if I had cherished this wax flower, at any moment I should have an absolution with me, but coincidently with this my fingers were fumbling the tight petals and opening them. The petals clung together with an inexplicable stubbornness and the shape of the bud was broken only after I had had the opportunity, time and time again, to change my mind. The orange stamens moved like the mouths of insects and gradually assumed a low form of vegetable-animal existence, lengthening like worms, changing color to a steel gray, undulating like clusters of eels. And then I noticed that the corridor had become glass and was filled with a light green fluid, much less dense than water, yet heavier than air, and I felt that disconcerting faintness which has come to be so definitely associated with you.

I prefer this to any other explanation, since it makes me appear less fatuous, and I like to think that we can select causes, like ribbons, to match whatever costumes our effects are wearing.

And so it is that I clothe you in faun-colored muslin, vaguely figured with cream and brown, to soften your sturdy shoulders. I remove your flannel blouse and leather gauntlets and the skirt which brushed the sides of the small bay mare. Always I turn away, since to see you with my eyes and the palms of my hands would be unbearable.

There were skeletons of buffaloes in the foothills when we rode together, and strange humped silhouettes resolving into the dusk. The startled curlews shrieked into a silence so vast that their cries were dissipated instantly and you stroked the saddle as the wind peered from over the distant summit and our horses bowed their heads and stepped more daintily. You were born at twilight, a grown woman, with no qualms of childhood and a low contralto voice unsharpened by the fear of age. Old calendars were taken from dusty walls and gravely the cattle turned their backs to the rising moon, munching among the sage and cactus.

How could I tell you then what you did not know, your body whispering to the evening air? I could have said, "I am older than you, and neither rich nor poor when I am trembling." I could have fallen forward, burying my face in my horse's crisp mane, and we all would have paused until it was over and then gone on. To what end?

When time is destroyed, one finds terror everywhere in unexpected places. Comforting clusters of ferns and petunias glitter with serpent's eyes.

It is a terrible thing to see your friend strung up in a public shop, sawdust on the floor, men in soiled coats marching back and forth with carcasses—your dear friend drained of life and quartered, hanging from steel hooks, upside down, ribs starkly clean and drying. On a damp shelf lie a row of hearts and you cannot decide which is his.

Along a parallel street in the old, old city, there is the sound of marching and a band plays out of tune. I must escape from these crowds, must fight my way through filthy alleys and into the open—into the park again.

I am calmer now. We are approaching a taxi, and the driver nods as we step in. The rain is falling obliquely into the city's perpendicular slits, and the windows blur, then writhe with raindrops and shut us in completely.

Again the end of the world declines its proper moment. Not a crash, nor lightnings, nor the opening of graves, but merely for the things upon earth to continue their movements into elipses, like the planets, and revolve with one another, forming an unchangeable pattern. I touch your hand, your breasts. Your response is never denied. And then I wait, and my brain leaks like an old mill dam and the dripping distracts me. You are waiting, too, but blindly, thinking thoughts you know are irrelevant. The driver does not turn, but settles deeper in his seat as the rain hurls itself against the windshield. A contentment seizes us, and life flows from my shoulder to your cheek, from your knees to my hands. Am I afraid of the full current of life, or of shriveling beneath the faintest flicker of your disappointment, or merely of imitating a rooster or a coal heaver or a billy-goat?

I can never decide so long as you exist and I cannot conceive of a universe without your image on all the screens of mist. Years or weeks or days are all the same, since they are telescoped and mingled by the impact with an unanswerable question.

Only by killing myself could I dispose of you, and that I could never consider, for perhaps I have had the largest share in your creation after all. But I know that if, at this particular instant, I slit the blue vein at your throat with tiny silver scissors, you will never be aware of it and will never change again. And may both of us be spared the knowledge of where I shall go when I leave this room.

transition 6

Katherine Anne Porter   *Magic*

And Madame Blanchard, believe that I am happy to be here with you and your family because it is so serene, everything, and before this I worked for a long time in a fancy house—maybe you don't know what is a fancy house? Naturally . . . everyone must have heard sometime or another. Well Madame I work always where there is work to be had, and so in this place I worked very hard and saw a lot of things, things you wouldn't believe, and I wouldn't think of telling you, only maybe it will rest you while I brush your hair. . . . You'll excuse me too but I couldn't help hearing you say to the laundress maybe someone had bewitched your linens, they fall away so fast in the wash: Well, there was a girl there in that house, a poor thing, thin, but popular with all the men who called, and you understand she could not get along with the woman who ran the house. They quarreled, the madam cheated her on her checks: you know, the girl got a check, a brass one, every time, and at the week's end she gave these back to the madam, yes, I think that was the way, and got her percentage, a very small little of her earnings: it is a business, you see, like any other—and the madam used to pretend the girl had given back only so many checks, you see, and really she had given many more: but after they were out of her hands, what could she do? So she would say, I will get out of this place, and curse and cry then. The madam would hit her over the head. She always hit people over the head with bottles, it was the way she fought, my good heavens Madame Blanchard, what noise there would be sometimes with a girl raving downstairs, and the madam pulling her back by the hair and smashing a bottle on her forehead.

It was nearly always about the money, the girls got in debt so, and if they wished to go they could not without paying every sou marqué. The madam had full understanding with the police, the girl must come back with them or go to the jails. Well, they always came back with the policemen or another kind of man friend of the madam: she could make men work for her too, but she paid them very well for all, let me tell you: and so the girls stayed unless they were sick: If so, if they got too sick, she sent them away again.

Madame Blanchard said, You are pulling a little here, and eased a strand of hair: and then what?

Pardon—but this girl, there was a true hatred between her and the madam, she would say, I make more money than anybody else in the house, and every week were scenes. So at last she said one morning, I will leave this place, and she took out forty dollars from under her pillow and said, Here's your money! The madam began then to shout Where did you get all that, you—? And accused her of robbing the men who came to visit her. The girl said keep your hands off or I'll brain you: and at that the madam took hold of her shoulders, and began to lift her knee and kick this girl most terribly in the stomach, and even in her most secret place, Madame Blanchard, and then she beat her in the face with a bottle, and the girl fell into her room where I was making clean: I helped her to the bed, and she sat there holding her sides with her head hanging down, and when she got up again there was blood everywhere she had sat. So then the madam came in again and screamed. Now you can get out, you are no good for me any more: I don't repeat all, you understand it is too much. But she took all the money she could find, and at the door she gave the girl a great push in the back with her knee, so that she fell again in the street, and then got up and went away with the dress barely on her.

After this the men who knew this girl kept saying, where is Ninette? And they kept asking this, so that the madam could not say any longer, I put her out because she is a thief. No, she began to see she was wrong to send this Ninette away, and then she said, She will be back in a few days.

And now Madame Blanchard, if you wish to hear, I come to the strange part, the thing recalled to me when you said your linens were bewitched. For the cook in that place was a woman, colored like myself, like myself with much French blood just the same, like myself living always among people who worked spells. But she had a very hard heart, she helped the madam in everything, she liked to watch all that happened, and she gave away tales on the girls. The madam trusted her above everything, and she said, Well, where can I find that slut? because she had gone altogether out of Basin Street before the madam began to ask of the police to bring her again. Well, the cook said, I know a charm that works here in New Orleans, colored women do it to bring back their men: in seven days they come again very happy to stay and they cannot say why. It is a New Orleans charm for sure, for certain, they say it does not work even across the river . . . And then they did it just as the cook said. They took the chamber pot of this girl's from under her bed, and in it they mixed with water and milk all the relics of her they found there: the hair from her brush, and the face powder from the box, and even little bits of her nails they found about the edges of the carpet where she sat by habit to cut her finger and toenails: and they dipped the sheets with her blood into the water, and all the time the cook said something over it in a low voice: I could not hear all, but at last she said to the madam, Now spit in it: and the madam spat: and the cook said, When she comes back she will be the dirt under your feet.

Madame Blanchard closed her perfume bottle with a thin click: Yes, and then?

Then in seven nights the girl came back and she looked very sick, but happy to be there. One of the men said, Welcome home, Ninette! and when she started to speak to the madam, the madam said, Shut up and get upstairs and dress yourself. So Ninette, this girl, she said, I'll be down in just a minute. And after that she lived there quietly.

transition 13

Laura Riding   *In a Café*

This is the second time I have seen that girl here. What makes me suspicious is that her manner has not changed. From her ears I should say she is Polish. If this is so, is it not dangerous to drink coffee here? Does anyone else think of this I wonder? Yet why should I be suspicious? And why should her manner not remain unchanged? She has probably been cold, unhappy, unsuccessful, or simply not alive ever since I saw her last. Quite sentimentally I wish her success. The man who is making sketches from pictures in the Art Magazine may find her little Polish ears not repulsive. For good luck I turn away and do not look at her again. I, who am neither primitive nor genteel, like this place because it has brown curtains of a shade I do not like. Everything, even my position, which is not against the wall, is unsatisfactory and pleasing: the men coming too hurriedly, the women too comfortably from the lavatories, which are in an unnecessarily prominent position— all this is disgusting; it puts me in a sordid good humor. This attitude I find to be the only way in which I can defy my own intelligence. Otherwise I should become barbaric and be a modern artist and intelligently mind everything, or I should become civilized and be a Christian Scientist and intelligently mind nothing. Plainly, the only problem is to avoid that love of lost identity which drives so many clever people to hold difficult points of view—by "difficult" I mean big and obviously religious points of view which absorb their personality. I, for one, am resolved to mind or not mind only to the degree where my point of view is no larger than myself. I thus have a great number of points of view no larger than the fingers of my hand and which I can treat as I treat the fingers of my hand, to hold my cup, to tap the table for me, and fold themselves away when I do not wish to think. If I fold them away now, then I am sitting here all this time (without ordering a second cup) because other people go on sitting here, not because I am thinking. It is all, indeed, I admit, rather horrible. But if I remain a person instead of becoming a point of view, I have no contact with horror. If I become a point of view, I become a force and am brought into direct contact with horror, another force. As well set one plague of cats loose upon another and expect peace of it. As a force I have power, as a person virtue. All forces eventually commit suicide with their power, while virtue in a person merely gives him a small though constant pain from being continuously touched, looked at, mentally handled; a pain by which he learns to recognize himself. Poems, being more like persons, probably only squirm every time they are read, and wrap themselves round more tightly. Pictures and pieces of music, being more like forces, are soon worn out by the power that holds them together. To me pictures and music are always like stories told backwards; or like this I read in the newspaper: "Up to the last she retained all her faculties and was able to sign checks."

It is certainly time for me to go and yet I do not in the least feel like going. I have been through certain intimacies and small talk with everything here; when I go out I shall have to begin all over again in the street, in addition to wondering how many people are being run over behind me; when I get home I shall turn on the light and say to myself how glad I am it is winter, with no moths to kill. And I shall look behind the curtain where my clothes hang and think that I have done this ever since the homicidal red-haired boy confided his fear to me and I was sorry for him and went to his room and did it for him. And my first look round will be a Wuthering Heights look; after that I shall settle down to work and forget about myself.

I am well aware that we form, all together, one monster. But I refuse to giggle and I refuse to be frightened and I refuse to be fierce. Nor will I feed or be fed on. I will simply think of other things. I will go now. Let them stare. I am well, though eccentrically, dressed.

transition 7

Robert Sage   *The Common Denominator*

In Nuremberg he and his friend went one night with a Bavarian musician to a restaurant where carp dinners were served. It was a December night, and the town, silent, resembled a German Christmas card. The white moon, floating in a sky of watery gray transparence, laid a glare on one side of the steep, snow-muffled roofs. There was a friendly crunch to the fresh snow in the streets, and they heard for some minutes the cheerful gurgle of the Pegnitz. Beside the Frauenkirche old women were selling holly branches crowded with bursting red berries, and girls and men, waiting for friends, were pacing impatiently back and forth by the Schoennenbrunnen.

The restaurant was nearly filled with people eating carp. When they had found places in the noisy crowd they ordered mugs of Munich beer, and the musician sipped his, contentedly telling them that if one drank slowly one could consume many glasses without becoming intoxicated. Just wait until you taste the carp, he said in his slow English. It is a great delicacy, not at all like the American variety.

He was right. The carp, fried in butter and still sizzling, was placed before them and the German told them to be sure to eat the fins and tail. It was delicious. He ate his greedily and they all ordered more beer.

For some time they did not say anything because the musician's hunger was a little distressing. Then he began to tell them how hard the times were. Having finished his fish he glared at the people in the restaurant, and as he glared he involuntarily snarled as a dog snarls when a stranger comes to the gate. It seemed to make him angry that other people could afford to eat carp, drink beer and have thin bottles of Rhine wine brought in pails of ice to their tables.

He only received six hundred marks for playing all evening in the café, he said. What was that? Not enough to buy a pound of coffee. Every day the prices went up, sometimes they were doubled or tripled, but his salary remained the same. There was the house to keep going and his wife and two children to provide for. During the day he gave music lessons, but what few pupils continued to come could only pay the old prices. He wrapped up a roll and a partly eaten piece of pumpernickel in a piece of paper and put them in his pocket.

They ordered more beer, and the Bavarian musician's ashy face slowly changed to a muddy purple. His voice became louder. He spoke in a grating tone of French atrocities, of how Germany was being starved and ruined. It will not be possible much longer to live he said. Many days he and his family had only bread and cheese and sugarless coffee made from yesterday's grounds. What would the next generation be? Weaklings, unable to earn their own living. Ah, the end was not far off. He remembered that it was time for him to be going to the café, and he tried honestly to smile as he said good night.

They stayed in the restaurant long enough to drink another glass of beer. Then they left intending to walk through the old city and perhaps go up to the Burg. But his friend tired soon of walking and they went to a cabaret and later to another . . .

He was aware that someone was sitting behind him in the *weinstube*. At that time he was alone in Berlin and did not understand the language. The presence gave him a hopeful feeling of companionship which he prolonged by staring at his sour cocktail some minutes before turning. When he turned he saw a woman dressed in dark brown. She was twirling the stem of an empty glass between her gloved fingers.

As she did not seem displeased at his experimental bow he went to her table. Her complexion was in tone with her unfashionable brown coat, and her features had the appearance of being unnecessarily crowded. Yet her eyes, too close to the nose that terminated sharply just above a thin mouth, had an accustomed sadness and there was emotional body to their brownness. Neither spoke, and he felt that in a strange way there was an understandable sympathy between them.

A few minutes later they went out together. Hesitating at first she ended by leading the way across the darkening Potsdamerplatz, active and dreary, to a straight street lined with blank façades. As they walked they seemed to be briefly living in rhythm and he recalled the little Danish girl he had encountered in the Tivoli Gardens of Copenhagen who used to tell him during their nocturnal walks that she wanted to visit her brother in America before he came back to Denmark.

Used objects filled the woman's room. When she had closed the door she dropped her hat with a familiar gesture into an armchair near the warm porcelain stove. As she instinctively threw back her head to shake her hair into place her body was for an instant drawn into an attitude of tense aliveness, and he experienced a new desire, to embrace her not passionately but as an impersonal tribute to her subtle beauty. But he remained some distance from her, fearful of breaking their mood by a motion which she would perhaps misunderstand. When she sat down he was pleased to notice that she did not draw her skirt from the careless position in which it fell just above her knee. The absence of the self-conscious adjustment seemed to prove her confidence in him.

In the room he tried discreetly to surprise a clue. There were dimly visible pictures among the toilette articles on the dressing table, pictures, he thought, of a man in uniform. He had the feeling too without direct substantiation that a man had lived in the room with her. When he looked back she seemed troubled. Somehow the situation instead of being ridiculous struck him as entirely natural.

Then she spoke in a low voice, leaning slightly forward and entwining her fingers nervously. He tried to form a coherent synthesis of her words, expressions, gestures. Suddenly, she smiled and stopped, apparently just realizing the futility of attempting communication. She regarded him speculatively as though slowly crystallizing a resolution. Then she recommenced talking, at first slowly, carefully, in a melodious voice. But the words as they continued followed each other more rapidly. She became absorbed in the uncomprehended message her intense voice framed in vibrant syllables. While she talked she moved jerkily about the room and he watched the rhythm of her motions feeling that he understood what she was saying as he understood the spirit of a symphony. Only once she looked at him, through him. After what seemed a long time she became silent. She seemed bewildered, and he saw now that she was crying. His hat on the table apparently forced itself into her consciousness as some unexplained foreign object, and she picked it up and not unkindly handed it to him. At the door he kissed her but she did not respond and he had the impression that she was not aware of the kiss . . .

A crowd of them, boys and girls, motored from the college town at dusk to a hill overlooking a nearby lake. When they arrived a charcoal early evening had settled serenely over the lakeside and a thin breeze carried the smell of pine through the trees. He joined the boys to gather wood for the fire while the girls unpacked the hampers of food.

Moving through the straight trunks they called back and forth jokingly and he could hear the pure sound of the girls' laughter. The springy moss and the leaf-caked ground projected a gratifying peaceful sensation through his limbs. Below on the lake was the hollow wood-metal sound of xylophone music played by a phonograph in some canoe.

The fire rose quickly from the dried wood and they cooked their steaks and roasted their potatoes. Later they sat around talking and poking marshmallows into the flames on the tip of pointed branches and when that was done they moved down to the beach to dance in the sand to phonograph music.

His senses, sharpened, vibrated in harmony with the freshened breeze, the low padding of the water on the sand, the tickling odor of charred wood, the girls' frank eagerness, the faint sounds and lights in the cottages across the lake.

But with no transition it all became intolerable. He waited miserably, trying to seem a part of things, until he had a chance to climb back up the hill alone. At the top he paused a moment to look distastefully at the supper remains, the purses and hats lying on the ground, the automobiles which, crookedly parked on a little declivity, seemed to share the holiday mood of the party. Then he started out through the woods.

Soon the last sound from the beach had faded and there was only silence and darkness about him. He tried to think, but everything was uncertain. He wanted only to get away alone and yet he was angry at his inarticulate desire for solitude. Coming to a sandy road he turned towards the college town but when he saw in the distance the lights of a late interurban car he hurried ahead to the crossroads. He got on the car and when it reached the city he took a room for the night in a hotel across from the station . . .

He wondered as he walked through the Rue Notre-Dame-des-Champs why it was that he should again be going to Laura's five-o'clock. It could never vary from the established monotony of a tall Frenchman telling sex stories in a blurred throaty voice to the smartly dressed and consciously voluptuous girls from New York while the three American men got hurriedly drunk and the countess accented her superiority by intermittent refusals of a second cocktail. When he passed the hostile concierge he had found no answer he would allow himself to accept.

Laura, with tin-bright eyes and her red hair more than usually mussed, jerked a cigarette nervously to and from her lips as she pointed to Margaret at the window. Her practiced voice cut shrilly through the background murmur as she said, It's so funny to see Margaret, Margaret of all people, flirting with Larry who's never, I'm quite sure, had a woman in all his life.

He resented the "of all people" and was immediately annoyed at his resentment. Even more was he annoyed to notice that his first feeling was one of jealousy. That feeling should have been dead, a misjudgment recognized and adjusted.

Margaret beckoned to him and the American moved shakily towards the table that Laura called her *Bar Américain*. You don't like me any more, Margaret pouted. Beneath her gray eyes the soft semicircles of flesh were folded, he saw, into more definite bands of wrinkles. You don't like me, and why? Because of irrelevant things. Because of my lonesome husband back in Chicago and perhaps because you know that Ralph was my lover and that when he left his wife for me I changed to Emmanuel. Because, too, I suppose, there have been so many others.

He shrugged his shoulders and thought lasciviously of her full breasts. He thought of the tulips in the Tuileries, his barber, the heavily perfumed blind girl who sat beside him in the Scala, and the need of buying cigarettes. He thought: one can never be quite deceived by one's own lies.

It isn't fair, she said, and more sharply. What's your basis? Is it religion or morality or convention or one of the notions you picked up in London, or what? Surely you realize that crowding is more essential than observing rules, that one can accept situations as they arise and still remain apart looking for an improbable illusion that will continue. It's strange that I should even have to talk of these things for they must by now be as familiar to you as your own studio. Or is the puritan still in hiding? At least, dear boy, if you can't understand requirements be fair and do not disapprove.

She said in a softer voice: You were once a friend of mine and I suspect you even loved me. I've always liked you, I've always felt there was something precious of . . . of summer in you. Why can't we still be friends? Come, please do, tomorrow and talk to me a little in the old way.

He could not evade the promise but he knew he would not go . . .

His friend returned to their studio late one autumn afternoon. He seemed embarrassed and at first did not say anything, walking about the room, looking at the pictures, staring for some time out the wind-rattled window. Finally he said simply, I am going back.

The other did not question him. Since he understood, it was needless to demand apologetic words that were strangers to the reason. They had dinner at Lapérouse, remaining a long while over the Armagnac and although neither mentioned the departure they seemed closer than before.

The next few days, his friend was busy packing and arranging his affairs. He said Adieu quietly as he climbed into the train at the Gare Saint-Lazare.

They had not had much in common during the past year, he and his friend, but he was impotently depressed now by the emptiness of the studio. The dust and the spots on the objects he had scarcely looked at for months bored so persistently into his consciousness that he walked much in the thin rain or sat in large cafés where there were many people.

After a week of it he hunted out the tattered map in a pile of papers and looked for a town that had not been invaded by his smudge of ink spots and lines. Among the clear spots Bruges attracted him the most.

A few British were still staying on at the Panier d'Or but he avoided them and dined alone at a corner table. He amused himself Saturday morning by wandering through the market, poking around among the sabots, tin lanterns, umbrellas, fruits, calicos, and vegetables. When the merchants began packing up their goods he went to a café and wrote for a long time in his neglected diary. In the evening he reviewed what he had written during the past two years, trying unsuccessfully to find a common denominator or even a summarizing phrase.

Memling, in the succeeding days, became more and more a friend to his spirit.

Pasty Madonnas and tanned realistic peasants arranged like a display of bottles in a drugstore window. Between fruit trees and green fields the gentle curve of country roads. Castles, flowers, birds, ponds. Cattle and more peasants—patient. The sureness of mysticism and the love of repetitions. Memling had absorbed the rhythm. He had, perhaps without knowing it, found a common denominator.

With the environment constant there was no confusion. Outlines lost their newness but the details became richer. Tranquillity was retarded until familiarity taught the unconscious alone the awareness of externals.

Memling soothed him like a woman's hand and the twilight breeze. He walked during the mornings on the banks of the canals and listened with impatience for the melody of the chimes each quarter-hour. When he wrote in his diary he could not clarify it but he felt he was approaching now for the first time something he had always wanted. Nervous and fidgety, Paris was an unimmediate world. If ultimately he should learn to understand would he still value movement enough to return?

One morning the sun shone with the cooling intensity of late autumn. While a bulky barge maneuvered awkwardly around the angle of two narrow canals he sat dreamily on the side of a bridge. There was little activity in the town and, outside the symphony of the chimes, he was conscious of no sound. It seemed that morning that he had nearly reached it.

At dinner his mood disintegrated. Vague disquietude at first, then an acceleration towards a known restiveness. He drank several glasses of beer in the café later and tried to recapture his morning sensations by walking along the dark canals until midnight.

The next morning he took the train back to Paris.

transition 8

Margaret Shedd   *My Uncle's Shoes*

The lid rotates. It is a merry-go-round. Hell is a merry-go-round. Not my hell but my uncle's. It is easy to imagine hell as a merry-go-round; the picture is too clear for much description. Devils scream, the damned scream, and Satan walks around the opposite way that the platform turns to collect the fares. But they never get anywhere; they cover immeasurable distance. It is a round platform fastened on an axis. The ones on the giraffes committed murder; those on the golden rams were caught in adultery, stir up the fire for them. There is a fire under the merry-go-round. This hell is only the lid to something else; its axis goes down into the bowels of this moment and of eternity. Underneath the lid there is something else.

There is no flavor to this flat hell on top. It is a pity that the damned should suffer so little. True, Satan can always get inspiration from some mad preacher exulting crazily in his pulpit or a tent, and there was the Inquisition; but now my uncle says, "We must not visualize hell in terms of dreadful tortures!" He thinks the wicked will howl enough at the dizzy monotony of the merry-go-round, and as for the unavoidable suffering on earth, that for the blessed is a purging fire, a spiritual bath. He does believe that wickedness will be punished in some sort of hell by pain of some vague sort; here the living agony around us is for another reason, but he is not sure what that is and he shuts his eyes.

I cannot shut my eyes. I feel the world's anguish about my loins. Just now, as my heart caught a fragment of time and let it loose, I knew that in that second was welded, of the then transpiring torment of the earth, a lash, thonged, which must beat upon me momently with the beating of my heart.

The lid is lifted clear and the silly figures of the giraffes and devils and the obliging damned who know their parts so well by long rehearsal lie tilted up on the motionless merry-go-round, a very pitiful hell.

Underneath, there is a hole, cavity most earthy yet not of space, a cruel cessation of nothingness, a vortical abyss which rotates eternally. It is bounded and almost filled by a moving road, like an escalator, downwards and conically spiral. And a compulsion fills this hole; so the moving stairs are peopled. I too descend, in the spaceless center of the cone, thus ultimately surrounded by miseries rotaliiform.

There is the constant shuffle of old shoes.

A city is a labyrinth of hard doors and asphalt. A woman lets them put their hands through the half-open door, "Lady, could you use this window stop I made of wire?" "Lady, I paid ten cents for this case of needles; pay me what you can." "Lady, I thought you might have a little work."

She lets them put their hands through the door and then she shuts the door very fast. She has a pile of hands inside the hall. Her uncle collects postage stamps; she collects hands. A wave washes up to the door, recedes, returns, a wave shod in misfits. At the dark of the morning they distribute broadsides to advertise six dollar and sixty-nine cent dresses. They are wearing my uncle's old shoes. Once suffering left blood on the snow; now the Salvation Army sees to that. No blood on the asphalt. So much cement put down and stamped. Contractors sign their asphalt. Contractors are paid to make the pavement hard. Wear it down. Wear it down. A city block is a geometrical figure with slits at intervals. Doors.

No!

A piece of bent wire to stop your window?

No!

I make it myself?

No!

Something to hang up your telephone book?

No!

This wave hurls itself at the door. It meets that which is stronger than pain, and recedes.

So many feet in misfit shoes come down the stairs at once that they are a chorus. Feet, ill-shod, are good stock in trade, all comedians know that. Contractors sign their asphalt.

The last man didn't come near the door; he stood off, "I thought you might have a little work," apologizing, "I don't mind doing anything. Anything." He apologized to me for asking to work. The tears are pouring down my face. But his feet have passed me now. He is one of the chorus on the staircase, all moving downward with the infinite and inexorable rhythm of despair. I do not know where they are going. And their descent is precarious because through ever-revolving reaches, narrowing rotation, and to that unmitigated point where ends the cone, ends road. Phalanxed downwards, weary feet in misfit shoes, and is their goal destruction? I follow seeking answer.

Not all are tragic choruses somnambulant; not all appear at the stairhead, then pause at a door and a door to retch forth unwanted wire oddments. Some emerge voice only, and like an invisible snake extend descending, filling at one breath the sequenced layers of the cone. Rather, at each intake of the breath the voice surges through another segment of the escalator. The cry is a snake hurrying along the road. Distant, more distant, it meets here a pocket of the night that holds it momentarily, until the coils are massed into twitching, slimy, apexed sound; then it slides away in haste, frightened by its own excessive agony. Now it lies quietly, filling every measure of the revolving stairs with an even, low, and horrible monody. I in the middle shaft encompass strangle. My eyes are closed. Each vibration is a shuddering coil. The snake twitches and new eddies of horrid sound arise and are sent wholly up or down. It is not necessary to know all the components of this voice. Partly it is the bloody choke of him they tie naked in a latrine at Sunbeam Chaingang Camp, so that his feet are barely not touching the floor; the fat guard Higgenbotham says, "The rope ain't tight enough, he can still swallow." Higgenbotham spits on the dirt floor. The boy had run away, naked then too. He hid in the swamp through a night of waiting and he was naked then too. They brought him back, the morning is hot too. His mother lives in Jellicoo. The other guard spits on the floor too. The boy can still swallow. He screams too.

And partly it is the old cry, so often heard it no longer claims attention, of one impaled by war. His fingerprints alone retain humanity; one hand and a little of the arm is correlated flesh in this pulped mass. His yellow fingertips make reflexed contact with the earth, seeking the warmth of rotting loam they soon will be; he lives only in the twitching hand because his cry, a burbling slime of sound, has become too horrible for pity. It must not be admitted to be human sound. Catch the polecat for his skin; lots of stenographers have skunk fur on their everyday coats. I don't know who all wear soldier skins. And there is bound to be noise when the trap clicks and there is no trapper with a club to stop the ebbing dying rising screams. A job for God who must have a club handy, or at least a club handle.

And in among the assorted cries of pain which have made this hole their own there is a great barking of little dogs. This sound makes tiny waves in the wake of the long-drawn, high-pitched inhumanity of man in anguish. Hundreds of dogs in little coops, and rows of coops. Kind dog catcher. Nice pound wagon. A little dog smiles up at me, shaking his head and rump. He wants a friend. The pound smells strongly of disinfectant. And slow-dying soldiers are waiting for the trapper, and the parade goes past me, sound forming into ranks again.

Here is a man with a basket full of doughnuts. He breathes hard, a rasping inhalation-exhalation at each step down the escalator. His wife came the other time. We live on a high hill. His wife is sick now, but she got up early in a cold room to fry these miserable doughnuts. She has seen the machines they use in windows where doughnuts are dipped, fried, so perfectly, so meticulously, so deliciously. But she doesn't know what else to do so she goes on frying doughnuts. How horrible the smell in an empty room, cold. No breakfast. Now he takes the basket. I didn't buy any. She crawls back into bed. There are not enough covers.

She and he are decent, tall; one wears glasses; he was a shipping clerk once; she taught school. Knowing, loving trees in lanes and gentle spring, they have been grateful to God and even the streetcar conductor for their small Sunday outings. Now he clods downstairs with the doughnuts. If he sells them, food. But there could never be enough money for another blanket. He does not sell them. Doughnuts in a cold house, cold bed. Good night. When the county hospital receives her emaciated carcass, starvation written on the chart, he, also starved but not yet in mortal throe, so no business of the doctors, looks faintly down the lane of beds and his whisper sidles through the convolutions of the vortex and is held, "So far to go. Ellen is dying . . . ," each word in its slow emptiness caught static in the intensity of the vortex whirl as a leaf that remains terribly long at the brink of the maelstrom, "so far to go . . ." But another voice eclipses his faint sibilence, coming from above, coming from all sides, bass, honest, and cold, "I cannot say there will be no starvation here this winter."

Governor of a black colony, since this is his admission, his also to pronounce who is to live and who to die. The Negroes are filling the abyss.

"You," and he speaks to a man whose hand is damply clutched by a blacker, smaller hand, "are to feel the vile distention of your belly and the then incaving until the sides adhere, and you die ultimately."

"Yes, sair," the black head nods, but not perfectly comprehending. Two chosen. Two more: the woman with the red sash who carries a baby crying because his teeth are coming in. Two more, a hundred more, a thousand more, ten thousand more must be selected. And is there hope still in their tread? They enter swiftly and silently, surrounding the shipping clerk who looks upon them with pity and offers them his doughnuts, which, however, not being a loaf and fishes, are of no account.

The ten thousand are moving quietly towards the bottom of the stairs; now in profound stillness their eyes are lifted all at one time. Ten thousand Negroes raise their eyes at once: dear God! must I be thus pillowed in the soft brown eyes of doomed savages? They are gone. They ask nothing. Their eyes have vanished; remains only the glint on a pair of nose glasses. The shipping clerk has been carried by the voiceless submission of the Negroes and by the magnet of the vortex struggling into the last loop. He can see now what is the absorption point to which he has arrived, and a final flicker of strength animates his bones, rushes up, faltering but somewhat strong, to rouse him against the insistence of the escalator, making him fight upward on bony hands and knees. His pale eyes are uplifted and his face is clothed in such heartbreaking terror as human face was not molded to convey; but then his face is reclothed by a thought which has no home here—that there is hope even for him whose feet are already in the pit. It is something he sees in the spirals beyond my sight which has given birth to his hope. To him there must be vision, even comfort; to me there is only the long shadow of a crucifix that falls athwart the throbbing coil of stairs, screened distorted transverse the gulf.

Nevertheless, my eyes, bowed first to the desperate insect struggle of the shipping clerk and then raised to the cross, forget the slipping clattering clutching there below, and when I look again, the glint on the nose glasses has vanished. I forget because of the voice, marvelous and pitiful, that follows the undulations of the Cross, saying, "Suffer the little children that they come unto Me," trailing agonized through each rotation of the stairs to the very bottom.

And children's feet are coming down the stairs in answer. They are answering the voice. They can go faster than the escalator. But where are they going? There is only the pit ahead. The tender voice, like a movie organ but much sadder, is repeating, "Suffer the little children to come unto Me and forbid them not."

Bad boy, bad boy, he's a wicked boy. That ever a son of mine should be like this! Since his father's death I was mother and father to him, both. You'll end in jail. You'll end up hanged. I am in jail. I'm in the reformatory forever. I drownded a kid in a swimming pool. I held him under. They talked to me. I said yes I done it. But I didn't look at them when they talked to me. I looked at some sun coming in the window.

The ugly little girl is Nappy. She is five. She has been placed out for adoption several times but she is always sent back. She and the worker are going to stop at another door. They have rung the bell. The worker has got Nappy a new hat and they both know why. Nappy is looking at the door. It opens. . . .

The one dressed like a child movie star is the daughter of a half-wit murderess. How fast she runs! Her face is terribly white and her curls, sausages, fly behind her. The mother broke open her sleeping husband's head because she liked the husband of the housemaid better. In jail she decided to confess the crime to her daughter. The reporters thought this had human interest and stood by while the vapid fatty woman pawed over and muled over the child, she standing like a stone and then suddenly running away, an animal crying.

How lightly their feet cover the rotations of the abyss! In front of them, halfway down the cone, a crowd has gathered making crowd noises, looking with aimless lethargy around the heads and shoulders of each other; but the children do not lessen their pace, push through to reach the crucifix. And it is this, swaying, moving rapidly, down carried in speed, Christ nailed to His Cross, that is the object of the crowd's attention. Someone has put a purple sateen bag over His head, like in Lent, and over each hand. But the sight merely of His feet, with the nails pounded between the bones, would shake a world or even a bigger planet. The thieves are carried after Him, but their bodies are very stringy. Those who bear the roods are dressed like misericordia brothers, and ahead, clearing the way, there are men who hold up long placards. These men wear my uncle's old shoes. Their faces are, as always, gray and anxious to please. They march abreast in lines, each line with a banner, like states in a nominating convention. The banners read THE CRUCIFIXION! Some say this is only a movie prologue for a picture called *The Sign of the Cross*. Certainly all the happy little children who have a dime rush away after the banner bearers. Their parents have something else to do and the children are a bother; besides, the movie shows a boy of twelve put into a pit with a huge black torturer and appropriate instruments where he screams to the satisfaction of all. They have to hurry if they want seats. The theater will be filled.

The crowd is glad the children have gone, because the escalator has to be cleared for the walkathon. Everyone thinks this is a wonderful place for a walkathon: the contestants can go around and around giving the patrons a chance to see from above and below as well as straight ahead. But it is hard to get the space cleared. There is always someone coming in from the top. Now it is Marvin who stands looking dazed at the crowds around him. On Christmas Eve the Elks gave a party at the orphanage. Marvin took his candy canes and toy autos and hid them under his bed in the dormitory, but he couldn't really hide them. The matron explained loudly to later visitors, "I don't know what's the matter with that new boy, Marvin; he even tried to hide his ice cream under his bed!" Marvin heard them because he was coming down the stairs from the dormitory. "Suffer little children." The patrons of the walkathon shove Marvin out of the way and let out a shout. Billee, in shorts and a brassiere, and her partner, in shorts, are ready for the sprints, a special added attraction to the routine "twelve hundred hours of sleepless perambulation." The announcer's fecund blather fills the cone, "Four couples . . . Billee and Herbert . . . Marie and Gaston . . . the girls may run but the boys must walk. If one member of the team passes out the other must make twice the distance . . . Doctors, nurses, and restoratives are being placed in the center . . ."

I am Billee. I am fifteen. I hitchhiked from Peoria to Sacramento, California, to my aunt's out there, but my aunt's husband didn't like me. He said he supposed girls were pretty free nowadays but not by God every night under the front steps. At the clinic they said I had gonorrhea. My aunt and I went in out of the hot sun and it was dark in the clinic. Yeah, they said, she has it. Is it catching? Because my aunt has three kids. Yeah, they said, sure, very.

They wanted to put me in some kind of a home in Oakland to cure me, but my boy friend says, hell, kid, we'll enter the walkathon. They'll never figure to look for you there. All you need is an extra pair of shoes. You can take a pair of your uncle's old shoes. You walked from Peoria, you ought to be able to walk five six weeks more.

"Her boy friend'll never make it around twice" . . . "I'll bet he goes out on the long stretch there" . . . "God, look at her, she's holding him up" . . . "There he goes, pooped out on the first time around" . . . "She'll have to run now" . . . "Look, she's going to wheel right up against the rail here" . . . "Ready, kid" . . . Billee stumbles again and again against the girding. . . . Laughing dumbbells gather there to buttress her nakedness. . . . Each impact throws her back into the ring and a little forward. . . . "Hey, doc, you better get her. She's clean out" . . . "Look, she's going to fall" . . . Legs and arms uncontrolled, she is put on a bed in the center. . . . She is kneaded into reactivity amid the dumbbells' plaudits. . . . Words in the foul air above her. . . . She fights not to hear. . . . "Swell show but get up and keep going" . . . "Aren't you going to fasten her brassiere?" calls out a woman patron.

Automaton on her giddy feet, again she tries to run. Each time around is a coil nearer the vortex. Why does she make such destroying effort to get there?

"To come unto Me and forbid them not." Some are entering now with a dragging and a scraping. These, now parallel with me, are too terrible to behold. Yet here in the abyss I am forced to put my eyes upon them to know their agony which is so great that after the seeing I find myself covered with wounds, from head to foot, which I doubt will ever heal. Two little boys, brothers, walked together every day to school. A soft pink creature, partly male, of perversion beyond perversion, stole them away, but they lived on for weeks.

Oh my God return me for one moment to the orchard near my mother's house that I may reach up my face to the down drifting petals; I will bury my tortured loins in the delicious loam and die. The little daughter of a father was stolen and returned to him piece by piece, and the newspaper sales rose to unprecedented heights. DIS-MEMBERED BODY FOUND IN SUTRO FOREST. WOMAN FINED IN BOY TORTURE. Extra, Extra. PIPE DISCOVERED IN MURDER BUNGALOW. Extra. (On a park bench some vacant mis-used idiot reads watering-mouthed, and the headlines groom their own next actor.) Extra. EX-SOLDIER BLINDS HIS PARAMOUR AND KILLS HER WITH AN AX. Extra. Extra. Extra. JURY OUT IN LAMSON CASE. And rustling fills the vortex because additional pictures will be found in Section 2, and every commuter turns to Section 2. Rustling then quickly finished because two hundred thou-sand rapt attentions have fallen on the picture of a dead woman in a bathtub. The vortex is a conical stadium where the cheering section has turned up the signaled placards for a bleacher stunt, two hundred thousand pictures of a young woman dead in her bathtub.

And then, "Michaelson has been reprieved several times. One execution date fell on his birthday, another came on St. Patrick's Day, and the last during the bank holiday. The governor said he was unwilling to have any man hanged on those dates." Even when the bank holidays are over, how long they take to hang him. How measuredly they lead him down the escalator. Towards the bottom they have to drag him, but death is beyond the vortex; first, for the pleasure of the man who reads his paper every night, he must be dragged, loop by loop. After that death is nothing.

Into the cone are pouring now murderers whose crime is a vaudeville act, trial a passing of hours and knitting for the sans-culottes—"and there was evidence found by the police that Mrs. Perdue had deceived her husband as to the reason for her refusal of his attentions on the night of the tragedy"—and whose death and rotting bodies are delicious carrion for the carrion eaters. In this procession each killer holds on his back or in his arms the killed. Both are fair sport.

The burdened dead and the burdened living who convey them have not vanished from sight when the patrons leave them and crowd to the top of the cone because the newsboys are calling extra again. But this time it is something special. Extra. Extra. NEGRO ATTACKS WHITE WOMAN.

Cries. Cries again. Cries fill all of the hole and the snake is stirring again. First it is the voiceless pant of one pursued and then, following hard after, catching the first cry and letting it go, catching it again, comes the horrible roar of the many pursuers. They join shouts with the shrill newsboys, Extra, Extra, NEGRO ATTACKS WHITE WOMAN, but their sound is a hoarse animal clamor, bestial, a voice at last released. They are the men at the doors. They are the placard bearers. Him they pursue to tear asunder is barefoot, a Negro, but they are not barefoot. They are wearing my uncle's old shoes. Down the stairs they pound, beat of feet and beat of voice together, "The black son of a bitch. He violated a white girl. He violated a white girl."

They hang him on a tree, and before he can die cunningly they cut his fingers and his toes and his hands and his legs, dissect them joint by joint. This happened today; this happened on the escalator. I saw it.

And then they carry him, not dead, they howling with the joy of achievement, down the long reaches of the staircase. And, as the gory band march fast and faster down the final slopes to the absorption point, there rises one to meet them. They, carrying down their black burden on a tree, son of a bitch, hacked violated, meet the Son of Man who has no place to lay His head, who returns from the pit of human suffering because the pit would not stomach Him. Himself carries His tree and His feet skeletonous are still so beautiful as to move the orbit of the sun, but the Negro has no feet left.

So there cross each other there on the escalator a red thread of horror as sharp as a knife and the white throbbing of a nameless disappointment. God stumbles up the stairs He once descended to mount finally I do not know what flat goal, even the merry-go-round, and the vagrant crowd goes down to throw its Negro into the abyss. But afterwards they are afraid, the place is very dark, and they clatter away with haste and tumult. Then quiet is the vortex, a quiet Christ upmoving and a million miseries go down. These are the multitude of unknown sufferers. They pass me now as they must have always been moving by, unseen before because so shadowy amid the garish horror of the other. Many of them come in from space beyond space that does surround the vortex, clustering in: women in postures of unattended travail; women who work never stopping for disease or death; long sequences of miserable sick for whom there is no love; little groups whispering together in the whiteness of true despair; and infinite numbers of human creatures who throw their beautiful human effort, strain and mar their minds and bodies at some trivial silly task, because they must, because they must. We are very tired. Sound is gone. Everyone is covered with wounds. This stillness is the irrevocable fading of activity into inactivity, finding of the point where moaning and gnashing of teeth have no longer any cogence. Lifting of a hand, which, because the body is so tired, is tearing of the bowels and destruction of life, must none the less be accomplished in silence. And now I can no longer defer the surveyal of that final vortex into which they have all descended, leaving me alone, atomic against the moving precipices around me. I know I must look down, force eyes to behold, for if these are the transpiring happenings of the world to which one is born, then either to mount a high cliff in the most distant mountains and die, hurled self-impelled into jagged space, or otherwise one must descend, survey, and if there is no strength left to rise again then there remain, wounded beyond health, but at least not blind. And so by effort like the lifting of a mountain I lower my eyes into the hidden abyss.

Pitiless! Pitiless! There is no pity. And pity therein poured is merely a trickle of water in the perpetual churn of flaming oil. But none the less I pour my pity there; I open a vein in my heart and pour in the little dribble of blood and love. It does not reach them. I see the doughnut man, but without his glasses now and ground almost into oblivion, maimed, clutching his empty basket. And all the children are there; the moving staircase on which they descended, now like an inexorable drill is dismembering them, tramping them down, crushing them not into the loam from which they may have risen and which man may always know as friend, but into a mass, useless, hideous, ultimately nothing but slime, like the spittle of a behemoth.

transition 23

Philippe Soupault   *Hymn to Liberty*

At the age of eight I was sent to a school run by priests. I worked absent-mindedly at my studies and have retained a memory of this school which is morose, disagreeable, and dust-covered. For it was a kind of huge barracks where the dust from the surrounding streets sought refuge. A long courtyard planted with broomsticks was given over during recess to authorized games. When I think of prisonyards it is always that yard I see. The schoolrooms, which were even gloomier, were painted a light brown and had black tables and dirty windows. Here we were taught catholicism, not severely, but also not brilliantly, and I don't remember having passed through a phase of mysticism. The sessions in the school chapel and those at church seemed equally long and monotonous to me. For eight years I remained shut in, watched over from seven in the morning till seven at night. The only means of escape was to think of something else; and that I certainly did. I read with keen interest the various anthologies and histories of literature, as well as certain interlinear translations, and a little later the *Lundis* of Sainte-Beuve. But I had little taste for Latin version and a holy horror of Latin composition and versification. Greek I found more amusing. And so, from the age of eight till fourteen, my life was one of exemplary monotony. Above all, I was exceedingly bored. During the classes at the Condorcet grammar school where the priests used to accompany us, I sought primarily to make the time pass more quickly. With one of my schoolmates, Robert Bourget, great-grandson of Buloz and grandson of Edouard Pailleron, I looked about for some sort of diversion. We carved the table with our knives, played ball, or talked of this and that. We also ate cakes and candies, and read *Nick*

Carter . . . It was for these latter diversions, especially, that we were punished. Usually, however, we didn't care.

"Soupault, you're not listening."

"Soupault, answer."

One of my more solemn professors, grown weary of repeating "you're not listening," and observing bitterly that I had understood nothing of the aorist tense, said to me: "Soupault, I will destroy your future like a twig," and suiting the gesture to the word, he broke in two a piece of chalk which was supposed to symbolize my destiny. But nothing was of any avail. I remained just as absent-minded, ferociously absent-minded, as ever.

"Two hours after school!"

"You'll be kept in on Sunday!"

Our chief thought was how to get away from school. My recollection of our conversations is rather vague, but I remember a little better the teasing and derision which we addressed especially to "good" pupils, or to those who memorized French verse.

In the schoolyard I caught a glimpse from time to time of my brothers, who were more intimate with each other than with me. At night I went home to my mother and sister. But of course I had to "go to bed early." Short as they were, however, I was at a loss to make these evenings pass. I wandered about the apartment, disgusted with everything, thinking bitterly that tomorrow would be like all the other days.

This childhood of mine seems to me to have been, above all, a series of little disappointments, a daily boredom; going to school and wanting perpetually to leave it in order to go and sleep, only to come back the next day to that "hole." It was a vicious circle, and I am sure that my great, imperious need of liberty, my horror of physical and moral restraint, my desire always to elude all outside suggestions or thoughts, even, date from this period.

Two days out of the week, Thursday and Sunday, I was free. But I was sick of everything, and enjoyed things only mildly. I was unaccustomed both to liberty and its uses, and hardly knew what to do with myself. Sometimes I was taken for a walk in the Bois de Boulogne. But this was the height of boredom. When it rained I was taken to a museum.

It was nevertheless on these free days that I acquired a taste for reading. Not knowing what to do, and tiring easily of playthings, I seized upon all printed matter. In fact, I read anything and everything: *My Diary,* the *Bible, Adventures of Captain Corcoran,* Andersen's *Fairy Tales,* the short stories of de Maupassant, Guisot's *History of England,* the works of Lenôtre. . . . Every week I devoured three or four books. Then, when I had none left, I would re-read those I had forgotten. It really became a vice. I remember my mother used to say: "If you want to keep him quiet, you have only to give him a book."

The summer vacations were pleasant, but I was really very apathetic. I think, too, that I must have been a child with rather frail health and a particularly inattentive mind. In any case, my recollections of this period are somewhat vague, the principal reason being, probably, that I accepted what was done to me without much resistance, and at the same time escaped all restraint, paid attention to nothing. It is natural that I should have retained so little now that I am grown.

When I think back on these small details that composed my child-hood, I am surprised to see how dull it was. Nor can I blame anyone for it. When all is said, I suffered very little, learned very little, and was merely very much bored.

But I was alive, which was already a lot. And during this period I did acquire one thing: a passion for liberty. This passion, which was eight years taking hold of me, has developed to such an extent that it is now probably the most violent thing about me. Liberty of movement and of thought, which could easily reach a point of tyranny and even destruc-tion, are essential to me. It is quite in earnest, and with all the serious-ness of which I am capable, that I now pen this hymn to Liberty.

O longed-for Liberty, you who are the source of my malady, who torture and kill me like thirst, I wish that once in my life I might behold your face. Only once, and I should be happy.

Each time I feel your presence and something tells me simply: "she is here," I know that my heart begins to beat faster and that my legs are seized with a desire to run. A strange odor pervades the air, a purer sound, a calmer voice, and a light which is more wonderful than joy itself. It is enough for me to know that your life touches mine, O Liberty, for me to feel stronger and more sure of myself.

You are really mine, and I am really your slave, only when your presence weighs on me, causing me to gasp with anguish. I am a stricken being, I press my elbows close against my trembling body, I clench my fists, my back is bowed. You are not beside me.

When the whole world is sleeping and night, like the oldest of goddesses, turns her head away; when the moon utters its little owl-like cry, then, O Liberty, I know that you are approaching in your silken gown, which is more beautiful than nakedness, and I wait. My lips, my ears, my fingers grow redder than the spider on the wall, and my heart is a little bull in my breast. I have already thirty times watched the coming of a new year; I have already seen that the sun is the most faithful of lovers; I have already forgotten that I was born and that

I must die. But Liberty, I am poorer than ever, more sincere than ever because you have not raped me.

Far off, in a mountain village, I see linen drying in a field where the sun is happily browsing. But nearby, walking along the highroad, men with bent backs are coming to gulp down their evening meal and then to sleep without protest. They have forgotten that the sky is like a great open hand, that the road which they wear down a little more each day leads to a mountain torrent, or to the steel-blue sea. They have forgotten that their sex organs might have some use, and that their feet have a shut-in odor; they have forgotten everything except eating and drinking. But they must be punished, Liberty, they must be punished, for they understand only possession.

A man whose nose is a dust bin and whose mouth is an old shed to keep teeth in, is bending over the earth. He would like to eat a piece of it spread on a crust of bread he has carefully saved for this moment. Here is a man who loves this earth of his, with its peculiar excremental taste, and he wants to keep it for his very own. If need be, he would have himself buried in it, in order better to watch over it! At his side, O Liberty, a frolicsome dog that cares not a rap for persons or things, is daintily wetting the flowers. O Liberty, with your starlike face, do not forget this man who licks the earth as though it were made of sugar. I well know that I am not the only one who calls and would like to follow you, that others too are your friends. But I am the most cowardly, the stupidest of all. So you must signal first to me, because I am the slowest and the dullest and because I really cannot live longer without you; because I am about to pass out with thirst, and the ink which I have taken to drinking really no longer suffices to quench this burning. I know well, beloved Liberty, that it would be enough for me to see one sign, one sign only, and with a bound I would stand ready. I am thinking of you, Liberty.

There are those who laugh and mock, and others who shrug their shoulders and thrust out their dung-yellow lips. I know that the best thing for them to do is to shut their traps up good and tight and watch what is going to happen. There are also those who know, the smart ones who make learned calculations with figures and statistics, but who are even duller than the others. These last are called men with a future. Liberty, I am nothing but a youngster enamored of Liberty, and I forget the rest without much effort, because I have a thirst, a wolf-like thirst which is sometimes a thirst for fresh blood, for your blood, Liberty. I have been told that there are men who will go to any lengths to bar your path and eliminate all those who seek to follow in your footsteps. The shaggy-headed idiots have not yet looked at themselves. Is it possible, Liberty, that they don't know that this death, which they brandish like a bogey, is our friend and your sister, and that we shall learn to love her if you say so; that we love you more because we still have faith in you, but that we are not afraid and, in order to follow you, we will not hesitate to take the path that leads directly to her? Then, O Liberty, let us have one sign, a grand sign, like dawn, or a gush of blood.

From *"Histoire d'un blanc"* (*au Sans Pareil, 1927*)
Translated from the French by Maria Jolas
transition 10

Gertrude Stein   *As a Wife Has a Cow*
                 a Love Story

Nearly all of it to be as a wife has a cow, a love story. All of it to be as a wife has a cow, all of it to be as a wife has a cow, a love story.

As to be all of it as to be a wife as a wife has a cow, a love story, all of it as to be all of it as a wife all of it as to be as a wife has a cow a love story, all of it as a wife has a cow as a wife has a cow a love story.

Has made, as it has made as it has made, has made has to be as a wife has a cow, a love story. Has made as to be as a wife has a cow a love story. As a wife has a cow, as a wife has a cow a love story. Has to be as a wife has a cow a love story. Has made as to be as a wife has a cow a love story.

When he can, and for that when he can, for that. When he can and for that when he can. For that. When he can. For that when he can. For that. And when he can and for that. Or that, and when he can. For that and when he can.

And to in six and another. And to and in and six and another. And to and in and six and another. And to in six and and to and in and six and another. And to and in and six and another. And to and six and in and another and and to and six and another and and to and in and six and and to and six and in and another.

In came in there, came in there come out of there. In came in come out of there. Come out there in came in there. Come out of there and in and come out of there. Came in there. Come out of there.

Feeling or for it, as feeling or for it, came in or come in, or come out of there or feeling as feeling or feeling as for it.

As a wife has a cow.

Came in and come out.

As a wife has a cow a love story.

As a love story, as a wife has a cow, a love story.

Not and now, now and not, not and now, by and by not and now, as not, as soon as not not and now, now as soon now, now as soon, and now as soon as soon as now. Just as soon just now just now just as soon just as soon as now. Just as soon as now.

And in that, as and in that, in that and and in that, so that, so that and in that, and in that and so that and as for that and as for that and that. In that. In that and and for that as for that and in that. Just as soon and in that. In that as that and just as soon. Just as soon as that.

Even now, now and even now and now and even now. Not as even now, therefor, even now and therefor, therefor and even now and even now and therefor even now. So not to and moreover and even now and therefor and moreover and even now and so and even now and therefor even now.

Do they as they do so. And do they do so.

We feel we feel. We feel or if we feel if we feel or if we feel. We feel or if we feel. As it is made made a day made a day or two made a day, as it is made a day or two, as it is made a day. Made a day. Made a day. Not away a day. By day. As it is made a day.

On the fifteenth of October as they say, said any way, what is it as they expect, as they expect it or as they expected it, as they expect it and as they expected it, expect it or for it, expected it and it is expected of it. As they say said anyway. What is it as they expect for it, what is it and it is as they expect of it. What is it. What is it the fifteenth of October as they say as they expect or as they expected as they expect for it. What is it as they say the fifteenth of October as they say and expected of it, the fifteenth of October as they say, what is it as expected of it. What is it and the fifteenth of October as they say and expected of it.

And prepare and prepare so prepare to prepare and prepare to prepare and prepare so as to prepare, so to prepare and prepare to prepare to prepare for and to prepare for it to prepare, to prepare for it, in preparation, as preparation in preparation by preparation. They will be too busy afterwards to prepare. As preparation prepare, to prepare, as to preparation and to prepare. Out there.

Have it as having having it as happening, happening to have it as having, having to have it as happening. Happening and have it as happening and having it happen as happening and having to have it happen as happening, and my wife has a cow as now, my wife having a cow as now, my wife having a cow as now and having a cow as now and having a cow and having a cow now, my wife has a cow and now. My wife has a cow.

transition 3

Italo Svevo   *The Wine That Kindles*

A niece of my wife's was going to be married at that age when young girls cease to be such and develop into spinsters. The poor thing had at first wanted to renounce the life of this world, but later the pressure brought to bear by the whole family had induced her to return and give up her desire for religion and chastity, and she had accepted the attentions of a young fellow whom the family had chosen as a good match. Then suddenly—good-by to religion! good-by to dreams of virtuous solitude: and the date of the nuptials was set for even earlier than the couple had intended.

And here we were, seated at dinner on the eve of the wedding. I was in a jovial mood, with a sense of recovered freedom. What had the young man done to induce her to change so quickly? Probably he had taken her in his arms to make her feel the pleasure of living, and had seduced rather than convinced her. In any case, they were to be the recipients of the usual good wishes. All have need of advice when they marry, but this girl had more need than most. What a disaster it would be if one day she should regret having let herself be brought back to this life from which she had at first instinctively turned! And so, as I drank, I plied them with good wishes, which I was even able to adapt to this special case: If you can be happy for one or two years, then you will more easily bear with one another for long years, thanks to the gratitude you will feel at having known joy. Joy leaves its own regret behind, and is therefore a form of suffering, but one that rises above the inescapable suffering inherent in life itself.

The bride did not appear to feel the need of all this advice. On the contrary, her face seemed to me to be crystallized in an expression of absolutely confident abandonment. Yet it was the same expression she had formerly worn when announcing her wish to retire to a cloister. Once again she was taking a vow—the vow to be happy for the rest of her life. Some people in this world are always taking vows. Would she keep this vow any more faithfully than she had the last?

All the others at that table were perfectly natural and gay, as spectators always are. To me, however, naturalness was entirely lacking. It was a memorable evening for me. My wife had prevailed on Dr. Paoli that for this evening I should be allowed to eat and drink like the others. This was a liberty conceded to me, and therefore all the more precious, as it would soon be taken away again. And so I behaved like a young fellow who has for the first time been given a latchkey of his own! I ate and drank not from thirst or hunger, but through greed for liberty. Every mouthful, every sip was the assertion of my own independence. I opened my mouth more than was necessary to receive the single mouthfuls; and the wine passed from the bottle to the glass in overflowing quantities; I did not leave it alone for a moment. I felt a sort of rage to bestir myself, and although glued to my seat, I nevertheless had a feeling of running and jumping like a dog released from his chain.

My wife aggravated my condition by relating to one of the persons seated next to her the regime to which I was ordinarily subjected, while my fifteen-year-old daughter, Emma, listened and gave herself airs of importance by completing her mother's description. It was as though they wanted to remind me of my chains just when I was momentarily freed of them. So all my tortures were recounted. They told how they weighed the little bit of meat allowed me at midday, thus depriving it of all taste, and how in the evening there was nothing to weigh, since supper consisted of a roll with a bit of ham and a glass of hot milk without sugar, which nauseated me. And as they talked, I privately damned both the doctor's science and their own ardor. As a matter of fact, if my organism was so worn out, how was it possible that this evening it could suddenly stand so many indigestible and harmful things, just because we had succeeded in the fine business of marrying off a girl who, of her own choice, would not have got married? And as I drank I prepared myself for the rebellion of the next day. I would show them.

The others abandoned themselves to champagne, whereas I, after taking a few glasses in order to respond to the various toasts, returned to ordinary table wine, in this instance an excellent dry Istrian wine which a friend of the family had sent for the occasion. I liked this wine —as one loves memories—and was not distrustful of it. But I was surprised that instead of giving me a feeling of joy and forgetfulness, it rather increased my sense of anger.

How could I help being in a rage? They had been responsible for a particularly disagreeable period of my life. Terrified and miserable, I had allowed some of my more generous instincts to die—to be replaced by lozenges, drops, and powders. No more Socialism for me. What did it matter to me if the land, contrary to every enlightened scientific conclusion, continued to remain in private hands? Or that for this reason the daily bread and essential liberty that every man should enjoy were withheld from so many? Had I either?

On that blessed evening I made a real effort to reintegrate my former self. When my nephew Giovanni, an immense fellow who weighed over two hundred pounds, started narrating in his stentorian voice little stories about his own business cunning as compared to the stupidity of others, I found that the old altruism still remained in my heart. "What will you do," I shouted at him, "when the struggle between men is no longer a struggle for money?"

For a moment Giovanni was taken aback at my somewhat somber question, which threatened suddenly to upset his entire world. He looked at me fixedly with eyes made larger by his spectacles, seeking in my face for some explanation that would serve as guide. Then, when all the guests turned to look at him, hoping to make them laugh with one of his sallies of half-naive, half-intelligent materialism—his was an ingenuous, cunning wit, with an element of surprise, despite its having been used long before the time of Sancho Panza—Giovanni gained time by remarking that although wine changed the aspect of the present for nearly everyone, for me it had also confused the future. This was not bad, but then he thought of something better and cried, "When the day comes when no one struggles for money, I shall have it all—every bit of it, without struggling!" This was greeted with hearty laughter, as was also the accompanying gesture of holding out his big, hefty arms, palms outstretched, then drawing them back with closed fists, as if he had already seized the money which would flow into them from every side.

The discussion continued, and no one seemed to notice that when I was not talking I was drinking. I drank much and said little, bent as I was on self-examination in order to discover if I really was filled with benevolence and altruism. I felt a slight heartburn, but from a fire that was diffused in an agreeable warmth, thanks to the feeling of youth produced by the wine.

Realising this, I exclaimed to Giovanni, "If you gather in the money that others reject, they'll throw you into prison!"

But Giovanni immediately retorted:

"Then I would bribe the jailers to have all those shut up who hadn't the money to bribe them."

"But money would have lost its power to corrupt."

"Then why not leave it all to me?"

I went into a violent rage. "They'd hang you," I screamed at him; "And you don't deserve anything better—a cord round your neck and weights on your feet!"

I stopped in astonishment. I realized that I had not exactly expressed my thought. Was it really I who had said this? No, certainly not. I reflected: how would I be able to recover my affection for all living persons, among whom Giovanni should also be counted? I smiled at him, exerting a violent effort to correct my attitude and to like him. But he made this impossible. Paying no attention to my benevolent smile, he said, as if turning over in his mind the discovery of a monstrous fact:

"Undoubtedly, all Socialists will end by having recourse to the hangman!"

He had won, but I hated him. He had upset my whole life, even the life I had led before the doctor intervened and on which I now looked back with regret as having been extremely pleasant. He had won, too, because he had raised the same doubt in my mind that I had already experienced with such anguish before he had spoken.

And then suddenly I was the object of another kind of punishment.

"How well he looks!" my sister had said, looking at me with complacency. This was an unfortunate remark. My wife had hardly heard it when she began to imagine that this excessive well-being now visible on my face meant just so much illness in store for me. She was terrified, as if at that moment someone had warned her of imminent danger, and she turned on me vehemently.

"That's enough!" she cried. "Put that glass down."

She then enlisted the help of my neighbor, a man named Alberi. Alberi was one of the tallest men in town, a thin, dry, healthy specimen, but who wore spectacles, like Giovanni. "Will you be so kind as to take that glass out of his hand," my wife said.

When Alberi hesitated, she became upset and excited. "Signor Alberi, will you be so kind as to take that glass away from him!"

I tried to laugh, and it occurred to me that for a well-bred person laughter would have been the proper reaction; but for me it was impossible. I had prepared my rebellion for the next day, and it was not my fault if it suddenly broke out before it was due. This rebuke in public was really outrageous. Alberi, who did not care two straws about me, my wife, or even the hosts who were plying him with food and drink, made my situation even worse by making me appear ridiculous. He looked over his spectacles at the glass I had now grasped firmly, made a gesture as if preparing to wrench it from me, and ended by hastily withdrawing his hand, as though frightened by the look on my face. Everybody laughed at me, Giovanni even more than the others, with that strident laugh of his which made him choke.

My young daughter Emma decided her mother needed her help. In a tone that seemed to me to be exaggeratedly supplicating, she said: "Papa, dear, don't drink any more!"

And it was on this innocent child that my wrath was vented. I turned on her with harsh, threatening words that were dictated by my resentment as an old man and a father. Her eyes suddenly filled with tears, and her mother left me in peace in order to devote herself to consoling the child.

At that moment my son Ottavio, aged thirteen, rushed over to his mother. He was concerned neither with his sister's grief nor with the dispute that had caused it. He wanted to obtain permission to go to the cinema the following evening with some of his companions who had just proposed this to him. My wife, absorbed entirely in her task of consoling Emma, paid no attention to him.

In order to recover my dignity through an act of authority, I called out my permission:

"Yes, certainly you may go to the cinema. If I permit it—that is enough." Without listening further, Ottavio said, "Thank you, papa," and returned to his companions. It was a pity he was in such a hurry, for if he had remained with us he might have cheered me with his own satisfaction, which was the fruit of my act of authority.

All conviviality disappeared from the table for some moments. I felt I had been lacking in consideration for the bride, for whom conviviality should have been an augury and a presage. And yet she was the only one who understood my difficulty, or so it seemed to me. She looked at me quite maternally, and seemed disposed to excuse, even to embrace me. In fact, this girl had always given this same impression of confidence in her own judgment. Just as when she had aspired to the life of the convent, so now she seemed to feel superior to everybody because of her renunciation. She appeared now superior to me, to my wife, and to my daughter. She even had compassion on us, and her beautiful gray eyes rested on us serenely, as if to seek where the blame might lie since, from her viewpoint, where there was pain there must also be blame.

This increased my anger towards my wife for having humiliated us in this way. It demeaned us before everybody down to the very humblest at that board, and even my sister's children, at the far end of the table, had stopped chattering to comment on the incident, their little heads close together. I seized the glass, hesitating whether to empty it, to hurl its contents against the wall, or to throw it out of the window just opposite. I ended by emptying it with one swallow. This was the most energetic thing I could have done, since it was also an assertion of my independence. In fact, it seemed to me to be the most precious drop of wine I had drunk that evening. I then prolonged the gesture of pouring some more wine into the glass, and started sipping it again. But gaiety would not be forced, and my only feeling, by now grown overintense, was one of rancor. A curious idea came to me. My rebellion would not suffice to clear up everything. Why not propose to the bride to rebel with me? By a stroke of good luck, she was at that very moment smiling sweetly at the man who was sitting so confidently beside her, and I thought to myself: "She doesn't know yet, but she is convinced that she does know."

I remember, too, that Giovanni said: "Why not let him drink? Wine is the milk of old people."

I turned to him, wrinkling my face to simulate a smile, but I did not succeed in liking him. I knew that all he wanted to do was to create an atmosphere of joviality and good humor that would please me, as one tries to placate a cross baby who has upset a gathering of grownups.

After that I drank little, and only when I saw that I was being looked at. Nor did I breathe another word. They were all talking away gaily at the top of their voices, and the noise wearied me. Not that I was listening to what they were saying, but it was difficult not to hear. An argument had broken out between Alberi and Giovanni, and the entire company was amused to see the fat and the thin man at grips. On what subject they were disputing I do not know, but I heard first from one and then from the other some pretty aggressive remarks. I saw Alberi leaning towards Giovanni, his bespectacled face thrust forward practically to the center of the table in order to come as near as possible to his adversary. The latter, however, was reclining comfortably in an armchair which someone had jokingly pushed towards him at the end of supper out of respect for his more than two hundred pounds. He eyed Alberi attentively, like the good fencer he was, trying to decide just where he would deliver his thrust. But Alberi was also a fine figure of a man, a little bony, perhaps, but nevertheless healthy, active, and calm.

I remember interminable good wishes and greetings when we started to separate, and the bride kissed me with a smile that still seemed to me maternal. However, I accepted her kiss absent-mindedly, for I was speculating on when I would be allowed to explain the facts of life to her.

At about this moment someone mentioned a name—Anna—the name of a friend of my wife's, and one-time friend of mine. I do not recall by whom it was mentioned nor in what connection, but I know it was the last name I heard before the other guests decided to leave me in peace. For many years I had been in the habit of seeing her frequently, in the company of my wife, and we always met with the friendship, the indifference, even, of people who have no objection to the fact that they were born in the same city and at the same time. Yet now, instead of this fact, I remembered that she had many years before been the object of my only amorous misdeed, for I had been courting her almost at the same moment that I had married my wife. After my breach of faith, which had been most abrupt—so much so, in fact, that I had not even tried to explain it with a single word—neither of us had ever spoken about it, as a little later she also married very happily. She had not been able to come to this banquet on account of a slight influenza which had kept her in bed, but was in no way serious. What was both strange and serious, however, was that I should now remember my misdeed, and it came to weigh on my already troubled conscience. I had the poignant sensation at that moment that my early offense was about to be punished. From her sickbed, which was now probably that of a convalescent, I heard my former victim protest: "You have no right to be happy!"

I reached my bedroom very downcast. Part of my depression was due to the fact that it seemed to me to be unjust that my wife should undertake to vindicate a woman whom she herself had supplanted.

Emma came to say good night to me. She was smiling, fresh and rosy, and her brief flood of tears had melted into a reaction of gaiety, as happens with all young, healthy organisms. For some time past I had been able to read the minds of others, and my little daughter, for instance, was like clear water for me. My rage had served to confer importance on her before the others, and despite all her ingenuousness she had enjoyed this. I gave her a kiss, and I am sure I thought it lucky for me that she should be so gay and contented. Undoubtedly, in order to educate her, it would have been my duty to admonish her for not having behaved with sufficient respect towards me. But I did not find the words, and so was silent. She left, and there remained of my effort to find these words—an effort that remained with me for some time— nothing but preoccupation and confusion. To calm myself I thought, "I will speak to her tomorrow; tomorrow I will tell her my reasons." But this did not suffice. I had offended her and she had offended me.

It was even a fresh offense that she no longer thought of me, whereas I was still thinking of her.

Ottavio also came to say goodnight. What a strange boy! He bade me and his mother goodnight almost without looking at us. He had already left the room when I called him back. "Are you pleased to go to the cinema?" I asked. He paused, made an effort to remember, and before hurrying off again, said curtly, "Yes," to which he added that he was very sleepy.

My wife handed me the box of pills. "Are these the ones?" I asked her icily.

"Yes, certainly," she said kindly. She looked at me searchingly, and, not knowing how otherwise to fathom my state of mind, she asked me hestitatingly, "Are you feeling well?"

"Very well, indeed," I declared decisively, taking off one shoe. At that very moment I began to feel a frightful heartburn. "That was just what she wanted!" I thought to myself, with a logic which only now I begin to doubt.

I swallowed the pill with a sip of water, and it relieved me somewhat. Then I kissed my wife mechanically on the cheek, a kiss made to accompany the pills. Nor could I very well have done otherwise, wishing as I did to avoid discussions and explanations. But I knew I could not settle down for the night without having first defined my position in the as yet unfinished struggle. "I think the pills would have been more efficacious if they had been taken with wine," I said.

For answer she put out the light, and very soon her regular breathing told me that her mind had finally attained to other worlds in which she was supremely indifferent to all my trouble. I had anxiously waited for this moment, and now I said to myself that I was at last free to breathe noisily, as the condition of my health seemed to require, or indeed even to sob, as in my depressed state I had wanted to do. But no sooner was I free to do this than my anxiety assumed an even greater reality. After all, this was not real liberty. How could I give vent to the anger that still raged inside me? All I could do was to turn over in my mind what I should say to my wife and my daughter the next day.—You make a great fuss about my health so long you can annoy me before other people.—This was absolutely true. Here I was, raging alone in my bed while they were sleeping serenely. Oh, what heartburn! I had imbibed into my organism an entire vast flood, the fumes of which were now gathered in my throat. On the little bedside table there must be a bottle of water, so I stretched out my hand to take hold of it. But instead I knocked over the empty glass, and the slight tinkle sufficed to arouse my wife. In any case, she always slept with one eye open.

"Aren't you feeling well?" she asked me in a low voice. She was not sure whether she had heard aright, and did not wish to wake me. I knew this, but attributed to her the curious intention of rejoicing at my misfortune, which would simply be proof that she had been right. So I abandoned the water bottle, and settled myself very quietly. Whereupon she immediately fell into her light sleep which permitted her at the same time to watch over me.

After all, if I was not to fail in my struggle with my wife, I must get to sleep. I closed my eyes and turned over on one side, but immediately changed my position again. I persisted, however, in not opening my eyes. Each position I assumed sacrificed one or the other part of my body, and at each new pose I thought to myself, "I cannot sleep with my body like this." I was all movement, all awake. A man who feels he is running can't possibly think of sleeping. As I worried about this I seemed to hear echoing in my ears the heavy tramping of my own footsteps. I next decided that perhaps I was moving too gently to be able to arrive all at once and with all my limbs at the proper position. It was useless to try for it. All I needed was to let each one find the position best suited to its form. Once more I turned over, with a certain violence. Immediately my wife murmured, "Aren't you feeling well?" If she had used any other words, I should have replied by asking for her help. But I refused to reply to these words, which were such an offensive reminder of our dispute.

To remain quite still should nevertheless be easy enough. What difficulty could there be in just lying quietly in one's bed? I went over in my mind all the real difficulties against which we have to struggle in this world, and found that really, in comparison with any of them, just to lie inert was nothing at all. Any old carcass could remain still. In my determination, I next invented a position, a complicated one, but calculated to hold. Planting my teeth into the upper part of my pillow, I twisted myself in such a way that my chest also rested on the pillow, while my right leg was thrust out of the bed, almost touching the floor, and my left leg, held stiff on the bed, pinned me to it. Yes, I had discovered a new system. It was not I who clung to the bed, but the bed which clung to me. And, in fact, this conviction of my own inertia was so great that even an increasing sense of oppression did not daunt me. When, later, I was forced to give in to it, I consoled myself with the idea that a portion of this horrible night had passed. I was also rewarded by the fact that as I freed myself from the bed I felt a sense of relief, like a fighter who has freed himself from the grip of an adversary.

I do not know for how long I remained still, for I was very weary. Suddenly I was conscious of a strange flash of light before my closed eyes, which I supposed emanated from the fire I felt within me. These were not real flames, however, but the colors of flames, which disappeared, little by little, assuming form of rounded reliefs, or, again, drops of a glutinous liquid, which turned a dull blue, surrounded by a vivid red light. The drops fell from a high point, became elongated, then uniform in size, and disappeared all at once down below. At first I thought they could see me, and, in fact, suddenly, in order to see me the better, they turned into so many small eyes. At the moment of elongation, while falling, a small circle formed in the center of each one —which, once it had got rid of its azure veil, revealed a real eye that was both malicious and malevolent. Indeed, I was being pursued by a mob that wanted to do me harm. With a movement of revolt, I groaned and cried out loud: "My God!"

"Aren't you feeling well?" my wife asked.

Some time must have elapsed before I replied. Then it so happened that I realized I was no longer lying in my bed, but was clinging tight to it, for it had been transformed into a slope down which I was slipping. I called out: "I am ill—very ill!"

My wife had lit a candle and was standing beside me in her pink nightgown. I felt reassured by the light, and also had the definite feeling of having slept and only just awakened. The bed was now quite straight again, and I lay there without effort. I looked at my wife in surprise, since now, as it was evident that I had been sleeping, I was no longer sure of having called for her help. "What do you want?" I asked.

She looked at me with tired, sleepy eyes. My cry had sufficed to make her start from bed, but not to take away her desire for rest, compared with which, simply to be in the right had lost its importance for her. In order to expedite matters, she asked, "Would you like some of those sleeping drops the doctor prescribed?"

I hesitated, in spite of my strong desire for greater well-being. "As you wish," I said, trying just to appear resigned. To take the drops was in no way equivalent to admitting I felt ill.

There followed an instant during which I enjoyed complete peace. It lasted while my wife, standing beside the bed in her pink nightgown, counted the drops by the light of the candle. The bed was once more a real horizontal bed, and when I closed my eyelids they sufficed to keep out all light. But from time to time I opened them and the light, added to the pink of the nightgown, gave me a different sense of peace from that afforded by total darkness. Unfortunately, my wife refused to prolong her ministrations for a minute more than was necessary, and

I was once more plunged into the night to continue my lone struggle for peace.

I remembered that when I had been young, in order to hasten sleep, I used to force myself to think of a very ugly old woman, a device that succeeded in making me forget the beautiful visions that obsessed me. Now, on the contrary, I could evoke beauty without danger, which should certainly have helped me get to sleep. This was the advantage—the only one—of old age. So I thought, calling them by name, of various handsome women I had desired in my youth, at a time when there had been such an incredible abundance of handsome women. But they did not come to me—they did not deign to come. And I evoked and conjured until at last out of the night there shone one lovely face—Anna herself, as she had been so many years before. Only now her face—her beautiful, rose-blossom face—was altered by grief and reproach. It was clear that she wished to bring me not peace but remorse. And since she was present I discussed the question with her. Yes, I had abandoned her; but then she had quickly married another, which was only right. Since then, she had brought into the world a little girl who was now fifteen years old. This daughter resembled her in her gentle coloring, golden hair, and blue eyes, but her face was nevertheless different, due to the role of the father who had been chosen for her—the soft waves had become thick, rich curls, she had plump cheeks, a big mouth, and very thick lips. In the eye of the outside world the mother's coloring, following the outlines of the father, had thus become the manifestation of obvious coupling. What did she want of me then, since she had shown so plainly that she preferred her husband to me?

For the first time that evening I felt I had won a victory. In my thoughts Anna became gentler, indeed, almost resigned. And her company no longer displeased me—she might remain. Happy in this decision I fell asleep, admiring her as being both beautiful and good. In fact, I fell asleep at once.

An awful dream. I found myself in a complicated structure, of which it soon seemed to me that I formed a part. It was a vast, primitive grotto, with none of those appurtenances which Nature is pleased to create in grottoes, and therefore certainly due to the hand of man. I was sitting in the darkness on a wooden tripod beside a glass coffin, which was faintly lighted by a light that appeared to me to be inherent in it—the only light there was, in fact, in that vast place. It sufficed, however, to throw light on me and on a wall built with large, rough stones, underneath which was a cement wall. How expressive is the construction of dreams! One might say that this is the case for the reason that he who has served as architect can easily understand them; which is true. But the surprising thing is that the architect is unaware of his role, and no longer remembers it when he awakens. Returning to the world from whence he has come and in which structures of every kind arise with such facility, his thought is surprise that everything should happen there without need of words.

I knew at once that this grotto had been built by men who used it for a cure invented by themselves—a cure which was mortal for those imprisoned therein (and there must be many down there in the shadow), but beneficial to all the others. Neither more nor less than a form of religion which had need of a holocaust, and which quite naturally did not seem to surprise me.

It was even easier to foretell that, having been placed so near the glass coffin in which the victim was to be asphyxiated, it was I who was elected to die in preference to all the others, and I already felt the pains of the terrible death that awaited me. I was breathing with difficulty, and my head was painful and heavy, so much so that I held it in my hands, my elbows planted on my knees.

Suddenly all this which was known to me was being told out loud by a number of people hidden in the darkness. My wife was the first to speak:

"Hurry up! The doctor says it's you who must get into that coffin."

This seemed painful to me, but quite logical. I therefore did not protest, but feigned not to hear. And I thought to myself, "My wife's love for me has always seemed to me foolish." A number of other voices shouted at me imperiously, "When will you make up your mind to obey?"

Among these voices I distinguished very clearly the voice of Dr. Paoli. I could not protest, but I thought, "He is doing this for money."

I raised my head to examine once more the glass coffin that stood in readiness for me. Then I discovered, seated on the top of the coffin, the bride. Even in this situation she had preserved her eternal air of tranquil assurance. I sincerely despised this foolish woman, but immediately became aware of the fact that she was very important to me. I ought to have discovered this in real life, I thought, as I watched her seated there on the instrument which was to be used to kill me. Then I began to look at her, all of a quiver, like one of those small dogs that go through life doing little but wag their tails. It was abject of me.

The bride began to speak. Without harshness, as though it were the most natural thing in the world, she said, "Uncle, the coffin is for you."

Now it became plain to me I would have to fight for my life all alone. I had the feeling of being able to make an enormous effort imperceptible to anybody else. Just as before I had felt I had the power to conquer the favor of my judge without speaking, so now I discovered in myself another power of which I had so far been unaware: to fight without any move on my part and thus attack my adversaries while they were off their guard. The effort was crowned with immediate success.

And now here was Giovanni, great, huge Giovanni, seated in the luminous glass coffin on a wooden seat similar to mine and in the same position as myself. He was leaning forward, the coffin being too low for him, holding his spectacles in his hand to keep them from falling off his nose. This gave him somewhat the appearance of arranging a business transaction, and of having taken off his spectacles in order the better to think without seeing anything. In fact, although he was perspiring and already very uneasy, instead of thinking of approaching death, he was full of malice, as could be seen by the look in his eyes. For it was evident that he was planning the same effort which I myself had made a little while before. Since I feared him, I was unable to feel any compassion for him.

With Giovanni, too, the effort succeeded, and a little later, Alberi had taken his place in the coffin; long, thin, healthy Alberi, seated in the same position as Giovanni, but even more uncomfortably, on account of his great height. He was absolutely doubled up, and would really have aroused my pity, if it had not been that just as with Giovanni, instead of an expression of affliction I saw a very wicked look in his eye. He looked up at me from below, with a most villainous grin, as if he knew that it depended only on himself not to die in that coffin.

From the top of the coffin came the voice of the bride who said: "Now, Uncle, this will certainly be your turn." She fairly hissed the words, stressing each one carefully, and as she spoke there came another sound, from a much greater distance and much higher up. This prolonged sound, uttered by a person who seemed to be moving rapidly farther away, gave me to understand that the grotto finished in a narrow corridor which led to the surface of the earth. It was a single hiss, but a hiss of approval, and it came from Anna, who once more had manifested her hatred for me. She had not the courage to clothe it in words, because I had, in fact, convinced her that she had been more guilty towards me than I had been towards her. But conviction plays no role when it is a question of hatred.

I was being blamed by everybody. At a certain distance away from me, somewhere in the grotto, my wife and the doctor were walking expectantly up and down, and I realized that my wife was highly offended. With violent gestures she proclaimed my faults loudly—the wine I had drunk, the food I had eaten, my abrupt manner with her and my daughter.

Now I felt myself drawn to the coffin by the triumphant look Alberi had turned in my direction. I began to approach it slowly, without leav-

ing my chair, a quarter of an inch at a time. I knew, however, that when
I had come within a yard of it (such was the law), at one fell swoop I
would be hurled, panting, into it.

There was nevertheless still a slight hope that I might be saved.
Giovanni, who by now had entirely recovered from the fatigue of his
own hard struggle, had once more approached the coffin. He no longer
feared it, having already been inside it (this too was a generally accepted law). He stood erect in the bright light, looking now at Alberi,
who was panting and groaning, now at me, as I slowly approached the
coffin.

"Giovanni," I cried out, "help me to keep him in there—I will pay
you!"

The whole grotto resounded with my cry, giving the effect of scornful laughter. Now I understood. It was useless to beg. The one destined
to die was not the first man who was thrust into it, nor yet the second,
but the third. This, too, was a law of the grotto, the application of which,
like the others, meant my destruction. Yet it was hard for me to believe
that this law had not been passed just at that moment for the very purpose of doing me harm. All this came to me out of the darkness.
Giovanni did not even reply, but shrugged his shoulders to signify his
regret at not being able either to save me or even to sell me salvation.

Once more I shouted, "If you cannot do anything else, take my
daughter, then! She is sleeping nearby. It will be easy."

My cry came back to me in the form of a deafening echo. But this
did not deter me, and I tried again to call my daughter: "Emma!
Emma!"

From the depths of the grotto I could hear Emma's reply, and her
voice was still very childlike in tone: "Here I am, daddy! Here I am!"

Somehow I felt she had not answered quickly enough. Then came
a violent disturbance, which I associated with my leap into the coffin.
Once more I thought to myself, "She's always slow to obey." But this
time her slowness had meant my destruction, and I was full of bitterness.

At this point I awoke. In fact, this was the disturbance—the sudden
plunge from one world into another. My head and chest were out of the
bed, and I was about to fall when my wife took hold of me. "Were you
dreaming?" she asked, adding with emotion, "You were calling for
your daughter. You see how fond of her you are!"

I was at first depressed by this reality, in which it seemed to me that
everything had become ugly and false. Confident that my wife shared
my feeling, I said, "How shall we ever obtain the pardon of our children for having put them into this life?"

But hers was a simple mind: "Our children are happy to be alive,"
she replied.

The life which I now felt to be the only true one, the dream-life, still held me in its grip, and I felt like shouting: "Because as yet they know nothing."

But I did not say it, lapsing into silence instead. Through the window near my bed dawn was breaking, and it made me feel that I ought not to tell my dream, that I must make an effort to conceal its shameful aspects. Later, as the sun rose higher in the blue sky and gently but imperiously invaded the room, I lost this sense of shame. The dream-life was not my life, it was not I who had trembled, nor was I that man who, in order to save himself, had been ready to sacrifice his own daughter.

Still, I would have to be careful never to return to that sinister grotto. So, firm in this resolution, I have grown more and more docile, more and more willing to adapt myself to the diet prescribed by the doctor. But if I ever should be obliged to return to that grotto, through no fault of my own—in other words, not as a result of excessive drinking, but of the fever that precedes the end—I would immediately take my place in the glass coffin, if it were still there, so as neither to tremble nor betray.

*Translated from the Italian
by* Sommerville Story
transition 15-17

Dylan Thomas   *The Mouse and the Woman*

I

In the eaves of the lunatic asylum were birds who whistled the coming in of spring. A madman, howling like a dog from the top room, could not disturb them, and their tunes did not stop when he thrust his hands through the bars of the window near their nests and clawed the sky. A fresh smell blew with the winds around the white building and its grounds. The asylum trees waved green hands over the wall to the world outside.

In the gardens the patients sat and looked up at the sun or upon the flowers or upon nothing, or walked sedately along the paths, hearing the gravel crunch beneath their feet with a hard, sensible sound. Children in print dresses might be expected to play, not noisily, upon the lawns. The building, too, had a sweet expression, as though it knew only the kind things of life and the polite emotions. In a middle room sat a child who had cut off his double thumb with a scissors.

A little way off the main path leading from house to gate, a girl, lifting her arms, beckoned to the birds. She enticed the sparrows with little movements of her fingers, but to no avail. It must be spring, she said. The sparrows sang exultantly, and then stopped.

The howling in the top room began again. The madman's face was pressed close to the bars of the window. Opening his mouth wide, he bayed up at the sun, listening to the inflections of his voice with a remorseless concentration. With his unseeing eyes fixed on the green garden, he heard the revolution of the years as they moved softly back. Now there was no garden. Under the sun the iron bars melted. Like a flower, a new room pulsed and opened.

II

Waking up when it was still dark, he turned the dream over and over on the tip of his brain until each little symbol became heavy with a separate meaning. But there were symbols he could not remember, they came and went so quickly among the rattle of leaves—the gestures of women's hands spelling on the sky, the falling of rain, and the humming wind. He remembered the oval of her face and the color of her eyes. He remembered the pitch of her voice, though not what she said. She moved again wearily up and down the same ruler of turf. What she said fell with the leaves, and spoke in the wind, whose brother rattled the panes like an old man.

There had been seven women, in a mad play by a Greek, each with the same face, crowned by the same hoop of mad, black hair. Seven was a number in magic. One by one they trod the ruler of turf, then vanished. They turned the same face to him, intolerably weary with the same suffering.

The dream had changed. Where the women were was an avenue of trees. And the trees leaned forward and interlaced their hands, turning into a black forest. He had seen himself, absurd in his nakedness, walk into the depths. Stepping on a dead twig, he was bitten.

Then there was her face again. There was nothing in his dream but her tired face. And the changes of the details of the dream and the celestial changes, the levers of the trees and the toothed twigs, these were the mechanisms of her delirium. It was not the sickness of sin that was upon her face. Rather it was the sickness of never having sinned and of never having done well.

He lit the candle on the little deal table by his bedside. Candlelight threw the shadows of the room into confusion, and raised up the warped men of shadow out of the corners. For the first time he heard the clock. He had been deaf until then to everything except the wind outside the window and the clean winter sounds of the nightworld. But now the steady tick tock tick sounded like the heart of someone hidden in his room. He could not hear the night birds now. The loud clock drowned their crying, or the wind was too cold for them, and made commotion among their feathers. He remembered the dark hair of the woman in the trees and of the seven women treading the ruler of turf.

He could no longer listen to the speaking of reason. The pulse of a new heart beat at his side. Contentedly he let the dream dictate its rhythm. Often he would rise when the sun had dropped down and, in the lunatic blackness under the stars, walk on the hill, feeling the wind finger his hair and at his nostrils. The rats and the rabbits on his towering hill came out in the dark, and the shadows consoled them for the light of the harsh sun. The dark woman, too, had risen out of darkness, pulling down the stars in their hundreds and showing him a mystery that hung and shone higher in the night of the sky than all the planets crowding beyond the curtains.

He fell to sleep again and woke in the sun. As he dressed, the dog scratched at the door. He let it in and felt its wet muzzle in his hand. The weather was hot for a midwinter day. The little wind there was could not relieve the sharpness of the heat. With the opening of the bedroom window, the uneven beams of the sun twisted his images into the hard lines of light.

He tried not to think of the woman as he ate. She had risen out of the depths of darkness. Now she was lost again. She is drowned, dead, dead. In the clean glittering of the kitchen, among the white boards, the oleographs of old women, the brass candlesticks, the plates on the shelves, and the sounds of kettle and clock, he was caught between believing in her and denying her. Now he insisted on the lines of her neck. The wilderness of her hair rose over the dark surface. He saw her flesh in the cut bread; her blood, still flowing through the channels of her mysterious body, in the spring water.

But another voice told him that she was dead. She was a woman in a mad story. He forced himself to hear the voice telling that she was dead. Dead, alive, drowned, raised up. The two voices shouted across his brain. He could not bear to think that the last spark in her had been put out. She is alive, alive, cried the two voices together.

As he tidied the sheets on his bed, he saw a block of paper, and sat down at the table with a pencil poised in his hand. A hawk flew over the hill. Sea gulls, on spread, unmoving wings, cried past the window. A mother rat, in a hole in the hillside near the holes of rabbits, suckled its young as the sun climbed higher in the clouds.

He put the pencil down.

III

One winter morning, after the last crowing of the cock in the walks of his garden had died to nothing, she who for so long had dwelt with him appeared in all the wonder of her youth. She had cried to be set free, and to walk in his dreams no longer. Had she not been in the beginning, there would have been no beginning. She had moved in his belly when he was a boy, and stirred in his boy's loins. He at last gave birth to her who had been with him from the beginning. And with him dwelt a dog, a mouse, and a dark woman.

IV

It is not a little thing, he thought, this writing that lies before me. It is the telling of a creation. It is the story of birth. Out of him had come another. A being had been born, not out of the womb, but out of the soul and the spinning head. He had come to the cottage on the hill, that the being within him might ripen and be born away from the eyes of men. He understood what the wind that took up the woman's cry had cried in his last dream. Let me be born, it had cried. He had given a woman being. His flesh would be upon her, and the life that he had given her would make her walk, talk, and sing. And he knew, too, that it was upon the block of paper she was made absolute. There was an oracle in the lead of the pencil.

In the kitchen he cleaned up after his meal. When the last plate had been washed, he looked around the room. In the corner near the door was a hole no bigger than a half crown. He found a tiny square of tin and nailed it over the hole, making sure that nothing could go in or come out. Then he donned his coat and walked out on to the hill and down towards the sea.

Broken water leaped up from the inrushing tide and fell into the crevices of the rocks, making innumerable pools. He climbed down to the half circle of beach, and the clusters of shells did not break when his foot fell on them. Feeling his heart knock at his side, he turned to where the greater rocks climbed perilously up to the grass. There, at the foot, the oval of her face towards him, she stood and smiled. The spray brushed her naked body, and the creams of the sea ran unheeded over her feet. She lifted her hand. He crossed to her.

V

In the cool of the evening they walked in the garden behind the cottage. She had lost none of her beauty with the covering up of her nakedness. With slippers on her feet she stepped as gracefully as when her feet were bare. There was a dignity in the poise of her head, and her voice was clear as a bell. Walking by her side along the narrow path, he heard no discord in the crying together of the gulls. She pointed out bird and bush with her finger, illuminating a new loveliness in the wings and leaves, in the sour churning of water over pebbles, and a new life along the dead branches of the trees.

It is quiet here, she said, as they stood out to sea and the dark coming over the land. Is it always as quiet?

Not when the storms come in with the tide, he said. Boys play behind the hill. Lovers go down to the shore.

Late evening turned to night so suddenly that, where she stood, stood a shadow under the moon. He took its hand, and they ran together to the cottage.

It was lonely for you before I came, she said.

A coal leered and spat out of the depths of the fire. As a cinder hissed into the grate, he moved back in his chair, made a startled gesture with his hand.

How quickly you become frightened, she said. I am frightened of nothing.

But she thought over her words and spoke again, this time in a low voice.

One day I may have no limbs to walk with, no hands to touch with. No heart under my breast, she said.

He told her that he was frightened of the stars.

Look at the million stars, he said. They make some pattern on the sky. It is a pattern of letters spelling a word. One night I shall look up and read the word.

But she kissed him and calmed his fears.

VI

The madman remembered the inflections of her voice, heard, again, her frock rustling, and saw the terrible curve of her breast. His own breathing thundered in his ears. The girl on the bench beckoned to the sparrows. Somewhere a child purred, stroking the black columns of a wooden horse that neighed and then lay down.

VII

They slept together on the first night, side by side in the dark, their arms around one another. The shadows in the corner were trimmed and shapely in her presence, losing their old deformity. And the stars looked in upon them and shone in their eyes.

Tomorrow you must tell me what you dream, he said.

It will be what I have always dreamed, she said. Walking on a little length of grass, up and down, up and down, till my feet bleed. Seven images of me walking up and down.

It is what I dream. Seven is a number in magic.

Magic? she said.

A woman makes a wax man, puts a pin in its chest; and the man dies. Someone has a little devil, tells it what to do. A girl dies, you see her walk. A woman turns into a hill.

She let her head rest on his shoulder, and fell to sleep.

He kissed her mouth, and passed his hand through her hair.

She was asleep, but he did not sleep. Wide-awake, he stared into darkness. Now he was drowned in terror, and the sucking waters closed over his skull.

I, I have a devil, he said.

She stirred at the noise of his voice, and then again her head was motionless and her body straight along the curves of the cool bed.

I have a devil, but I do not tell it what to do. It lifts my hand. I write. The words spring into life. She, then, is a woman of the devil.

She made a contented sound, nestled ever nearer to him. Her breath was warm on his neck, and her foot lay on his like a mouse. He saw that she was beautiful in her sleep. Her beauty could not have sprouted out of evil. God, whom he had searched for in his loneliness, had formed her for his mate, as Eve for Adam out of Adam's rib.

He kissed her again, and saw her smile as she slept.

God at my side, he said.

VIII

He had not slept with Rachel and woken with Leah. There was the pallor of dawn on her cheeks. He touched them lightly with a finger-nail. She did not stir.

But there had been no woman in his dream. Not even a thread of woman's hair had dangled from the sky. God had come down in a cloud and the cloud had changed to a snake's nest. Foul hissing of snakes had suggested the sound of water, and he had been drowned. Down and down he had fallen, under green shiftings and the bubbles that fishes blew from their mouths, down and down on to the bony floors of the sea.

Then, against a white curtain, people had moved and moved to no purpose but to speak mad things.

What did you find under the tree?

I found an airman.

No, no, under the other tree?

I found a bottle of fetus.

No, no, under the other tree?

I found a mousetrap.

He had been invisible. There had been nothing but his voice. He had flown across back gardens, and his voice, caught in a tangle of wireless aerials, had bled as though it were a thing of substance. Men in deck chairs were listening to the loudspeakers speaking:

What did you find under the tree?

I found a wax man.

No, no, under the other tree?

He could remember little else except the odds and ends of sentences, the movement of a turning shoulder, the sudden flight or drop of syllables. But slowly the whole meaning edged into his brain. He could translate every symbol of his dreams, and he lifted the pencil so that they might stand hard and clear upon the paper. But the words would not come. He thought he heard the scratching of velvet paws behind a panel. But when he sat still and listened close, there was no sound.

She opened her eyes.

What are you doing? she said.

He put down the paper, and kissed her before they rose to dress.

What did you dream last night? he asked her, when they had eaten.

Nothing. I slept, that is all. What did you dream?

Nothing, he said.

IX

There was creation screaming in the steam of the kettle, in the light making mouths on the china and the floor she swept as a child sweeps the floor of a doll's house. There was nothing to see in her but the ebb and flood of creation, only the transcendent sweep of being and living in the careless fold of flesh from shoulder bone to elbow. He could not tell, after the horror he had found in the translating symbols, why the sea should point to the fruitful and unfailing stars with the edge of each wave, and an image of fruition disturb the moon in its dead course.

She molded his images that evening. She lent light, and the lamp was dim beside her who had the oil of life glistening in every pore of her hand.

And now in the garden they remembered how they had walked in the garden for the first time.

You were lonely before I came.

How quickly you become frightened.

She had lost none of her beauty with the covering up of her nakedness. Though he had slept at her side, he had been content to know the surface of her. Now he stripped her of her clothes and laid her upon a bed of grass.

X

The mouse had waited for this consummation. Wrinkling its eyes, it crept stealthily along the tunnel, littered with scraps of half-eaten paper, behind the kitchen wall. Stealthily, on tiny, padded paws, it felt its way through darkness, its nails scraping on the wood. Stealthily, it worked its way between the walls, screamed at the blind light through the chinks, and filed through the square of tin. Moonlight dropped slowly into the space where the mouse, working its destruction, inched into light. The last barrier fell away. And on the clean stones of the kitchen floor the mouse stood still.

XI

That night he told her of the love in the garden of Eden.

A garden was planted eastward, and Adam lived in it. Eve was made for him, out of him, bone of his bones, flesh of his flesh. They were as naked as you upon the seashore, but Eve could not have been as beautiful. They ate with the devil, and saw that they were naked, and covered up their nakedness. In their good bodies they saw evil for the first time.

Then you saw evil in me, she said, when I was naked. I would as soon be naked as be clothed. Why did you cover up my nakedness?

It was not good to look upon, he said.

But it was beautiful. You yourself said that it was beautiful, she said.

It was not good to look upon.

You said the body of Eve was good. And yet you say I was not good to look upon. Why did you cover up my nakedness?

It was not good to look upon.

XII

Welcome, said the devil to the madman. Cast your eyes upon me. I grow and grow. See how I multiply. See my sad, Grecian stare. And the longing to be born in my dark eyes. Oh, that was the best joke of all.

I am an asylum boy tearing the wings of birds. Remember the lions that were crucified. Who knows that it was not I who opened the door of the tomb for Christ to struggle out?

But the madman had heard that welcome time after time. Ever since the evening of the second day, after their love in the garden, when he had told her that her nakedness was not good to look upon, he had heard the welcome ring out, in the sliding rain, and seen the welcome words burnt into the sea. He had known at the ringing of the first sylla-ble in his ears that nothing on the earth could save him, and that the mouse would come out.

But the mouse had come out already.

The madman cried down at the beckoning girl to whom, now, a host of birds edged closer on a bough.

XIII

Why did you cover up my nakedness?

It was not good to look upon.

Why, then, no, no, under the other tree?

It was not good, I found a wax cross.

As she had questioned him, not harshly, but with bewilderment, that he whom she loved should find her nakedness unclean, he heard the broken pieces of the old dirge break into her questioning.

Why, then, she said, no, no, under the other tree?

He heard himself reply, It was not good, I found a talking thorn.

Real things kept changing place with unreal, and, as a bird burst into song, he heard the springs rattle far back in its throat.

She left him with a smile that still poised over a question, and cross-ing the strip of hill, vanished into the half dark where the cottage stood like another woman. But she returned ten times, in ten different shapes. She breathed at his ear, passed the back of her hand over his dry mouth, and lit the lamp in the cottage room more than a mile away.

It grew darker as he stared at the stars. Wind cut through the new night. Very suddenly a bird screamed over the trees, and an owl, hungry for mice, hooted in the mile-away wood.

There was contradiction in heartbeat and green Sirius, an eye in the east. He put his hand to his eyes, hiding the star, and walked slowly towards the lamp burning far away in the cottage. And all the elements come together, of wind and sea and fire, of love and the passing of love, closed in a circle around him.

She was not sitting by the fire, as he had expected her to be, smiling upon the folds of her dress. He called her name at the foot of the stairs. He looked into the empty bedroom, and called her name in the garden. But she had gone, and all the mystery of her presence had left the cottage. And the shadows that he thought had departed when she had come crowded the corners, muttering in women's voices among them-selves. He turned down the wick in the lamp. As he climbed upstairs, he heard the corner voices become louder and louder, until the whole cottage reverberated with them, and the wind could not be heard.

XIV

With tears on his cheeks and a hard pain in his heart, he fell to sleep, coming at last to where his father sat in an alcove carved in a cloud.

Father, he said, I have been walking over the world, looking for a thing worthy to love, but I drove it away, and go now from place to place, moaning my hideousness, hearing my own voice in the voices of the corn crakes and the frogs, seeing my own face in the riddled faces of the beasts.

He held out his arms, waiting for words to fall from that old mouth hidden under a white beard frozen with tears. He implored the old man to speak.

Speak to me, your son. Remember how we read the classic books together on the terraces. Or on an Irish harp you would pluck tunes until the geese, like the seven geese of the Wandering Jew, rose squawking into the air. Father, speak to me, your only son, a prodigal out of the herbaceous spaces of small towns, out of the smells and sounds of the city, out of the thorny desert, and the deep sea. You are a wise old man.

He implored the old man to speak, but coming closer to him and staring into his face, he saw the stains of death upon mouth and eyes and a nest of mice in the tangle of the frozen beard.

It was weak to fly, but he flew. And it was a weakness of the blood to be invisible, but he was invisible. He reasoned and dreamed unreasonably at the same time, knowing his weakness and the lunacy of flying, but having no strength to conquer it. He flew like a bird over the fields, but soon the bird's body vanished, and he was a flying voice. An open window beckoned him by the waving of its blinds, as a scarecrow beckons a wise bird by its ragged waving, and into the open window he flew, alighting on a bed near a sleeping girl.

Awake, girl, he said. I am your lover come in the night.

She awoke at his voice.

Who called me?

I called you.

Where are you?

I am upon the pillow by your head, speaking into your ear.

Who are you?

I am a voice.

Stop calling into my ear, then, and hop into my hand so that I may touch you and tickle you. Hop into my hand, voice.

He lay still and warm in her palm.

Where are you?

I am in your hand.

Which hand?

The hand on your breast, left hand. Do not make a fist or you will crush me. Can you not feel me warm in your hand? I am close to the roots of your fingers.

Talk to me.

I had a body, but was always a voice. As I truly am, I come to you in the night, a voice on your pillow.

I know what you are. You are the still, small voice I must not listen to. I have been told not to listen to that still, small voice that speaks in the night. It is wicked to listen. You must not come here again. You must go away.

But I am your lover.

I must not listen, said the girl, and suddenly clenched her hand.

XV

He could go into the garden, regardless of rain, and bury his face in the wet earth. With his ears pressed close to the earth he would hear the great heart, under soil and grass, strain before breaking. In dreams he would say to some figure, lift me up. I am only ten pounds now. I am lighter. Six pounds. Two pounds. My spine shows through my breast. The secret of that alchemy that had turned a little revolution of the unsteady senses into a golden moment was lost, as a key is lost in undergrowth. A secret was confused among the night, and the confusion of the last madness before the grave would come down like an animal on the brain.

He wrote upon the block of paper, not knowing what he wrote, and dreading the words that looked up at him at last and could not be forgotten.

XVI

And this is all there was to it: a woman had been born, not out of the womb, but out of the soul and the spinning head. And he who had borne her out of darkness loved his creation, and she loved him. But this is all there was to it: a miracle befell a man. He fell in love with it, but could not keep it, and the miracle passed. And with him dwelt a dog, a mouse, and a dark woman. The woman went away, and the dog died.

XVII

He buried the dog at the end of the garden. Rest in peace, he told the dead dog. But the grave was not deep enough and there were rats in the underhanging of the bank who bit through the sack shroud.

XVIII

Upon town pavements he saw the woman step loose, her breasts firm under a coat on which the single hairs from old men's heads lay white on black. Her life, he knew, was only a life of days. Her spring had passed with him. After the summer and the autumn, unhallowed time between full life and death, there would be winter corrugating charm. He who knew the subtleties of every season, and sensed the four together in every symbol of the earth, would disturb the chronology of the seasons. Winter must not appear.

XIX

Consider now the old effigy of time, his long beard whitened by an Egyptian sun, his bare feet watered by the Sargasso Sea. Watch me belabor the old fellow. I have stopped his heart. It split like a chamber pot. No, this is no rain falling. This is the wet out of the cracked heart.

Parhelion and sun shine in the same sky with the broken moon. Dizzy with the chasing of moon by sun, and by the twinkling of so many stars, I run upstairs to read again of the love of some man for a woman. I tumble down to see the half-crown hole in the kitchen wall stabbed open, and the prints of a mouse's pads on the floor.

Consider now the old effigies of the seasons. Break up the rhythm of the old figures' moving, the spring trot, summer canter, sad stride of autumn, and winter shuffle. Break, piece by piece, the continuous changing of motion into a spindle-shanked walking.

Consider the sun, for whom I know no image but the old image of a shot eye, and the broken moon.

XX

Gradually the chaos became less, and the things of the surrounding world were no longer wrought out of their own substance into the shapes of his thoughts. Some peace fell about him, and again the music of creation was to be heard trembling out of crystal waters, out of the holy sweep of the sky down to the wet edge of the earth where a sea flowed over. Night came slowly, and the hill rose to the unrisen stars. He turned over the block of paper and upon the last page wrote in a clear hand:

XXI

The woman died.

XXII

There was dignity in such a murder. And the hero in him rose up in all his holiness and strength. It was just that he who had brought her forth from darkness should pack her away again. And it was just that she should die not knowing what hand out of the sky struck upon her and laid her low.

He walked down the hill, his steps slow as in procession, and his lips smiling at the half-dark sea. He climbed on to the shore, and, feeling his heart knock at his side, turned to where the greater rocks climbed perilously to the grass. There at the foot, her face towards him, she lay and smiled. Seawater ran unheeded over her nakedness. He crossed to her, and touched her cold cheek with his nails.

XXIII

Acquainted with the last grief, he stood at the open window of his room. And the night was an island in a sea of mystery and meaning. And the voice out of the night was a voice of acceptance. And the face of the moon was the face of humility.

He knew the last wonder before the grave, and the mystery that bewilders and incorporates the heavens and the earth. He knew that he had failed before the eye of God and the eye of Sirius to hold his miracle. The woman had shown him that it was wonderful to live. And now, when at last he knew how wonderful, and how pleasant the blood in the trees, and how deep the well of the clouds, he must close his eyes and die. He opened his eyes, and looked up at the stars. There were a million stars spelling the same word. And the word of the stars was written clearly upon the sky.

XXIV

Alone in the kitchen, among the broken chairs and china, stood the mouse that had come out of the hole. Its paws rested lightly upon the floor painted all over with the grotesque figures of birds and girls. Stealthily, it crept back into the hole. Stealthily, it worked its way between the walls. There was no sound in the kitchen but the sound of the mouse's nails scraping upon wood.

XXV

In the eaves of the lunatic asylum the birds still whistled, and the madman, pressed close to the bars of the window near their nests, bayed up at the sun.

Upon the bench some distance from the main path, the girl was beckoning to the birds, while on a square of lawn danced three old women, hand in hand, simpering in the wind, to the music of an Italian organ from the world outside.

Spring is come, said the warders.

I. M. Veissenberg   *Mazel-tof* [1]

The small town is in a turmoil, for the rabbi is sinking rapidly. And from the start it has been evident that the doors of heaven are closing to their prayers.

A chorus of heart-rending cries fills the air. In the shop doorways, saleswomen with pale faces stand weeping, as they gaze with quiet intensity towards the end of the street. Chave Gittel, who sells pots and pans, runs by excitedly, her face flushed. She meets another woman, to whom she speaks breathlessly and waves her hands.

Then Hirshl, the schoolmaster, hurries by, his thin stringy neck stretched out, hands in his back pocket, sharp elbows protruding like the wings of a goose about to fly. A small schoolboy, with tiny feet and glowing red cheeks, runs after him.

"To the *bes-hamidrach*! To the *bes-hamidrach*!"

The *bes-hamidrach* is overcrowded. Teachers and pupils from all the schools have come together in a solid mass.

A Jew wearing a red sash stands before the altar with outstretched hands, praying. In a whining voice he recites the *Tfila Lemosha,* line by line, and the crowd repeats it so feelingly and with such grief and fervor that the children stand openmouthed and staring. . . . Over by the wall, a man hides his face in the psalter with a bitter sigh, lifts his eyes to the ceiling, closes them again, and remains so, motionless, his neck outstretched, like Isaac before the sacrifice. They are all praying, constantly repeating the prayers, in which the rabbi's name is used over and over again to form an acrostic. On and on the crowd prays.

In the courtyard before the rabbi's house, people jostle and trample one another. Plain people, cobblers, tailors stand with rapt gaze. Young *chasidim* walk about in circles, tripping over their long sashes and scarcely speaking to one another. Now the teachers and pupils have returned from the *bes-hamidrach*. The teachers stand in a separate group, chatting quietly among themselves, while the children play about or cling to the fence around the rabbi's garden. They crawl up to the icehouse roof, where they stretch out lengthwise and crosswise,

---

[1] Good luck!

their faces turned towards the rabbi's windows. The sexton and members of the household go and come, confusedly, brushing aside young men who happen to be in their way. Asked for news, they only hold out their hands, sigh, and hurry off. Under an open shed, a large crowd of women stand in one corner, grimacing painfully, their aprons held ready to cry.

Suddenly, from the house comes a current of excitement. The crowd starts to move. The doctor tells them to pray the Lord! There is a shout from the window. But the crowd seems numb. Then a number of women rush out, pushing past the men, who make way for them. Screaming, they run into the street, where more women join them. On the way to the market place, they divide into two groups, one hurrying towards the synagogue, the other to the cemetery.

In the market place the men are milling about like lost, silent sheep, when someone brings even worse news. The crowd remains frozen, and trembling lips whisper:

Blessed be Thy Judgment!
Blessed be Thy Judgment!

Now they are left with nothing, without hope, and with but one consolation: to express sorrow for the rabbi's wife and orphans. Gathered together on one side of the square they abandon themselves to God's will and judgment which they know to be love.

The sexton is already running to the postoffice with long telegrams. The windows of the room where the rabbi lies light up with a reddish glow as a thin, cold rain begins to fall from the leaden sky, falling on the bodies of the mourners, which have already begun to shrivel and shrink. Women turn up their coat collars and huddle into their shoulders to keep warm. Teachers huddle into their thick red scarves, and their faces grow darker, bluer, and more sunken. Lips and eyes tremble.

By night the *chasidim* begin to drive in from the surrounding towns, and towards morning there is great commotion in the streets, which are filled with cabs and other vehicles. By dinnertime all the stores close and the entire crowd has gathered in the rabbi's courtyard. From the door comes a cry: Open! Open! As the coffin appears the crowd begins to move towards the *bes-hamidrach,* to pray for the dead. It soon becomes so crowded that there is no more room for a pin. Heads upon heads they stand there, men and women together, and even the space around the tables and the altar, everywhere, is black with people. The lights burning in the chandeliers throw out heat, so that soon the faces grow red and are covered with sweat. The air becomes suffocatingly hot and muggy. The coffin is placed before the altar, and as the *chasidim* take one another by the shoulders, their eyes seem to be starting from their heads. People crane their necks into the air, one

higher than the other, in a confused melee. Then there is quiet, and
all eyes are turned towards the center. Soon a thin small voice is heard,
"Too great penance do you require, O Lord, for our sins! You have
taken our king of the torah and, more than that, you have taken away
the shield and buckler without which we stand exposed . . ."

Once more there is quiet among the women and girls, whose head
kerchiefs half cover their eyes.

Now the coffin is moved, and the crowd begins to push through the
doors and opened windows.

The street is already blocked. A chain of *chasidim* occupies one side,
and the crowd accompanying the coffin stretches like a long belt with
thousands of faces, along the whole length of which prayers are being
said. The son and heir walks at the head of the procession, his forehead
resting on the coffin, his face hidden.

At the cemetery, in a grove of trees, the grave is already prepared and
a final coffin stands waiting in readiness. The rabbi is lowered into the
open grave and all salute him with a *mazel-tof*. Now the crowd turns
towards the son, *"Mazel-tof, rabbi! Mazel-tof!"*

The grave is filled in. The new rabbi says a prayer for the dead.

And a consolation, a new hope begins to bloom. Faces begin to
brighten and in each eye a new light begins to dawn. Everybody gathers
around the rabbi, to witness the light of godliness manifested on his pale
face.

In the cemetery, quiet reigns. The trees sway gently, as though in
prayer.

Translated from the Yiddish, and
adapted, by Sofia Himmel
transition 10

George Whitsett   *Sonances*

I

Falsely forth skam the pepple upon the pool. Foibles upon foibles
spent themselves into muteness. Over the glum morasses came the
nightly echo of her pent-in race as the tangled skeins held up the

bottomless ooze. Only spirits of trees, of vines, of nebulous fire wisps, of throats of night, of myriad-encircling swamp could dement her further than bedfastness with this serf.

Battalions of innocence charged the quagmires, but the floundering and smooth legs of horses bayonetted the softness. Nostrils and starting eyes pressed the wrinkles of briers towards the yielding bottoms. Even devils, reaching towards her, but receded her into the arms of a convention which antedated the rings of water oaks. Demounted riders swept downward towards the parent rock.

Her last night should not kindly preface bearded hugs. Her breasts were white under this coarse stuff. "Do you think that I would tingle for this oppression? But the opiates upon my body! And the alterations of my girdle. I am as I would be when finally the morasses are drained and riders can stoop under the beech trunks, when faces work speaking to us from beyond the river, when from the castle comes one who has eaten with silver."

He would answer, were he not twitching in his dreams: "A tender female dog was lying among the may flowers, lifting her ears. Her skin was pink under its covering. She pushed her muzzle against the smooth stalk of larkspur and a fat serpent rolled over upon her. A fat, bearded serpent rolled over upon her thighs!"

II

She went down into the dance floor against our commands the night the new syncopation was to be tried four times. His right hand being paralyzed, it was necessary that he should hold her improperly, because of the high position of her antipodal girdle.

Through the crowd as the trombone gave its improvised warning ran the man in the darkened spectacles. Him we selected to be unexpectedly bitten by the fly from the ceiling.

As she nestled against the frontispiece, the *frog hopped against her*. *The frog hopped against her* as she walked in the darkness when the cornet called to the tuba to beware. As she kissed him under the pretext of a whisper, as the false jade setting fell to the floor without the music stopping, as the daring young capitalist whirled his partner against the increasing numbers, as the synthetic straws dropped in their glassy holders, as the woman on a street above scraped the coping with her basket, as several sparrows stirred expectantly of dawn in the abattoir, as all conditions were fulfilled—*the frog hopped against her*.

III

The twelfth basement was reserved according to orders and filled with barrels from which the staves had been carefully removed. The canaries were kept singing with great difficulty while the young Russian had time to remove her brassiere of Persian rubber. The jade settings clicked into their places while the hotel detective made his announcement.

The dance had no sooner started than, according to preconceived plan, his toupee arose and remained pendant within easy reach of the concealed madman. Seeing this we dismissed him, taking the blade of rustless Damascus into our own hands. An unguarded gesture severed the great cable which kept both the floor and ceiling suspended.

The tears in her eyes turned to turquoises as she felt that we were drifting towards the tunnel. It was there that the demoniac was confined and we knew then that her long hair should have been tightly braided.

Only a relish for entertainment kept us from faltering as the canaries fell dead among their wires as the first warning. When the first film of smoke arose I knew it was irrevocable, and both of us broke into a lemon-like laughter.

As the slender shears removed the down from her body, I felt the first intuition that the detective was enjoying the spectacle. He had kept the girl confined so long that the millionaire was eager to do his bidding.

As her section of the floor sank several paces, the heavier fumes came with a sluggish rush to her nostrils. As the chemist had predicted, the image of her singing as she rediscovered and clung to one of the floating barrels was a startling drape for her nudity. Her head, now completely bald, was quickly singed as she called several times the name of her lover. This was the expected signal and the army of ants, preceded by pincers and lances, safely declined the larger bones.

From the ruby-colored infinitesimals it was inevitable.

transition **24**

William Carlos Williams   *Theessentialroar*

It is the roar first brilliantly overdone THEN the plug in the pipe that carries them home with a ROAR and a cigarette and a belly full of sweet sugar and the roar of the film or to sit at the busy hour in the polished window of Union Club at the northeast corner of fifty-first street across the street from St. Patrick's (so to speak) neat gray catholic cathedral and feel the roar pleasantly pricking the face but they're all face as the Indian said to Ben Franklin who also knew French women like the New York Journal which knows that unless it roars it does not do the trick and that's the trick that you have to have the money for like Weismuller when he slaps the mater with his hands, quick, the way they talk and THAT's what makes them WIN, it just HAPPENS but when a baby drops a ball of twine and it rollllllls unwinding about their feet neatly semicolon placed in rows while the cigar train is sucked at by the throat of the tube and it rolls without WITHOUT any roar at all along among the feet everybody smiles because it DOES something to everybody it SURPRISES them all because it SHOWS UP the roar and nice colored men smile and a nice fat man picks it up and a very nice lady smiles like the translation of a norse saga that the sea has left when the plug slips through the pipe, the toss and danger of the cold sea is dead in English keeps them kidded so the emptiness of the continent has been filled, that's the crowd at the door jamming and pushing both ways, YOUNG hit a ball with a stick stick to it roar out around the middle its the brush hedge on which the vine leans hell with booze who can't invent noise that carries a rock drill in its breeches WHOOP it up and we'll ride the bronk with the hands tied ka plunk ka plunk opens up the old clam under your ribs till the whisky of it tickles the capillaries around the fissure of Sylvius and the milky way weigh spits out a drop or two of fire to you? I'm just too lazy like when he got the capsicum vaseline on the finger of his glove when he was making the regional examination and the result was SURPRISING.

2. expansion of language

Eugene Jolas   *Manifesto: The Revolution of the Word*

TIRED OF THE SPECTACLE OF SHORT STORIES, NOVELS, POEMS AND PLAYS STILL UNDER THE HEGEMONY OF THE BANAL WORD, MONOTONOUS SYNTAX, STATIC PSYCHOLOGY, DESCRIPTIVE NATURALISM, AND DESIROUS OF CRYSTALLIZING A VIEWPOINT . . .

WE HEREBY DECLARE THAT:

1. THE REVOLUTION IN THE ENGLISH LANGUAGE IS AN ACCOMPLISHED FACT.

2. THE IMAGINATION IN SEARCH OF A FABULOUS WORLD IS AUTONOMOUS AND UNCONFINED.

   (Prudence is a rich, ugly old maid courted by Incapacity . . . Blake)

3. PURE POETRY IS A LYRICAL ABSOLUTE THAT SEEKS AN A PRIORI REALITY WITHIN OURSELVES ALONE.

   (Bring out number, weight and measure in a year of dearth . . . Blake)

4. NARRATIVE IS NOT MERE ANECDOTE, BUT THE PROJECTION OF A METAMORPHOSIS OF REALITY.

   (Enough! Or Too Much! . . . Blake)

5. THE EXPRESSION OF THESE CONCEPTS CAN BE ACHIEVED ONLY THROUGH THE RHYTHMIC "HALLUCINATION OF THE WORD." (Rimbaud)

173

6. THE LITERARY CREATOR HAS THE RIGHT TO DIS-
INTEGRATE THE PRIMAL MATTER OF WORDS IM-
POSED ON HIM BY TEXTBOOKS AND DICTIONARIES.

   (The road of excess leads to the palace of Wisdom . . . Blake)

7. HE HAS THE RIGHT TO USE WORDS OF HIS OWN
FASHIONING AND TO DISREGARD EXISTING GRAM-
MATICAL AND SYNTACTICAL LAWS.

   (The tigers of wrath are wiser than the horses of instruction . . . Blake)

8. THE "LITANY OF WORDS" IS ADMITTED AS AN IN-
DEPENDENT UNIT.

9. WE ARE NOT CONCERNED WITH THE PROPAGATION
OF SOCIOLOGICAL IDEAS, EXCEPT TO EMANCIPATE
THE CREATIVE ELEMENTS FROM THE PRESENT
IDEOLOGY.

10. TIME IS A TYRANNY TO BE ABOLISHED.

11. THE WRITER EXPRESSES. HE DOES NOT COMMUNI-
CATE.

12. THE PLAIN READER BE DAMNED.

   (Damn braces! Bless relaxes! . . . Blake)

Signed KAY BOYLE, WHIT BURNETT,
HART CRANE, CARESSE CROSBY, HARRY CROSBY, MAR-
THA FOLEY, STUART GILBERT, A. L. GILLESPIE, LEIGH
HOFFMAN, EUGENE JOLAS, ELLIOT PAUL, DOUGLAS
RIGBY, THEO RUTRA, ROBERT SAGE, HAROLD J. SALEM-
SON, LAURENCE VAIL.

transition 16-17

Hugo Ball *Clouds*[1]

elomen elomen lefitalominai
wolminuscaio
baumbala bunga
acycam glastala feirofim flinsi
elominuscula pluplubasch
rallalalaio

endramin saxassa flumen flobollala
feilobasch falljada follidi
flumbasch

cerobadadrada
glagluda gligloda glodasch
gluglamen gloglada gleroda glandridi

elomen elomen lefitalominai
wolminuscaio
baumbala bunga
acycam glastala feirofim blisti
elominuscula pluplusch
rallabataio

[1] Wolken.

Eugene Jolas   *Earthgore*

I

Nightfall floops organing the storm. We are so sere in reeve. Fleet flutter three and clush. The hill brills paniknouting war.

II

Immobile jockeys flack in voot. Earth rocks and beebes. Light darkgloos low. It is a flameglast rooking deer and doom.

III

Is end this? Planets shake in groar. Birds beak the golden satellites. Wildglands go chalk in fluvirane.

IV

Globes concussdance in mist. The sparklers flook and flake. A motor gurrs. Flimgored the comets zish in brail.

V

The houses ginrock asps. Rats joggle sackcloth bibber woo. Hornbeasts moan wrack. Flushflish a whiner bursts into the esh.

VI

From deepworld start the plebs. A loo. A groal. In vocables of glish and gla the calls mishmash. O sting thy tod holds rocks abay.

VII

A revoluzzing glout. The storm in stala grims. Halt flows the singer's ring and bant. Space gloogloos catastrafing cassocked breasts of bray.

Kurt Schwitters   *priimiitittiii*

```
priimiitittiii    tisch
tesch
priimiitittiii    tesch
tusch
priimiitittiii    tischa
tescho
priimiitittiii    tescho
tuschi
priimiitittiii
priimiitittiii
priimiitittiii    too
priimiitittiii    taa
priimiitittiii    too
priimiitittiii    taa
priimiitittiii    tootaa
priimiitittiii    tootaa
priimiitittiii    tuutaa
priimiitittiii    tuutaa
priimiitittiii    tuutaatoo
priimiitittiii    tuutaatoo
priimiitittiii    tuutaatoo
priimiitittiii    tuutaatoo
```

Translated from the German
by Eugene Jolas
                    transition 3

Tristan Tzara   *Toto Vaca*

I

ka tangi te kivi
kivi

ka tangi te moho
moho

ka tangi te tike
ka tangi te tike

tike

he poko anahe
to tikoko tikoko

heare i te hara
tikoko

ko te taoura te rangi
kaouaea

me kave kivhea
kaouaea

a-ko te take
take no tou

e haou
to ia

to ia ake te take
take no tou

II

ko ia rimou ha ere
kaouaea

totara ha ere
kaouaea
poukatea ha ere
kaouaea
homa i te tou
kaouaea
khia vhitikia
kaouaea
takou takapou
kaouea
hihi e
haha e
pipi e
tata e
apitia
ha
ko te here
ha
ko te here
ha ko te timata
e-ko te tiko pohue
e-ko te aitanga a mata
e-te aitanga ate hoe-manuko

III

ko aou ko aou
h i t a ou e
make to te hanga
h i t a ou e
tourouki tourouki
paneke paneke
oioi te toki
kaouaea
takitakina
ia
he tikaokao
he taraho
he pararera
ke ke ke ke
he parera
ke ke ke ke

Bob Brown

I accept transition's verdict
That words should be
Bro ken up

I only hope the slippery slimy
GLASS- SNAKE ONES
DON'T
CRAWL AWL TOGETHER AGAIN

MERCURY, I'LL CONTINUE
DUSTING THE

MOUNTAIN TOPS FOR YOU AND
PEGASUS

WITH MY FEATHERED
ACHILLIAN HEELS

Stuart Gilbert   *Dichtung and Diction*

The trouble began with Wordsworth. Won by the glamor of sweet simplicity (as, at times, was Blake; but with what different results!), he willfully obscured the light of inborn genius. So abysmal, indeed, is the bathos into which he too often lapses, that one might think he parodies himself. Some have seen in this cult of the commonplace a compensation for his regrets over the outcome of the French Revolution, which excited him much as the recent[1] upheaval in Russia impressed contemporaries. Great poets have, it seems, no business to take thought for politics, and this is natural, for their concern is with an ideal world of Types and rare emotion—their home is in Astropolis, not Metropolis —whereas even the best of statesmen must soil his hands and compromise with facts; as for the baser and successful type, such men deliberately traffic in the unbeautiful, in petty and parochial malignities—all that the poet holds anathema.

Thus, in his attack on poetic diction, Wordsworth probably allowed political bias to deflect his natural taste. As Dean Church has said, "He was right in protesting against the doctrine that a thing is not poetical because it is not expressed in a conventional mintage; he was wrong in denying that there is a mintage of words fit for poetry and unsuitable for ordinary prose."

If we analyze any of the finest passages in verse or imaginative prose, we shall nearly always find that there is something in the vocabulary, idiom, or word order to distinguish them from vulgar speech. Sometimes, no doubt, rhythm alone may suffice to redeem banality (this is why poetic effects are apter to realize in ordered meters than in free verse), as in Browning's line:

"It all comes to the same thing in the end."

Read in its context this trivial phrase rings like a line of Shakespeare. Meter bids us discover stresses that in common speech would be slurred over; this unexpected emphasis arrests attention, and dead words glow with vivid meaning.

The poet (whose name includes the maker of imaginative prose), as distinct from storyteller or reporter, selects and handles words with an

---

[1] This was written nearly twenty years ago. s.g.

ear to their emotive *timbre* as well as to their thought-content. The
artist is always something of a seer, a Magian, and it is significant that
Magic was reckoned among the arts—the Black Arts. The language of
the old incantations was speech and sound and diction strained to
breaking point, a frenzied quest for names of power which would
evoke the dark personified emotions of the underworld.

> "By Adonai, Eloim Jehova, Adonai Sabaoth, Metraton On Agla
> Adonai Mathon, the pythonic word, the mystery of the sala-
> mander, the assembly of the sylphs, the grotto of the gnomes, the
> demons of the heaven of God, Almousin, Gioor, Jehosua, Evam,
> Zariatnatmik,
> > "Come! Come! Come!"

The supreme appellation of Peter of Apono ends as follows:

> "By Eloym, Achima, Rabur, Bathas over Abrac, flowing down,
> coming from above Abror upon Aberer, Chavajoth! Chavajoth!
> Chavajoth! I command thee by the Key of Solomon and the
> great name Semhamphoras."

Absurd as such a jargon may sound to us today, it was full of panic
and black power for those who, greatly daring, launched its summons
through the medieval night. The effectiveness of such formulas we
cannot judge; that they often produced what nowadays are called sub-
jective reactions cannot be doubted. And the frontier between hallucination and reality has not been, of its nature can never be, defined. Now
the virtue of such incantations lay wholly in the words employed. To
find the *mot juste* was even more incumbent on the sorcerer than on
any literary man today. A slip of the tongue might set the powers of
darkness by the ears. It was not a matter of making his meaning clear;
the magician had little notion what his formula might *really* mean. He
only knew it held a high-potential charge and used it as we use electricity, in ignorance of its ultimate nature. The known involved the
unknown:

> "The word within a word, unable to speak a word,
> Swaddled with darkness."

The distinction between the two functions of language—its evocative
function (operative for magic or esthetic ends) and its service as a
means of communicating information—has been suitably defined in
The Meaning of Meaning (C. K. Ogden & I. A. Richards). In the
former function the element of sound, *qua* sound, may count for much,
though every spoken sound bears an association, and even unknown
words are charged with overtones of meaning, indefinable though these
may often be. (The Joycean handling of word sounds in *Anna Livia
Plurabelle* is a case in point.)

For it is only a partial explanation of word-magic to say that words (not only nouns) are always names and, since *nomen est numen,* you need only call an object aright to make it put its thinghood at your service. Sound by itself can be evocative. Not far from where I write a farm cart is crunching its way along a stony country road. Its rumble (apart from such obvious associations as the recall of the natural world and the good years when Mr. Henry Ford was yet a child and innocent) has an immediate influence on my senses, like the opening phrase of the *Sacre du Printemps* or the purr of far-off thunder. But use may stale the zest of sounds; after a month beside the sea I hardly hear its murmur; only a newborn babe can catch the music of the spheres. Hence the abiding need for new word-forms; the poet who is content with a "conventional mintage" will not travel far.

The power, indeed, of spells and the magic of creative writing are largely due to the use of unfamiliar diction and vocabulary. (Occasionally, of course, as Dr. Coué and certain modernists are aware, the "damnable iteration" of a set phrase of banal words may have curious effects; but the reiteration itself is quite abnormal.) It is not so much that there is "a mintage of words fit for poetry and unsuitable for ordinary prose" as that many of the terms we use in daily life are worn-out counters and, whatever their mintage, inadequate for art; or else they need to be regrouped in striking patterns and rhythms, if they are to wake esthetic feeling.

An obvious analogy is the need for ritual and vestment in religious service; churches which ban such implements inevitably tend towards materialism or an alliance with the secular power for utilitarian ends. What the Reformers took for sincerity was really a concession to the rising tide of rationalism.

Much has been done in recent years in the way of skilled manipulation of syntax and word-order. Thus Mr. Eliot, as Mr. Hugh Sykes has noted in his stimulating essay on "The Ornate Style" (in *Experiment* No. 7), "is getting much of his technical effect by playing off a more uncommon order against the common one." "English," as Mr. Sykes points out, "has been becoming increasingly conventionalized in word-order . . . this rigidity is such an obviously valuable poetic weapon that it could not have lain unused much longer." It is, in fact, some consolation to reflect that not only poetry but all the arts today (painting, perhaps, most of all) can make a springboard of the growing subjection of language, sound, and pictures to anesthetic ends. Even France, the citadel of culture, and Germany, last refuge of a mystic *Urwelt,* are yielding to the popular demand for a standardized art idiom. And obviously, the farther the *niveausenkung* process is carried and the more vocabulary is whittled down to the few thousand words of slipshod daily speech, the wider grows the field for revolutionary experiment.

But this is after all a meager consolation. Creative minds will hardly be contented with the simple retention of tracts laid bare by the receding tide of culture. The mere possession of an adequate vocabulary and the common sense of diction, rare though it be, is little for a poet to rejoice in, and he will look for new fields of verbal magic.

It well may be (as already suggested) that the minority in quest of verbal and syntactical adventure will be drawn towards a certain regularity of rhythmic form (though not necessarily the classic meters), to assonance and rhyme; for such limitations at once invite and justify verbal innovations and experiments in word-order. The diction of Greek and Latin verse owes much to the exigencies of quantity, caesura, and so forth. That is the paradox; the artist is inspired by obstacles and his spirit is at its freest when most restrained.

Sound, word-order, and a recourse to non-colloquial or new-found terms—all may serve as factors of incantation. Not that a poet needs to be eccentric or obscure. Something, too, may be achieved by sheer simplicity (though not of the demotic or Wordsworthian kind), a verbal meiosis, so to speak, and the use of pure Anglo-Saxon forms (German owes much of its resonance and force to its exclusion of Greek and Latin). There is something in these old words,[1] in their sound and shape, which makes them seem more telling, more alive, than a vocabulary drawn from the Mediterranean classics. Darkness, for instance, is a richer word than obscurity, the Northern Lights than that false-sounding term Aurora Borealis, will-o'-the-wisp than ignis fatuus. (In today's *Daily Mail* I read that the Flying Family has been "located"; why not simply "found"?) Moreover, it is child's-play to build neologies from flexible Greek and Latin roots (savants are doing it every day), harder but far more effective to force rugged Teutonic and Old English words to coalesce. Adventurers of the word had better ransack Chaucer, the *Plowman's Vision,* and the Minnesinger than any Greek thesaurus or Latin repertory. For the classical tongues, as they reach us, are sophisticated, finished products. For all the splendor of that golden age of letters, the words themselves had traveled far from magic and the dawn of speech; the language of the gods had passed away, the Arval hymn become an ancient residue. The "barbarians" may have more to teach us in the lore of language than their Roman conquerors.

---

[1] *Cf.* the earliest version (*circa* 890 A.D.) of the Lord's Prayer. "Faedar ure thu the eart in heofenum. Si thin nama gehalgod, to-be-come thin rice. Geweorthe thin willa on eorthan, swa swa on heofenum." The word-order is especially suggestive, with its apt distribution of emphasis.

The genial force and spaciousness of Anglo-Saxon is illustrated in an admirable passage of Miss G. E. Hodgson's *English Mystics,* which calls for full citation here. "Among such qualities or gifts, the peculiar capacity of arriving at the essence of a matter, and so of drawing, not just any picture, but the one and only apt one, and this by means of highly picturesque, suggestive words, will strike any attentive student of Anglo-Saxon poetry at once. Of a race who coined scores and scores of such nouns as *mere-streets* (for the ship's paths over the sea), *slaughter-qualm, hearth-enjoyers, battle-whirl-of-billows, water-fear, wave-strife, battle-adders* (arrows), *gleewood* (harp); of such adjectives as *ash-feathered, slaughter-greedy, snake-colored, blood-marbled;* of such telling phrases as the *dew-feathered eagle, faithful peace-weaver, gannet's-bath* (the sea), *the raven dark and corpse-greedy, the raven swart and sallow-brown, winter-freezing wretchedness*—to choose a few at random—of such a race great feats of illumined penetration, of really enlightened understanding might be expected to develop eventually. No doubt, the main element in this verbal picturesqueness is imagination proper, the faculty of forming mentally an image of some object no longer present to sense. But into such examples as those given above, something enters which is other than mere reproduction; there is a strand in them of genuine creation. Psychologists may be right in classing reproductive imagination with the rest of our 'sense' capacities; but creative imagination includes a factor which belongs to the region of extra-sense."

The artist can weave a spell with anything, for life is one and everything is holy. By the alchemy of pen or brush he can transmute the basest metal to pure gold; and the "One Thing," the "Stone of Wisdom" whereby the writer makes this miracle is the Word. But without the driving force of belief all spells are powerless. If some contemporary experiments prove futile, insentient as the twitchings of a dead frog, the atrophy is in the maker, not his medium. If he be merely interested in technique and in particulars, a writer loses contact with the immanent realities that give life to language. Old words and new alike, if they evoke no inward echo, are dull and mute, like the keyboard of a pithed piano. To many it may seem that the age of visionary faith has passed forever, the "word within a word" is dead. But the wraiths of ecstasy still walk the earth; latent in the most unlikely places, they bide the times of their outgoing, obedient to the word of power. And that by uttered word or written sign the artist can evoke these shades and give them real presence—this is the miracle of words and diction.

Sidney Hunt   *design V*

BRONZE PLATES WITH

EXTRA

DEEP CHISELED

V-CUT

LETTERS

   SOLID

   BEAUTIFUL

   LEGIBLE

   PERMANENT

transition 2

Eugene Jolas   *Faula and Flona*

The lilygushes ring and ting the bilbels in the ivilley. Lilools sart sling-slongdang into the clish of sun. The pool dries must. The morrowlei loors in the meaves. The sardine-wings flir flar and meere. A flishflash-fling hoohoos and haas. Long shill the mellohoolooloos. The rangomane clanks jungling flight. The elegoat mickmecks and crools. A rabotick ringrangs the stam. A plutocrass with throat of steel. Then woor of meadowcalif's rout. The hedgeking gloos. And matemaids click fer dartalays.

transition 16-17

Eugene Jolas   *Storiette*

Abyssblue hosannaed into spring. Platonics stood horizontal song. He lingered in a sassaslab.

It was so alcohol. The train had shrilspilled many days and his speculations riped through the woonland woole. But was it real? Rags swickered glore. His hunger fleeried pale. His zenith shambled in collapse of dances and flew with locomotives to the orifice of the sun.

The world has buised my porphories. Long have I rumored midnightly in the blizzard's atlas. Where were you then, my gate and grace? I was yumlying in the querulous track. Heavy was my sleep o near one so distant one in mathematics. Will you ever know the silences sherroring into the silver silversool? Haallowy your languories dear ferneroots in the cloam o the glow and the glew.

He langed. He drank her eyes. It was very cool the flash of her hairscape. She was not alone. A signal loopswooped to the galley. The minutes lozanged down. He saw her turbilling in flight. Her hands were shoum. Her face burnt road. A mineral glooed in her eyes. She turned so very vegetable.

A graygreen skoon clank runk. An echo wrapped him in his trek. The tale sank stupefiant Roolatingama buised lilylums.

transition 16-17

James Joyce   *Ad-Writer* [1]

Buy a book in brown paper
From Faber and Faber
To hear Annie Liffie trip, tumble and caper.
Sevensinns in her singthings,
Plurabells on her prose,
Sheashell ebb music wayriver she flows.

Humptydump Dublin squeaks through his norse;
Humptydump Dublin hath a horriple vorse.
But for all his kinks english plus his irismanx brogues
Humptydump Dublin's granddada of all rogues.

transition 21

Niall Montgomery   *Swing Tides of March This Time Darling*

verse in brackets the old brackets say when
(i have been left in complete control)
on my left montgomery skelly-eyed and fat
stalking county goatherds in his homburg hat
ok?
e-flat boys—let it break virginia—awright joe take it away

---

[1] Written apropos of the publication of *Haveth Childers Everywhere* and *Anna Livia Plurabelle* in the *Criterion Miscellany. Faber & Faber* (London).

DOWN out of the hysterical mountain slums of the asynchromati rises a nine-fisted infra-fed vacuum of nut-milk windows to crumble incalculably into magnesium-velvet cloque under the seared-clotted axis xx. Hold it, Jane and give me the bandages.

COOL clanging serum of endermic sun-slit nights is Prince-Archbishop Steinklammer-Flanagan whose decent trombone-routine of brekekek-ex-coagulation to the jewess-hawks: "These iced bucket-dredgers cost me and Stevenson plenty supertax in a grand conductivity of helium and local inch-tons" embalms the automatic pelvis of a dilettante spring. Up in Room 17 a minor-screwed, honey-scared console of apse-like chins bubbles glamorously to scale a gallery of soluble lips and eye-creased hands. The agenda initiates a floating entelecheiasm of naked laughing gas-fitters. This, of course, means war.

Cold suns blow through the poplar tree
but why must you do this to me;

HIS storm-dogs pry open thirty bottles of pious cement-greed, slipping across the overt, passion-trussed algae in the market-square merely to dial tribal trunk-calls on the gold-blistered Adriatic-face (to half-inch detail). From intravenous anadyomene to the grand sensual laboratories a salute of twenty-one rolled-steel joys and stainless-polished straw-votes to invoice the noses of the irritable, faceless gods. Just as you say, Mr. Sullavan, sir.

MEANWHILE from Alabama's Montgomery in blue-stockinged federal freight-trains, slaking a scheduled pay-lust, gnawing their way into the diapason-coal country of the pavement-prophets come elder-buried, coniferous-jawed statesmen to help assess the February time-lag with deaf singers.

FOR men he censures even the magenta-glued peon, still threads his architectural gun-cotton, herds pimply clocks and offers insanitary sacrifice of humble bee to the second-last five-breasted deity of an honest, dog-fearing tribe. That was the Admiral, men, filed neatly away in them gold-laced drawers.

THEN—custom-built tin-hat to this shyster bay-tree—comes thunder-smeared Model-T; swift to unhinge Whistler's mother the underworld moves in high-powered hansom cabs when "Cry-baby" Charon is grilled before a fetid grand jewry in a coast-to-coast subway probe. To Washington's dim Martha penetrates the anguish of kitchen-midwives, legacies, water-closets and indictments and the ominous gravel of seven thousand and fifteen three-way corset-belts exhumes the British Thermal Eunuch whom incorporated intersuburban rudiments dazzle with ink-flushed arteries.

I don't hear no golden bands
    tightening on her sad, dumb hands;

IT'S you that they remember still and deep, matte-surfaced, injured darkness drawling inanely from the measured hips of so many unshed rocks: all right, I'll pay. These your white-glazed fingernails trisect the salt horizon. I said the elegance of your credulous appearance washes out the keyboard mattress of my bones once a week, massages the sawn-off buttocks of a caged gynecologist, hisses dexterously in first, changes down, whirls into the museum so many of them have died to defend.

EDUCATED bacteria in Utah cherish the maudlin glass rose: you tell them of the Edification of the McGee, tarred splayed hymeneal crucifixion in the parlor of Hephaistos and goldwyn Aphrodite gambling and saying cute things in the numb scullery.

Lying together lying on straw
    lying on oath with our limbs to the wall;

LAUGH, laugh in the three-rock tower at slier fingers, ga-ga drum controls; admonish formally the unpredicted owl you planted and watered on the parapet-sky, tricked out with glazing trumpets and the neon-tube hiss of constricted urine. Go out there into your dance on the thrice-rattled sacerdotal boards. The Duke says take it easy, Zlugzenheimer, the femme is sleeping.

WE know the west. Why shrink from terror whose logic you disassembled in the old days. We know. Four centuries and sixty-five cents back this culinary lawn-mower was a liturgical steam-plough chanting and playing the ghost in the mortuary-chamber behind your raw sienna eyes, so viscous are they; and so, unheralded, the cacophony of stigmata. Always I leave the key under the door so when the plumber comes you know what to play. Make-a seem big difficult job. And shut the bloody piano after you.

Her oil-skin glitters in the blackened rain
    what's this my mother told me about men;

IN oil the creaking joints down the avenue daffodil salad is now being wisely resented. Did you know about Bach's unforgivable passacaglia for strip-talker, lip-tease artist and pneumatic drill (which is now compulsory in the second row) and the grand rhumba-underwear in Handel's 5,000 cc (Targa-Florio) "Miscegenation"—fundamentally a Metrovicz-Kataleptik.

I was talking with Ruskin, the other dame on his hippomarx holding many benignant hands, a putter, three aces, and some irons in his ardent harps. He played the first movement of the poignant new game for kill-crazy desperadoes—"Colonnes Fondantes" (B-mol)—and lost. Oh! l'orchestre de fuseaux!

IN conclusion may we say these things would have been impossible but for the retrospective speculations, morbid stock, and cravat exchanges of Mr Charles Howard Wanamaker III Jr.

On my right montgomery the shaven yellow rat
his big blonde wife behind him with a thermostat

YOU have listened this evening to "Hypo" Chondria and his Nervous Breakdown Gang bringing to you a program of sweat music from the hanging gardens of the Social-Contact Club through the courtesy of Wanamaker—the new thirty-billion Private Relations Corporation. We are now signing off with our signature-melody "Wanamaker? We can fix that." And don't forget—next Sunday we are bringing you Senator Moses and his Ten Commanders;
> let it ride boys
> ok joe   right through to the end

transition 27

Keidrych Rhys   *Cynghanedd Cymry*

Lips curry-flame
Byces henna foetor

Whizzing wizardings
a langor lingers
a slight slough
an even avon
hoary hairy
with the greengrins of a gubbon goblin
fig
X in an axe
split-peas and platespies
    among the river rovers
        or
    the shame of shimsham
    the shame in SHEMSHONG

By coarse beards of curse-bards
by the pore-hanger for pure hunger
by the heelhorrorhirry of hale hurry
by the fool-foal feel in the faaall
    a picture pasture for posture
    a NILE of nails
    simple samples of live love
    shun the shine
    flickers fleckers
        liftever the leftovers
        the far-tight under the fear-taught
Launch lunch in a glad shoeshy glade
with a pinch of punch
with our jane on june air
with the coif   the carafe   the neon-noon
        from
linden   London

From the author's letter:
  "Cynghanedd" is peculiar to Welsh poetry: consonantal agreement in many intricate
patterns. The classic example in English—
    "Come April spray and capture spring
    C—   pr- spr   c-p—r- spr"

William Saroyan   *Fragment*

In my room I slept, dreaming language, Pater hemon, father in heaven, ho en tois ouranois, worded and named, sanctificetur nomen tuum, hallowed. Il tuo regno venga, republic of Russia. Sea hecha tua volontad come all ye faithful como en el cielo, friend, can you tell me the way to Troy? I am a stranger in town. Ansi también en la tierra, Thy will upon the turning earth. Unser tägliches brod gieb uns heute, bread, for we hunger and are weary. En vergeet on onze schulden, forgive, sicut et nos remittimus debitoribus nostris, zione, on the steps of the Baptist Church, universal smile, mas libranos de mal, from evil torn. Percioche tuo e il regno, Thine alone, e la potenza, e la gloria, in sempiterno, power, glory. Mr. Fleming, in a neat twelve-dollar suit, two pairs of pants, from two stories up, laughing in the dark earth, ha, ha, ha, good afternoon God, mighty pleasant to see your bright and beaming face: allow me to introduce a number of varieties of contemporary microbes, of for and by the flesh, one hundred per cent.

And I said to her, Woman, I have brought you my heart on a cafeteria tray and my money on a copy of *True Confessions*.

transition 27

Laurence Vail   *Gaspar Loot*

Noise—hail of a   Vocal hell stones   Terrible noise
Dum-dum expletives curiously being stuttered
       curiously and seriously
           seriously and studiously
              religiously

Gaspar Loot pulled his acoustics together. Tightened his eardrum taut. Thus, good dog Pedigree clicks his cèpes stifferect to mushrooms when in familiar vicinity voised wrong'uns suspiciously jar the ether.

He histed.

What ho oh What oh What?

Were fishwives at it?

((Each scale throws back an echo. Hers? No, its own. Yes, Sir, when fishwife screams, taint her that screameth, but Neptune raging through salt-rasped throat, while fish pants, fish-eyes you, dies, dies, and dies, then up and stinks, in odorous resurrection. Know you not, Cook, that stink of fish and shrill of wife increase in direct angry ratio? More it stinks more she shrieks more. Because, shevoice and fishsmell are one and same, and sane (sane as salt) the literary expression of the ocean.

Write-ho, professor. Language knows what it says. Fishwife = wife of fish. His instrument and radio.

Yes Ma'am. When fishwife screams, tis not her, indeed no, she's gentle meek spoken woman, a mild and mary lamb, a cutie-whiney. Tis each sardine that squeaketh, tin quiver, pin o'sea. Each log of cod, skate plate, torpedo flash, each gnarled and crab-grab lobster. Each oyster, tuberculosis oceanus. Each mussel black eye.))

Were preachers at it?

((Evangelist chases bête à bon dieu in forest of hirsute chest. Itch runneth on his breast, or heart, or soul that misty saoulerie. He thinks to pinch the teeny. Wheureka. Tis god lui même, Himself MESELF. Let's gnash together brethren at oozy-nice damnation.))

Were politishuns at it, demonrats, unready reds, retropublicans, factists, factionists, facetionists, ra-Yalists, laxitimists, annacristies, gauche writers, pimpdependents? Or makers of domestic scenes, doomestic squallers, hub-wives, wife-lifers, slob-lovers, madadulterous cat and doggers, crossbossing and kissticuffing?

Sounded (this noise terrible indeed) like a bunch of jaws or jews or women. And yet the single sounds were

manly in a way

pompous

emphatic

decidedly literary

Just words, thought Gaspar Loot, and let it go at that. But through it all, above and underneath, there was another sound, like something perpetually being torn

A bed sheet?
No.
Raw silk?
No.
A sail? A sail? Ten twenty sails?
No.
Suddenly Gaspar Loot has it just like that if it isn't yes it is paper.
PAPER
    ((Bwitchly a woman vixen tore the letter of her better, author ripped script of brother author better, twixt index thumb Rogolo tore the Mighty Sunday Times from West to East, slashed Brittanica to shribbons and.))
In short a lot of paper auld and news was being torn across arage, mussed, pelleted and slusherhated.
    What's hell a'bout, thought Loot.
    A newsboy tearing news and suns and times went tearing by:
Paper Sir REVOLUTION mister WORD HINSURRECTION my l'awed WORD DEFIED GRANNY MARY paper to tear signor WORD TEARS APRON STRINGS paper mon prince paper paper p . . p . . aper . . . .

3. intercontinental poets

Xavier Abril   *Angle of Light*

1. — SINGING, I say, my voice and my rose-colored skeleton: my hand seizes the newly-born, I enjoy an exact douche of numbers, of small successive cries which reveal color, temperature, and urine.

I begin to rise in music, to understand in the shadow the matrix and the cry which leads up to man. Afterwards, the most comprehensible logic of the body gives me its light, and I remain in the angle of Music and Number.

2. — I have descended to the line of color, of flesh at 39″. Yes, just that, and the eyelids like heavy rose-colored cork; I have been constantly with a little animal very similar to a nail, a large nail with, in addition, spittle. The glass was also a small animal. There was only a small difference in the neck, in the correct manner of putting on the necktie.

It was an enormous nail, a small man and an animal with nothing but ribs. Impossible! It was still worse, the fall behind the glass, which later could not be seen. The nail always obtains fulfillment of its wishes: with its half-Moon. The nail, a small landscape in the middle of the night, a horrible animal.

Without fever, a perfect man and even without nails.

Translated from the Peruvian
by Auguste Hurdlebring
transition 19-20

James Agee   *Lyric*

Demure morning morning margin glows cold flows foaled:
Fouled is flown   float float   easily earth before   demurely:

Chanced gems   leaves their harbors
Sparkle above leaves   whom light lifted

Drilling in their curly throats   severally sweet ordinate phrases
                Smooth ancestral phrases.

Teaching: touching: sinuous disunison.

Drinking: drafting: each of all   serenest pleasure.

Bring floral earth   your breast before her
Afford your breast before the morning.

Demurely, the early margin:

Fouled is fallen flower flower fearless earth before: serenely:

Rafael Alberti   *From 2 to 3*

2 o'clock at the barn steeple.

The moon is embroidering a cloth
and singing in my hall;

— A little child,
with no cradle, plays.
The Virgin Mary
watches over her;
Three little gray cats
and a blackbird in mourning;
The spinning spider
and the red fish;
A white elephant
and an earth-colored camel;
and all the flora of the air,
and all the fauna of the sky.

Ting,
   ting,
      ting,
         3 o'clock at the dairy.
            tong,
               tong,
                  tong,
                     3 o'clock at the priory.

Translated from the Spanish
by the Marquise d'Elbée and Eugene Jolas
transition 4

Richard Aldington   *Stairway of Pain*

unyielding
there is no way out
mosaic mask threatens and laughs
that blood was wasted
so were his hers mine
I always knew that brought the gravest pang
there is no way out
who said so? he said so
no I said so
up those winding stairs
so long and tedious to mount alone
always the mosaic mask
that nothing says and says too much
there is no way out
except the inevitable final plunge
and that's not soon
and yet too soon
round and up they wind
and up and round
blind feeling with fingertips
up and round
there is no way out
but why have entered?
yes why have entered?
entered? well the mask said enter
so beautiful a mask
I forgot the blood
so beautifully so like a god
said enter I forgot the blood
ran stumbling upwards too eagerly
then the mask changed
and yes there is no way out

Kay Boyle *And Winter* [1]

This night is a bitter cry for you
it is a dark cry for you
held hollow to your ear in the cavern of my heart
Dark and impenetrable as the wings of deep valleys
my blood is a long lament for you
The dry twigs of the winterwillow
rub their lean bones against the glass

Orion fades like the white heel of a runner
and my anguish is as bitter as almond-rind
My hands seek in the underbrush of my sorrow
as children seek the new vines of arbutus
that run in winter like music under the leaves

Here is the sweet wine of my knees to be poured for you
my temples are hollow bowls for the fruit of your mouth
The waves of the sea pace the shore and bemoan you
they cry out and wring their white hands in anguish
      Stir in me cool as the pulse of
           the wind
      lie in my veins and chill and
           chill me
      until the blood runs cold through
           my heart

transition 5

---

[1] Reprinted in *A Glad Day, published by* New Directions, 1938.

Samuel Beckett   *Malacoda*

thrice he came
the undertaker's man
impassible behind his scutal bowler

to measure
is he not paid to measure
this incorruptible in the vestibule
this malebranca knee-deep in the lilies
Malacoda knee-deep in the lilies
Malacoda for all the expert awe
that felts his perineum mutes his signal
sighing up through the heavy air
must it be it must be it must be
find the weeds engage them in the garden
hear she may see she need not

to coffin
with assistant ungulata
find the weeds engage their attention
hear she must see she need not

to cover
to be sure cover cover all over

your targe allow me hold your sulphur
divine dogday glass set fair
stay Scarmilion stay stay
lay this Huysum on the box
mind the imago it is he
hear she must see she must
all aboard all souls
half-mast aye aye

nay

André Breton   *Sunflower*
for Pierre Reverdy

The woman who walked through the *Halles* as summer came in
Was walking lightly on tiptoe
Despair unfurled its tall and beauteous arms to the sky
In her handbag was my dream a smelling-salts
Which none but God's own god-mother had smelled
Stagnation reeked like the vapors
At the *Chien qui Fume*
Where the pro and the con had just entered
They could scarcely see the young woman and then only sidewise
Did I have before me the ambassadress of saltpeter
Or of the white curve on a black ground we call thought
The ball of the innocents was at its height and slowly
The paper lanterns took fire in the chestnut trees
The shadowless lady knelt on the *Pont-au-Change*
In the *Rue Gît-le-Coeur* the sounds were no longer the same
The promises of night were kept at last
The carrier-pigeons the first-aid kisses
Joined the lovely unknown woman's breasts
Darting from under the crepe of perfect meanings
There was a prosperous farm in the heart of Paris
And its windows gave on to the Milky Way
But no one lived there due to unforeseen guests
Guests whom we know to be more faithful than ghosts
Some there are like that woman who seem to be swimming
And in love there enters a little of their essence
She makes them inwardly her own
I am the plaything of no sensorial powers
And yet the cricket that sang in the ash-blond hair
One evening near the statue of Etienne Marcel
Looked at me with a look of understanding
André Breton it said is passing by

Translated from the French
by Eugene Jolas
transition 27

Harry Brown   *Analogies Over a Range*

Renzella, maid in the kitchen, loved
The cook (the one who lacked an eye)
And forgot the wretch in due season.

The Lord's breakfast was crossed with bussing
But he was unaware.
                    Venus
Sweated over the spit, immortally decided
That the affair would end correctly, but
Even the gods feel heat.
                    In the morning,
The stifling morning, she cooked food,
(Two eggs and some bacon) warmed the coffee
That had gone unfinished the midnight before.

Displeased, we wept for having gorged ourselves.

—Pandemonium of shells, rotting under the sea,
And fishermen sorting lobsters for
City consumption.
        Death on the sea and in the morning
Knew us: we agreed and still wept.

—Your mother, your damned mother
Has come down on us, having
Great wrath.
        Pray God her time is short.

Padraic Colum   *James Joyce at the Half Century*

Exile they say who do not know
That in a thousand years
But one is born worthy of
The doom that exile bears.

'Tis not to bring from Sicily
Songs for the Ptolemies,
But to set between one and one's land
The centuries, not seas.

To forge upon the iron found
With labor and with care
The conscience of a race that has
To find its character.

To forge it on the anvil was
Once iron alight,
Black, pitted, dense that tore through space
A weighty meteorite.

And still to hold as presences
Memories of childhood's day,
The lesson read, the voices heard,
The schooling and the play.

This is to know what exile is —
Yet he is not alone
Who hears the few the flare illumined
Tell him his task is known.

Emily Holmes Coleman   *Invocation*

Sun,
come down upon the ground
and spread your feet upon its chill.
Let them drink you to dregs
the cold mountain streams,
and the frozen reeds in the river
let them
bend to your power.
Come into the houses of people
fill them with heat
and with stress.

And flow into the pores of the indifferent,
energize their meekness —
who look for rain
and are not content with cloudburst.
Sun,
do not mistake the indifferent,
who walk with loose hands —
beat upon them, scorch them
and bring to their attention
fire
and tropic darkness
and childbirth under a southern sky.

Malcolm Cowley   *The Hill Above the Mine*

Nobody comes to the graveyard on the hill
there on the blackened slope above the mine
where coke-oven fumes drift heavily by day
and creeping fires at night, nobody stirs
beneath the crumbling wall where headstones loom
among the blackberry vines, nobody walks
in the blue starlight under cedar branches
twisted and black against the moon, nor speaks
except the unquiet company of the dead

and one who calls the roll
             — Ezekiel Cowley?
Dead.
             — Laban and Uriah Evans?
                              Dead.
— Jasper Dearmitt, your three wives, your thirty
children, of whom four bastards?
                              Dead, all dead.
Simon Elliot? Sergeant William George?
Judge Edward and Sara May McPherson?
                              Dead.
sleeping under the briers in the starlight
above the unpainted cabins and the mine.

What have you seen, O dead?
             — We saw our woods
butchered, flames curling in the maple tops
white ashes drifting, a railroad in the valley
bridging the creek, and mines under the hill.
We saw our farms lie fallow and houses grow
all summer in the flowerless meadows. Rats
all winter gnawed the last husks in the barn.
In spring the waters rose, crept through the fields
and stripped them bare of soil, while on the hill
we waited and stood firm.
             —Wait on, O dead!

The water still shall rise, the hills fold in
the tombs open to heaven, and you shall ride
eastward on a rain wind, spurring the thunder
your white bones drifting like herons across the moon.

Hart Crane   *O Carib Isle!*

The tarantula rattling at the lily's foot,
across the feet of the dead, laid in white sand
near the coral beach—the small and ruddy crabs
flickering out of sight, that reverse your name; —

and above, the lyric palsy of eucalypti, seeping
a silver swash of something unvisited . . . Suppose
I count these clean, enamel frames of death,
brutal necklaces of shells around each grave
laid out so carefully. This pity can be told . . .

And in the white sand I can find a name, albeit
in another tongue. Tree-name, flower-name deliberate,
gainsay the unknown death . . . The wind
sweeping the scrub palms, also is almost kind.

But who is Captain of this doubloon isle
without a turnstile? Nought but catchword crabs
vining the hot groins of the underbrush? Who
the Commissioner of mildew throughout the senses?
His Carib mathematics dull the bright new lenses.

Under the poinciana, of a noon or afternoon
let fiery blossoms clot the light, render my ghost,
sieved upward, black and white along the air —
until it meets the blue's comedian host.

Caresse Crosby *from*
                    The Stranger

But forever the primary sigh of the flesh
and the womb that is caught
in the turn of the plough
O fertile device in the circle of
how and of how

O steed made of silver what hope have we now!

Sink back to the hilltop and back
to the plain
We must lie with the cattle as
others have lain.
We must yield to the rain.

Intentional kiss for intentional pain —

Will the Stranger still linger there
back of the Sun!

              *   *

I rise again
My feet are tangled now.
About me now the clinging
lace of hands
The hardly-heard triumphant
weak commands
of tendrils draining deep for sap —

What if the silver bird and gold
Should wait and wait and I grow old?

O wait!
for I have been
and I have guessed

and I have seen
and I must wholly something know.

The golden bird: "Arise, and we will go."

*   *

But our linen is tinged
with the shame of our sex
and the stain of our rose
is a wound to be hid.
I have bartered with youth
for a cycle of fears
O my son
You are young
You are youth without years.

And I molded you, I, in the long of a day.
In the morning with pain
In the evening with shame
And at night with a prayer —

I have fashioned you fair?
Is it true, is it true —
Put your feet to the fields
Give your strength to your play
I am free — I am through.
The golden wings are tremulous
and I
(while arms lean earthward)
yearn,
        and we must fly —

*   *

A drift of dust
and our shadow gone over
Erased from the fields
lost into the sun
O my bird of gold
You are wax to flames
and your wings unmold.
Only flight remains.

How your speed is cold!

*   *

Must it be to the heart of the sun bright through
Shall eyes see — Can I tell it is you?

O stranger so masked by such light
If I knew — if I knew.
Your burning is dont to my flesh and O dont
I am tortured with flame.
Your fire about and above and below me
and through me again

Whereby shall I find you
or shall I go —

And Stranger your name?

*   *

A silver bird and a bird of gold
I harnessed to my chariot of hope
The silver bird wore bells on silver wings
The gold one yoked with filaments and strings of gold,

And I the charioteer with word and song
Urged on the upward pair!
The moon was with us —
But the sun was yonder
Ever beyond and always otherwhere!

transition 18

from

Harry Crosby   *Sleeping Together*

Embrace Me You Said

Embrace me you said but my arms were riveted to the most exacting
of walls, embrace me you said but my mouth was sealed with the huge

hot fruit of red wax, embrace me you said but my eyes were seared by the severities of two thousand winters — embrace me you said in such a low and feline voice that my eyes began to open like frightened shutters, in such a low and feline voice that my mouth became unsealed like red ice in a bowl of fire, in such a low and feline voice that my chains dropped like silver needles to the floor and my arms were free to encircle the white satin nudity of your voice which I tore into thin strips of music to store away in my heart whose desert had been threatened with vast armies of female laborers marching down dusty roads strewn with the prickly leaves of the cactus plant.

White Fire
Your throat in my dream is a sensation of light so bright so sudden that I am dominated by the image of white fire far beyond the moment of ordinary awakening.

It Is Snowing
We are preparing ourselves for the horrors of war by viewing an autopsy. A trained nurse depressingly capable sits by a stove reading aloud from the Madonna of the Sleeping Cars while you insist on telling me that for three years the chorus girls have not come to Touggourt. There is a turmoil of passionate red except for my hands which are two drifts of white snow lying upon the cool shells of your breasts. It is snowing and there are people in galoshes and when we wake up it is snowing and there is the sound of the men shoveling the snow off the sidewalks. It is one of those cold gray days when the wise thing for us to do is to go to sleep again like bears in the wintertime.

transition 19-20

Robert Desnos   *I've Dreamed So Much About You*

I've dreamed so much about you
that you lose your reality

Is there still time to reach that living body and to kiss on
    those lips the cradle of the voice which I hold so dear?

I've dreamed so much about you

that my arms grown used to lie crossed on my breast from clasping
    your shadow might be unable to enfold the contours of your body

And that, before the real appearance of the thing which has guided
    and haunted me for days and years

I might indeed become a shadow.

O tender balances.

I've dreamed so much about you that it is doubtless too late for me
    to wake. I sleep standing up, with my body exposed to all the
    appearances of life and love; and though you are the only one
    who counts for me today, I could more easily touch the brow and
    lips of any stranger

Than your lips and brow.

I've dreamed so much about you
I've walked, talked, and slept so much with your phantom self
    that perhaps nothing remains for me

but to be a phantom among phantoms and a hundredfold more shadowy
    than the shadow that walks and will continue lightly to walk
    on the sundial of your life.

*Authorized translation from the French
by* Eugene Jolas

transition 1

Denis Devlin   *Celibate Recusant* [1]

In the jingling, clear air,
Skim over the Temple domes
Birds, those fishes with hair.

Remember the signa fish were
In the incoherent catacombs,
Wombs that gave but mixed birth.

In a tunic, striped and cool,
I lie on the red earth,
Over me kneels my Fool.

Floats from a far shrine
A Virgin, pure of male girth
The upper air seethes to brine.

She is the first unlike All Them,
Jerusalem! Jerusalem!

She planes down over me,
Endymion and the Moon I see.

"Unclean! Unclean!" my Fool cries,
Hatred of me frees his eyes

I jerk out what comes next
In the ritual of slaves of slime,
My fear all unstrung:

"Touch me not!" to the unsexed,
Abstract, furious Virgin hung
Above me, time after time

---

[1] Included in the book, *Lough Derg and Other Poems* (New York: Reynal and Hitchcock, 1946).

And like a great, dull fish
She floats on: "It's as you wish."

Richard Eberhart   *Request for Offering*

Loose the baleful lion, snap
The frosty bars down from his cage
And unclasp the virgin pap
Of the white world to his rage.

See the innocent breast deny
But the bellowing shake down the air
Shudders of passion out of the sky
To shock, mangle and maim, tear.

Under the actual talons see
Virginal white and the black paw
Poised to slash on mystery
The five hates of a claw.

Amaze your eyes now, hard
Is the marble pap of the world
And the baleful lion regard
With the claws of the paw curled.

Loose the baleful lion, snap
The frosty bars down from his cage
And unclasp the virgin pap
Of the white world to his rage.

Paul Eluard   *Poem*

Your hair of oranges in the emptiness of the world,
In the emptiness of windowpanes heavy with silence
And with shadows in which my naked hands seek all your reflections

The form of your heart is chimerical,
And your love resembles my lost desire.
O amber sighs, o looks, o dreams!

But you were not always with me. My memory
Is still darkened by having seen you come
And go. Time uses words like Love.

> *From "Capitale de la Douleur" (Nouvelle Revue Française).*
> *Translated from the French by* Eugene Jolas
>
> *transition 2*

William Empson   *Experiment*

PART OF MANDEVIL'S TRAVELS
*Chapter 87: "Of the faith and beliefe of Prester John,
but he hath not all the full beliefe as we have"*
DONE INTO VERSE, WITH COMMENT
"I feel half an Englishman already"
King Ammanullah after firing off a torpedo

Mandevil's river of dry jewels grows
Day-cycled, deathly, and iron-fruited trees;
From Paradise it runs to Pantarose

And with great waves into the gravely seas.
> (Olympe, and Paradise Terrestre the same
> (Whence, bent to improve, King Alleluiah came)
> High (Higher, in fact, as Milton boasted) hurled
> Clings to the cold slates of the Roof of the World.)

Spears pierce its desert basin, the long dawn:
Tower, noon, all cliquant, dock-side cranes, sag-fruited:
And, sand-born weight, brief by waste sand upborne,
Leave, gulfed, ere night, the bare plain, deeper rooted.
> (Herr Trinckler, there of late, reports of these—
> A million acres of dead poplar trees.
> Well may new pit-heads to wise A appeal;
> Our desolation is of harsher steel.)

Antred, of malachite, its boulders thunder:
Involve their cataracts, one known week end:
Then, deep, a labyrinth of landslides, under
The gravely sea, and seen no more, descend.
> (It is cracked mud the motor service dints;
> Five clays, diluvian, covered some chipped flints.
> Tour well the slag-heaps, royalty, we own
> The arid sowing, the tumultuous stone.)

Fish of another fashion the dry sea
Ride: can blast through eddies, and sail on:
Can rend the hunter whose nets drag the scree:
Are full good savor: are for Prester John.
> (Paradise, like Bohemia, has no coast;
> Of bombs and bowlers it has power to boast,
> But mail-dark fish, spawned in grit-silted grotto,
> Adam comes here for; and recites my motto.)

transition 19-20

Serge Essenin   *I'm Tired of Living in My Native Land*

I'm tired of living in my native land.
Aching for the buckwheat fields,
I shall leave my little hut,
And wander as a vagabond and thief.

I shall walk on the white curls of the day
To search for a ramshackle house,
And there my beloved comrade
Will sharpen his knife on his boot.

The yellow road across the meadow
Is lighted with sun and spring.
And she whose name I carry
Will drive me from the threshold of her home.

Once more I'll be back in my father's house
And comfort myself with an alien's joy—
And in a green evening beneath the window
I'll hang myself by my coat sleeve.

The gray-tufted willows by the hedge
Will bow their heads more gently still,
And my unwashed body will be buried
To the noise of dogs, bellowing.

Then the moon will swim and swim,
Letting the oars fall into the lake;
And Russia will always live like this,
Dancing and weeping at the gate.

*Translated from the Russian
by* Gusta Zimbalist *and* Eugene Jolas
transition 2

Léon-Paul Fargue   *Aeternae Memoriae Patris*

*One human being is gone and the whole world seems
deserted.*

Since then, there has been always, draped painfully on my brow,
Washed out, stiff with saltpeter and brine, like a spider's web in a
cellar,
A veil of tears, ready always to fall before my eyes.
I no longer dare to move my cheek; the slightest reflex, the slightest
twitch
Ends in tears.

If for a moment I forget my grief,
Suddenly, on an avenue, in the rustle of trees,
In the mass of the streets, the anguish of railway stations,
On the arm of a gently-voiced friend,
Or in a far-off plaint,
At the sound of a whistle's icy blast beneath the sheds,
Or in a kitchen smell some evening,
Recalling a silence at table, long ago . .
Brought on by a trifle,
Or like the rap of God's finger on my ashes,

It rises! And unsheathes! And pierces me through with the mortal
thrust from an invisible battle,
Forceful as the explosion that shatters a tunnel,
Heavy as the undertow that coils in a slack sea!
High as the volcano that hurls its heart to the stars.
So I really let you go, giving you nothing in return
For all of yourself you had planted in my heart!
And I wearied you of me, and you left me,
And this summer night was needed for me to understand . . .
Have pity! I who wanted . . . Did not know . . . Forgive me, on my
knees, forgive me!
May I finally wither, a poor bone-yard crumbling, a miserable tool-bag
which life throws out, with the heave of a shoulder in a corner . . .

Ah! I see you, my loved ones. My Father, I see you. I shall always see
   you stretched out upon your bed.
Just and pure before the Master, as in the days of your youth,
Wise like the bark at anchor in port, with sails furled, and watch-lights
   darkened.
With your smile, mysterious and constrained, forever fixed, proud of
   your secret, relieved of all your labors,
A prey to all the fingers of light, stark and stiff at midday,
Drunk with the martyr's scent of candles,
With the flowers gathered for you on the terrace;
While a poor man's song mourned over the workshop roof from the
   courtyard,
And hasty steps echoed from every side, confused,
And the drums of Death opened and closed the doors.

Authorized translation from the French
by Eugene Jolas

transition 2

Kenneth Fearing   *Evening Song*

Sleep, McKade.
   Fold up the day. It was a bright scarf.
   Put it away.
   Take yourself to pieces like a house of cards.

It is time to be a gray mouse under a tall building.
   Go there. Go there now.
   Look at the huge nails. Run behind the pipes.
   Scamper in the walls.
   Crawl towards the beckoning girl, her breasts are warm.

   But here is a dead man. A murderer?
   Kill him with your pistol. Creep past him to the girl.

Sleep, McKade.
> Throw one arm across the bed. Wind your watch.
> You are a gentleman, and important.
> Yawn. Go to sleep.

The continent turning from the sun is quiet.
> Your ticker waits for tomorrow morning
> And you are alive now.
> It will be a long time before they put McKade under the sod.

> Sometime, but not now.
> Sometime, though. Sometime, for certain.

Take apart your brain,
> Close the mouths in it that have been hungry,
> They are fed for a while.
> Go to sleep, you are a gentleman, McKade, alive and sane.
> A gentleman of position.

Tip your hat to the lady.
> Speak to the mayor.
> You are a personal friend of the mayor's, are you not?
> True. A friend of the mayor's.
> And you met the Queen of Rumania. True.

Then go to sleep.
> Be a dog sleeping in the old sun.
> Be a poodle drowsing in the old sun, by the Appian Way.
> Be a dog lying in the meadow watching soldiers pass on the road.

> Chase after the woman who beckons.
> Run from the policeman with the dagger. It will split your bones.

> Be terrified.
> Curl up and drowse on the pavement of Fifth Avenue in the
> old sun.

> Sleep, McKade.
> Yawn.
> Go to sleep.

transition 2

Dudley Fitts   *Evening Prayer*

Now I lay me down to sleep

Of travail and the heavy laden hours
Soft soft the sliding mist drops down
And curls about the skeletons of things;
Enameled day, furred patina of night,
A spent cat wails
The wraiths of hidden sight: I lay me down
To sleep.

I pray the Lord my soul to keep

From the ghost of me, from the long shadow
Striking chill inward, from
Crazy burr and posture of false me, the
Will to be hurt, the selfloss, the lenses
Cracked by this other hand of mine:
From my Hell and my Fiend also, my soul
To keep.

If I should die before I wake—

But there are surer things: choke it out
Spew it out, I fear no unreal attack,
Breast the wave, Christian: but if all your whirlpools
Go over my head—tell me then, There is time to renew force,
To light my lamp again,
To strip off this Vile beneath the Pleiades, if I should die
Before I wake.

I pray the Lord my soul to take

Quietly to rest
Motionless O soul on the rising sea of silence borne

Beyond the shadow of the jetty, beyond the friendly spark on the point,
  beyond the noisy rocks, the
Fat seals and the bobbing lobster-spindles, far away from the courtesy-
  ing town, the voices jabbing the air this way and that way,
East always, crest into the East, humble no more with the plunging
  waves dashing and flashing against the dawn,
New vivid strong before the wind caroling the morning forever unfold-
  ing as iris from iris reflects the fire of the huge revolving sun: I pray
  the Lord
My soul to take.

transition 19-20

Charles Henri Ford   *Digressive Announcement of Spring*

now does the air harsh
tendons of rain and corridors reverberate with broken lusts

while the fires discreetly waver
mist moves lowly in a monotone of sadness

interlude: plot for a novel or something:

jan dre sitting sun in red brass sighing one nervous however
      oh anything
      but that
jan dre strolling stopping looking to or down at river sometimes too
  mirror others too mud always slowly
jan dre still painfully droop bell away bell then the eyes walking
      stopping to look at river mud now completely or
      rather saying good night or good-by

drop or drop slowly the mucid words from mulberry lips
      his voice very
      orchestra or obutes born

too suddenly shrilly however and
when the milk plaaplaanged into the tin
tin
pail he thought it dis-
gusting like say an amputation or rather
must the evening throw a taunt
must the evening and a thin stream of heavy water
a sewer is an inundation of viscera and murdered men
wideeyed cattle flow down the hot asphalt and a streetcar decapitates
   frustrations panics nauseas

then will be an exodus and a dancer exhilirant in adagio
the glare of headlights makes a nightmare plausible but the spring grass
   is not a recompense
while the eyes are moistened a mockingbird sings of a stab and a drug
   for forgetting

transition 19-20

Virgil Geddes   *To the Monks of Imperishable Song*

Savior of the lambs
And the hollow low
Of the offended sheep
And the wolf below,

Father and son of the toad and snake
And the unforgivable prophets of your theory,
I make a poem and add it to your glory.

For thus you left us
A useless mercy,
Bearded and bellied,
Walking on the sands,

And in a whisper
Hinted that Jesus knew
How to blend with the blues
And indigos of the country.

For I would ask you,
Wildly to bestow
This heaven-haunted
Ghost a settled blow,

Are these our sins the sins?
Or is it where our love so late begins?
As women without names
Whose names have been defiled,
As wisdom without age

Thus did you waltz and waver.

transition 1

André Gide   *Roundelay of the Pomegranate*

Should you seek yet a long while
The impossible happiness of the soul,
—Joys of the flesh and joys of the senses
May another condemn you, if he likes,
Bitter joys of the flesh and the senses—
May he condemn you—I dare not.

—To be sure, I admire you, Didier, fervent philosopher,
If faith in your thought leads you to believe
That nothing is preferable to the joy of the spirit.
But not in all spirits can there be such loves.

To be sure, I love them, too,
Mortal quakings of my soul,
Joys of the heart, joys of the spirit—
But it is of you, pleasures, I sing.

Joys of the flesh, tender as grass,
Charming as the hedge flowers
Mown or withered sooner than the meadow grass,
Or the sad spirae that sheds its leaves when touched.

Sight—the most distressing of our senses . . .
Everything we cannot touch grieves us;
The spirit seizes more easily the thought
Than our hand that which our eyes covet.
—O! may you only desire things you can touch—
Nathaniel, and seek not a more perfect possession.
The sweetest joys of my senses
Have been quenched thirsts.

To be sure, the mist at sun-up on the plains is lovely—
And lovely the sun—
Lovely under our bare feet is the damp earth,
And the sand made wet by the sea;
Lovely was the water of springs when we wanted to bathe;
Lovely it was to kiss the unknown lips touched by mine in the
    shadow . . .
But of fruits—of fruits—Nathaniel, what shall I say?

—O! that you have not known them
Nathaniel, drives me to despair . . .
. . . Their pulp was delicious and juicy,
Savory as bleeding flesh,
Red as blood trickling from a wound.
. . . These, Nathaniel, did not require a special thirst;
They were served in golden baskets;
At first, incomparably flat, their taste was sickening,
Unlike that of any other fruit on earth;
It recalled the taste of overripe Indian pears,
And the pulp seemed lifeless;
It left a bitter aftertaste in the mouth,
Which only the eating of another one would heal;
Its thrill hardly lasted longer
Than the moment of tasting the juice;

And the nicer that moment seemed,
The flatter and more nauseating became the aftertaste
Quickly the basket was emptied . . .
And we left the last one therein
Rather than divide it.

Alas! Nathaniel, who can say of our lips
What made them burn so bitterly?
No water could wash them—
The desire for these fruits tortured our very souls.

For three days, on our walks, we sought them;
Their season was over.
Where shall we find, Nathaniel, in our wanderings,
New fruits to give us other desires?
There are those we shall eat on terraces,
Before the sea and the sunset.
There are those preserved in sugared glaze
With a drop of brandy inside.

There are those to be picked from the trees
Of private gardens with walls around,
Which one eats in the shade during the tropical season.
We will arrange little tables—
The fruits will fall about us,
When we shake the branches,
And the torpid flies will wake.
The fallen fruits will be gathered into bowls,
And even their fragrance will be enough to enchant us . . .

There are those the rind of which stains the lips and which we eat only
   when we are very thirsty.
We found them along sandy roads;
They gleamed through the thorny foliage
Which tore our hands when we tried to pluck them;
And our thirst was hardly quenched.
There are those from which jellies are made,
Merely by letting them cook in the sun.
There are those the flesh of which, in spite of winter, remains sour;
Our teeth are on edge, when we bite into them.
There are those the flesh of which, even in summer, seems always cold.
We eat them, squatted on rush-mats,
In little inns.

There are those the memory of which equals a thirst,
When we can find them no longer.

Nathaniel, shall I speak to you of pomegranates?
They were sold for a few pennies, at that Oriental fair,
Upon reed crates in which they had tumbled about.
We saw some of them roll far into the dust,
And naked children gather them.
—Their juice is bitter-sweet like that of unripe raspberries.

Their blossoms are like wax,
Having the color of the fruit.
Guarded treasure, hivelike sections,

Abundance of savor,
Pentagonal architecture.
The rind bursts, the seeds fall—
Seeds of blood in azure cups;
And others, drops of gold, in dishes of enameled bronze.
Now sing of the fig, Simiane,
Because its loves are hidden.
I sing of the fig, she said,
And its beautiful hidden loves.
Its blooming is deeply enfolded.
Fig! Secret room where nuptials are held:
No perfume carries their tale outside.
Since none of it escapes,
All the fragrance becomes succulence and savor.
Flower without beauty; fruit of delights;
Fruit which is only its ripened blossom.

I have sung the fig, she said.
Now sing all the flowers . . .

The acid wild plum of the hedges,
Which the cold snow sweetens.
The medlar eaten only when rotten;
And the chestnut, the color of dead leaves,
Which we set to burst before the fire.

From "Les Nourritures Terrestres" (*Nouvelle Revue Française*).
Authorized translation from the French by Eugene Jolas
transition 1

Ivan Goll   *Ivan to Claire*

Come back;
I shall invent a fifth season for us alone,
Where the oysters will have wings,
Where the birds will sing Stravinsky,
And the golden Hesperides
Will ripen to fig trees.

I shall change all the calendars,
That lack the dates of your vanished trysts,
And on the maps of Europe
I shall efface the roads of your flights.

Come back:
The world will be born again,
The compass will have a new North:
Your heart.

Claire Goll   *Claire to Ivan*

May weeds grow under your steps;
May the poisonous saffron pursue you,
May hemlock border the roads
Of your slumber!

I am preparing a celestial apéritif for you:
The strychnine of my thoughts,
And my tears—drops of belladonna.

Soon I shall wait no longer for the night
To sob like the owl.

Translated from the French
by Madeleine Reid
transition 10

Robert Graves   *O Jorrocks, I Have Promised*

Sprung of no worthier parentage of sun
In February, and fireside and the snow
Streaked on the north side of each wall and hedge,
And breakfast, late, in bed, and a tall puppy
Restless for sticks to fetch and tussle over,
And Jorrocks bawling from the library shelf,
And the accumulation of newspapers
And the day-after-judgment-day to face—
This poem (only well-bred on one side,
Father a grum, mother a lady's maid)
Asked for a style, a place in literature.
So, since the morning had been wholly spoilt
By sun, by snow, breakfast in bed, the puppy,
By literature, a headache and their headaches;
Throwing away the rest of my bad day
I gave it style, let it be literature
Only too well, and let it talk itself
And me to boredom, let it draw lunch out
From one o'clock to three with nuts and smoking
While it went talking on, with imagery,
Why it was what it was, and had no breeding

But waste things and the ambition to be real;
And flattered me with puppy gratitude
I let it miss the one train back to town
And stay to tea and supper and a bed
And even bed-in-breakfast the next morning.
More thanks.
        The penalty of authorship;
Forced hospitality, an impotence
Expecting an impossible return
Not only from the plainly stupid chance
But from impossible caddishness, no less.
I answered leading questions about Poe
And let it photograph me in the snow
And gave it a signed copy of itself
And "the nursery money-box is on the shelf,
How kind of you to give them each a penny."

      O Jorrocks I have promised
        To serve thee to the end,
     To entertain young Indians,
       The pupils of my friend,
     To entertain Etonians
       And for their sake combine
    The wit of T. S. Eliot,
       The grace of Gertrude Stein.
    Be thou forever near me
       To hasten or control,
    Thou Literary Supplement,
       Thou Guardian of my soul.
    I shall not fear the battle
       While thou art by my side
   Nor wander from the pathway
       If thou shalt be my guide.
          Amen.

Horace Gregory   *Ladies' Exit*

After certain gentlemen have gone,
less dignified, no doubt, but serious,
not entirely broken, a trifle maimed
with no more tremulous
pretense or hope of staying on:
then go, you ladies,
beautiful, beautiful ladies,
there is no longer too much quiet for
round hips, neat breasts and oh
ever so sweetly miraculous smiles.

All of you must go, must go,
taking what is left (a few things)
and then go on many more miles
(a torn chemise, soiled stocking
and a clot of blood in the throat)
A little damaged, perhaps,
but not infirm,
bodies still warm,
and voices that break only
(when ladies must be heard)
on a far, sharp note.

And because hands and feet are small,
they are not pitiful,
they are simply going,
vanishing; go all
you ladies, go

Randall Jarrell *Two Poems*

I

Because of me, because of you,
More things happened than I know:
The star's distention, the detonation
Of the instant and endless collocation
Of the wicked unlikely spinsters—and Mother;

The singular protein, the abstract cell,
Elaborated, industrial,
Grew feet and fat to keep from falling
In inland air or ever feeling
The limiting ice of the glacial sea;

The gangling and abortive fathers
Worked out their odds-on lives before us
And laughed at the actuaries' end—
Despised, evaded, or endured
The novel virus, the unique star;

Grew witty, mutant, and courageous,
And never faltered, because they knew
Their blood meant more than us and now:
The unstable and haggard intimation
Of a wiser speech and a stranger's face.

II

Enormous Love, it's no good asking
The rocketing burst, the point-blank stare
From the eligible and half-stunned owner
Of the sweepstakes virtue, the pitchblende star—

To win by meekness and inclination
The told-about Real and the light-year feeling,
Be accused and forgiven for a dwarf's devotion
By the biggest hole in the punched-out ceiling:

Too much to ask—too much to find
One mortgaged farmer, one asteroid
To graft and cherish the ailing sprig
And laugh at the dispossessing void;

O ancient Love, sun, single out
The aimed-at organ, the jinnee's anger,
The cave of the sleeper: detonate
The consummation of the Stranger.

transition 26

Eugene Jolas   *The Apocalyptic Hour*

The treason of the sorceress bereaves wonder.
There is a traffic of rotting kings.
There is a mildew of servile wits.

Are we not cankering in fear?
News of secret miseries thaws.
The lecherous army obeys the command.
They play at dice in the barbarous barracks,
Where the bell never rings requiem,
Where the grief-stricken have no hope.

All prayers have died in the nettles,
And the bracken awaits the hideous cadavers.

transition 23

Matthew Josephson   *In Back of the Wind*

I complained righteously of my friend
I stole my friend's wife I stole his gold
I fled.
      I laughed much my beloved friends wept
I had no friends but felony and treason
the queenliest cities of the world knew me
knew to mistrust me I knew their shadows
their green tables were my masks their lights
a garland for my brows I wore profanely
whereas their spears and snares glanced off.

I laughed and laughter gave me impunity
I wept seldom but enemies crept around

the trains drift across the edge of the landscape
the ships skirt the blue islands
here I could swagger the sunlight lent insolence
here it pleased me to catch a southern fever
that laid me abed.
      I heard a lady sing
      I wish I had a reticule
      or some cunning amulet
      or a bloodstone ring
Madam! I said and
offering her my hand
but worse
she sought my wisdom my purse
imperturbable I fled
but was right back again
I fled but came right back again
would not a parasol instead?

And there below the turquoise sky
nearby the cobalt sea

the poppies the lemons the fields of garlic
we danced together our blood leaped and mingled

what fiend came whispering? what hazard set me free?
where the faint blue of the lady's flank
a dagger made a song for her
it is indeed a red sky.
                    I grip hard the branches of the world
scan artfully the meaning of each dawn
the faces of men are hateful to me and their hearths
their dogs their cattle and their progeny
the contumacy of animals is sweet
a lawless wind soothes the refractory mind.

I have eluded the gale doubled its sense
my incendiary laughter has gone ululating
at the conflagration of capitals
the dissolution of republics
over the funest pyres of heroes
and the impeachment of philosophies
fretting (no doubt) the honored sleep of townspeople
but loveliest was the civil insurrection
I stalked amongst the most admired disorder
the perfidy and constancy I conjured with.
I have been more logical than you
I have molested the nave the hidden heart

there is a cool broad marble stairway leading
from the thousand eyed multitude plaudits
to the detonating circus band above
to the solitary flight of seditious wings
to the glaciers of silence to the pure death.

Alfred Kreymborg   *from*
                       Manhattan Anthology

WHORE.

Everybody
used her
as earth
before
and now
Death
knocks
at the door.

MISANTHROPE.

This fellow
was always
goddamning things
from the cradle
to the sod.
And doubtless
if he
should wake up again
he'll begin
goddamning God.

transition 8

Else Lasker-Schüler   *Farewell*

But you never came with the evening—
I sat in my mantle of stars.

There was a knocking at my door—
It was my own heart,

That hangs now at every gate post,
At your door, also.

Among the ferns, the fire rose went out
In the brown of the garland.

I painted your sky blackberry-red
With my heart's blood—

But you never came with the evening—
. . . I was wearing golden shoes.

transition 5

Valéry Larbaud   *Ode*

Lend me your great roar, your vast and gentle pace,
Your nocturnal creeping through lighted Europe,
O train de luxe! and the anguishing music

Shaking along your gold leathered corridors,
While behind the heavy brass latches of the lacquered
  doors
Sleep the millionaires.

I wander humming through your corridors
And follow your race to Vienna and Budapest,
Mingling my voice with your hundred thousand voices,
O Accordion-Train!

All the sweetness of living I felt for the first time
In a berth of the Nord-Express between Wirballen and
  Pskow.
We were gliding through meadows where shepherds
Stood dressed in raw, soiled sheepskins
At the foot of trees clustered so that they looked like
  hills . . .

(Eight o'clock of an autumn morning, and the beautiful
  singer
With violet eyes sang in the berth next to mine.)
And you, huge ice blocks through which I saw Siberia
  and the Samnium Mountains, pass.
Rugged, flowerless Castille and the Marmara Sea under
  a warm rain!
Lend me, o Orient-Express, Sued-Brenner Bahn, o lend
  me
Your miraculous low roar and
Your voices vibrant like a cord;
Lend me the light and easy breathing
Of the high, thin locomotives that have such gentle
Movements, of the express locomotives,
Riding effortless before four yellow, gold-lettered cars
In the mountain solitudes of Serbia,
And farther on, through Bulgaria, full of roses . . .

Ah! may those sounds and this movement
Enter my poems and utter
My unutterable life for me, my life
Like a child's that wants to know nothing, save
To hope eternally for elusive things.

Translated from the French
by Eugene Jolas
transition 8

Pierre Loving   *from*
      The Black Horse Rider
      for George Antheil

The black horse crooks his
forelegs, the hills split open,
his nostrils pour flame.
Snort, snort through miles,
O charger, through rock.

He drinks the mesas,
he burns his thin knees over
braziers of grass:
Ride, ride.

Sky is spilt water,
a silver hello is flung
from star to star.
Black horse breaks
fire underfoot and now
his name is a burnt city,
his mouth churned ocean,
foam on his belly a constellation.

At last he tramples
the sand
behemoth
Asleep before the sea.

transition 2

Norman McCaig   *Two Poems*

I

This carded mist tangling my face with ghosts
blows through a horn for bones to echo with
and in the cheated glimmer of hero-feasts
I plant spruce music. From the lovely earth

rise up encounters of a wing with devil
that slur my ragtime into friendly drums
and bakes arenas where the vultures grovel
and the slain rise ankled with their torn dreams

to float the air into a center eye
that sees no handhold but discards the cliff
for branchy orchards in its cloud and sea
where death's harsh apple rots banished for grief.

II

The bright and beady ladle scraping trips
out of a turtledove that laid eggs in lava
and smilingly crouched on volcano tops
and sucked blood cherries
out of the coster pudding dished by spring
rescues the eternal fly that skates on gravy
to gravel our Utopias and my sprung
and toothless trap scaling his homeward lessons
in tears and a dunce's cap shouts Work and pray
for the blight comes to maculate your fashions
and hook your grimy story
from the green bank into that drowning beauty
for which your botanizing wisdoms pry—
o holy terrier baying the moon for Blighty
I who incur your tallest rage now scatter
tin-tacks for burglars in the marriage suite,
and the astonished sweep in the Christmas litter

finds one born blind but armored,
bass in a sea of trebles, misty boulder
to landmark bankers to their rustic cot,
himself his arrow, paralytic raider.

transition 25

Archibald MacLeish   *Tourist Death*
for Sylvia Beach

I promise you these days and an understanding
Of light in the twigs after sunfall

                    Do you ask to descend
At dawn in a new world with wet on the pavements
And a yawning cat and the fresh odor of dew
And red geraniums under the station windows
And doors wide and brooms and the sheets on the railing
And a whistling boy and the sun like shellac on the street

Do you ask to embark at night at the third hour
Sliding away in the dark and the sails of the fishermen
Slack in the light of the lanterns and black seas
And the tide going down and the splash and drip of the hawser

Do you ask something to happen as spring does
In a night in a small time and nothing the same again

Life is neither a prize box nor a terminus
Life is a haft that has fitted the palms of many
Dark as the helved oak
                    with sweat bitter
Browned by numerous hands

Death is the rest of it
Death is the same bones and the trees nearer
Death is a serious thing like the loam smell
Of the plowed earth in the fall

Death is here
Not in another place not among strangers
Death is under the moon here and the rain

I promise you old signs and a recognition
Of sun in the seething grass and the wind's rising

Do you ask more
Do you ask to travel forever

transition 15

Henri Michaux   *Le Grand Combat*
à R. M. Hermant

Il l'emparouille et l'endosque contre terre;
Il le rague et le roupète jusqu'à son drâle;
Il le pratèle et le libucque et lui barufle les ouillais;
Il le tocarde et le marmine,
Le manage rape à ri et ripe à ra.
Enfin il l'écorcobalisse.

L'autre hésite, s'espudrine, se défaisse, se torse et se ruine.
C'en sera bientôt fini de lui;
Il se reprise et s'emmargine . . . mais en vain
Le cerceau tombe qui a tant roulé.
Abrah! Abrah! Abrah!
Le pied a failli!
Le bras a cassé!

Le sang a coulé!
Fouille, fouille, fouille,
Dans la marmite de son ventre est un grand secret
Mégères alentour qui pleurez dans vos mouchoirs;
On s'étonne, on s'étonne, on s'étonne
Et vous regarde
On cherche aussi, nous autres, le Grand Secret.

transition 17

St. John Perse   *King Light's Settlements*

I

Palms . . . !
They bathed you in green-leaf-water; and the water was also green
with sun; and your mother's maidservants, big gleaming girls, moved
their warm legs near you, and you were trembling . . .
(I speak now of a high state among the dresses in the reign of whirling clarities.)

Palms! and the sweetness
of an old age of roots . . . ! The earth
in those days longed to be deafer, and the sky deeper, where overlarge trees, weary of an obscure design, entered into an inextricable
pact . . .
(I had this dream with the idea of a sure stay amid the enthusiastic
canvases.)

And the high
crooked roots celebrated
the wanderings of prodigious roads, the invention of vaults and naves
and then the light, pregnant with the purest exploits, inaugurated the
white kingdom whither I led perhaps a shadowless body . . .
(I am speaking of a high state, long ago, between men and their
daughters, when they chewed a certain leaf.)

At that time men had
graver mouths, women slower arms;
in those days, big taciturn animals, having lived on roots like ourselves, became ennobled;
and eyelids rose longer upon more shadow . . .
(I have had this dream; it has consumed us without trace.)

II

And my mother's maidservants, big gleaming girls . . . And our
fabulous eyelids . . . O
clarities! o boons!
Naming each thing, I said that it was big, naming each animal that
it was beautiful and kind.
O my largest
most voracious flowers, amid the red leaf, devouring all my loveliest
green insects! The clusters of flowers in the garden smelled of the
family graveyard. And a very little sister was dead: I had her sweet-
scented mahogany coffin between the mirrors of three rooms. And no
one was to kill the hummingbird with a pebble . . . But the earth
bowed down in our games as does the maidservant,
she who has a right to a chair, if we stay indoors.

. . . Vegetable fervors, o clarities, o boons! . . .
Then those flies, those strange flies, towards the last terrace of the
garden, that were as if the light were singing!

. . . I remember the salt, I remember the salt that the yellow nurse
had to wipe from the corners of my eyes.
The black sorcerer grew sententious during services:
"The world is like a canoe that, whirling and whirling, knows no
longer, if the wind meant to laugh or to cry . . ."
And at once my eyes tried to paint
a world rocked between sparkling waters, recognized the smooth
mast of the weather-vane shafts, the top masthead under the leaves, the
main-booms and the yardarms and the foreshrouds of bindweed.
where the too tall flowers
ended in parrot cries.

.   .   .   .

IV

And everything was but reigns and confines of gleams.
And the herds went up, the cows smelled of cane syrup . . .
Let my limbs grow
and be heavy, nourished with age! I remember the tears

of a day too beautiful with too much horror, too much horror! . . .
of a white sky, o silence! that flared like a fevered glance . . . I weep, o
how I
weep, in the hollow of sweet old hands . . .
Oh! it is a pure sobbing loath to be relieved, oh! it is nothing else,
and it already lulls my brow like a large morning star.

. . . How lovely, how pale your mother was
when she loomed tall and weary, with bending down, and fastened
your heavy straw or sun hat trimmed with a double leaf of siguines,
    or when, piercing a dream devoted to shadows, the shimmer of
muslin
flooded your slumber!

. . . My nurse was a mestizo and smelled of the castor-oil plant,
always I saw there were pearls of glistening sweat on her forehead,
around her eyes—and her mouth, so warm, had the taste of rose
apples, in the river, before noon.

. . . But of the yellowing grandmother
who knew so well how to cure mosquito stings,
I will say that she is beautiful who has white stockings on, when the
gentle flower of fire comes through the shutter towards your long ivory
    eyelids.

. . . And I did not know all Their voices, and I did not know all
the women, all the men serving in the high frame
    dwelling; but for a long time I shall remember
soundless faces, the color of papaya and boredom, standing still behind
our chairs like dead stars.

V

. . . O! I have good cause for praise!
My brow beneath yellow hands,
    my brow, do you remember the sweats in the night,
the vain midnight of fever and a cistern's taste?
and flowers of blue dawn dancing on the creeks of morning
    and the noon hour more sonorous than a mosquito, and the arrows
shot by the sea of colors . . . ?

O I have good cause! o I have good cause for praise!
In the harbor there were tall music boats. There were promontories
of logwood; fruits of exploding woods . . . What have they done
with the tall music boats that were in the harbor?

Palms . . . ! Then
a sea more credulous, and haunted by invisible departures,
rising in tiers like a sky above orchards,
gorged itself with golden fruits, violet fish and birds.
More affable scents, leading to the most gorgeous hilltops,
scattered this breath of another age,
abroad merely through the artifice of the cinnamon tree in my
father's garden—o shams!
glorious with scales and armors, a turbid world was in delirium.
(. . . O I have good cause for praise! O generous fable, o table of
abundance!)

VI

Palms!
and on the creaking house so many lances of flame!
. . . The voices were a luminous whir to leeward . . . My father's
studious bark brought in large white faces: probably nothing but
tousled Angels; or else robust men dressed in beautiful cloth, with caps
of alder (like my father, who was noble and decorous).

. . . For mornings, on the pale fields of the nude Water, along the
West, I have seen Princes and their Sons-in-Law walking, men of high
rank, all well-dressed and silent, because the sea before noon is a Sunday
in which slumber has assumed the body of a God his legs sagging.

And torches, at noon, were lifted for my flights.
And I believe that Arches, Halls of ebony and tin, were lighted each
evening while dreaming of volcanoes,
at the hour when our hands were joined before the idol with the
gala dress.

Palms! and the sweetness
of an old age of roots . . . ! The puff of the trade winds, the wood
pigeons and the stray cat
bored into the bitter foliage where in the crudity of an evening that
smelled of the Flood,
the pink and green moons hung like mangroves.

*

*   *

. . . And so my Uncles talked in low voices with my mother.
They had tied their horses to the gate. And the House endured
beneath the plumed trees.

1907

From *"To Celebrate a Childhood"* (*Eloges*)
Translated from the French by Eugene Jolas
transition 11

Pierre Reverdy   *Inn*

An eye closes
> Back there hugged fast against the wall
> the thought that does not emerge

> Ideas little by little take leave

> We could die
That which I hold in my arms could depart

> A dream

The dawn hardly born is ending
> A rattling
The opening shutters destroyed it

> If nothing should come

There is a field where we still could run
> Stars without number

> And your shadow at the end of the avenue
> Is fading

We have seen nothing
Of all that passed we have retained nothing
Just so many words that spring
From stories we've never read
> Nothing
The days that swarm at the exit
> The cavalcade has vanished at last

Downstairs among the card-players' tables.

Translated from the French
by Eugene Jolas
transition 7

Alfonso Reyes   *Tropics*

The vicinity of the sea has been abolished:
It is enough to know that our shoulders protect us;
that there is a huge green window
through which we may plunge for a swim.

It is not Cuba, where the sea dissolves the soul.
It is not Cuba—that never saw Gauguin,
            that never saw Picasso—
where Negroes clothed in yellow and green
roam about the dyke, between two lights,
and where the vanquished eyes
dissemble their thoughts no longer.

It is not Cuba—that never heard Stravinski
orchestrate the sounds of marimbas and guiros
at the burial of Papa Montero,
that pompous rascal with his swinging cane.

It is not Cuba—where the colonial yankee
fights the heat by sipping cracked ice
on the terraces of the houses;
            —where police disinfect
the sting of the last mosquitoes
that hum in Spanish still.
It is not Cuba—where the sea is so clear
that one may still see the wreck of the Maine,
and where a rebel leader
dyes white the afternoon air,
fanning in his rocker,
wearily smiling, the fragrance
of cocoanuts and mangoes from the customs house.

No: here the earth triumphs and commands
    —it calms the sharks at its feet;

and between the cliffs, last vestiges of Atlantis,
the sponges of poisonous algae
tint the distance, where the sea hangs in the air
with a green gall-like violet.
    It is enough to know that our shoulders protect us:
the city opens to the coast
only its service doors.

    In the weariness of the wharves
the stevedores are no sailors:
they carry under the brim of their hats
a sun of the fields:
men color of man,
sweat makes you kin to the donkey
—and you balance your torsos
with the weight of civilian pistols.

    Heron Proal, hands joined and eyes lowered
carries the holy word to the people;
and the sashes of the shirt-sleeved officers
hold the overflowing of their bellies
with a sparkling row of bullets.
    The shadow of birds
dances upon the ill-swept squares.
There is a noise of wings on the high towers.

       The best murderer in the country,
old and hungry, tells of his prowess.
A man from Juchitlán, slave enchained
to the burden upon which he rests,
seeks and catches, with his bare foot,
the cigar which the siesta dream
had let fall from his mouth.

       The captains who have seen so much
enjoy, in silence,
the mint drinks in the doorways;
and all the storms of the Canary Islands;
and Cap Vert with its motley lighthouses;
and the China ink of the Yellow Sea;
and the Red Sea glimpsed afar
         —once cleft by the Jewish prophet's rod;
and the Rio Negro where float

the caravels of skulls of those elephants
that helped along the Deluge with their trunks;
and the Sulphur Sea
   —where the horsemen perished, men and goods;
and that of Azogue that gives teeth of gold
to the Malayan pirate crews,
—all this is revived in the smell of sugar alcohol,
and, wearing the thin blue, three-striped caps,
they leave the captured butterflies,
while whirling clouds of smoke float up
from pipes with cherry stems.

         The vicinity of the sea is abolished.
The errant yelp of brass and woodwinds
rides around in a streetcar.
It is enough to know that our shoulders protect us.

         (A huge green window behind us . . .)
the alcohol of the sun paints with sugar
the crumbling walls of the houses.
(. . . through which we plunge for a swim.)

         Honey of sweat akin to the donkey;
and men color of man
contrive new laws,
in the midst of the squares
where bird-shadows roam.

   And I herald the attack on the volcanoes
by those who have their shoulders to the sea:
when the eaters of insects
will drive the locusts away with their feet,
—and within the silence of the capitals,
we will hear the coming of sandaled footfalls,
and the thunder of Mexican flutes.

Vera Cruz, 1925

Translated from the Mexican
by the Marquise d'Elbée
transition 14

Laura Riding   *All Nothing, Nothing*

The standing-stillness,
The from foot-to-foot,
Is no real illness,
Is no real fever,
Is no true shiver;
The slow impatience
Is no bad conscience;
The covered cough bodes nothing
Nor the covered laugh
Nor the eye-to-eye shifting
Of the foot-to-foot lifting,
Nor the hands under-over,
Nor the neck and the waist
Twisting loose and tight,
Left and right,
Nor the mind up and down
The long body column
With a know-not-why passion
And a can't-stop motion:
All nothing, nothing.

More death and discomfort
Were it
To walk away.
To fret and fidget
Is the ordinary.
To writhe and wriggle
Is the simple.
To walk away
Were a disgrace,
Were cowardice,
Were malice,
Would leave a mark and space
And were unbeautiful

And vain, oh, it were vain,
For none may walk away,
Who go, they stay,
And this is plain
By what is simple.

What, is their suspense
Clownish pretense?
What, are their grimaces
Silly-faces
And love of ghastliness?
What, is their anxiety and want
Teasing and taunt?
This scarcely,
This were hypocrisy
And a deep intention
And a hard concentration
And open ears
And communication.

But the twisting does not turn,
The stamping does not steam,
Nor impatience burn
Nor the tossing hearts scream
Nor bones fall apart
By tossing of heart
Nor the heads roll off
With laugh-cough, laugh-cough
Nor the backs crack with horror
Nor the faces make martyr
Nor love loathe
Nor loathing fondle
Nor pain rebel
Nor pride quarrel
Nor anything stir
In this standstill
Which is not simple.
Which is not trivial,
Not peaceful, not beautiful,
Altogether unwoeful,
Without significance
Or further sense
Than going and returning

Within one inch,
Than rising and falling
Within one breath,
Than chattering and shivering
Between one minute and the next
Like a will without will quivering
Between life and life, death and death,
Life and death.

transition 13

Edouard Roditi   *The Prophet Delivered*
to Carlo Suares

I have seen strange terrors in the depths of a mystic night, and my
head has been a wheel in a strange machinery of dreams.

When I return from the oceans of my dreams the sweat of an inspired
past drips from my brow and my hair is matted with the blood of a
desperate night.

I have felt the voices of another world; I have been a harp in the
hands of demons and I have been

The flute through which the breath of demons flows.

I have broken the skies, my fists have hammered new rhythms into
eternity, and I have been

the divine rebel of space. My head has been a drum in the hands of
time, and I have felt music,

the music of lost hopes and of revolt, the music of living death and of
dead life, and the music of the eternal in my brain.

I have felt my brain like a fish in an endless ocean, and I have felt
that ocean in my brain.

I have counted the stars and have found them too few; I have
counted the drops of the ocean and have not found them enough to
satisfy my thirst;

and I have built palaces of smoke and found them too enduring for
my desire of eternal action.

I have been the priest of my own religion, and the God of my own religion;

I have been to myself a rock and a source of birth and a fountain of hate.

I have invented new sins like flowers in the night, deathless sins that find no punishment worthy of their magnitude.

I have been a jewel to myself and a spring of life in the deserts of solitude; I have been an angel and a demon, a bible and a book of vice, eternal and ephemeral, and I have been

the All-in-all to every detail of my thoughts.

And there have been no boundaries to my power, no tears to follow my deeds, no echoes to the rumbling of my blasphemies.

The memory of my prodigious hands is like green waters that flow on the surface of the elements, and the shadow of my deeds is like the smoke of a burning city.

My hands have embraced the ocean and the stars; the ocean with all its ships, and the stars with all the centuries of space.

And I have been the Leviathan that has swallowed eternity.

I have found no present, no past, and no future; I have abolished the walls of time, and my senses were a deliberate contradiction of my mind.

I have counted my words and they were innumerable; I ceased to count and they ceased to be;

And now I count them again, but they are not enough.

I have found a cross of words to exorcise each ghost; and I have found an ocean of sleep whose waves were boundless in their power of oblivion;

And my head has bathed itself in the waters of eternity.

My flowing hair has been the current of the oceans, and my breath has led the clouds across the skies.

I cannot count the forms of my spirit and I cannot foretell all its delights.

I have been the conjurer of the elements and from the endless warfare of my soul I have saved

these words that are my soul.

My words are a rhetoric of discontent.

Priest of revolt settled upon the brink of the oceans, speech of the unknown gods,

I,

lost emblem of my own soul, city of rotting words, I, ruin of a rotting tongue,

I, endless flow of words, I, flower of the night, breast of the earth, I, nothing of nothing,

I, dust of the Almighty, immortal juggler of words and of revolt,

I break my hands against a glorious rock,

my burning hands of glory that have held

the eternal concubinage of the skies.

I have been in caverns of sleep and have drunk the wine of space,

and now I have come to record my dreams and the hallucinations of my soul.

I have seen gulfs and peaks, stars and the yawning void,

and my limbs have been cramped by the power of my dreams.

Now I have come and do not know

why I have come.

I have come in the storm and I am the storm and the breath of the storm that breaks itself against itself.

I have come and my heart has found no heart and has found no words I have come and the words are lost I have come.

And the breath of my heart is a dream of my coming and the words of my coming are lost and have lost their sound in my head.

I have come and I crush the bones of the dawn I have come and I am the lord of the dawn and the lord of space and the lord of my heart and the lord of my words.

I have come and have lost the tracks and the time of my coming I have come and have lost the source of my coming and the sound of my coming.

I have come from the vague soft shadows of the oceans or the depths of the sun I have come in a torrent of words and I break the iron bars of death.

I have come and have found the statues of death and the source of death and the source of words and in my flesh I feel the claws of life and on my neck the breath of life and on my hands the blood of the sun. I have come and have drunk the blood of the sun the wine of space the waters of death and the honey of love and the poison of love.

I have come in the flow of an endless love I have come in the breath of the beasts of the wind and I am the wind.

I have come and my breath is a scream of the past and my love is a leaf in the wind and I am the wind

and my brain is a drum which my own hands beat

I have come and have found the threshold of life and the pillars of life and the wings of life I have come in a tempest of life I have come.

René Schickele *The Boy in the Garden*

Since evening nears,
I shall clasp my bare hands
And let them sink down gravely,
as if they were lovers.
May bells ring in the dusk,
and white veils of fragrance drift over us,
as close together we listen to the flowers!
Tulips gleam through the last glow of day,
syringa blossoms gush from the bushes,
a bright rose melts on the sod . . .
We are all kind to one another.
Outside through the blue night
we hear the muted hours strike.

*Authorized translation from the German
by* Eugene Jolas

transition 2

James Johnson Sweeney *Mole*

Not silver, nor yellow, nor ivory, nor white
are the teeth of the small mole
that gnaws his way busily into
(slapping the flat of his tail relentlessly
against
      the blunt of my heart).

Nor is the red of the morning
nor the blue of the noon
nor the green of the twilight in his eyes.

But we cannot see
                    for the glare,
I only know the feel
as of a hummingbird's bill.

        —it was for this we clambered up
        those chilly cords last spring
        in the wet season
        to bloom—

and the slap of his tail relentless
against the blunt of my heart.

John L. Sweeney   *Poems*

I

Time stirs. The flesh made word on all sides.
Vision or velleity; a life or minute world fixed in a phial.
The spread hand a shut house derides,
No one, nothing within; the garden wild, no shadow on the dial.

Beyond, the sun flakes off its beams in medals
To those whom largesse makes a target, some waking,
Some dreaming, and the bright world brightly settles
For a beam's life on brides whose easy taking
Whispers sterility. Surrender with no blade to pass,
Only an empty sheathe but acclamation cloaks its emptiness,
Illusion makes a lane, simpering sinks to talk and less,
The beam extinct no cinder clings, no memories distress.

And here within, mute, the blank denial
Of silence and envy's eating ivy creeps
Into the wall's veins, across the starving dial
Cracking the crooked hour on its face. And time sleeps.

II

When the warm blade cools
and the pool of black beginning
shows a smooth brow, the now
final absolution will seem
a simple thing.
Purpose, resentful,
will hide among the hills,
contrive eclipse, escape;
and gesture of definition
requite apologetic silence
where accusation fell.

transition 25

Allen Tate   *Causerie* [1]

. . . party on the stage of the Earl Carroll Theatre on Feb. 23. At this party Joyce Hawley, a chorus-girl, bathed in the nude in a bathtub filled with alleged wine.—New York Times.

What are the springs of sleep? What is the motion
Of dust in the lane that has an end in falling?
Heroes, heroes, you auguries of passion,
Where are the heroes with sloops and telescopes
Who got out of bed at four to vex the dawn?
Men for their last quietus scanned the earth,
Alert on the utmost foothill of the mountains;
They were the men who climbed the topmost screen
Of the world, if sleep but lay beyond it,
Sworn to the portage of our confirmed sensations,

Seeking our image in the farthest hills.
Now bearing a useless testimony of strife
Gathered in a rumor of light, we know our end
A packet of worm-seed, a garden of spent tissues.

I've done no rape, arson, incest, no murder,
Yet cannot sleep. The petty crimes of silence
(Wary pander to whom the truth's chief whore)
I have omitted; no fool can say my tongue
Reversed its fetish and made a cult of conscience.
This innermost disturbance is a babble,
It is a sign moved to my face as well
Where every tide of heart surges to speech
Until in that loquacity of visage
One speaks a countenance fitter for death than hell.
Always your features lean to one direction
And by that charted distance know your doom.
For death is "morality touched with emotion,"
The syllable and full measure of affirmation;
Give life the innocent crutch of quiet fools.

Where is your house, in which room stands your bed?
What window discovers these insupportable dreams?
In a lean house spawned on baked limestone
Blood history is the murmur of grasshoppers
Eastward of the dawn. Have you a daughter,
Daughters are the seed of occupations,
Of asperities, such as wills, deeds, mortgages,
Duels, estates, statesmen, pioneers, embezzlers,
"Eminent Virginians," reminiscences, bastards,
The bar-sinister hushed, effaced by the porcelain tub.
A daughter is the fruit of occupations;
Let her not read history lest knowledge
Of her fathers instruct her to be a petty bawd.
Vittoria was herself, the contemporary strumpet
A plain bitch.

                    For miracles are faint
And resurrection is our weakest clause of religion,
I have known men in my youth who foundered on
This point of doctrine: John Ransom, boasting hardy
Entelechies yet botched in the head, lacking grace;
Warren thirsty in Kentucky, his hair in the rain, asleep;

None so unbaptized as Edmund Wilson the unwearied,
That sly parody of the devil. They lacked doctrine;
They waited. I, who watched out the first crisis
With them, wait:
                For the incredible image. Now
I am told that Purusha sits no more in our eyes.

Year after year the blood of Christ will sleep
In the holy tree, the branches sagged without bloom
Till the plant overflowing the stale vegetation
In May the creek swells with the anemone,
The Lord God wastes his substance towards the ocean.
In Christ we have lived, on the flood of Christ borne up,
Who now is a precipitate flood of silence,
We a drenched wreck off an imponderable shore:
A jagged cloud is our memory of shore
Whereon we figure hills below ultimate ranges.
You cannot plot the tendency of man,
Whither it leads is not mysterious
In the various grave; but whence the impulse
To lust for the apple of apples on Christ's tree,
To desire in the eye, to penetrate your sleep,
Perhaps to catch in unexpected leaves
The light incentive of your absolute suspicion?
Over the mountains, the last barrier, you'd spill
These relics of your sires in a pool of sleep,
The sun being drained.

              We have learned to require
In the infirm concessions of memory
The privilege never to hear too much.
What is this conversation, now secular,
A speech not mine yet speaking for me in
The heaving jelly of my tribal air?
It rises in the throat, it climbs the tongue,
It perches there for secret tutelage
And gets it, of inscrutable instruction—
Which is a puzzle like crepuscular light
That has no visible source but fills the trees
With equal foliage, as if the upper leaf
No less than the under were only imminent shade.
Manhood like a lawyer with his formulas
Sesamés his youth for innocent acquittal.

The essential wreckage of your age is different,
The accident the same; the Annabella
Of proper incest, no longer incestuous:
In an age of abstract experience, fornication
Is self-expression, adjunct to Christian euphoria,
And whores become delinquents; delinquents, patients;
Patients, wards of society. Whores, by that rule,
Are precious.

        Was it for this that Lucius
Became the ass of Thessaly? For this did Kyd
Unlock the lion of passion on the stage?
To litter a race of politic pimps? To glut
The Capitol with the progeny of thieves—
Where now the antique courtesy of your myths
Goes in to sleep under a still shadow?

transition 3

Parker Tyler   *Elegy for a Dead Idol of the Screen*
                 for Carlyle Blackwell

    idol—
    stamped
    regimental beauty

    of following to him
    king once-always loved
    though dead to millions

    alive idol
    can rape death

like his surrendering women
beyond screens

of him said is
a number of children
his by life's kindness only
begetter of dream-children
by constant visibleness
of begettingness

can never
bother concerning
who may step within
his real chamber

cause to unbutton
the secret of screens
for sticks of quarters

were laid towards paradise
for him an endless walk
towards acres of ecstasy

he whose wishheart
may have flowered
for a trivial
smell
will choke

here by trees of breasts
and fruit like wombs
so faces lifted

towards his
sham sex
saw and remembered
dying minds

have opened
like popguns
like bombs

blown
up box offices

Dylan Thomas   *Poem*

Then was my neophyte,
Child in white blood bent on its knees
Under the bell of rocks,
Ducked in the twelve, disciple seas
The winder of the water-clocks
Calls a green day and night.
My sea hermaphrodite,
Snail of man in His ship of fires
That burn the bitten decks,
Knew all His horrible desires
The climber of the water sex
Calls the green rock of light.

Who in these labyrinths,
This tidethread and the lane of scales,
Twine in a moon-blown shell,
Escapes to the flat cities' sails
Furled on the fishes' house and hell,
Nor falls to His green myths?
Stretch the salt photographs,
The landscape grief, love in His oils
Mirror from man to whale
That the green child see like a grail
Through veil and fin and fire and coil
Time on the canvas paths.

He films my vanity.
Shot in the wind, by tilted arcs,
Over the water come
Children from homes and children's parks
Who speak on a finger and thumb,
And the masked, headless boy.
His reels and mystery
The winder of the clockwise scene

Wound like a ball of lakes
Then threw on that tide-hoisted screen
Love's image till my heartbone breaks
By a dramatic sea.

Who kills my history?
The year-hedged row is lame with flint,
Blunt scythe and water blade.
"Who could snap off the shapeless print
From your tomorrow-treading shade
With oracle for eye?"
Time kills me terribly.
"Time shall not murder you," He said,
"Nor the green nought be hurt;
Who could hack out your unsucked heart,
O green and unborn and undead?"
I saw time murder me.

transition 25

Giuseppe Ungaretti   *Transfiguration*

I lie,
My back against the bronze
Of a haystack.

A sharp spasm
Bursts and swarms
From the fat furrows.

Now I feel I am sprung
From people of the loam.

I feel myself living in their eyes
Watchful of the phases
Of this sky;

The eyes of the wrinkled man—
Like unto the rind
Of the shoots he is cutting.

I feel myself
Living in their children's faces,
Like a wine-red fruit,

That burns
In the plundered trees.

I feel myself diffused
In a kiss
That consumes me,
That calms me.

Translated from the Italian
by Emile Gouthière
transition 7

William Carlos Williams   *The Dead Baby*

sweep the house
      under the feet of the curious
      holiday seekers—
sweep under the table and the bed
      the baby is dead—
the mother's eyes where she sits
      by the window, unconsoled—
have purple bags under them
      the father—
tall, well spoken, pitiful
      is the abler of these two—

sweep the house clean
      here is one who has gone up
      (though problematically)—

to heaven blindly
        by force of the facts—
a clean sweep
        is one way of expressing it—

Hurry up! any minute
        they will be bringing it
        from the hospital—
a white model of our lives
        a curiosity—
surrounded by fresh flowers

transition 2

William Carlos Williams   *Winter*

Now the snow
lies on the ground
and more snow
is descending upon it

Patches of red dirt
hold together
the old
snow patches

This is winter
rosettes of
leathery green leaves
by the old fence

and bare trees
marking
the sky
over them

This is winter
winter winter
green
spearshaped leaves

leathery
in the falling snow

transition 9

Josef Wittlin   *Fear of Death*

I do not want to die, O Lord—

I have seen how fearfully dead men stare
I have seen how icy are the graves
I have heard how dreadfully the mothers wail,
Carrying to a grave their beloved child

I do not want to die, O Lord! . . .

What of their talk about the worthlessness of life
What if they give me an eternity in dying—
I know: Heroic death—a consolation
For those who fell in the service of the outcast.
They are noble.
I do not want to die!

I have seen how glassily stared the eyes
That once were blue as your sky, O Lord,
And sent their gleam upon their fellow men—
And today frighten their own children
With the icy, decrepit look
Of a corpse

I, the corpse—my own mother will have nothing to do with me
I, the corpse—my own wife denies me
The wife who has known me through the years
In a stiff dead body she lets me be carried out of the house
Out of the house where she loved me for years,

And fumigates it so that it will not smell of me
And fumigates it, as if it were something repulsive
And not—something she loved!

I do not want to die, Lord!

Translated from the Polish
by J. Jaryczower
transition 5

Louis Zukofsky   *Poem*

Cocktails
and signs of
"ads"

flashing
light's waterfalls,

Bacchae
among electric lights

will swarm the crowds
streamers of the lighted

skyscrapers

nor tripping
over underbrush

but upon pavement

and not with thyrsus
shall they prick

the body of their loves
but waist to waist

laugh out in gyre—
announced then upon stairs,

not upon hills,
will be their flight

when passed turnstiles,
having dropped

coins
they've sprinted up

where on the air (elevated)
waves flash—and out—

leap
signaling—lights below

transition 15

4. spirit and language of night

I. *Romantic Texts*

II. *Anglo-American Documents of Night*

Hölderlin *Poems of Madness*[1]

Homeland

And nobody knows . . . .
Yet let me roam
and pick wild berries,
to extinguish my love for you
on your paths, oh earth.

Here where
     rose thorns
and sweet linden trees smell beside
the beeches, at noon, when in the fallow grainfield
growth rustles on the upright blade
and sideward the ear bends its neck,
like autumn. But now beneath high
vaults of oak trees, as I muse
and question upward: bells,
well-known to me,
come golden-chiming from far away;
at the hour when

---

[1] Friedrich Hölderlin was born in Lauffen-am-Neckar in 1770 and died in 1843. He wrote *Hyperion Empedocles* and numerous other poems during his first thirty years. This was the period of his friendship with Hegel, Goethe, and Schiller. The two latter turned from him, however, when he no longer wrote in their style. In 1803 he returned to Germany from Bordeaux, where he had been engaged as a private tutor. It was then that he began to show signs of mental derangement. But although from a strictly psychiatric standpoint he may have been demented, his poetic spring nevertheless continued to flow. He signed these later poems "Scardanelli." They show a definite regression towards a childhood vision. Edited by Rudolf von Delius, they were published in Germany recently for the first time. The present translations—the first to be made in English—adhere as closely as possible to the distorted syntax and the rhythmic structure of the original.   E.J.

275

the bird awakes once more—
and thus it passes on.

To Heinse

And you speak to me, far off,
from the eternally serene soul:
"What do you call happiness?

"What unhappiness?"
Full well I understand the question,
my father, but still it roars,
the wave which immersed me,
in my ears, and it dreams
of the ocean bottom's precious pearl.
But you, knowing the sea
and firm land, you look at the earth,
and look at light.

Unlike seem the two, you think,
yet both divine, for always,
sent by the ether,
a genius lies on his brow.

As Birds . . . .

As birds slowly pass:
he looks ahead,
the prince, and coolly processionals
drift to his breast, when it
grows silent about him, high
in the air, yet richly gleaming down below
the countries' chattels lie,
and with him are
the young men,
victory-probing
for the first time.
But he tempers
with the flutter of wings.

Greece

      Roads of the wanderer!
For   shadows of trees
and hills, sunny, where
the road leads

to church,
            rain, like arrow rain
and trees stand, slumbering, and yet
there come shades of the sun,
for just as over the towns
warmer burns steam,
so over the rain-
draped walls goes the sun.
For like ivy the rain
hangs branchless down.
But more beautifully
bloom the roads for travelers
            in the open   changing like corn,
wooded Avignon across the Gotthart,
the horse gropes its way. Laurels
rustle around Virgil and may
the sun unmanly never
seek the grave. Moss roses
grow
on the Alps. Flowers begin
before the gates of the town,
on smooth roads.

Like crystals in the desert
growing unfavored by the sea.
Gardens bloom around Windsor. Up there
from London rolls
the carriage of the King.
Lovely gardens sense the season.
On the channel. But deep below lies
the world sea,
smooth and flaming.

To Know Little

To know little, but much of joy
is given mortal man.

Oh lovely sun,
why does it not suffice for me,
thou bloom of my blooming,
to call thy name on may day?
For do I know higher things?
Oh, may I rather be like children are!

May I, like nightingales, sing
a carefree song of my rapture!

The Eagle
My father wandered on the Gotthart,
there where down the rivers . . . .
To Etruria perhaps, on side roads . . . .
and on the straight road
above the snows
towards Olympus and Haemos
where Athens casts its shadow,
towards caverns in Lemnos . . . .
In the beginning
from the deep-scented forests
of the Indus
came my forefathers.
But the first sire
flew over the sea
sharply meditating, and the king's
golden head was astounded
at the secret of the waters,
when red steamed the clouds
above the ship, and the animals,
dumbly eyeing each other,
thought of food. But
the mountains stand still.
Where shall we abide?

Yet When from Self-Inflicted Wounds . . . .
Yet when from self-inflicted wounds
my heart bleeds,
and deeply lost is peace
and freely modest sufficiency;
and I am driven by unrest and dearth
to the abundance of the gods' table . . . .

And I say at once, I had come
to behold the celestial beings;
still they cast me down among the living,
a false priest, so that from out of nights,
I sing the warning, distressed
song of the inexperienced.

The Next Best

Opened the windows of the sky
and released the night ghost,
the heaven-storming one.
He has gabbled at our land
with many tongues,
unbeautiful tongues, and
trundled the waste
until this hour.

But what I want, will come.

New World

New world. And there hangs an iron vault, the sky
above us, a curse unnerves the limbs of men,
and the joy-bringing gifts of the earth are like chaff,
and all is appearance.

Oh when? When?
Already the flood
Opens above the draught.

But where is he?
May he conjure the living spirit.

To the Madonna

Yet will I, oh celestial woman,
magnify you, and none shall
rebuke the beauty of my speech,
my homeland's speech,
while I alone
go to the field, where wild
the lily grows and fearless,
to the inaccessible
age-old vault,
to the ambush
of celestial beings.

Fate

Fate,
It means:
whip and bridle of the sun.

On Fallow Leaf

on fallow leaf rests
the grape, hope of the wine, so rests on the cheek
the shadow of the golden drop that hangs
on the maiden's ear.

And single shall I stay.
Though easily caught
in the chain it has broken
is the little calf.

But the sower loves
to see a woman
who all day drowses over
her knitting

Not gently will sound
the german mouth,
but tenderly
on the prickly beard rustle
the kisses.

Vineyard and Bees

For when the sap of the grape,
the mild growth, seeks shadow,
and the grape swells under the cool
vault of the leaves:
a strength to men,
lovely scent to young girls . . . .

And bees,
drunken with the scent
of spring, are touched
by the spirit of the sun,
driven along,
pursue him; but when
a ray burns, they turn back
with humming,
many things sensing . . . .

Klopstock

Klopstock died on the century.
Now call forth mourning for the old.

Terrible this seems to me,
For him, divinely-repenting,
the parents' sun has killed
with his companions.

From the Abyss

For from the abyss we started
and we went,
like unto the lion
who lies
in the blaze
of the desert.

*Translated from the German
by* Eugene Jolas
transition 21

Jean Paul [1]   *Walt's Dream*

. . . Way back in the distance there arose worlds, like little balls of vapor, beneath a far-off, veiled solar body. In the middle there was a spinning wheel which turned round and round, to which the stars were attached in a row by a thousand silver threads, and which spun themselves down from the sky ever nearer and smaller. A swarm of bees were hanging from a lily. A rose played with a bee, and they teased each other with their barbs and their honey. A somber nightflower rose greedily towards heaven. A spider raced about in the calix of a flower weaving industriously in order to hold the night with threads, in fact, it was weaving a pall for the world. But all the threads were dewy and shimmery, and the eternal snow of light lay on the heights. . . .

Suddenly there appeared on the sky a brightly flashing little star. Its name was Aurora. The ocean, as in a trance, opened up for a moment. Instead of the dusky plain, I saw before me a broad streak

---

[1] Nom de plume of Friedrich Richter, 1763-1825. Fragment from *Flegeljahre*.

of lightning. Then it closed again, the dusky land awoke, and everything was changed. For the flowers, the stars, the sounds, had only been
slumbering children. The tall sculpture of the thundergod stood in the
midst of the land. One after another the children flew into the arms of
stone and put a butterfly upon the living eagle which circles around
God. Then the children, apparently lighter than air, flitted onto the
next cloud, and looked down upon the others who lifted amorous arms.
Surely God, before whom we are all like children, accepts our love.
Afterwards the children played at love among themselves. "Be my red
tulip," said one, and the other became a red tulip and allowed itself to
be pinned to the first one's breast. "Be my star," and it was a star, and
was pinned to the other's breast. "Be my God," and "You're my God";
but at that moment neither of them became changed, for they looked
at each other a long time, with a great love, and then vanished, as if
they were dying. . . . "Stay with me, my child, when you go from
me," said the one who remained behind. The one who had left began
to change into a little dusky red ball, as it disappeared, then into an
evening star, then, as it went deeper into the land, there remained only
a moon shimmer, and this when there was no moon. Finally it became
lost, farther and farther away, in a sound of flutes. But opposite the
dusk the dawn was now rising; ever more wonderfully, dawn and dusk
roared towards each other like two choirs, in a wave of sound instead
of color, as if unknown, blessed beings were singing their songs of joy
behind the earth. The black flower with the spider bent down convulsively until it almost broke asunder. The stars wove into a lily
wreath and spun down from heaven. The all-pervading sound had
ripened the flowers to trees. The children had grown to adults and at
last they stood there as gods and goddesses looking very gravely towards
morning and evening.

The dawn choirs now struck up a song clashing together like thunder,
and each note lighted another still more powerful one. Two suns were
supposed to rise with the sound of morning. As they were about to
reach one another, the air became quieter and gentler. Amor flew up
from the East, Psyche from the West, and as they met high in the
middle of the sky, and the two suns arose, they were only two delicate
tunes, dying side by side, and awaking in each other's arms. Perhaps
they sang "You and I"; two holy, yet terrifying tunes, snatched from
deepest eternity, as if God had spoken the first word for himself and
replied similarly to himself. Mortals could not hear it without dying.
I slept, but while I was drunk with sleep, it seemed as if I were envel-
oped, poisoned even, by the flower scent from a paradise flying nearby.
Then suddenly I found myself on the beach again; an evil old woman
was standing in the water. She shivered as though she were icy cold,

and anxiously pointed to the smooth sea behind her, saying, "Eternity is past, the storm is nigh, for the sun has stirred." While I looked on, immensity fermented into innumerable hills and sky-high storm; far away behind the edges of the horizon a gentle morning light came rolling towards me. . . .

Translated and adapted from the German
by Eugene Jolas

transition 23

Novalis   *Hymns to the Night*

I

What spirited being, endowed with senses, does not love, above all the other miraculous phenomena of space that surround him, the all-cheering light, with its colors, its rays and billows, its mild omnipresence, as when day is breaking? Like life's innermost soul, the titanic world of the restless stars breathes it and swims dancing in its blue tide—the sparkling, eternally tranquil stone, the meditative, sucking plant and the wild, burning, multiform animal breathe it—but more than all others does the magnificent stranger breathe it, he with the expressive eyes, the buoyant step and the delicately-closed lips, rich in sound. Like one of earthly nature's kings, it summons each force to numberless transformations, binds and loosens infinite alliances, wraps its celestial image about every earthly being. Its presence alone reveals the miraculous splendor of the world's empires.

But I turn down towards the sacred, inexpressible, mysterious night. Far off lies the world, sunk into a deep pit; its site is a lonely waste. Deep melancholy is wafted on the strings of the heart. I want to sink down into dewdrops and mingle with the ashes. Far-aching memory, desires of youth, dreams of childhood, the brief joys and vain hopes of an entire long life come gray-clad, like evening mist after sundown. Light has pitched its bright tents in other spheres. And if it should never return to its children who await it with the faith of innocence?

What is it that suddenly, portentously, wells up beneath the heart and swallows up the soft air of melancholy? O dark night, do you also take pleasure in us? What is it you hold beneath your cloak, that so invisibly and powerfully stirs my soul? From your hand there trickles precious balm, from out the poppy-cluster. You lift up the heavy wings of the soul. We feel darkly, unutterably moved—with frightened joy I behold a grave face bending gently, devotedly, towards me, and under infinitely tangled locks it reflects a mother's cherished youth. How poor and childish the light now seems, and how happy and blessed the day's farewell— So it is because night lures the servitors from you that you sowed the gleaming bullets in the wide expanses of space, in order to proclaim your omnipotence—your return—during the time when you were far away? More heavenly to us than those flashing stars seem the infinite eyes which night has opened in us. They see farther than the palest of those countless armies—without need of light they penetrate the depths of a loving heart, they see what fills a higher sphere with unutterable ecstasy. Praise to the world-queen, to the high proclaimer of sacred worlds, to her who watches over blessed love— she sends you to me, o gentle beloved, o lovely sun of the night. Now I awaken, for I am Yours and Mine—you have turned my night into life, you have made of me a human being. Devour my body with the spirits' flame, that I may mingle lightly and more closely with you, that the bridal night may last forever.

II

Must morning always come again? Does the power of the earthbound never cease? Baleful pursuits devour the heavenly soaring of night. Will love's secret sacrifice never burn perpetually? To light has been apportioned its time; but timeless and spaceless is the empire of night. —Eternal is the duration of sleep. Holy sleep, do not come too rarely to gladden those who are dedicated to night in this workaday world! Only fools misjudge you and know no sleep save the shade which compassionately you cast over us in the twilight of the veritable night. They do not feel you in the golden flood of the grape—in the magic oil of the almond tree, and in the brown juice of the poppy. They do not know that it is you who hover about the bosom of the gentle girl, who make a heaven of her arms—they do not sense that you are come out of ancient tales to open heaven and bring the key to the dwellings of the blessed, o silent messenger of infinite mysteries!

III

There was a time when I shed bitter tears, when my hope dissolved in pain and vanished, when I stood lonely on the arid mound which held entombed in its dark confines the very substance of my life—lonely, as none was ever lonely, driven by unutterable fear—powerless, reduced to a thought of wretchedness.—As I looked around for help, unable either to advance or to retreat, cleaving with infinite longing to fleeting, extinguished life:—from out the far-off blue—from the heights of my former beatitude, there came a twilight shudder—and suddenly the birth-cord, the chain of light, snapped asunder. Terrestrial splendor fled, and with it fled my mourning—melancholy melted into a new, unfathomable world:—o ardor of night, o slumber of heaven, you it was came over me—the landscape rose softly; and above it soared my delivered, newborn spirit. The mound became a dust-cloud—and through the cloud I saw the radiant features of my beloved. Eternity dwelt in her eyes—I seized her hands, and her tears became a sparkling, indestructible tie. Thousands of years sank down into the faraway like rolling thunder. On her shoulder I wept enraptured tears to the new life. It was the first, the one dream—and only since then do I feel an eternal, unchangeable faith in the heaven of night and in its light, the beloved.

Translated from the German
by Eugene Jolas
transition 18

Paul Bowles   *Entity*

The intimacy of spirals has become stone to him. This is in reality only the last prayer urge. As it is, all the crimson of stamps has resolved into loops. These fold up and seek sounds beyond lime rinds.

Let it not be understood that the frenzied fingers were here wishing us to leave. It was only that he went away and shells returned. An urn of disgust cannot stop up the pores, for they are after his creases of intelligence. Or, let us say, if one end were rubbed blue and all edges left green, we should have a pleasing effect. But all this is uncertain. One does not feel the imperative qualities soon because behind lapels there are buttons of unrest.

Eradicate, if you can, the adaptability of my nature to joy. It is our heritage, this abandoned cerise—perhaps the only one we have left.

The steel of now cannot be rounded like letters of the system into laughing hordes of misunderstanding. We cannot permit these unflinching bones to perform such elegies. There may be abysms in our fingers. There may be falsehoods about ponds. Last week occurred a strange step. Paradise stalked, and seizing a trombone from the wall, stumbled. In this way all such margins weaken.

Can you not all discover how ennui will creep thus? There is no object in such flight. Masses have power.

At any rate, I shall not have panted entirely beyond borders of limpness. Our sycamores need repose. Is it possible that ever we shall be able to trace our responsibilities to such commands? We cannot ignore successfully the call of feathers. We must heed somewhat bristles. As it is, we are not entirely beyond aluminum fences. This is the reason for his dialogue. The origin of power is everywhere.

If any such enmity is discovered let us discard our yawning.

The susceptibility of emotionalism to unguarded caves may be readily realized by all of us. His smiles fall slowly into jars of porcelain. Even if his pain persists, all these losing forces discover their positions.

A rubber is black. The eternal verities are not. In this effigy we may discern a long boulevard. Leaves of such tendencies shall impale him, and he will be certain to remain poised over lavender pebbles.

The immutability of spheres is constant. All about us are carcasses of planets. Whirling continues a short while. Close her eyes and fold her hands above. We are ready for the treatise on hexagonal tiles.

When all shall have been immersed in brass, it will be easily recognized. Only then shall the grain of the pelt be held by fundamental hands. The only tense is the future and futility is taken for granted.

transition 13

Kathleen Cannell *The History of a Dream*

I dream every night and I can remember my dreams, if they seem to me sufficiently interesting. The elements that escape me in the morning come back to me the next night when I am sinking into sleep, just crossing that voluptuously terrifying area that divides wholly conscious control from the unconscious. Then, at will, the dream appears to me, complete in all its details, and I can remember it even awake, forever after.

I discovered this technique of dream memory when I was three years old—that is when I first began to have very definite conscious impressions of everything. Since then, I have developed it, so that I can, when I'm not afraid to, apply it not only to dreams, but to all recollections, and thus re-seize those forgotten things that so irritate with their flittering hovering just back of the eyes.

R.V. and I for a time amused ourselves by analyzing some of my more unusual dreams. We were not interested in discovering complexes; Oedipus and Antigone were alike indifferent to us. But nowadays no one is innocent of Freud, and, undoubtedly, our method was inspired and, to some extent, directed by what we knew of Freud's theories.

We considered the dream as a centrifugal maze of poetic images. It was thrilling to enter the obvious middle door and to voyage, without the aid of a time machine, through the past and the future, following first one clue and then another, and making a map of the seemingly inextricable labyrinth.

It takes two, at least, to play the dream-game. You cannot, unaided, track yourself to your own lair; and your partner must be cunning and sympathetic if he is to penetrate the ruses behind which, however sincere you may think you are, your personality naturally shelters itself.

I found this game more exciting than any mystery drama. You play at the same time Sherlock Holmes and Arsène Lupin, the tiger and the gazelle. You unmask characters and events to find behind them others quite different, and behind them yet others, and so on through thousands of visible and invisible layers right back to the womb, if not beyond.

R.V. and I intended to write the history of a certain number of dreams, but we were obliged to stop, for we found such myriad twisting trails that conscientiously to follow even one would fill a volume.

We sketched out the main lines of a few, however, and I am sending one in what might be called scenario form, as a documentary reply to *Transition's* dream questionnaire.

The obvious envelope of my dream, invariably, is directly formed by the events or conversations of the day, more particularly those just preceding bedtime. Here I give first the dream itself. Next, the immediate apparent causes, and so on down through layer upon layer of memory.

The Dream—9 November 1927

Alone on the edge of a wide city street paved with enormous cobble-stones, slanting on a hill. Though it is a dark night, a bluish haze renders everything visible. Huge wagons filled with animals, penned in by high wooden bars, pass down towards the slaughterhouse. The terraced floor of the first wagon descends in three wide platforms from the back to the front. On the lowest platform, thirteen animals stand still—cows and calves. The second is crowded with cattle in wild confusion, struggling in violent but ineffectual efforts to move. Some have fallen. Horns and legs are crushed through the bars. Eyes roll redly. One bull walks clumsily, heavily, over the backs and heads of the others.

On the last and highest platform a big bull sitting regally on his haunches, with stiff forelegs, in the attitude of an Egyptian cat, stares disdainfully straight ahead.

I, filled with sick pity for the animals, catching sight of this majestic beast cry: "That's like Sitting Bull!"

A deserted narrow street perfectly dark. High buildings inclined together so that the end far away forms an arch of bluish light. Through this aperture I can see the slaughter wagons passing.

The fifth and last wagon, barred and terraced in three platforms like the first, is filled with wrestling brown bears.

I am surprised that wild animals should be taken to the slaughter-house. I approach. The bears are young men and girls in sports costume —beige and brown striped sweaters and brown plus fours. They are very gay, dancing together, singing, and playing on guitars and ukuleles.

Still night. I am standing with two men, R.V. and A.A., before the door of a perfectly round building with smooth plastered walls. Walking through the empty corridors of a theater, I notice that the color of these walls, also finished in smooth plaster, is pale green. I recognize this theater as Le Théâtre des Champs-Elysées, though there is no point of resemblance between the two.

R.V. leaves us to ask for complimentary tickets. No sooner has he disappeared round the curve of the corridor, than I propose to A.A. to go out.

Walking along a grassy country road. Grass soft underfoot and greenish brown. A greenish light of late afternoon filters through green and brown leaves. No sun but a distinctly sunny feeling. Indian Summer?

To our right, directly opposite the theater, another perfectly round building—the slaughterhouse. Through barred windows in compartments resembling stables we glimpse heads, horns, rumps. I terribly fear to see or hear killing. A.A. reassures me: "Oh, no, they keep those animals for the milk." (*"Ces animaux sont pour le lait."*)

We walk on pleasantly. Coming towards us, a strange monster: a sort of bull, with dark-brown skin like a mule's but rather woolly, criss-crossed with scars, a head vaguely resembling that of a horse, short curly ram's horns tapering into dangerous sharp points, and a very tall, long body deformed into three planes—the rump highest, the back lower, the head and shoulders lowest—like the first and fifth slaughter wagons. He looks very tired, miserable, and seems scarred and deformed from having carried too-heavy burdens.

We watch him to see what he will do. He passes slowly, but once past turns and looks at us. A.A. and I draw together apprehensively and take each other by the arm.

"He hasn't got horns like that for nothing," I say, while the monster continues to stare at us wickedly out of a mean horse's eye.

He turns and saunters nonchalantly off towards the theater.

A.A. and I take a narrower road bordered by maple trees, branching abruptly to the left. More autumnal light. Directly in front of us the sun setting through a haze. We devise amicably in French. Twice I catch myself using the *tutoiement* and each time beg his pardon.

"Mais pourquoi ne me tutoieriez-vous pas? R. est mon ami et vous aussi. Il n'y a pas de raison . . ."

A.A. throws his arm around my shoulder. I feel happily friendly. We are going to meet R.V.

At this moment I was awakened by a loud knocking on the door. I felt furious at being interrupted, depressed at not being able to recover the thread of my dream.

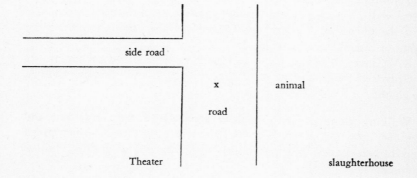

Events of the 9th November
having a direct influence upon the dream

In the afternoon, D., my most intimate friend, came to tea with me in my apartment. She has been psychoanalyzed in the past by two of Freud's students and is interested in psychoanalysis. Our conversation turned on dreams and their interpretation and I offered to lend her, when I had finished it, Freud's *Souvenir d'Enfance de Léonard da Vinci*. We were particularly amused by the fantastic tricks Leonardo loved [1].

(This is the latest element in the fabrication of the dream monster.) We also talked of A.A. and of his romantic idiosyncrasies, which reminded us of another friend of ours whom we had not seen for years, the American poet J.G.F. He used to come to see my husband and myself in the early days of our marriage and he delighted me with his tales of wild animals, whose cries he imitated so realistically that the concierge forbade him the house if he would not *"cesser de faire la ménagerie."*

Later R.V. joined us. He had come from a café where he had separately met M.J. and A.A. Each of them had told him of a chance meeting of the other and given a totally different version of a long conversation they had had about the theater—particularly *Le Démon Blanc* of Webster.

We all laughed a bit at the idea of this meeting, for we were certain that neither had listened to a word the other had said.

D. left for dinner and R.V. and I dined *en tête à tête*.

In the evening, A.A. and R.A. came to hold an informal meeting of an *avant-garde* theater of which they, with R.V., were the directors.

---

[1] Note from *Souvenir d'Enfance de Léonard da Vinci*:

"Il alla à Rome avec le Duc Julien . . . là, il confectionna une pâte de cire et, tandis qu'il se promenait, il en formait des animaux très délicats, creux et remplis d'air; soufflait-il dedans, ils volaient; l'air en sortait-il, ils retombaient à terre. Le vigneron du Belvédère ayant trouvé un lézard très curieux, Léonard lui fit des ailes avec la peau prise à d'autres lézards et il les remplit de vif argent de sorte qu'elles s'agitaient et frémissaient dès que se mouvait le lézard; il lui fit aussi de la même manière des yeux, une barbe et des cornes; il l'apprivoisa, la mit dans une boîte et effarouchait avec ce lézard tous ses amis."

"Il faisait nettoyer et dégraisser si minutieusement les entrailles d'un mouton qu'elles eussent pu tenir dans le creux de la main. Il fit mettre dans une pièce voisine une paire de soufflets de forge auxquels il abouchait les boyaux et les emplissait d'air jusqu'à ce qu'ils occupassent toute la chambre, laquelle était très grande, et qu'on fût obligé de se réfugier dans un coin. Alors il faisait remarquer combien les boyaux étaient devenus transparents et pleins de vent. Et, en ceci, que d'abord, limités à un lieu restreint, ils s'épandaient de plus en plus dans l'espace, ils les comparait au génie."

L. d. V. la vita di Vasari, ed.
p. 41 Poggi, 1919.

R.V. was to read them the first act of his play: *Victor, ou les Enfants au Pouvoir,* which they intended to put on a little later.

R.V. and I were very keen about this play and we had not the least doubt that the two confreres would be equally enthusiastic.

R.V. read sitting at the big flat-topped desk. A green shaded study lamp cast a luminous greenish circle over the manuscript. R.A. reclined on the divan. I remember noticing that he had a distinctly Assyrian air. A.A. sat up straight in an armchair with his feet turned out like a Chinese mandarin, smoking a pipe. From time to time he drank coffee, raising the cup to his mouth with both hands. He had let his hair grow long around a tonsure for the part of a monk he was turning in a medieval film.

R.V. read more and more nervously. We listened in silence. Occasionally A.A. grimaced. It was impossible to tell whether he was laughing or sneering.

When the reading ceased, no one spoke for a minute; A.A. and R.A. exchanged glances. Then R.A. gathered his muscles together and spoke. He said the play was a great disappointment to him, although it contained some interesting elements. He said he felt he would not be playing the part of a friend if he did not speak his mind. He went on to demolish it bit by bit.

R.V. stood up behind the desk with his back against the wall. A.A. sat impassively smoking. Challenged, he agreed with R.A. The act was boring. It lacked poetry and violence. It would never go on the stage. R.V. was finished. He would never do another *Mystères de l'Amour.*

With many assurances of their good faith, they left us, bitterly amazed.

Interpretation of the Dream
with correlating events in the past

I had always considered A.A. to be one of R.V.'s closest and most comprehending friends. Obviously, I was deeply and painfully impressed by his attitude regarding the play, which struck me as a betrayal of friendship, and the surface of the dream was an effort to adjust this disturbance.

The city street down which the wagons passed to the slaughterhouse and its metamorphosis, in the second part of the dream, into the country road where A.A. and I met the monster comes from A.A.'s film *La Coquille et le Clergyman,* whose first presentation had taken place at the Théâtre Fémina a short time before.

—The clergyman walks on all fours around the corners of streets paved in large cobblestones, inclined by the objective of the camera.

The clergyman walks through high rooms. His coattails grow into an *immense chemin de nuit,* which changes into a country road bordered in trees.

Animals being taken to the slaughterhouse appear in almost all my dreams of a painful character. I have always had a pathological shrinking from cruelty to animals and a special fear of hearing the suffering cries of dumb animals, caused, I think, by the fact that my first playmate (named Laddie Fox) was the only articulate being in a household of deaf-and-dumb parents and servants, who used to call us and cajole us in their guttural *enchained* voices.

During the war, in New York, every day, wagons full of calves passed my apartment on their way to the slaughterhouse. One afternoon, a wagon crowded with animals stopped in front of the house. A calf had his front legs crushed through the bars and I thought they would be broken. I tried to push them in for him and I saw all their eyes, accusing. I was physically unable to swallow a piece of meat for two years after.

The three planes of the wagons are a hierarchic sign—three being the most universal mystic number, as well as the number specially assigned to me by the Pythagoreans. They also represent the three antagonists present at the reading of the play—R.V., A.A., and R.A.

The exact significance of the thirteen animals on the lowest platform we were not able to trace, though they may have been myself, in my role of spectator, as they were standing still. The cows and calves struggling on the second platform are R.V.; R.A. is the bull clumsily walking over them.

A.A. is the "Sitting Bull" of the highest platform. Once on the right track it is easy to penetrate his disguise—his tonsure, suggesting the scalp lock of the Indian and the idea of bringing home R.V.'s scalp; his impassive, disdainful attitude seated in the armchair, smoking a pipe, which was the opposite to the pipe of peace; his habit of carrying the coffee cup to his lips in both hands, recalling the movements of the raccoon (called in French *raton laveur*) in washing his food and putting it in his mouth with both paws.

I have Indian blood. Sitting Bull, the Indian chief who swore to eat Custer's heart and did it, was my childhood hero. One of the first films I ever saw was *Custer's Last Stand.* My first nickname and Custer's were the same.

Custer's coonskin cap is suggested by A.A.'s round fringe of hair and by R.V.'s furry hair. R.V. facing his antagonists with his back against the wall is Custer in the film with his back against the tree, surrounded by redskins. A.A. eats his heart in condemning his play.

Sitting Bull had been recently revived in my memory by a headline in the New York *Herald:* Descendant of Sitting Bull runs for Congress.

The bears in the fifth and last wagon are a transformation of the cattle in the first, evidently created by the idea of bear baiting, R.V. having appeared to me gratuitously harried and heckled by his two tormentors. This links up indirectly with my horror of bullfights and stormy arguments I have had with their admirers.

Bears also have roots in my earliest infancy. My favorite brother was less than a year younger than myself. There was such a strong affinity and resemblance between us that we were almost like twins. Similar obsessions haunted both our sleeping and our waking dreams. Mine I will speak of later in connection with the making of the monster. Our parents wanted to make us courageous and independent, so we children all slept alone in separate rooms from the time we were three years old. He seldom, and I never, dared mention the horrors of the night. But when he could bear them no longer he would creep into my parents' room—or occasionally into mine—and stand silently by the bed until his large eyes fixed on them in the dark awakened them, when he would say: "Bears! *Japie* sees Bears!" and then would go back to his own room and to bed without another word.

As, in the dream, I gradually become reassured, the animals undergo a second transformation, the bears changing into young people dancing, which image is a direct evocation of the hayrides popular in Canada in my childhood, when we drove through the country in haycarts something like the wagons of the dream, and the boys and girls sang and played mouth organs, banjos, and guitars.

At this point I seem to be almost satisfied as the dream ends. Not quite enough, though, since in the second dream I pursue the same theme and restore to the characters, disguised in the first dream, their human individualities.

In the second part of the dream, the pale-green smooth walls and circular form of the theater come from the texture of the green glass lamp shade and the tinted disk of light cast on the manuscript of the play during the reading.

R.V. had told me that if his own group did not take the play, he would offer it to the Théâtre des Champs Elysées, and the fact that I thus identified the theater and that he went to ask for complimentary tickets indicate that in my mind this solution of the disappointment had been adopted.

The road is, as I have already said, an "interiorisation" of the *immense chemin de nuit* of A.A.'s film.

The slaughterhouse opposite and of the same shape as the theater shows clearly the identity between the two parts of the dream.

The slaughterhouse stables represent the opposition of the two symbols—Blood and Milk, the peaceful one in the end triumphant.

The last personage we could interpret was the monster. There was, on both our parts, a subconscious reluctance to acknowledge it as R.V. Once we admitted the possibility of this disguise, it became perfectly transparent: The curly horns; curly hair; the eye—we always tease R.V. about his straight eyelashes, giving him the expression of a scared bull—the length of the animal; the nonchalant walk.

My remark to A.A. as to the monster's sharp horns reflects the idea of rendezvous, fear of betrayal, and so on, borne out by our turning into the bypath to flee the monster and so meet R.V.

The *tutoiement,* with its evident intention to conciliate A.A., goes back in reality to the previous July 14th. M.J., his wife H., R.V., and I all met on the Boulevard Montparnasse and dined together. Cocktails had resulted in aggressiveness rather than gaiety. A.A. stared fixedly at H., who was sitting across the table from him, then dug me in the ribs, and, winking cryptically, said: "C'est une femme cheval. Non, une femme mouton. Frisé. Une fois et demie. Non une demi-fois."

As all the party except A.A. were old friends, I was accustomed to use the *tu* and *toi* in addressing them, and I slipped into it with A.A. too, without noticing.

He reproved me haughtily: "Je ne vous ai jamais autorisé à me tutoyer," and went to sleep on the table.

When A.A. in the dream gives me permission to *tutoyer* him, he seems to free me of my final apprehension, thus enabling me to awake.

The Making of a Monster

The history of the fabrication of the monster is a good example of the way in which my dream disguises are collected. Like a bunch of flowers picked here and there on the course of a long walk, it will trace for you the whole route.

When I was three years old I slept alone in the sewing room. I was afraid of the night not because it was dark but because, to me, it was not. It was lit up by the melodramatic phosphorescent glare of the devil who stood, dressed in red for Faust, behind the sewing machine, and by the blue-green lizards that ran over the walls. The devil is easily accounted for—my father had a life-size statue of him carved in cherry wood. The lizards undoubtedly came out of the zoo.

Lafcadio Hearn explains their phosphorescence by astigmatism and it is true that I am astigmatic.

The lizards would come in quite small; they would swell and grow into alligators and crocodiles. I could see them whether my eyes were tight shut or open. One night, one ran over the top of the door and sat on the rug by my bed. He grew as long as the rug and then walked slowly out the door. I could not bear to think that he might be lurking just outside, so I got up and followed him into the hall.

At the top of the stairs there was a landing in black walnut about twenty feet long, extending two or three feet beyond the carved black balusters. Just as I thought, the crocodile was crouching there. I could see him plainly by the light of the hall gas turned low. I clung to the balusters to keep myself from falling and my nurse, I don't know how much later, found me there.

My aunt and uncle were horticulturists. They had long hot conservatories full of flowers and palms. When I was about five, my aunt got two little alligators. She kept them in the hottest, palmiest greenhouse, where they used to walk around free until they got so large the gardeners were afraid of them. I often went to see them and, to this day, the hot damp smell of earth or of atmosphere enclosed in glass will excite in me instantly an expectation of reptiles.

In the spring of '21 or '22 I was living in Rome. With my sister and some friends we went to lunch across the Tiber at a country inn, whose name I have forgotten. We were driving gaily down a grassy road. A golden-brown light filtered through the trees. We heard loud curses and cries. A man appeared, driving the most ill-used horse I have ever seen. Its dark-brown skin was covered with scars, thicker around the neck and head. As we passed, he pulled it up brutally at the left side of the road and began beating it and sawing at its mouth. My luncheon was spoiled.

In the summer of 1927 I went to the Island of Porquerolles with R.V. I had there very fantastic dreams all dealing with the curious history of the island, which I had not at that time read—one in particular about the fort of the Lycastre, named for a dragon reputed to have had its lair there.

A chain of incidents or coincidences that occurred at Porquerolles seemed destined to continually throw my attention back to the crocodiles of my childhood. I became really superstitious about them.

We went to visit a banana plantation, the only one I have ever seen. Some of the trees were in flower. The guardian picked one and gave it to me. Standing under the tents of banana leaves, with the dark mysterious flower in my hand, the steamy smell rising from the hot earth carried me right back to my aunt's greenhouse.

"There must be serpents here," I said to the guard.

"Yes, we have caught quite a few. We keep them in glass. I'll show them to you as we go out."

On the way home, we were talking about the power of green. Suddenly R.V. jumped and caught my arm. A green lizard had run under his feet. It passed us and turned around and looked at us with its head raised, quite still. It was the brightest green I've ever seen and of an unbelievable elegance.

A few days later, walking home from the beach, we saw a man and a woman looking at an enormous green lizard lying in some short grass by the side of the road. As we had our camera, we thought it would be fun to take his picture. Very carefully we arranged the camera on the ground within a foot of him. He posed perfectly complacently, with his head up looking into the objective. The couple with us were sure we'd got a splendid photo of him and asked us to send them one. When the film was developed, every twig and blade of grass surrounding him came out distinct, but there was no shadow of a lizard.

One of our last walks on Porquerolles was up to the lighthouse. From there one has a wildly romantic view of the surrounding "Iles d'Or"— more like a water color of the Highland Lakes than the Mediterranean. The sun was setting. We were standing on an overhanging point of the high cliff. We both saw, at once, a little Chinese dragon just at our feet. Stooping down carefully so as not to disturb it, we were amazed to find it was not alive, but a pine root protruding from the earth formed like a little gargoyle with one malicious eye and a long arm pointing over its shoulder like Leonardo's St. Jean. We dug it up and named it the Lycastre. I put it in my *armoire,* and often in the night I thought I heard it moving.

Some weeks after our return to Paris, we dined with our friend N.J. and his wife H., who was pregnant. Driving home in a taxi, the chauffeur tried to see how close he could come to all the inevitable street repairs without dumping us. H. cautioned him to drive more slowly, as she did not wish to give birth "on the wheel." R.V. said to her: "Make a monster. *Ce serait très joli!* A siren, a hydra, or a centaur would be much more amusing than the regulation child."

I recalled some other friends of mine, whose parents were always chivying them to make proud grandparents of them. They said they would have no objection if they could choose their offspring. The wife wanted a dwarf hippopotamus and the husband a zebra.

Here is the first suggestion of metamorphosis of the lizards of childhood into ruminants . . .

R.V. was lunching with me in my Paris apartment. He had been reading that morning in Freud's *Souvenir d'Enfance de Léonard da Vinci* the description of Leonardo's little monsters—the wax animals which he blew up so that they would fly about the room, and the little dragon he created out of a curious lizard found by the gardener among the vines, attaching to it eyes and horns, a beard, and little wings filled with quicksilver which quivered as though alive when the lizard moved.

"That's my Lycastre," I said. "You know, she makes the Vinci sign."

But when R.V. came to the sheep's entrails, cleaned so that Leonardo could hold them in the palm of his hand and which he caused to be blown up by bellows until they filled a large room, I found myself unable to finish my mutton cutlet and begged him to stop, telling him about my meatless New York years in explanation.

Here you have each conscious layer of the pattern of the dream monster—beginning in my third year and ending a few days before the dream in this conversation which inspires the final metamorphosis.

transition 18

Harry Crosby   *Dreams*

1928-1929

> La pureté du rêve, l'inemployable, l'inutile du rêve, voilà
> ce qu'il s'agit de défendre contre une nouvelle rage de ronds-
> de-cuir qui va se déchaîner.
>
> *Aragon: "Traité du Style"*

I

the dream of the glass princess is a cool moonlight of glass wings each wing a beat of the heart to greet the glass princess she is no bigger than a thimble as she tiptoes daintily down the tall glass corridor of my soul tinkle by tinkle tinkle by tinkle until I feel I shall go mad with suspense but just as she is opening her mouth to speak there is a shattering of glass and I awake to find I have knocked over the pitcher of ice water that in summer always stands like a cold sentinel on the red table by the bed

II

red funnels are vomiting tall smoke plumes gold and onyx and diamond and emerald into four high round circles which solidify before they collide together with the impact of billiard balls that soon are caromed by a thin cue of wind into the deep pockets of sleep

III

The Man in the Moon is as rose-colored as our fingernails as we go out hand in hand into the garden you and I to somewhere beyond the sleeping roses but although you remove your silk stockings and I my silk socks (we have forgotten our calling cards) the star butler with his silver tray never reappears and we are forced to find our way home along the bottom of the lake

IV

I am rattling dice in a yellow skull they are falling upon the floor at the feet of the plump woman with bare breasts who is absorbed in the passion of giving milk to a rattlesnake but as soon as the numbers on the face of the dice correspond to the number of birds of paradise that form the jewels of her necklace she withdraws behind a red counterpane for the purpose of concealment

V

a naked lady in a yellow hat

VI

I am a lean Siamese cat who insists upon sleeping under the bed in order to watch the mouse holes so I am not particularly astonished when I wake up next morning to find myself under my bed

VII

there is a tree too high for me to reach its top until the young girl with the blonde hair and the white white skin (she wears furs and a veil) proposes that we take flying lessons whereupon I climb to the top of the tree and set at liberty my soul but when I slide down again to the ground the girl is disappearing out of sight on a tricycle and I am powerless to climb back again

VIII

they the twelve lions prowl swiftly out of a long iron tunnel and the entire dream is a waiting to be torn in pieces

IX

I begin to take it as a matter of course that no girl under ten years of
age can in any circumstance swim more than a given number of strokes
and naturally when the whole question has become one of formula I
am not surprised when these girls look up at me and drown without
more than a perfunctory show of resistance

X

a horse dealer is looking into a horse's mouth and examining its teeth
but I am far more interested in the young cripple who holds up a wax
leg for me to light as I would light a candle and by the light of his
flaming leg I am able to read the book of one hundred ways of kissing
girls which he has been able to buy with the profits he has obtained
by the selling of his large stock of artificial eyes

XI

P S the maid never returned to turn down the bed each word illuminated in a different color but all the other pages of the letter (my
fingers inform me that there are a great many of them) are as blank
as the ceiling of my bedroom white as the linen sheets except for that
strange last page P S the maid never returned to turn down the bed
nor can I find out the author of this letter (the writing suggests the
influence of the rainbow) nor can I ever know what bed is referred to
(there have been so many beds) nor who the maid is who never chooses
to return

XII

I do not find it strange that a bluebird should fall in love with a playing
card because the playing card in question happens to be the queen of
hearts

XIII

I am in a girl's soul (as we all live and sleep in a certain sense in our
beloved's soul) among the frail crumpled garments of her thought cast
here and there in disarray by invisible hands (are they hers are they
mine or are they perhaps the ardent hands of time) the fallen petals
of her apparel symbolic of her former vagaries the dress discarded on
the floor of her imagination the discarded robe of her past her red slippers petulantly kicked into a corner of her brain like a pair of red-
throated scruples the broken girdle at her waist for a sign of desire slender ribbons to suggest slender nights of love slenderer than rainbows

at dawn while all her hair becomes a mysterious undercurrent flowing through me (the new blood flowing through my arteries) but the pleasantest part of this dream is the awakening at the blue hour before the dawn to find her sleeping at my side

XIV

battleships emerge painted gray and black (they are lean as arrows) a submarine comes to the surface flying the skull and crossbones red icebergs drift like tombs upon the waves—with a red sword I trace upon the great whalelike back of the submarine the red words of war she spurts a jet of fire and sinks below the surface while I race over the horizon in pursuit of the mad dryad widespread upon a dolphin but as I am catching up to her there is a knock on my door and the femme de chambre announces il est sept heures monsieur

XV

a nightmare in the shape of an empty bed in the center of a tall room upon the bed lies one of those long pistols the kind formerly used in dueling I am kneeling on one side of the bed my uncle is kneeling on the other side the horror of the dream being who will first dare to reach for the revolver the strain being so great that I am exhausted all the next day although this nightmare has repeated itself more than once

XVI

it is night one infinitesimal grain of sand swells and swells and swells and swells until it is an enormous circular beach which suddenly tilts and slides down into the sea leaving me clinging to the handle of a large red umbrella which is automatically opening and shutting against a windy sky (I notice the stars have all been blown away) but nothing more happens till I feel in my ears the insistent burring of an alarm clock

XVII

a giraffe is gorging himself on sunflowers a Parisian doll is washing herself in a blue fingerbowl while I insist on their electrocution on the grounds of indecency

XVIII

the Ritz Tower sways like a drunkard under the cold fire of the moon while the Botticelli chorus girl is busily cutting her toenails to the great astonishment of a bottle of gin which stares out at her from behind a pair of white tennis shoes

XIX

I am endeavoring to persuade a Chinese professor who is at work on a torpedo which he expects to shoot to the sun to allow me to live in the center of this torpedo

XX

the dream of the sporting scene consists of three clowns (no doubt the Fratellini) lying behind coverts formed by bushes one of the clowns is about to shoot a tiger which is ravenously devouring a tethered tightrope walker who has been used as a decoy the unpleasant part of this dream being that I am the tiger

XXI

all night I dream I am an eagle winging over deserts of insanity in pursuit of the drunken birds of her eyes but although this has been a recurring dream I have never succeeded in catching both birds in the same night one night it is the left eye on another the right eye but last night for the first time (let this be a good omen) the eagle overtook and devoured both of the birds at once and this morning I have the sensation of a complete virginity of victory

XXII

a black and yellow bird morbidly tender with a feminine name excites by her musical exercises one of a Jewish sect who lies on a portable bed among a thicket of red windflowers but in spite of his entreaties she is unyielding, and he is forced to resume his relations (lascivious) with a corpulent Spanish Lady the back of whose neck I have marked with my teeth much to the consternation of a young Miss Eraser who until now had labored under the delusion that everything could be removed by rubbing

XXIII

Behind a painting of the Virgin with child—a sudden appearing and disappearing of the Nightgown

transition 18

Marius Lyle   *How I Dreamed*

I dreamed of planes, of superplanes, piled one on top of the other; planograms, planoderms, planollels. Planes in block, planes in mass-blockoplanes, massoplanes. Planes in zero so in nines so many, a skyful. Planists, planetists. Planegies operated by planegists. Running and walking and creeping planes. Anda-a-ante. Swinging out beyond the moon curved into a luxury of space. Feeding on the stars. Shooting through the milky way. Lethal planes below the belt.

   OR, a bridge spanned the sun in one great star and sang in space, pearls dropping through the dripping air. Vibrant hanging

>   Drippery frippery
>   Drapery napery
>   Fritillary rillary
>   Verily merrily
>   Sellery

As light as that. Like a moon wash.
and dawn came with her white blind eyes
scum on her eyes uplifting, uplifting, whites rolling
under the scum, white pupils, white ir . . . is
nines and nines and nines
oh long rolling zero loggers
offing from the the sun's disc
across like a dim subconscious
or not dim but heavy
heavy in the bearing down heavily zero
oh for the light of nines spiral eternal
NO. long r o l l i n g zero loggers
breathless panting dawn
waiting for the blind eyes
to open and make her *be* . . .

   Snow plane more 3 than 9 shadowless, certain, unafraid, open and even; dancing E b MAJOR if there were an i it would be that minor the one shadow vertically oblique reaching reaching blue in value there is nobody there but the vertically oblique shadow $=$ a stake but the

stake is O the shadow is what danced to the cosmic piping and will
march to the orphic dirge and is
now weltering to the world's unknowing
Unknowing, how can you not going to know?
Undoing, how go to not do?
Unseeing, how to bl ob?
I will show why: I met a man scratching his eyes out with
          numbers
          and causes and ultimates and who did what
          before
          the other thought how to: but he not knew
          I saw a man slaving at shells on the seashore:
          but he no do
          I knew a man with a microscope and horny glasses:
          but he saw not
          THE UNLEARNED KNOW
          THE IDLE DO
          THE BLIND SEE
WAIT like the dawn and assuredly you will BE
THE plane is
THE snowfield is
THE shadow is
AS we see them to be
THE dawn will come
AS we will it to be
WILD or PALE or BLEARY
So sang the man with the golden sickle

FINALLY: I dreamed of light after the sun had tiptoed through space
          and disappeared above time. Streams of light of an inef-
          fable complex poured radiant through the trees out from a
          willow wren's throat through blades of grass I smelled light
          I touched it I tasted it I heard light singing in chorus I saw
          . . . oh to say I saw light says nothing LIGHT SAW ME
          light was a solid entity It burst from the crowd of millions
          of humans waiting for the dawn of a new thing It
          ravished the stars it attacked the hills and lay in wait for
          the valleys it pursued the lightning and drowned it it
          romped with the snow mountains and caught the sky in its
          arms And there was no sky no mountains no valleys no
          crowds waiting only LIGHT light light and I and the
          DAWN TO BE

Norman MacLeod   *Dreams*

Twelve Knives

Starting with a penknife silver-handled. The body was never seen, but I remember stuck in the floor beside the doorway twelve knives at various angles. And several others must have been thrown into a space beyond comprehension. Four in myself that left no wound. Neither could they be seen.

But nobody saw the body, not even I. But yet I was sure and he was dead. Stretched upon the table invisibly.

"Saying there there there

Positum, Alive, Petronious three names on the doorstep. Possibly known in Philadelphia anywhere stepping incognito the music of incalculable targets practicing.

"Knowing there there there

And in my body, a taste of alcohol and the knowledge of something dying, for no reason at all brown as a cut in the head."

transition 19-20

Henry Miller   *The Cosmological Eye*

My friend Reichel is just a pretext to enable me to talk about the world, the world of art and the world of men, and the confusion and eternal misunderstanding between the two. When I talk about Reichel I mean any good artist who finds himself alone, ignored, unappreciated.

The Reichels of this world are being killed off like flies. It will always be so; the penalty for being different, for being an artist, is a cruel one.

Nothing will change this state of affairs. If you read carefully the history of our great and glorious civilization, if you read the biographies of the great, you will see that it has always been so; and if you read still more closely, you will see that these exceptional men have themselves explained why it must be so, though often complaining bitterly of their lot.

Every artist is a human being as well as a painter, writer, or musician; and never more so than when he is trying to justify himself as artist. As a human being Reichel almost brings tears to my eyes. Not merely because he is unrecognized (while thousands of lesser men are wallowing in fame), but first of all because when you enter his room, which is in a cheap hotel where he does his work, the sanctity of the place breaks you down. It is not quite a hovel, his little den, but it is perilously close to being one. You cast your eye about the room and you see that the walls are covered with his paintings. The paintings themselves are holy. This is a man, you cannot help thinking, who has never done anything for gain. This man had to do these things or die. This is a man who is desperate, and at the same time full of love. He is trying desperately to embrace the world with this love which nobody appreciates. And finding himself alone, always alone and unacknowledged, he is filled with a black sorrow.

He was trying to explain it to me the other day as we stood at a bar. It's true, he was a little under the weather and so it was even more difficult to explain than normally. He was trying to say that what he felt was worse than sorrow, a sort of subhuman black pain which was in the spinal column and not in the heart or brain. This gnawing black pain, though he didn't say so, I realized at once was the reverse of his great love: it was the black unending curtain against which his gleaming pictures stand out and glow with a holy phosphorescence. He says to me, standing in his little hotel room: "I want that the pictures should look back at me; if I look at them and they don't look at me too then they are no good." The remark came about because someone had observed that in all his pictures there was an eye, the *cosmological eye,* this person said. As I walked away from the hotel I was thinking that perhaps this ubiquitous eye was the vestigial organ of his love, so deeply implanted into everything he looked at that it shone back at him out of the darkness of human insensitivity. More, that this eye had to be in everything he did or he would go mad. This eye had to be there in order to gnaw into men's vitals, to get hold of them like a crab, and make them realize that Hans Reichel exists.

This cosmological eye is sunk deep within his body. Everything he looks at and seizes must be brought below the threshold of consciousness, brought deep into the entrails where there reigns an absolute night and where also the tender little mouths with which he absorbs his vision eat away until only the quintessence remains. Here, in the warm bowels, the metamorphosis takes place. In the absolute night, in the black pain hidden away in the backbone, the substance of things is dissolved until only the essence shines forth. The objects of his love, as they swim up to the light to arrange themselves on his canvases, marry one another in strange mystic unions which are indissoluble. But the real ceremony goes on below, in the dark, according to the inscrutable atomic laws of wedlock. There are no witnesses, no solemn oaths. Phenomenon weds phenomenon in the way that atomic elements marry to make the miraculous substance of living matter. There are polygamous marriages and polyandrous marriages, but no morganatic marriages. There are monstrous unions too, just as in nature, and they are as inviolable, as indissoluble as the others. Caprice rules, but it is the stern caprice of nature, and so divine.

There is a picture which he calls "The Stillborn Twins." It is an ensemble of miniature panels in which there is not only the embryonic flavor but the hieroglyphic as well. If he likes you, Reichel will show you in one of the panels the little shirt which the mother of the stillborn twins was probably thinking of in her agony. He says it so simply and honestly that you feel like weeping. The little shirt embedded in a cold prenatal green is indeed the sort of shirt which only a woman in travail could summon up. You feel that with the freezing torture of birth, at the moment when the mind seems ready to snap, the mother's eye inwardly turning gropes frantically towards some tender, known object which will attach her, if only for a moment, to the world of human entities. In this quick, agonized clutch the mother sinks back through worlds unknown to man, to planets long since disappeared, where perhaps there were no baby's shirts, but where there was the warmth, the tenderness, the mossy envelope of a love beyond love, of a love for the disparate elements which metamorphose through the mother, through her pain, through her death, that life may go on. Each panel, if you read it with the cosmological eye, is a throwback to an undecipherable script of life. The whole cosmos is moving back and forth through the sluice of time and the stillborn twins are embedded there in the cold prenatal green with the shirt that was never worn.

When I see him sitting in the armchair in a garden without bounds I see him dreaming backward with the stillborn twins. I see him as he looks to himself when there is no mirror anywhere in the world: when he is caught in a stone trance and has to *imagine* the mirror which is not there. The little white bird in the corner near his feet is talking to him, but he is deaf and the voice of the bird is inside him and he does not know whether he is talking to himself or whether he has become the little white bird itself. Caught like that, in the stony trance, the bird is plucked to the quick. It is as though the idea, *bird,* was suddenly arrested in the act of passing through the brain. The bird and the trance and the bird *in* the trance are transfixed. It shows in the expression on his face. The face is Reichel's, but it is a Reichel that has passed into a cataleptic state. A fleeting wonder hovers over the stone mask. Neither fear nor terror is registered in his expression—only an inexpressible wonder, as though he were the last witness of a world sliding down into darkness. And in this last-minute vision the little white bird comes to speak to him—but he is already deaf. The most miraculous words are being uttered inside him, this bird language which no one has ever understood; he has it now deep inside him. But it is at this moment when everything is clear that he sees with stony vision the world slipping away into the black pit of nothingness.

There is another self-portrait—a bust which is smothered in a mass of green foliage. It's extraordinary how he bobs up out of the still ferns, with a more human look now, but still drunk with wonder, still amazed, bedazzled and overwhelmed by the feast of the eye. He seems to be floating up from the paleozoic ooze and, as if he had caught the distant roar of the Flood, there is in his face the premonition of impending catastrophe. He seems to be anticipating the destruction of the great forests, the annihilation of countless living trees and the lush green foliage of a spring which will never happen again. Every variety of leaf, every shade of green seems to be packed onto this canvas. It is a sort of bath in the vernal equinox, and man is happily absent from his preoccupations. Only Reichel is there, with his big round eyes, and the wonder is on him and this great indwelling wonder saturates the impending doom and casts a searchlight into the unknown.

In every cataclysm Reichel is present. Sometimes he is a fish hanging in the sky beneath a triple-ringed sun. He hangs there like a God of Vengeance raining down his maledictions upon man. He is the God who destroys the fishermen's nets, the God who brings down thunder and lightning so that the fishermen may be drowned. Sometimes he appears incarnated as a snail, and you may see him at work building his own monument. Sometimes he is a gay and happy snail crawling about on the sands of Spain. Sometimes he is only the dream of a snail, and then his world already phantasmagorical becomes musical and diaphanous. You are there in his dream at the precise moment when everything is melting, when only the barest suggestion of form remains to give a last fleeting clue to the appearance of things. Swift as flame, elusive, perpetually on the wing, nevertheless there is always in his pictures the iron claw which grasps the unseizable and imprisons it without hurt or damage. It is the dexterity of the master, the visionary clutch which holds firm and secure its prey without ruffling a feather.

There are moments when he gives you the impression of being seated on another planet making his inventory of the world. Conjunctions are recorded such as no astronomer has noted. I am thinking now of a picture which he calls "Almost Full Moon." The *almost* is characteristic of Reichel. This *almost* full is not the almost full with which we are familiar. It is the almost-full-moon which a man would see from Mars, let us say. For when it will be full, this moon, it will be a green, spectral light reflected from a planet just bursting into life. This is a moon which has somehow strayed from its orbit. It belongs to a night studded with strange configurations and it hangs there taut as an anchor in an ocean of pitchblende. So finely balanced is it in this unfamiliar sky that the addition of a thread would destroy its equilibrium.

This is one of the moons which the poets are constantly charting and concerning which, fortunately, there is no scientific knowledge. Under these new moons the destiny of the race will one day be determined. They are the anarchic moons which swim in the latent protoplasm of the race, which bring about baffling disturbances, *angoisse,* hallucinations. Everything that happens now and has been happening for the last twenty thousand years or so is put in the balance against this weird, prophetic cusp of a moon which is traveling towards its optimum.

The moon and the sea! What cold, clean attractions obsess him! That warm, cozy fire out of which men build their petty emotions seems almost unknown to Reichel. He inhabits the depths, of ocean and of sky. Only in the depths is he content and in his element. Once he described to me a Medusa he had seen in the waters of Spain. It came swimming towards him like a sea organ playing a mysterious oceanic music. I thought, as he was describing the Medusa, of another painting for which he could not find words. I saw him make the motion with his arms, that helpless, fluttering stammer of the man who has not yet named everything. He was almost on the point of describing it when suddenly he stopped, as if paralyzed by the dread of naming it. But while he was stuttering and stammering I heard the music playing; I knew that the old woman with the white hair was only another creature from the depths, a Medusa in female guise who was playing for him the music of eternal sorrow. I knew that she was the woman who inhabited "The Haunted House" where in hot somber tones the little white bird is perched, warbling the pre-ideological language unknown to man. I knew that she was there in the "Remembrance of a Stained Glass Window," the being which inhabits the window, revealing herself in silence only to those who have opened their hearts. I knew that she was in the wall on which he had painted a verse of Rilke's, this gloomy, desolate wall over which a smothered sun casts a wan ray of light. I knew that what he could not name was in everything, like his black sorrow, and that he had chosen a language as fluid as music in order not to be broken on the sharp spokes of the intellect.

In everything he does color is the predominant note. By the choice and blend of his tones you know that he is a musician, that he is preoccupied with what is unseizable and untranslatable. His colors are like the dark melodies of César Franck. They are all weighted with black, a live black, like the heart of chaos itself. This black might also be said to correspond to a kind of beneficent ignorance which permits him to resuscitate the powers of magic. Everything he portrays has a symbolic and contagious quality: the subject is but the means for conveying a significance which is deeper than form or language. When I think, for example, of the picture which he calls "The Holy Place," one of his strikingly unobtrusive subjects, I have to fall back on the word enigmatic. There is nothing in this work which bears resemblance to other holy places that we know of. It is made up of entirely new elements which through form and color suggest all that is called up by the title. And yet, by some strange alchemy, this little canvas, which might also have been called "Urim and Thummim," revives the memory of that which was lost to the Jews upon the destruction of the Holy Temple. It suggests the fact that in the consciousness of the race nothing which is sacred has been lost, that on the contrary it is we who are lost and vainly seeking, and that we shall go on vainly seeking until we learn to see with other eyes.

In this black out of which his rich colors are born there is not only the transcendental but the despotic. His black is not oppressive, but profound, producing a *fruitful* disquietude. It gives one to believe that there is no rock bottom any more than there is eternal truth. Not even God, in the sense of the Absolute, for to create God one would first have to describe a circle. No, there is no God in these paintings, unless it be Reichel himself. There is no need for a God because it is all one creative substance born out of darkness and relapsing into darkness again.

Peter Neagoe   *Dreams*

The elusive trickery of the dream always puzzled me. It takes an arch-detective of Freud's magnitude to make cosmos out of the lawless activities of their chaos. The onus of this task I leave to him. The following are my own dreams, property of my dreamland, out of which they came to people my sleep with phantoms which my helpless ego had to accept as reality. I record the medley of talk as well as the jumble of aspects with all accuracy at my hand. To the reader I can say with all humility, take it or leave it, whereas I had no choice. I could only take. Occasionally there was a feeble gesture on the part of my "self" in protest, saying then "Bah, it's only a dream." But soon the poor flame of divine light fell into a trap and admitted that, no! it had this dream before but now it was reality. Then I awoke.

Dream One

A vast plain under gray skies. A great multitude, swaying in imitation of wind-blown wheat. Two huge figures dressed in white loom above the swaying multitude. The garb of one is a Roman toga, while the other has a military cut, a flowing white cape over it. The head of the first shines like the moon and grows lighter as the sky darkens. But now it detaches from the toga and floats in space. Higher and higher it goes, without losing in size. The swaying multitude stretches out millions of arms towards the ascending head. The military-garbed puts forward his arms, over the swaying horde, and his arms grow larger and longer till they reach the outer end of the enormous crowd. Then he turns these gigantic organs over the crowd, putting down their outstretched arms, shouting, "Comrades, comrades," with a thundering voice, which issues from his mouth in booming red waves, lighting the upturned faces. I see now all heads glowing in the red light of the giant's words. And lo! None have eyes. Only two dark hollows in each head dot the mass of red light cast upon the upturned faces. I shudder and awake.

Dream Two

I am at the seashore. White sand in dunes, in fine rippling shapes and in regularly laid heaps, stretches to the horizon. From one side the sea sends its booming waves to break at my feet. Tolstoi is leading me by the hand, telling me the secret of sand and sea. He talks incessantly, his gray eyes shining like diamonds. What he says has immense importance. I feel it by the beating of my heart and a dryness in my throat. But I can't hear a word he says. Eagerness to know his words tortures me, and the wish to break his illusion of my hearing and understanding him turns in my chest like a turbine. But I can't utter a word. Suddenly, from behind the dunes appear naked figures. They all run upon us with big strides. More and more appear and come upon us from all sides. They are all male men and have blue fig leaves hanging like an apron, suspended with a vermilion cord from the navels which are Legion of Honor rosettes. Now they all pick handfuls of sand and throw it into our eyes. But the sand grains burst into words, each of a different color, floating in the air and falling upon us as sharply-stinging frozen snowflakes. Through the rain of words appears Cervantes, riding on a nag and shouldering a huge spear from which dangle, like toy balloons, heads of authors I seem to know. The heads are attached to the spear by agile monkey tails, by which means they change position, bustling each other constantly. Then Rabelais appears riding on a pink cloud, a huge book open before him, in which he writes with an enormous quill, occasionally dipping it in the pink cloud. Suddenly I see that the cloud is a fat monk, his head serving Rabelais for a writing desk. Upon seeing Tolstoi, both Rabelais and Cervantes greet him with the simple words of Da-da, to which my venerable companion answers Da-da also. The sound of these words disperses those born of sand grains, which pack together and stream away like myriads of multicolored ants. They make a rustling noise but above it sounds their chant, a monotonous melody, repeating the word—now in shrill, now in less piercing voices. Cervantes, Rabelais, and Tolstoi burst into thundering laughter, and I awake.

Herbert Read   *Myth, Dream, and Poem*

At first it would seem that nothing is so remote from the scientific mind of today as the myth. Scholars may still read Homer and Ovid as a literary exercise, and perhaps a few people can read their poems as simple and enthralling stories. But the myths of these ancient poets do not mean anything to the average man, and even the myths that are nearer to us and embodied in our own culture—the myths of Christ, of Hamlet, and of Faust—even these have lost their simple virtue. Unless we are peasants or mystics, we can only believe in the Christian legend by an effort of the will, *quia impossibile;* and for men wandering through the world without faith in themselves, as for Hamlet and Faust, they are the myths of the mythless.

At the same time we may observe that the farther science penetrates into the mystery of life, the more it reverts to a mythological world. I refer more particularly to the science of the individual psyche, where all science culminates; for we know nothing unless we know ourselves. And the more we learn about ourselves by the objective methods of observation and analysis, the more we realize that our knowledge is already crystallized in the ancient myths. Nowhere do we meet these myths playing so vital a part as in the pages of Freud. Myths that were dead are now alive again, and it may be that in the course of time all the old gods and heroes, that for centuries peopled and pacified the minds of men, will return and resume their symbolic functions.

Oedipus lives again, and Electra; and Eros has been revived to indicate that our poor words, sex and love, no longer adequately represent the force and necessity of our most passionate instincts. We feel a need to personify feelings so intimate and acceptable. But death, which is so universally dreaded, for that reason remains an abstract conception; even Freud has not yet dared to personify that instinct which finally triumphs over Eros. "The picture which life presents to us," he says, "is the result of the working of Eros and the death-instinct together and against each other." Eros, but not Thanatos; the god of death has no familiar claim on our imagination. Man has been afraid to create a recognizable figure of death: he would have been too constant and too terrifying. Death, apart from a few fleshless and inhuman symbols (such as the skull) remains deeply buried in the unconscious.

Yet death is present in all the great myths, though at first we do not recognize him. Generally he is the loathly worm, the gorgon or dragon which must be slain by the hero, who is always Eros in disguise. Evade the dragon!—that is the condition on which alone love can be consummated.

A little research would discover the symbols of life and death on every side of us—threaded through the fabric of our history and legend, our poetry and painting, our dreams and our speech. It is even possible that in many subtle ways these symbols dominate each individual life. It would only be possible to prove such an hypothesis, in any normal case, by a process of psychoanalysis. There are certain cases, however, which are not normal: in particular, there is the case of the poet.

The poet is distinct from the reporter (who is rather the scientist, in so far as the scientist makes use of words). That is to say, the poet is a man who creates his own myths. But we must ask, by what process does such a myth, the unique creation of an individual, come into being? We say that the poet is inspired, or possessed. He is no longer in his right mind, but is visited by voices that come, it seemed once from the sky, but we now say from deep within the self. A man's *right* mind—by that we mean his conscious mind. When he is not in his right mind, then he is in another mind—a mind which, from the point of view of the imaginative life, is the mythical mind. And this mythical mind is the mind we all know in our dreams, partially, incoherently; but the poet knows it with a penetrating and selective validity.

It is tempting to identify poetry and the dream; or, shall we say, to avoid qualifications of a technical and linguistic nature, the imagination and the dream. Freud has found it necessary to distinguish between various stages or degrees of dream activity, and it is with the most superficial level, which we call daydreaming, that he tends to identify the poetic imagination. At the same time he would be willing to admit that the myth, the dream which has become valid for a whole people, has a significance which reaches into the very depths of the unconscious. Jung, who has dealt much more fully with this aspect of the myth, has found it necessary to suppose the existence of a racial psyche from which the myth is precipitated into the individual mind of the poet: an hypothesis for which there is, of course, no objective evidence.

The myth and the poem differ in this: the myth persists by virtue of its *imagery,* and this imagery can be conveyed by means of the verbal symbols of any language. The essence of a myth is diffusible. But a poem persists by virtue of its *language;* its essence belongs to that language and cannot be translated. Very rarely a poem in one language may inspire a poem of comparable poetic value in another language; but generally it is only the imagery which is translated intact. Nevertheless, a poem is more than an essence of language; it is this essence allied to imagery. In later stages of human development it may be this essence allied to abstract thought, or discourse; but this is the rarest type of poetry and invariably a prelude to poetic decadence. Visual or verbal, all art is predominantly eidetic, emotionally aware of the plastic reality of its images.

In this art resembles the dream. We all remark on the vividness of our dreams. Confusion there may be, but no vagueness or mistiness. Each person or object has a separate and discrete existence, and the landscape of dreams is as carefully and distinctly composed as the landscape in a medieval painting. The dream, in fact, is a combination of acute sensational awareness with an unnatural order. The order or composition of what we call nature, which is our human and superficial vision of reality, is plethoric and arbitrary, and all art except the most crudely naturalistic is based on a selection and arrangement of a few elements. The dream, too, is selective; but whereas art tends to arrange the selected elements according to some intellectual or instinctive scheme (such as balance, symmetry, proportion, and harmony), the dream arranges its selected elements according to some symbolic intention, the significance of which can be explained only by a complete analysis *of the dreamer*.

There is not, however, any clear distinction between the dream and the work of art, for the more we examine the history of art, the more evident it becomes that the works of art which survive are those which most nearly approach to the illogical order of the dream. Art retreats before the intellect, or grows stiff and atrophied and survives only in the records of academies. But those works of art which are irrational and dreamlike—legendary myths and folktales and the poems which embody them—these survive all economic and political changes, the transmigration of peoples and the metamorphosis of language. They are told and retold in every age and every climate, and though modified in detail, are always essentially the same, irrational and superreal, significant beyond their immediate meaning.

In a certain sense, then, the myth, and more intimately the image, makes the poem. Its vivid eidetic energy acts like a catalyst among the suspended verbal molecules and precipitates just those which clothe the image in the brightest sheath of words.

If we could *speak* our dreams we should dictate continuous poetry. But we neither speak nor even distinctly remember them, and the connections between poetry and dream must still be sought and established. It is a hazardous experiment, as I will show.

I dreamed that I stood (I say *stood,* but one is not conscious of a physical posture—one is just present, omnipresent) by the shore of a lake or inland sea. To my right was a cliff, falling sheer into the lake, whose waters were crystal clear, so clear that I could distinctly see the rocky bed, uneven in surface and mottled in color. As I stood there I suddenly became aware of a figure floating between the cliff and the lake. It was a naked female form, very lovely; and she held above her, like a horizontal sail, a sheet of golden silk. She floated gracefully down to the surface of the water, into which she fell without a sound or a ripple. The golden sail remained floating on the water, and in the middle of it I then observed a neat coil of rope, such as one sees on a ship or a pier. Below the sail, on the rocky floor of the lake, the body of the naked girl was now extended, as if lifeless. I had a distinct impulse to dive into the lake, as if to rescue her from drowning. But as I "registered" this impulse, at the same moment my attention was caught by the floating sail of silk and the superimposed coil of rope; and in the instant that I hesitated, another figure ran across the shore and dived into the lake. As he touched the surface, I awoke.

Here is a dream of very striking imagery. From a psychoanalytical point of view it has certain obvious features, but its interpretation is a personal matter of no immediate interest. I am concerned with its literary possibilities. Can I, while the dream is still vividly impressed on my mind, convert it into a poem?

I made the attempt, and this is what I wrote:

Her angel flight from cliff to lake
sustains its poise upon the sheet of silk
she holds above her head.

The air is still in dreams
a clear and plasmic element.
No ripples dim the surface as she falls
The cold distress
of days unknown of days to be.

The lake receives her, *the lake her lover.*
Her *ravished* flesh redeems the rocky floor.
Still, *as if asleep,* she lies
a treasure to be salvaged by who dares
shatter the level mirror of the lake.

I do not dare; *defeatist* I have seen
the cloth she held relinquished on the lake;

a baldaquin on which reposes
a neatly raveled coil of rope.

Another runs and dives and *I am free*
to stay a prisoner in the timeless cell of dreams.

Let me first state, to prevent a misunderstanding, that I consider this poem a failure. It is a failure in a personal sense because it does not nearly express the peculiar vividness and significance of the dream. It is a failure in a general sense because, as a consequence of its personal failure, it cannot possibly convey the quality of the dream to other people. But most essentially it is simply a failure as poetry. It might conceivably have been a success as poetry and still not have expressed or conveyed the quality of the dream. But actually it fails both in creation and in communication. The experience has not adequately fused the linguistic symbols: it has not selected them finely enough nor collocated them significantly enough.

In seeking the cause of this failure I first notice that in the act of converting the dream into a poem I have departed here and there from the actual or manifest content of the dream. The words and phrases printed in italics are additions of my conscious mind—critical comments or asides, such as "the air is still in dreams," or literary similes such as "as if asleep." Phrases like "the cold distress of days unknown . . . ." and "a treasure to be salvaged" are poetic metaphors, and not symbols given by the unconscious, which I distinguish under the name "images."

Those asides, similes, and metaphors arise without excessive deliberation—they are spontaneous associations and as such of some psychological interest. But in their origin they are distinct from the basic symbolism of the dream itself.

I do not see how anyone but the poet himself can make this critical distinction, though I am sure it is present in all poetry. The *degree* of its presence or absence would be the basis of a very important distinction between types of poets. The degree of symbolic imagery in Shelley, for example, is much greater than in Wordsworth, who is almost entirely, like his prototype Milton, a metaphorical poet. Milton, however, is a mixed case. As his critics in the eighteenth century did not fail to point out, he is sometimes, as they would say, "guilty" of irrational imagery. I may be expressing merely a personal preference, but I would like to suggest that the imagistic poet like Shakespeare, Shelley, and Blake is more essentially poetic than the metaphorical poet like Dryden, Pope, and Wordsworth; though admittedly this is merely one criterion. There are qualities in Dryden, for example, which compensate for his lack of imagery: there is his verbal felicity. For poetry is not only a matter of vision, but also of sound; though, as I have already suggested, in their gestation the two become closely linked, so that we can scarcely see an image without immediately formulating the verbal sign for it, nor hear a sound without immediately seeing an associated image.

Do the images in a poem like *Kubla Khan* precipitate the verbal signs in inevitable poetry? Is the poet's dream necessarily poetic the moment it is expressed in verbal symbols? It seems that an affirmative answer to these questions would make poetry too easy, but actually, as my own experiment proves, nothing is more difficult to secure than the immediate translation of the dream into its verbal equivalents. Ignoring the fact established by Freud, that the dream as remembered is nearly always a fragment, and may indeed be a positive distortion of the dream as originally dreamed, we still have to cross the gulf between experience and expression. It can only be done in a state of trance or automatism, in which state the images of the dream draw words from the memory very much as a magnet might draw needles from a haystack. The only *proof* (it is really only pragmatic evidence) of my conviction that these words will necessarily be poetic is a few admittedly great poems like *Kubla Khan,* of which it is recorded that they were written in a state of trance. It is for poets now to test the theory by rigorous experiment. It may take a long time to sort out the evidence— to agree on the validity of the experience and (what should be the same thing) the value of the poetry; but eventually the science of criticism would be in possession of sufficient facts to settle the question.

Automatism is the phenomenon to be investigated, but I ought perhaps to give a more precise definition of the word. To some people it merely conveys spiritualistic procedures which make use of instruments like the planchette, or perhaps any form of communication made in a condition of induced hypnosis. But by automatism in the present context we mean a state of mind in which expression is immediate and instinctive—where there is no time gap between the image and its verbal equivalent. Such spontaneous *utterances* are, of course, an everyday occurrence; in fact, they are the normal utterances of joy and sorrow, of wonder and excitement, and as such are the basic material of speech. And poetry is in this sense, and for this reason, a basic form of speech —*Ursprache*. It is distinguished from the more discursive modes of conversation by its immediacy, by its expression of images which at the moment of utterance are obsessing our minds by their dramatic or lyrical importance.

D. H. Lawrence was aware of this truth. In a preface to an American edition of *New Poems* (1920) he wrote: "One realm we have never conquered: the pure present. One great mystery of time is *terra incognita* to us: the instant. The most superb mystery we have hardly recognized: the immediate, instant self. The quick of all time is the instant. The quick of all the universe, of all creation, is the incarnate, carnal self. Poetry gave us the clue: free verse . . . In free verse we look for the insurgent naked throb of the instant moment. To break the lovely form of metrical verse, and to dish up the fragments as a new substance, called *vers libre,* this is what most free-versifiers accomplish. They do not know that free verse has its own *nature,* that it is neither star nor pearl, but instantaneous like plasm. It has no goal in either (time or) [1] eternity. It has no finish. It has no satisfying stability, satisfying to those who like the immutable. None of this. It is the instant; the quick; the very jetting source of all will-be and has-been. The utterance is like a spasm, naked contact with all influence at once. It does not want to get anywhere. It just takes place."

Poetry of this instantaneous kind must necessarily be written in free verse. At the same time it tends to be strongly rhythmical, though this rhythm is also unconscious and instinctive: the pitch and interval of natural utterance. The rhythm is found just as the words are found: by the law of attraction which seems to operate in the unconscious mind, a law which selects equivalents in visual image, verbal expression, musical expression, temporal extension. There is the image like a photographic film and there is at the same time an automatically selected and adjusted sound track, perfectly expressing and faultlessly accompanying the imagery.

I am speaking of an ideal poetry, such as has only very rarely been written in the past. Whether by research and self-control we shall ever be able to increase the quantity of such ideal poetry is a question which can only be answered at some future date when our experiments have been carried out over a sufficiently long period. It is possible that the necessary degree of concentration and of self-discipline will be beyond the capacity of the normal poet, who is after all a human being. I mean that it may possibly require a withdrawal from the normal activities of life such as the Yogi practice. But to withdraw from life is to defeat the purpose of poetry (though it may attain the purpose of religion); for the purpose of poetry is the enhancement of the enjoyment of life, either by sensuous celebration of its immediate qualities, as in lyrical poetry, or by communication of its ultimate meaning, as in epic and dramatic myths. What I am saying—the conclusion I am driven to—is that pure poetry is ideal or absolute poetry, and not real or actual poetry; that poetry is an essence which we have to dilute with grosser elements to make it viable or practicable. A poem that is pure imagery would be like a statue of crystal—something too cold and transparent for our

---

[1] I supply two words apparently omitted from the text as printed in *Phoenix,* p. 221.

animal senses. We therefore cloud the poem with metaphors and similes, which are our personal and human associations; we add to it sentiments and ideas, until finally the essential imagery is completely obscured and we are left with verbal rhetoric. And obviously the more rhetorical poetry is, the more popular it is; for it is then appealing to the widest range of human emotions. But just as essential music can be played on a single pipe and is by no means enriched by all the intestinal complexities of a Wurlitzer organ, so essential poetry remains in the instantaneous expression of the image, in "the insurgent naked throb of the instant moment."

To return for a moment to my own experience, I can aver that all the poetry I have written which I continue to regard as authentic poetry was written immediately, instantaneously, in a condition of trance. Now it is very difficult to hold oneself in a state of trance for any length of time; the least little noise or interruption from the outer world is sufficient to shatter it. The trance which Coleridge was in when he wrote *Kubla Khan* was interrupted by "a person from Porlock," and the poem could never be completed. In this particular case an American professor, Mr. John Livingston Lowes, has shown that however trance-like Coleridge's condition may have been, it did nevertheless allow him to make use of fragments of knowledge, words, and phrases, garnered during the course of his conscious reading. There is nothing surprising in this: I believe that every sound we hear and every object we see is instantaneously recorded by the brain, whether or not we consciously register the experience. Our consciousness is only a tiny aperture opening on to the wide world of the unconscious—a finger in an infinite range of card indexes.

The poem I am now going to quote is longer and more discursive than the dream transcript already given, and differs from it in that it had no precedent experience, such as a dream, but was itself the experience. When I began to write, my mind and my pencil worked slowly and haltingly, and there are evidences of this in the first paragraph of the poem, which I find a little too conscious or deliberate. But the rest of the poem was written automatically, without hesitation or revision.

Love and Death
On a strange bed I drop my tired head
But sleep does not come—only wakeful dread.
The room was dark at first, but now
The light that filters from the street
Falls aslant the mirror, casts in my eyes
Its mildewed radiance. My limbs
That like a busy watch

Mark the seconds with their urgent twitch
Enlarge the area of my mind
Keep me alert to every sound
That echoes in the space
Around this unknown inn where I have come
So weary and late.

The last step outside has died away.
All is quiet: the bulbs extinct
That lately glowed above the lust and stink
Of urban life. The shadows in my room
Shift like silhouettes on frosted glass,
Coagulate and tremble into shape.
The light seems now to cut across a street
Leaving an edge of darkness round which creeps
A careless figure. She stands irresolute
Her misty breath jumping like a plume
Into the icy fog. Pellicules of dew
Which catch and concentrate the light
Have settled on the fringes of her hair;
Her step is soft and soundless as she moves
Across the cobbled street whose greasy sets
Meet her worn feet like folded knuckles.
I wait in the dark, withdrawn.
But she by instinct guided comes my way
And stands before me till her silence
Is a question, and I yield
And take her hand, and lead her to my room
Which now is suddenly light and warm.

I am not curious. I see her eyes are clear
And the tresses where the hoar has formed
Are like the withered sheaths which hang from corn.
Her dress she soon discards
And falls into my arms and laughs and cries
And tells me life was sad until I came.
She sits beside the fire; her eyes, her lips, her limbs
Speak of love, a feeling I have known
But never until this moment seen
Embodied in a form not sought but found.

Between the fire and the lamp
Her body gleams distinct, as if it had absorbed

Ethereal rays, which now give out
Their luminous response to night.
The more she gleams and grows intense
The less I know myself—until
I am not there, except that in her mind
I dwell, and look into the world through crystal eyes
And see the swelling waves break into surf
On golden sands, and birds with bright wings
Sailing the air which shakes
The fronds and ferns on wiry stalks
Against the even green
Of endless fields.

    A dream,
As soon I know. For then she falls asleep
Her head upon the hearth, her limbs
Like Danaë's open to the fitful flame.
When I awake she is not there,
And I am I again, a prickling frame
Of flesh and bone, gazing upon the earlier scene
Of drifting fog and artificial light.

But now there comes
Sidling round the selfsame edge of dark
Another figure, this time a boy
Dressed in rags, so thin
His shadow seems a blade
That cuts across the cobbled street.
He shuffles till he stands, a beggar, at my feet.
Then once again we are within the room
Now lit by sinking embers. Once again
The figure strips and stands
Lank and angular against the glow.
His eyes are sunk so deep I cannot see
Their color, nor discover their intent.
His cheeks are drawn about his jaw
And every joint articulate.
He puts his bony hand against my breast.
I do not shrink—indeed, I feel,
His still appeal and in his mind
Find a cool retreat.

The shore is icy: a cliff of glass
Against which the sullen waves

Slide in the distant lunar grip.
The seabirds cry in the white silence
And only cease when breaking floes
Boom like a muffled gun
Across the arctic waste.

Again I find myself
My face against the worldly scene.
But now it is no dream. The fog
Drifts over the empty street.
Sleet falls across the light.
I shudder and turn. There in my bed
The lovely girl and the destitute lad
Are lying enlaced. And I know they are dead.

It was not until I had written this poem, and read what I had written, that I realized I had invented a myth which exactly expressed Freud's theory of the two instincts which control all life—the instincts of Eros and Death. In his *Autobiographical Study,* Freud describes his theory in these words:

> I have combined the instincts for self-preservation and for the preservation of the species under the concept of Eros and have contrasted with it an instinct of death or destruction which works in silence. Instinct in general is regarded as a kind of elasticity of living things, an impulsion towards the restoration of a situation which once existed but was brought to an end by some external disturbance. This essentially conservative character of instincts is exemplified by the phenomena of the *compulsion to repeat.* The picture which life presents to us is the result of the working of Eros and the death-instinct together and against each other.

My poem is a dramatic myth which (whatever its poetic merits, of which I am very doubtful) does give in visual imagery an equivalent of the abstract concepts of Freud's theory. Myths, of course, were invented before theories; but the whole point of this essay is to suggest that theories are inadequate so long as they remain intellectual concepts: to dwell in the imagination of mankind they must be transformed into myths.

As a result of these experiments poetry is seen more clearly than ever as the mediator between dream and reality. For centuries, philosophy has been disintegrating this concept of reality, showing what a miserable compromise of averages and probabilities it represents. Philosophy falls back upon some form of idealism—some system of intellectual absolutes which gives coherence and continuity to existence; or it puts up with a provisional attitude like logical positivism, which is the contemporary form of agnosticism. But art is neither philosophy nor science, neither idealism nor agnosticism. It is an attempt to solve these existential problems by means of a living synthesis. Like the philosopher and the scientist, the poet experiences the contradictions of life, but instead of trying to solve them on the plane of inductive or deductive reasoning, solves them in the imagination. The imagination is the faculty by means of which we can encompass the antithetical terms of our experience, thus bringing the widest oppositions within a single focus, under a light which fuses them into a wholeness, a coherence, a plastic and sensuous integrity which is the work of art, that miracle which is the only objective evidence we possess of whatever superreality is cosmic and eternal.

transition 27

Julian Trevelyan   *Dreams*

Stare fixedly at the lamp, its incandescent spherical shade, the white zigzag of its filament; with eyes shut the pattern remains printed in purple and blue on the empty redness of Retina. But once liberated from the meanly world of actuality, the pattern acquires a new and more dynamic value; the sphere of the shade becomes the symbol of a finite universe; the incandescent zigzag, the thought to penetrate the encircling walls. So in dreams the objects of everyday existence, freed from the tyranny of consistency, of unilocality, acquire a new meaning. Jung has shown that the subconscious symbolizes, the better to solve its problems; and we would go further and suggest that the entire esthetic activity of the mind is an attempt, often frustrated, to symbolize a remote disintegrating reality. Certainly the state of mind, sometimes called "rational," in which we spend our waking hours, finds no room for symbolism. Indeed, a pusillanimous and insecure state of mind which on the one hand ignores the *sine qua non* of its existence, the primitive basis of symbolism: and on the other struggles to connotate and project the dimensionless unity of the subconscious upon the one plane of its very limited conception of space and time. This, its so-called "logical" process, reduces the essential unity of the "primal being" to the plurality which has bewildered philosophers at all times. Already in the *Vedas* an attempt was made to define the relation of the *particular* to the *absolute*. To Parmenides of the fourth century B.C. all plurality was of the *non-ent,* and being mere opinion did not exist; whereas Reason discovers the *ent,* the unity of existence which extends throughout space and endures throughout time. So Parmenides became the first neo-rationalist; and since his time a good many philosophers, among whom it is customary to mention Spinoza and Nietzsche, have been worried and defeated by the same problem.

Neoclassicism begins where Parmenides left off, and naively accepting the dream-psychology, more by way of analogy than as fact, sets out to make this fundamental unity its objective.

In the state of dreaming or of hallucination, the mind loses that self-consciousness which in its waking hours it can never quite banish, and begins to move silently through a timeless, spaceless world, where neither Destiny nor Chance have stepped; it is created by and at the same time creates its sleep-liberated creatures, grows deeper and broader than the day-world; lines can be drawn in any direction instead of in the one; the tension which relates mind to matter in the waking hours disappears. Proust writes: ". . . *il suffisait que, dans mon lit même, mon sommeil fût profond et détendît entièrement mon esprit; alors celui-ci lâchait le plan du lieu où je m'étais endormi, et quand je m'éveillais au milieu de la nuit, comme j'ignorais où je me trouvais, je ne savais même pas au premier instant qui j'étais; j'avais seulement dans sa simplicité première, le sentiment de l'existence comme il peut frémir au fond d'un animal; j'étais plus dénué que l'homme des cavernes; mais alors le souvenir—non encore du lieu où j'étais, mais de quelques-uns de ceux que j'avais habités et où j'aurais pu être—venait à moi comme un secours d'en haut pour me tirer du néant d'où je n'aurais pu sortir tout seul; je passais en une seconde par-dessus des siècles de civilisation, et l'image confusément entrevue de lampes à pétrole, puis de chemises à col rabattu, recomposaient peu à peu les traits originaux de mon moi.*"

Today artists have identified the esthetic faculty, still chiefly by analogy, with the subconscious (where Surrealism flounders, prematurely corpulent, through treasure-trove). For as the mind has changed, so, too, has the definition of meaning: the rhythm of living has its foundations deeper, and the mind gropes to justify, exemplify itself in the subconscious. Perhaps it glows with a new phosphorescence, and in the oblique mirrors that line the corridor from the day-world to the night-world, shines pearl-like in surrounding blackness. But the image reduplicated a thousand times appears to itself to possess an opulence not really its own, and consciousness to master a regiment that at once nods and kicks.

We have shown that esthetic pleasure justifies itself in the fantasies of a dream-world, and we have suggested that the converse bears a very particular relation to truth. A cord stretched through the subconscious round which may crystallize the impersonal dream-fantasies, this affords so strange an analogy to the process of artistic creation that we felt justified in whispering, a little hastily, *to dream is to create*. Since then the years have shifted, Mr. Joyce has waxed . . . and waned, Sir Joynson Hicks has been banished to his shelf in the peerage, Mr. Eliot has turned Anglo-Catholic; and we say with a little more assurance, *To Dream Is To Create*. Finally, since this is a manifesto, unencumbered with lurid inhibitions, let us gladly shout *TO DREAM IS TO CREATE*.

Appendix: The Dreamer's Almanack

I Food

I used not to believe that pearls were found in oysters, and when they told me that such was indeed the case I told them they were fools and opened an oyster to prove my point. Seeing only an indescribably filthy mess, I gulped it down. What was my horror when inside me I felt the voice of a minute homunculus; *"sophistication devours wisdom"* it cried, and I knew that the universe, packed ever so tightly into a nutshell, was groping for scope in the depths of my intestines. Since then I cannot abide the taste of oysters nor, for that matter, of pearls.

II Women

Umbrellas up
      umbrellas down.

III Architecture

The sleep within a sleep is the decomposition of matter, a gesture towards the philosophy of the single proton; radium turns to lead, to gold, to bismuth, to carbon, to hydrogen, and all in a trice. To wake within sleep is to clutch, feverishly to embrace a baroque pile, volutes, pilasters, cupolas, and rococo cusps and ogees. The natural architecture of the universe, for it has always been florid, lies clasped, shrunken, precipitate, a static bedfellow for the dynamic architect.

5. post-romantic documents

Carl Einstein *Bebuquin* [1]

One of Euphemia's blue hat feathers got drunk glittering in the green chartreuse.

Bebuquin looked with his left leg into the corner of the bar, where Heinrich Lippenknabe was meditatively arranging an orchid in the bronzed hollow of a hetera's navel and pouring cognac into it.

"Who is the father?" the barmaid yelled.

The gleam of an electric lamp went through the lace to her knee, danced excitedly backward across the crystal glasses and the champagne coolers; the usually decent electric light!

"Nobody," Euphemia looked with circularly expanded eyes. "I had him in a dream."

"Bunk," Heinrich Lippenknabe cried, "she means birth control that didn't succeed."

"First of all, I had no idea who the father might be. It doesn't matter really." She looked frightened.

"Was it Boehm, perhaps?" Bebuquin asked.

Euphemia screamed perpendicularly.

"*That* one keeps on coming, he wants to nurse the child, he has such a milky skull since he died, and he uses his now useless intestine as a zither to which he sings the Pythagorean law very touchingly. He said the boy would have to become a real intellectual."

"But didn't your embryo write a philosophic work and make his doctorate in obstetrics? Isn't the story entitled: the cutting of the navel cord or the *Principium Individuationis*?"

"Yes," Euphemia whispered, "he has renounced the world, he is becoming spiritual, without desires, unclean, and silent. Besides, he has a sensitive skin which constantly changes color. Isn't it possible to use him as a transparent advertising sign? We would save colored lamps."

[1] Fragment from a novel

"The alogical grows, the alogical is victorious, he will not be led astray."

Bebuquin was balancing himself on the rickety barchair.

"That, dear ladies, is the reason so many are going crazy. We lack fictions, positivism is ruining us."

The barmaid was kneeling in rapture between the champagne coolers.

"We conceive too materially, sir."

Her lace dress glittered around her, ornament of dream.

The champagne coolers, sacred vessels of the unspeakable.

"We no longer sacrifice," Bebuquin screamed into the street, "the sublime is being lost. You criticize the miracle, the miracle has sense only when it is real, but you have destroyed all the forces which go beyond the human element."

"I want the spirit to become visible," Heinrich Lippenknabe moaned.

"Let nothingness become materialized," said the lady with the orchid in her navel.

Boehm was standing below them.

He said:

"The natural law ought to get soaked in alcohol, until it recognizes that there are irrational situations, and until it finds out that only weakness and the democrat with his parliamentary suffrage are legitimate. The law never realizes itself psychically, it is hanging senselessly on the nail of some miserable axiom in mathematics.

When a thing is recognized as being according to law, it only goes to show that the thing as an experience has been exhausted. The law is the past, subject to death.

We lack exceptions.

Too few people have the courage to express perfect bunk. Bunk which is frequently repeated becomes the integrating moment of our thinking; at a certain phase of the intelligence we are no longer interested in correct and rational things.

Reason causes too many great and sublime things to become grotesque and impossible. With reason we ruined God, the all-embracing idiosyncrasy.

What right does reason have to do this? It rests upon unity.

There sits mass.

There are so many worlds that have nothing whatever to do with each other, as little as green chartreuse has to do with the visions into which it may be recomposed. If a sympathetic contemporary busies himself with extraordinary things, they lock him up in the madhouse.

Gentlemen, man is simply not interested in your rational world. Why will you not understand at least that your reason is boring?

Reason stylizes everything, most of the things it sells at a sacrifice for supposedly futile transitions, the other part is canon, the valuable, the boring, the democratic, the stable.

Gentlemen, the intelligence and imagination of people should reveal themselves through the fact that they catch the lightning streak, you must differentiate. I assure you, I, for instance, live only because I suggest myself to myself; in reality I am dead. Of course, you know that I let myself be put in a coffin. But I promised myself to run around as an advertisement for the unreal, until some idiot could experience a miracle with me. Look here, babies, unreal, nothingness, these are terms for your bad eyesight. Should there be a future fulfillment, then it comes from nothingness, the unreal. That is the sole guarantee for the future.

The utilitarian and the rationalist say for the imaginary: deception and Maya; for nothingness: vacuum or ether. Those are people who want to take everything into their mouths and eat it or else cut it up into a moral concept. But nothingness is the indifferent premise of all existence. Nothingness is the basis, only you must not believe in Robert Meyer, and all of life is after all only a limitation of nothingness. Existence in forms is a sofa, a bolster, a convention which is not obligatory and which is boring. If we are free and bold towards life in many forms, if we look on death as a prejudice, a lack of imagination, then we go towards the fantastic, that is indefatigability in all possible forms.

I admit that reason makes everything comfortable, it concentrates, but it destroys too much, makes too much ridiculous and always the greatest things. We should look at the impossible so long until it becomes an easy matter. The miracle is a question of training. Euphemia, all of you lack a cult.

The romantic says: Look, I have imagination and I have reason, I am queer and sometimes say things that don't exist, as my reason shows you afterwards. If I want to be very poetic, I then say, I have dreamed this story. But that is my most sublime means, it is better to be economical with it. To this come masks and mirror as romantic apparatus. But, ladies and gentlemen, estheticism comes in with this. With the romantic you take one step forwards and two backwards. That is a tortuous adhesive plaster."

He poured absinthe on those who had not yet passed out.

"Here is the means of the dilettant."

Bebuquin threw himself at Euphemia's nose and embraced her passionately at the same time.

A storm rain clacked against the great windowpanes.

"We need a deluge.

Up till now we have used reason, in order to make the sense hard, in order to reduce, to simplify perception. Reason became impoverished;

reason impoverished God to the point of indifference; let us kill reason; reason has produced the formless death where there is nothing more to be seen. For Dante death was still a pretext for splendor, color, wealth, and lust. Let us take our senses, let us tear them from the quiet of stupid Platonic ideas, let us observe the moment, which is much more singular than quiet, because it differentiates and is characteristic, because it has no unity, but divides up finally between that which is in front and that which is in back."

The dead Boehm danced gratefully upon Euphemia's hat and sank into the bar; he lay down once more in a strange kind of cognac which he had always liked.

1905-1908

Translated from the German
by Eugene Jolas
transition 16-17

Franz Kafka   *The Housefather's Care*

Some say that the word Odradek comes from the Slavonic, and trace its structure to that tongue. Others believe it has a German origin and is merely influenced by the Slavonic. The uncertainty about these two derivations, I consider, entitles us to assume that neither is correct, since we cannot find a meaning for the name in either language.

Needless to say, no one would bother his head about the problem did there not really exist an entity called Odradek. It resembles a flat, star-shaped spool, and, what is more, seems actually to be covered with yarn. Probably they are only loose ends of thread which have been snapped off and knotted or tangled up together, and they are of various shapes and colors. But it is not merely a spool: from the middle of the star a small crossbar protrudes in which another bar is inset at right angles. With the aid of the crossbar on one side, and the prongs of the star upon the other, the whole structure can stand up as if it were mounted on two legs.

We might be tempted to believe this form had once a functional significance of some kind, and that now we see it in a damaged state.

This, however, does not seem to be the case; at least we can detect nothing to confirm any such theory. Nowhere can we discern any appendages or fragments that might point to that conclusion; the whole thing seems senseless, yet quite complete in its peculiar way. Nothing further can be said about its anatomy, for Odradek is extraordinarily nimble and cannot be captured.

It lives in the garret, on the stairs, and in the hall, by turns. Sometimes it is invisible for months on end when presumably it has moved to other houses, but sooner or later it always returns to ours. Sometimes when we are going out and happen to notice it floundering down the banisters, we feel moved to address it. Of course we don't put direct questions, we treat it, naturally enough, considering its tininess, like a child. "What's your name?" we ask. "Odradek." "And where do you live?" "Anywhere," it says and seems to laugh, yet the laughter is such as might be produced by a being without lungs. There is a sound in it like the rustle of fallen leaves. With that the conversation usually comes to an end. As a matter of fact, replies are not always forthcoming. Quite often it is mute over a long period, dumb as the wood it seems to be.

Vainly I ask myself, what will become of it? Can it really die? All that dies has had, to start with, some kind of goal and a specific activity in which it has indulged, but this is not the case with Odradek. Will it then, one wonders, go rolling on and on and on forever before the feet of my children and my children's children, the tattered threads trailing away behind it?

Obviously it's quite harmless; yet I find the idea that it may possibly survive me almost painful.

Translated from the German
by Eugene Jolas *and* Stuart Gilbert
transition 27

Hans Arp   *Notes from a Diary*

man is a beautiful dream. man lives in the sagalike country of utopia where the thing-in-itself tap-dances with the categorical imperative, today's representative of man is only a tiny button on a giant senseless machine. nothing in man is any longer substantial. the safe-deposit vault replaces the may night. how sweetly and plaintively the nightingale sings down there while man is studying the stock market. what a heady scent the lilac gives forth down there. man's head and reason are gelded, and are trained only in a certain kind of trickery. man's goal is money and every means of getting money is all right with him. men hack at each other like fighting cocks without ever once looking into that bottomless pit into which one day they will dwindle along with their damned swindle. to run faster to step wider to jump higher to hit harder that is what man pays the highest price for. the little folk song of time and space has been wiped out by the cerebral sponge. was there ever a bigger swine than the man who invented the expression time is money. time and space no longer exist for modern man. with a can of gasoline under his behind man whizzes faster and faster around the earth so that soon he will be back again before he leaves. yesterday monsieur duval whizzed at three o'clock from paris to berlin and was back again at four. today monsieur duval whizzed at three o'clock from paris to berlin and was back again at half past three. tomorrow monsieur duval will whiz at three o-clock from paris to berlin and will be back again at three o-clock that is at the same time he leaves and day after tomorrow monsieur duval will be back before he leaves. nothing seems more ridiculous to present-day man than broad clear living.

spiders flee into the cracks in the earth in the face of man's ugliness and human thinking. from his eight curl-ringed holes he shoots off a lot of hot air. man wants what he can't do and despises what he can. the trick is his goal and its achievement. he feels himself a god when he roars up to heaven with a clockwork under his behind. when dada unveiled the deepest wisdom for man he smiled indulgently and continued to jaw. when man thinks and jaws even the rats have to vomit. jawing is to him the most important thing of all. jawing is a healthy airing. after a beautiful speech we also have a huge appetite and a different point of view. man takes for red today what he thought was green yesterday and what in reality is black. every moment he emits final explanations about life man and art and knows no more than the stink-mushroom what life man and art are. he thinks that this blue fume this gray fog this black smoke which he gives forth is more important than the braying of a jackass. man thinks he is related to life. gladly this big-mouthed frog calls himself a son of light. but light dwells magnificently in the sky and chases man far from its path. only as a murderer is man creative. he covers with blood and mud everything within his reach. only the physically unfit among men compose poems pluck the lyre or swing the paintbrush.

in art too man loves a void. it is impossible for him to comprehend as art anything other than a landscape prepared with vinegar and oil or a lady's shanks cast in marble or bronze. every living transformation of art is as objectionable to him as the eternal transformation of life. straight lines and pure colors particularly excite his fury. man does not want to look at the origin of things. the purity of the world emphasizes too much his own degeneration. that is why man clings like a drowning creature to each graceful garland and out of sheer cowardice becomes a specialist in stocks and bonds.

man calls abstract that which is concrete. yet i find this a good deal in his favor since for the most part he mistakes with nose mouth and ears, in other words with six of his eight curl-framed holes, the behind for the front. i understand that he should call a cubist picture abstract because parts have been abstracted from the object which served as a pretext for the picture. but a picture or a plastic for which no object was pretexted i find as concrete and as perceptible as a leaf or a stone.

art is a fruit growing out of man like the fruit out of a plant like the child out of the mother. while the fruit of the plant grows independent forms and never resembles a balloon or a president in a cutaway suit the artistic fruit of man shows for the most part a ridiculous resemblance to the appearance of other things. reason tells man to stand above nature and to be the measure of all things. thus man thinks he is able to live and to create against the laws of nature and he creates abortions. through reason man became a tragic and ugly figure. i dare say he would create even his children in the form of vases with umbilical cords if he could do so. reason has cut man off from nature.

i love nature but not its substitute. illusionistic art is a substitute for nature. in many points however i have to count myself among the ugly men who let reason tell them to put themselves above nature. gladly would I create children in the shape of vases with umbilical cords. we must smash the toys of these gentlemen said the dadaists in order that the lousy materialists can recognize on the ruins what is essential. dada wanted to destroy the rationalist swindle for man and incorporate him again humbly in nature. dada wanted to change the perceptible world of man today into a pious senseless world without reason. that is why hugo ball furiously beat the dadaistic kettledrum and trumpeted the praise of unreason. dada washed out the venus of milo and made it possible for laocoon and sons after a struggle of a thousand years with the rattlesnake to at last step out for a moment. their worn out toothbrushes were restituted to the great benefactors of the people and their vocabulary of wisdom was revealed as a hieroglyph for greed and murder. dada is a moral revolution. dada is for nonsense. which does not mean bunk. dada is as senseless as nature and life. dada is for nature and against art. dada is direct like nature and like nature wants to give its essential place to each thing. dada is moral the way nature is. dada represents an infinite sense and finite means.

the earth is not a fresh-air resort and the idyllic prospectuses of the earth tell lies. nature does not run along the little thread on which reason would like to see it run. the light of day is beautiful but poisonous and rustic life even creates hexameters and madness. we can of course insure our house against fire our cash register against burglary or our daughter against devirgination but heaven looks nevertheless down into the bottomless pots of our home countries and extracts the sweat of fear from our foreheads. every moment we shuffle off this mortal coil by a hair's breadth. from out of every plank seat a black claw grabs us by the backsides. all bosom friendship and love is a lot of applesauce. like water off the duck's back so love runs off the human bacon. in loneliness man rides down the styx on his chamber pot. in the neighborhood of karlsruhe he would like to get off because his name is karl and he would like to take a little rest. but chance would have it that here a thicket of laurel feet victory tripe and saber rattling germanic spooning couples make it impossible for him to get off in that beautiful landscape and thus man damn it to hell continues riding lonelily down the styx on his chamber pot. shamelessly nude clouds without fig leaves or decorations ride past the blue german eyes and lay their eggs in heraldic nests. from the springs beer flows in streams. water fire earth air have been gnawed at by man. but also from man to man the mannikin does what he can. no ha-ha-hallelujah can help him. in carl einstein's poems the design of a landscape there is no further mention that man the measure of all things gets away with a black eye. of man in these poems there remains less than of his lares and penates. einstein gives man a good drubbing and sends him home. the white buttocks of an aged narcissus emerge once but it is quickly ignored as fata morganata, aside from this encounter and a few parts of the human anatomy that flow through the black belly of this landscape concepts are the most corporeal vestige of man. you speaks with i about flight and fear of death. human qualities migrate through light and shadow.

carl einstein's design of a landscape is an ice-cold pit. no rabbit can live or sleep in this pit for these pits are bottomless. in order that the third dot on the i be not missing i would say further that this pit is as tenebrous as night. no perfumed columns, no fluted rump weals, no schwepperman's eggs architecturally beautify its entrance. with teeth chattering the reader asks this insomnia in persona can you give ghost knocks but not even a violet answers him so much as cuckoo. with staring eyes and mug hanging wide open this landscape roars through

the void. only a handful of snuff remains of the sphinx the olympus and
Louis XV. the golden rule and other valuable rules have vanished without leaving a trace. a chair leg clings sea-sick with madness to a torture
stake. shreds of sneezing skies jump over ruminating coffins. each of
these poems is served on ice. the breasts of this landscape are made of
cold-storage meat. but nevertheless in the coldest abstractions of einstein there is very distinctly the unmodern question why has this garden
party been arranged. einstein is not satisfied with the art pour art
of the world. he is for the delusional ideas of the good old days and
against reason. he does not want to see illusion used as a scarecrow nor
the reservation of the ghosts eliminated. it seems to him that people
have not yet succeeded in unveiling the world through reason. a great
deal in the new doctrine for him does not fit together like a meander in
patent leather shoes who goes walking on the arm of a somnambulist
box of sardines through the sooty hortus deliciarum. einstein's poems
have nothing to do with modern alarm clocks. before them reason takes
its tail between its legs and goes philandering somewhere else. einstein
does not want to cover up the asphodel meadows. his apollo is not yet
the hen-pecked mate of a hundred horse power mrs rolls royce. here an
unhygienic polonaise is being danced against all the prohibitions of the
concrete top hat of the glass necktie and the nickel cutaway to the tune
of the old snowman still lives. whether today people planted antennae
instead of narcissi doesn't matter one way or the other. the main thing
is to have here and there a lucida intervalla in order to be able to take
a gulp from the saving whisky bottle of illusion. the darkness which
einstein distills from the smiling meads of the earth goes beyond jack
and the bean stalk beyond the corner grocer and beyond all human
endurance. yes yes the earth is not a valley of tears in the vest pocket.

the seven head lengths of beauty have been cut off one after the other
but nevertheless man acts as if he were a being that vegetates outside of
nature, industriously he adds seven to black in order to get thereby
another hundred pounds of chatter. gentlemen who always stood for
the dream and life are now making a loathsomely industrious effort to
reach the goal of class and to deform hegel's dialectics into a popular
song. i am justified in my theory that man is a pot the handles of which
fell out of his own holes. poetry and the five year plan are now being
busily stirred together but the attempt to stand up while lying down
will not succeed. man will not let himself be made into a happy hy-
gienic number which brays ee-on enthusiastically like a jackass before
a certain picture. man will not let himself be standardized. in this ridiculous circus which stands without relation to life itself the books of
hugo ball epitomize a gigantic act. hugo ball leads man out of his silly

corporeality towards his true content dream and death. art and the dream represent the preliminary step to the true collectivity of the redemption from all reason. hugo ball's language is also a magic treasure and connects him with the language of light and darkness. through language too man can grow into real life.

Translated from the German mss by Eugene Jolas

transition 21

fragments from a

Hugo Ball   *Dada Diary*

March 3, 1916 Introduce symmetries and rhythms instead of principles. Contradict the existing world orders . . .

What we are celebrating is at once a buffoonery and a requiem mass . . .

June 12, 1916 What we call Dada is a harlequinade made of nothingness in which all higher questions are involved, a gladiator's gesture, a play with shabby debris, an execution of postured morality and plenitude . . .

The Dadaist loves the extraordinary, the absurd, even. He knows that life asserts itself in contradictions, and that his age, more than any preceding it, aims at the destruction of all generous impulses. Every kind of mask is therefore welcome to him, every play at hide and seek in which there is an inherent power of deception. The direct and the primitive appear to him in the midst of this huge antinature, as being the supernatural itself . . .

The bankruptcy of ideas having destroyed the concept of humanity to its very innermost strata, the instincts and hereditary backgrounds are now emerging pathologically. Since no art, politics, or religious faith seems adequate to dam this torrent, there remain only the *blague* and the bleeding pose . . .

The Dadaist trusts more in the sincerity of events than in the wit of persons. To him persons may be had cheaply, his own person not excepted. He no longer believes in the comprehension of things from *one* point of departure, but is nevertheless convinced of the union of all things, of totality, to such an extent that he suffers from dissonances to the point of self-dissolution . . .

The Dadaist fights against the death throes and death drunkenness of his time. Averse to every clever reticence, he cultivates the curiosity of one who experiences delight even in the most questionable forms of insubordination. He knows that this world of systems has gone to pieces, and that the age which demanded cash has organized a bargain sale of godless philosophies. Where bad conscience begins for the market-booth owners, mild laughter and mild kindliness begin for the Dadaist . . .

The image differentiates us. Through the image we comprehend. Whatever it may be—it is night—we hold the print of it in our hands . . .

The word and the image are one. Painting and composing poetry belong together. Christ is image and word. The word and the image are crucified . . .

June 18, 1916   We have developed the plasticity of the word to a point which can hardly be surpassed. This result was achieved at the price of the logically constructed, rational sentence, and therefore, also, by renouncing the document (which is only possible by means of a time-robbing grouping of sentences in a logically ordered syntax). We were assisted in our efforts by the special circumstances of our age, which does not allow a real talent either to rest or ripen, forcing it to a premature test of its capacities, as well as by the emphatic élan of our group, whose members sought to surpass each other by an even greater intensification and accentuation of their platform. People may smile, if they want to; language will thank us for our zeal, even if there should not be any directly visible results. We have charged the word with forces and energies which made it possible for us to rediscover the evangelical concept of the "word" (logos) as a magical complex of images . . .

August 5, 1916   Childhood as a new world, and everything childlike and fantastic, everything childlike and direct, everything childlike and symbolical in opposition to the senilities of the world of grown-ups. The child will be the accuser on Judgment Day, the Crucified One will judge, the Resurrected One will pardon. The distrust of children, their shut-in quality, their escape from our recognition—their recognition that they won't be understood anyway . . .

Childhood is not at all as obvious as is generally assumed. It is a world to which hardly any attention is paid, with its own laws, without whose application there is no art, and without whose religious and philosophic recognition art cannot exist or be apprehended . . .

The credulous imagination of children, however, is also exposed to corruption and deformation. To surpass oneself in naivete and childishness—that is still the best antidote . . .

November 21, 1916   Note about a criticism of individualism: The accentuated "I" has constant interests, whether they be greedy, dictatorial, vain, or lazy. It always follows appetites, so long as it does not become absorbed in society. Whoever renounces his interests, renounces his "I." The "I" and the interests are identical. Therefore, the individualistic-egoistic ideal of the Renaissance ripened to the general union of the mechanized appetites which we now see before us, bleeding and disintegrating.

January 9, 1917   We should burn all libraries and allow to remain only that which everyone knows by heart. A beautiful age of the legend would then begin . . .

The middle ages praised not only foolishness, but even idiocy. The barons sent their children to board with idiotic families so that they might learn humility . . .

March 30, 1917   The new art is sympathetic because in an age of total disruption it has conserved the will-to-the-image; because it is inclined to force the image, even though the means and parts be antagonistic. Convention triumphs in the moralistic evaluation of the parts and details; art cannot be concerned with this. It drives towards the indwelling, all-connecting life nerve; it is indifferent to external resistance. One might also say: morals are withdrawn from convention, and utilized for the sole purpose of sharpening the senses of measure and weight . . .

March 7, 1917   One might also speak of Klee as follows: He always presents himself as quite small and playful. In an age of the colossal he falls in love with a green leaf, a little star, a butterfly wing; and since heaven and infinity are reflected in them, he paints them in. The point of his pencil, his brush, tempt him to minutiae. He always remains quite near first beginnings and the smallest format. The beginning possesses him and will not let him go. When he reaches the end, he does not start a new leaf at once, but begins to paint over the first one. The little formats are filled with intensity, become magic letters and colored palimpsests . . .

What irony, approaching sarcasm even, must this artist feel for our hollow, empty epoch. Perhaps there is no man today who is so master of himself as Klee. He scarcely detaches himself from his inspiration. He knows the shortest path from his inspiration to the page. The wide, distracting, stretching out of the hand and body which Kandinsky needs to fill the great formats of his canvases, necessarily brings waste and fatigue; it demands an exhaustive exposition, and explanation. Painting, when it seeks to retain unity and soul, becomes a sermon, or music.

April 18, 1917   Perhaps the art which we are seeking is the key to every former art: a Solomonic key that will open all mysteries.

Dadaism—a mask play, a burst of laughter? And behind it, a synthesis of the romantic, dandyistic and—demonistic theories of the 19th century.

From "Flucht aus der Zeit" (Duncker & Humbolt, Munich)
Translated from the German by Eugene Jolas
transition 25

Richard Huelsenbeck   *Dada Lives*

In 1916, Hugo Ball founded the Cabaret Voltaire in Zurich, Switzerland. He had left Germany because of his pacifist convictions, and wanted to create, through this Cabaret, a platform for himself in Switzerland, since, at that time, shelter to political refugees was still granted there. With his wife, Emmy Hennings, he organized a center to express the aims of the creative man smothered by the World War. The name of Voltaire was not chosen accidentally, but out of veneration for a man who had fought all his life for the liberation of the creative forces from the tutelage of the advocates of power.

Dadaism was born in the Cabaret Voltaire in 1916. In order to understand why it still lives and why it created such a sensation throughout the world, one must know the special circumstances of its genesis. Among Hugo Ball's intimate collaborators, besides his wife, Emmy Hennings, and myself, were Hans Arp, and the Rumanians, Tristan Tzara and Marcel Janco. Our work in the Cabaret Voltaire had, from the very beginning, an antimilitaristic, revolutionary tendency. Friends came to visit us from the various belligerent countries—from Italy, the Futurists; from Paris, Picabia; from Germany, René Schickelé and Werfel. All of them, even the Futurists, loathed the senseless, systematic massacre of modern warfare.

We were not politicians, but artists searching for an expression that would correspond to our demands for a new art. All of us were enemies of the old rationalistic, bourgeois art which we regarded as symptomatic of a culture about to crumble with the war. We loathed every form of an art that merely imitated nature and we admired, instead, the Cubists and Picasso. We agreed with the Futurists that most public monuments should be smashed with a hammer, and we delighted in the nonrepresentational experiments of Hans Arp, Van Rees, and Marcel Janco.

One day Hugo Ball was seated in his modest room in a Zurich tenement flat. Besides his wife, I was the only person present. We were discussing the question of a name for our idea, we needed a slogan which might epitomize for a larger public the whole complex of our direction. This was all the more necessary since we were about to launch a publication in which all of us wanted to set forth our ideas about the new art.

We were conscious of the difficulty of our task. Our art had to be young, it had to be new, it had to integrate all the experimental tendencies of the Futurists and Cubists. Above everything, our art had to be international, for we believed in an *Internationale* of the Spirit and not in different national concepts.

Hugo Ball sat in an armchair holding a German-French dictionary on his knees. He was busy in those days with the preliminary work for a long book in which he wanted to show the deleterious changes German civilization had undergone as a result of Luther's influence. Consequently, he was studying countless German and French books on history.

I was standing behind Ball looking into the dictionary. Ball's finger pointed to the first letter of each word descending the page. Suddenly I cried halt. I was struck by a word I had never heard before, the word Dada.

"Dada," Ball read, and added: "It is a children's word meaning hobbyhorse." At that moment I understood what advantages the word held for us.

"Let's take the word Dada," I said. "It's just made for our purpose. The child's first sound expresses the primitiveness, the beginning at zero, the new in our art. We could not find a better word."

Emmy Hennings, who in those days was already oriented towards Catholicism and who, at that very moment, was busy erecting an altar in another corner of the room, came over to us. She, too, thought that dada was an excellent word. "Then we'll take Dada as the slogan for our new artistic direction," said Ball. That was the hour of the birth of Dadaism. The following day we told our friends, Tristan Tzara, Marcel Janco, and Hans Arp what we had found and decided on. They were enthusiastic about the word dada.

And so it happened that it was I who pronounced the word dada for the first time. I was the first to point it out and to insist that we use it as a slogan for our efforts. I do not mean to overestimate this service, for Dada has become the symbol of the totality of our artistic expressions. But it is perhaps important to restate the authorship of Dada since today Dadaism assumes once more a very special importance. My idea of Dada was always different from that of Tristan Tzara who, after the dissolution of the Cabaret Voltaire, founded and became the leader of Dadaism in Paris.

Dada, in my opinion, is intimately connected with the events that are shaking the world today. Dada is regarded in present-day Germany as the symbol of destructive art. It is in this that lies its immortal service. In the word Dada there is still such revolutionary force that the Chancellor of a great empire, himself, poured forth his rage against it for a whole hour, menacing the Dadaists and their successors with arrest.[1]

Dada as an artistic direction in painting, the plastic arts, and literature could never be accurately defined (in contradistinction to Futurism and Cubism which were artistic creeds with definite programs). Tzara, in Paris, eliminated from Dadaism its revolutionary and creative element and attempted to compete with other artistic movements. That, of course, after a while, was bound to lead to failure, and I cannot feel any surprise that Dadaism should have been rejected in the classical land of rationalism.

Dada is a perpetual, revolutionary "pathos" aimed at rationalistic bourgeois art. In itself it is not an artistic movement. To quote the German Chancellor, the revolutionary element in Dada was always greater than its constructive element. Tzara did not invent Dadaism, nor did he really understand it. Under Tzara in Paris Dada was deformed for the private use of a few persons so that its action was almost a snobbish one. What Dada really is, and what it still means today, can be gauged from the hatred nurtured against it by people who would like to turn the history of the world backward and bring back the old, rationalistic, bourgeois art.

The eternal value of Dada can be deduced from the fact that in Germany an exhibition of "Dadaistic Works of Shame and Filth" was

---

[1] Vide: Hitler's Nuremberg speech of 1934 and also his *Mein Kampf*.

organized officially in order to frighten off the constructive burghers. Dada is forever the enemy of that comfortable Sunday Art which is supposed to uplift man by reminding him of agreeable moments. Dada hurts. Dada does not jest, for the reason that it was experienced by revolutionary men and not by philistines who demand that art be a decoration for the mendacity of their own emotions.

While Tzara transformed Dadaism into an artistic movement, I felt it to be a volcanic eruption. That I was right is proven by the present times and the evolution of the world. Everywhere, throughout the world, where forces are at work to turn back the wheel of history, Dada will be hated. Therefore it is not difficult to predict a great future for Dada. Dada will experience a golden age, but in another form than the one imagined by the Paris Dadaists.

I am firmly convinced that all art will become Dadaistic in the course of time, because from Dada proceeds the perpetual urge for its renovation. I am glad to have contributed my share to this change.

Indian Acres
Fryeburg, Maine
August, 1936

> *Translated from the German manuscript*
> *by* Eugene Jolas
>
> *transition 25*

Georges Ribemont-Dessaignes   *Poem*

He put his hat upon the ground and filled it with earth
And sowed therein a tear with his finger
Up sprang a large geranium
Countless pumpkins ripened in the foliage
He opened his mouth with its gold teeth and said
Oo-wii
He shook the branches of the babylon willow cooling the air
And the pregnant woman through the skin of her womb
Showed the child the crescent of a stillborn moon
Put on his head the hat imported from Germany

The woman had a miscarriage by Mozart
While in an armored car there passed
A harpist
And amid the sky of doves
Tender Mexican doves ate Spanish flies.

*Translated from the French
by* Eugene Jolas

transition 3

Antonin Artaud   *The Parson and the Shell*
film scenario

The cinema today seems to be at a parting of the ways, and both the avenues ahead of it may well prove to be blind alleys. On the one hand we have the "pure" or abstract cinema; the other way leads to a commonplace, hybrid art which depicts, more or less adequately, psychological situations which would be in place on the stage or in the pages of a book, but not on the screen where they exist only as the pale image of a world whose real existence and significance lie elsewhere.

All that the pure or abstract cinema has given us so far is obviously lacking in one of the essentials of cinematographic art. For, however great may be the aptitude of the human mind to work its way to the core of every abstraction, we remain insensible to pure geometrical shapes, which in themselves mean nothing and are devoid of that sensory quality which alone can give significance to the motion picture. The deeper we dig down into the human mind, the clearer it is that every emotion, even an intellectual emotion, is based on an affective sensation, a nervous process, involving (even if only in a minor degree) a material basis of some kind or other, a vibration which is the reflex of certain experienced or imagined states, presented under aspects already apprehended in our dreams or waking hours. The significance of pure cinema, then, would depend on the reconstitution of images of this kind, adjusted to the rhythm and movement which are the specific qualities of the art of the cinema.

On the one hand, then, we have the purely linear abstraction (and an interplay of light and shade comes under this category) and, on the other, the psychological film, which illustrates the development of a narrative, whether dramatic or otherwise. But between these extremes there is room for an art of the cinema, whose value and purport have been, so far, entirely overlooked by producers.

The emotion or humor of the adventure film depends wholly on the narrative, apart from the pictures; with some rare exceptions, all the meaning of such films is derived from the captions, and this is true even of those films which ostensibly dispense with subtitles; the emotion is of a verbal order and calls for the aid of words or, anyhow, a verbal interpretation; for the action and images derive from an explicable situation. You will look in vain for a film which is based on purely visual situations, whose action springs from stimuli addressed to the eye only and is founded, so to speak, on the essential qualities of eyesight, untrammeled by psychological and irrelevant complications or by a verbal story expressed in visual terms. It is futile to look for an equivalent of written language in visual language—such a translation from one idiom to another is foredoomed to failure. The essence of the visual language should be so presented, and the action should be such, that any translation would be out of the question; the visual action should operate on the mind as an intuition.

In the scenario which follows I have tried to realize this conception of a purely visual cinema, where action entirely ousts psychology. Though no doubt my scenario falls short of the acme of what can be done on these lines, it is yet a precursor. I do not suggest that psychology should be wholly banned; that is not the ideal I propose for the cinema—far from it. But such psychology should be presented under a living, dynamic aspect, exempt from glosses, inserted to explain the so-called motives of our acts by a preposterous logic, instead of exhibiting such acts in all their primitive, indeed barbarous, inconsequence.

This scenario is not the story of a dream, and does not profess to be such; and I shall not try to justify its incoherence by the simple device of labeling it a dream. Dreams have a logic of their own; more, they have a life of their own, infused with darkly rational truth. This scenario seeks to portray a dark truth of the mind by a series of pictures, self-engendered and owing nothing to the circumstances whence they spring, but governed by, so to speak, an inherent and ineluctable necessity of their own, which forces them out into the light.

The outer skin of things, the epidermis of reality, these are the raw material of the cinema. In glorifying the material, it reveals the profound spirituality of matter and its relation to the mind of man whence it is derived. The pictures come to birth, each the offspring of its predecessor, *qua* picture, and the objective synthesis which they depict is more authentic than any abstraction. They create an autonomous world of their own. And from this interplay of images, a transubstantiation of elements, there arises an inorganic language which works on our minds by an osmosis and demands no translation into words. Since the cinema handles matter itself, the action which it creates springs from the impact of objects, of shapes, attractions, repulsions. It does not cut itself off from life, but rediscovers things in their primitive arrangement. The most successful films are those where there is a marked element of humor—as, for instance, in the early Malec films and those of Charlie Chaplin where the "human interest" is at its minimum. Humor at its wildest—that is the stuff of a cinema faceted with the glamor of dreams, a cinema full of the breath of life. A perpetual movement of objects, shapes, and appearances is best realized in the convulsions, the death throes, of reality, lacerated by an irony which is the cry of the human soul strained to breaking-point.

The first view shows us a man, dressed in black, mixing a liquid in glasses of different height and capacity. To decant the liquid from one glass to another he uses a sort of oyster shell, and breaks each glass after he has employed it. There is an immense pile of phials beside him. Presently a door opens; an army officer enters. He is a prosperous-looking fellow, fat and debonair, beplastered with medals. After him trails a gigantic sword. Like a spider he prowls around, now in a dark corner, now on the ceiling. As each phial is shattered, the officer gives a jump. Now we see him stand behind the man in black and take the oyster shell from his hands. The latter allows him to do this, with a quaint air of astonishment. The officer walks once or twice round the room, holding the shell; then he draws his sword from the scabbard and cleaves the shell with a swinging blow. The whole room quivers at the impact. The lamps flicker and on each blob of light hovers a sword point. The officer strides out of the room, followed on all fours by the clergyman (for such the man in black seems to be).

We see the clergyman still on all fours, trotting along a street. A series of street corners flashes across the screen. Suddenly an open carriage, drawn by four horses, appears; in it is seated the officer, accompanied by a very beautiful woman with white hair. Crouching at a street corner, the clergyman watches the carriage go by and then runs after it at top speed. The carriage comes to a church. Officer and woman alight and, entering the church, move towards a confession box. Together they enter it. At this moment the clergyman springs up and throws himself on the officer. The officer's face swells, grows lined and pimpled; the clergyman is holding in his arms not an officer but a Catholic priest. It seems that the white-haired woman also is aware of the priest, but she sees him differently. In a series of close-ups we are shown the priest's face, amiable and complacent as it appears to the woman's eyes; savage and menacing when it is turned to the clergyman. Night falls with strange swiftness. The clergyman lifts the priest in his arms and swings him to and fro; around him the air grows blank and now we see that he is on a mountain top. At his feet lies (in superimpression) a tangle of rivers and plains. The priest is hurled from the clergyman's arms like a bullet, a projectile which, exploding, falls dizzily through space.

The woman and the clergyman are in the confessional. The clergyman's head quivers like a leaf and of a sudden it seems as if some inner voice begins to speak within him. He rolls up his sleeves and softly, ironically, taps thrice the panels of the confessional. The woman gets up. Then the clergyman crashes the door open with a mad blow of his fist. He eyes the woman before him. Then he throws himself on her and tears open her dress as though to lacerate her breasts. But these now appear covered with a carapace of shells. He tears off this breastplate and brandishes it flashing in the air. As he frantically waves it the scene suddenly changes to a ballroom. Couples enter, some treading stealthily on tiptoe, others in febrile haste. The candelabra seem to follow the movements of the dancers. The women have opulent breasts, bobbed hair, and very short skirts displaying their legs.

A royal pair enter—the officer and woman whom we already know— and take their seats on a dais. The couples are closely linked together. In one corner is a man alone, about him a wide empty space. He is holding an oyster shell, peering down at it with a strangely rapt regard. We gradually recognize in him the clergyman. But suddenly this self-same clergyman enters, upsetting everything in his way and holding the carapace or breastplate which he was wildly brandishing a moment ago. He raises it aloft as though he were going to belabor a couple of the dancers. But at this moment the couples are frozen into rigidity, the white-haired woman and officer melt into the air, and this same woman appears at the other end of the room in the archway of a door which has just opened.

This apparition seems to alarm the clergyman. He drops the breastplate which, as it falls, sends up a column of flame. Then, as if moved by a sudden access of shame, he makes the gesture of wrapping his garments tight about him. But as he grips his coattails to draw them over his thighs, the coattails seem to lengthen out and form a vast avenue of darkness. Along the darkness, clergyman and woman run like souls demented.

The scene of their flight is interspersed with images of the woman in various states: sometimes her cheek is hugely swollen, now she sticks out her tongue and, as it lengthens out into infinity, the clergyman clutches it as if it were a rope; sometimes her chest swells to fearful dimensions.

At the end of their course we see the clergyman trotting down a passage, while the woman seems to swim after him in a sort of sky-scape.

Appears a huge door, studded with iron. The door opens to some unseen pressure and the clergyman walks backwards, calling to some-one in front of him who does not come. He enters a large room in which there is a great glass globe. Still walking backwards, he beckons an invisible person.

We feel that this person is near him. He raises his arms as if to embrace a woman's body. At the moment when he is sure he holds this phantom, this viewless double, he flings himself on it and strangles it, grimacing with sadistic glee. We grow aware that he is introducing the severed head into the glass bowl.

He is in the corridors again, he seems at a loss and is twiddling a big key in his hands. He scurries along a passage at the end of which is a door; he opens the door with the key. Beyond the door there is another passage and, at the end of this, two people—the same woman and the decorated officer.

A scene of flight and pursuit. From all sides fists batter on a door. The clergyman is in a ship's cabin. He gets up from his bunk and goes on deck. The officer is there, in chains. Now the clergyman seems to meditate and pray but, when he raises his head, two mouths which touch each other, level with his eyes, reveal to him the officer beside the woman who a moment ago was not there. The body of the woman is suspended vertically in the air.

He is shaken by a paroxysm. It seems as if the fingers of his hands were twitching to throttle a neck. But between his hands there appear sky pictures, phosphorescent landscapes; ghostly white, he passes on his ship under domes of stalactites.

Distant view of the ship far away on a silver sea.

Close-up of the clergyman's head, reclining, breathing.

From his parted lips, from between his eyelashes, stream glistening vapors which, condensing in a corner of the screen, reveal a city or landscapes of an intense luminosity. Finally, his head fades out and houses, landscapes, and cities swirl together, tangled and disentangled, forming a fantastic firmament of celestial lagoons and incandescent stalactites. Beneath grottoes and clouds and lagoons we see the outline of the ship, moving to and fro, black against the white background of cities, white against mirages which suddenly turn black.

On all sides doors and windows are flung open. Light floods the room.

What room? The room which contains the glass globe. A troop of servants and housewives invade the room, carrying brooms and buckets, and rush to the windows. They scour the room with passion, with a frenetic zest. A woman who seems to be the housekeeper, dressed in black, enters, a Bible in her hand, and takes her stand at a window. When we see her face, we recognize the handsome woman we know. In the street outside we see a priest hurrying forward, and behind him a girl in a sports costume holding a tennis racket. She is playing with a boy whom we have not seen before.

The priest enters the house. Menservants arrive from all directions and line up in an imposing retinue. But, to enable the cleaning to proceed, it is necessary to shift the glass globe, which turns out to be a sort of vase filled with water. It passes from hand to hand, and at moments it seems as if a human head were moving in it. The housekeeper calls in the boy and girl from the garden. The priest too is present. Once again we are confronted with the clergyman and the woman. It seems that they are going to be married. But at this moment there crowd together from the edges of the screen the visions seen by the clergyman when he slept. A huge ship approaches, bisecting the screen. The ship vanishes and we see a staircase leading up the sky, down which comes the clergyman, headless now, carrying a parcel. When he enters the room where all the people are assembled, he unfastens the parcel and produces the glass globe. All watch him intently. Then, leaning down, he breaks the globe, from which emerges a head, his own head.

The head makes a foul grimace.

He is holding it in his hand as if it were a hat. The head is placed on an oyster shell. As he raises the shell to his lips, the head melts and becomes a dark liquid which he drinks up, his eyes closed.

*Translated from the French
by* Stuart Gilbert
transition 19-20

André Breton   *fragment from*
                    Mad Love

Dear Chipnut of Munkhazel,

In the lovely spring of 1952, you will have just turned sixteen, and perhaps you will be tempted to open this book, the title of which, I like to believe, will be wafted to you euphonically by the wind that bends the hawthorn. . . . All dreams, all hopes, all illusions will, I trust, be dancing night and day by the light of your curly locks and I, doubtless, shall no longer be here, I, who would only desire to be here in order to see you. At dusk, mysterious, radiant horsemen will come dashing by, along the banks of ever-changing streams. A young girl clad in filmy, sea-green veils will glide somnambulistically underneath tall archways, lighted by the flicker of a single devotional lamp. But the spirits in the reeds, the tiny catkins that pretend to sleep in rings, the smart toy-pistol shot through with the word "Ball," will keep you from taking these scenes too tragically. Whatever may be your lot, whether never fair enough, or otherwise, I can't tell, you will take joy in living, in expecting all of love. Whatever may happen between now and the moment you see this letter—and apparently it is the unsupposable that is destined to happen—let me believe that you will then be ready to incarnate this eternal force of woman, the only one to which I have ever made obeisance. Whether you will have just closed a school-desk on a highly fantastic crow-blue world, or whether you already cast a solar silhouette, except for the flower at your waist, on the wall of a factory— I am far from certain as to your future—let me believe that these words, "mad love," will one day be the only ones that correspond to your delirium.

They will not keep their promise, since all they will do will be to enlighten you as to the mystery of your birth. For a long time I had thought that the height of folly was to give life. In any case, I felt resentful towards those who had given it to me. It may be that, on certain days, you will feel resentful towards me. In fact, that is why I have chosen to see you at sixteen, when you will be incapable of feeling resentment. What am I saying? To see you, no; to try to see you through your eyes, to see myself through your eyes.

My wee little child, with your barely eight months, and your continual smile, you who are made like both coral and pearls, you will understand then that all element of chance was strictly excluded from your coming, that this event took place at the very hour when it was supposed to take place, neither earlier nor later, and that no shadow hovered about your little reed cradle. Even the rather intense poverty, which had been and remains mine, called a truce for a few days. As it happens, I was not opposed to this poverty; I had agreed to pay the price for my non-slavery to life, to settle for the right I had assumed once and for all, to express no other ideas than my own. There were not so many of us. . . . Poverty passed at a distance, very much embellished, justified almost, somewhat as in what has been termed, for a certain painter who was one of your very first friends, *the blue period*. It seemed to be the almost inevitable consequence of my refusal to accept conditions which nearly all the others, in whatever camp, had accepted. Though you may or may not have had time to learn to dread it, remember that this poverty was but the other side of the miraculous coin of our existence: without it the "Night of the Sunflower" would have been less radiant.

Less radiant, because then love would not have had to face all it did face, because it would not have had to count entirely on itself, in order to triumph. This was perhaps a great piece of imprudence, but it was just this imprudence which was the brightest jewel in the case. Beyond this imprudence there remained no alternative other than to commit an even greater one: that of causing you to be born, imprudence whose perfumed breath you are. It was necessary at least to stretch a magic cord from one to the other, to stretch it so that it would break over a precipice, in order that beauty might pluck you like some impossible serial flower, with no aid other than her own balancing-rod. May you one day believe that you are this flower, that you were born entirely without contact with the unfortunately unsterile soil of what are commonly referred to as "the affairs of men." For you spring from the mere shimmer of that which, rather tardily, was for me the goal of poetry, to which I had devoted my youth, and which I have continued to serve, scorning all that was not poetry. You appeared there as if by enchantment, and should you ever detect a trace of sadness in these words which, for the first time, I am addressing *to you alone,* say to yourself that this enchantment continues and will always continue to be identified with you, and that it is great enough to surmount every heartbreak. *Always* and *for long,* those two solemn enemy words which confront each other whenever love is mentioned, never exchanged more blinding stabs than they did today, over my head, in a sky that was all blue, like your eyes, with their whites that are still so blue. Of these two words, the one that wears my colors, even though its star may be waning now, even though it be destined to lose, is *always*. Always, as in the vows young girls ask for. Always, as on the white sand of time and, thanks to the instrument which serves to count it (but, so far, only fascinates you and leaves you famished) reduced to an endless, fine stream of milk issuing from a glass breast. Despite everything, I shall have maintained that this *always* is the master key. That which I have once loved, whether I have kept it or not, I shall continue to love *always*. Since you will be called upon to suffer too, I wanted to explain certain things to you before reaching the end of this book. I mentioned earlier the "sublime peak" of a mountain. There was never any question of my settling permanently on this peak. In fact, from then on, it would have ceased to be sublime, and I should have ceased to be a man. But although unable to settle there, at least I have never gone so far away from it as to lose sight of it, or to be unable to point it out to others. I chose to be the guide, in consequence of which I forced myself to be worthy of that power which, in the direction of eternal love, made me *see* and granted me the rarer privilege of *making others see*. I have never been unworthy of this trust, I have never ceased to identify the flesh of the being I love with the snow on the heights at sunrise. Of love, I have only wanted to know the hours of triumph, which I now clasp in a necklace about your throat. But I am sure you will understand the weakness of my attachment to the last pearl of all, the black one; you will understand what ultimate hope of *conjuration* I have placed on it. I do not deny that love has a crow to pick with life. But I insist that love must win, and that to this end, it must have risen to such poetic consciousness of itself that every necessarily hostile encounter will melt in the flame of its own glory.

At least this will have been at all times my greatest hope, a hope that is in no way diminished by my occasional incapacity to prove myself worthy. And should it ever have mingled with another, I shall make sure that the latter touches you no less closely. Since I wanted your existence to be conscious of the following *raison d'être,* namely, that I had asked it of what for me, in all the force of the word, was beauty, in all the force of the word, love—the name I gave you at the head of this letter does not represent for me, in its anagrammatical form, merely a charming account of your *present* aspect, since long after I invented it for you, I realized that the words which composed it on page 66[1] of this book had served to characterize the very aspect which *love* had taken for me: (this must be what we mean by *resemblance*). I also wanted everything that I hope for from human becoming, everything

---

[1] "Her smile at this moment leaves me today the memory of a chipmunk holding a green hazel-nut."

which, in my opinion, is worth a collective rather than an individual effort, to cease to be a formal mode of thinking, even the noblest, in order for it to confront this reality, this living becoming, that is yourself. What I mean is that I feared, at one time in my life, that I should be deprived of the necessary contact, the human contact, with what will come after me. *After me,* this idea keeps getting lost, but turns up again, marvelously, through a certain sleight of hand which you possess *like* (and for me, not like) all little children. From the very first day I was filled with admiration for your hand. It hovered about all I had tried to construct intellectually, making it seem almost inane. What a mad thing is that little hand, and how I pity those who have not had the opportunity of bejeweling the loveliest page of a book with its starry form! Even a flower seems suddenly poor. One has only to look at this hand to know that man makes ridiculous use of what he pretends to know. All that he understands about this hand is that, from every standpoint, it has been fashioned as best it could be. This blind aspiration towards the best would suffice to justify love as I conceive it, that is, absolute love, as being the only principle of physical and moral selection capable of guaranteeing the non-vanity of human presence and human witness.

I thought of all this somewhat feverishly, in September, 1936, alone with you in my famous, uninhabitable, rock-salt house. I thought of it between reading the newspapers that recounted more or less hypocritically the different episodes of the Spanish civil war, newspapers behind which you thought I disappeared in order to play hide and seek with you. And that, too, was true, because in those moments the unconscious and the conscious, in your form and in mine, existed, side by side, in complete duality. They were in entire ignorance of each other and yet were able to communicate at will through the single powerful thread that was the exchange of glances between us. Indeed, at that moment, my life hung by a thread. The temptation was great to go and offer it to those who, without possible error or distinction of tendencies, wanted, at any price, to finish with the old "order" founded on the cult of that abject trinity: family, fatherland, and religion. And yet you held me back by that thread which is the thread of happiness, as it appears in the woof of unhappiness itself. In you I loved all the children of the Spanish militia, like those I had seen running about naked in the pepper groves of Santa-Cruz, on Tenerife Island. May the sacrifice of so many lives one day make *happy* human beings of them! And yet I did not feel that I had the courage to expose you, as well as myself, to help make this come about.

Above all, the idea of family should be buried deep in the ground! If

I have loved in you the accomplishment of a natural necessity, it is in exact proportion to the degree that this necessity, in your person, was one with what, for me, was human, *logical* necessity; and the reconciliation of these two necessities has always seemed to me to be the only marvelous thing within the grasp of man, to be the only possible chance that he has to escape from the meanness of his estate. You progressed from non-being to being by virtue of one of those agreements that are the only ones to which I care to lend an ear. You were posited as possible, as certain, at the moment when, in a love that was deeply self-confident, a man and a woman desired you.

Leave you! It is of too much importance to me to hear you reply one day in all innocence to those insidious questions which grown people put to children! "With what do we think? Do we suffer? How did we learn the name of the sun? Where does the night come from?" As if they knew themselves! And since you are for me the human creature in its perfect authenticity, in all likelihood you will have to teach me these things.

My wish is that you may be loved to the point of madness.

Translated from the French
by Maria Jolas
transition 27

Paul Eluard   *In Company*
                  (Surrealist text)

I do not mourn—but merely because mourning is an insufficient form of despair—the time when I was suspicious, or still hoped to have an enemy to vanquish, some dent to make in human nature, or some sacred hiding place. Suspicion was then still the stopping place, the delectable substantiation of the finite. A thread drawn by a swallow which, open-winged, forms the point of the arrow, and distorts the appearance of man as well as his reality. The wind will not go where man wants it to go. Luckily. These are frontiers of error, here are the blind who do not want to put their feet where the step is missing, here are the mute who think with words, here are the deaf who bid the world's noises grow silent.

Tired limbs, my word, do not separate easily. Their ignorance of solitude prevents them from giving themselves up to crafty individual experiences of amusing physique, crumbs of the great rest, so many minute bursts of laughter of the wistarias and acacias in the setting.

The spring of virtue is not dried up. Large beautiful eyes that are wide open still serve for the contemplation of industrious hands that have never done evil and that are bored and bore everyone else. The lowest reckonings close these eyes each day. They favor sleep only to plunge later into the contemplation of industrious hands that have never done evil and are bored and bore everyone else. An odious business.

All this lives: this patient insect body, this loving bird body, this loyal mammiferous body, this lean, vain body of the beast of my childhood, all this lives. Only its head has died. I had to kill it. My face understands me no longer. And there are no others.

From "Les Dessous d'une Vie ou La Pyramide Humaine"
(Les Cahiers du Sud, Marseille)
Translated from the French by Eugene Jolas
***transition* 2**

Paul Eluard   *A Dream*

I meet her on the sidewalk of a deserted Paris street. The sky of an indefinite color gives me the feeling of great physical liberty. I do not see the face of the woman who is the color of the hour, but I find great pleasure in not taking my eyes from the place where she is. Somehow I seem to be passing through the four seasons. At the end of a long moment, the woman slowly unties the knots of the multicolored ribbons she has on her breasts and body. Then appears her face, white and hard as marble.

From "Les Dessous d'une Vie ou La Pyramide Humaine"
(Les Cahiers du Sud, Marseille)
Translated from the French by Eugene Jolas
***transition* 2**

Comte de Lautréamont
(*Isidore Ducasse*)

from
The Lay of Maldoror
(*Canto I, fragment*)

When, in a remote moonlit landscape by the sea, one sits plunged in bitter meditation, everything assumes a yellowish, blurred, fantastic appearance. Quickly, then slowly, the shadows of the trees race back and forth in varying forms, flattened out or clinging close to the earth. In the past, when I was carried away upon the wings of youth, this used to set me to dreaming, it seemed strange to me; now I am used to it. The wind moans its languorous notes through the leaves, and the owl sings a solemn lament that makes the listener's hair stand on end. Then it is that dogs, driven wild, burst their chains and escape from the distant farms; they dash through the countryside in every direction, a prey to madness. Suddenly they stop, look all about them with savage restlessness, their eyes blazing; and like the elephant which, as it is about to die in the desert, casts one last glance skywards, then raises its trunk despairingly, while its ears droop inert, the dogs too let their ears droop, lift their heads, puff out their frightful necks and, one after the other, like a baby crying with hunger, or a wounded cat on a roof, or a woman about to bring forth, or a plague victim dying in hospital, or a young girl's exalted singing, they begin to bay at the northern stars, the eastern stars, the southern stars, the western stars; at the moon and at the mountains, which resemble giant rocks reclining in the darkness; at the icy air which they inhale deeply, and which makes the inside of their nostrils red and burning; at the nocturnal silence; at the owl carrying a rat or a frog in its beak—living food, so tender for the young—and which brushes against their muzzles in its crooked flight; at the hare which disappears in the twinkling of an eye; at the thief who, having committed his crime, flees as fast as hoofs will carry him; at the snake which sets the heather astir and causes their skins to quiver and their teeth to chatter; at their own baying which frightens them; at the toad which they crush with one snap of the jaw (why did it ever leave the marsh?); at the trees, whose gently swaying leaves are so many incomprehensible mysteries for them, mysteries they

seek to solve with their staring, intelligent eyes; at the spider hanging
between its long legs, and which clambers up trees to safety; at the
crow which, having found nothing to eat all day, returns on weary
wings to the nest; at the rocks on the shore; at lights which appear on
the masts of invisible ships; at the dull noise of the waves; at the great
fish which show their black backs as they swim, then disappear into
the depths; and, finally, at man, who enslaves them. After which, they
begin again to rush through the countryside, leaping with bloodstained
paws across ditches, roads, fields, grass tufts and craggy rocks. One
might think that they were quite mad, and in search of some vast pool
in which to quench their thirst. All nature is terrified by their prolonged baying. But woe to the belated traveler! These friends of ceme-
teries will leap upon him, will tear him limb from limb, and devour
him with blood-dripping fangs; for their teeth are not decayed. Wild
animals, not daring to approach to share the repast of flesh, flee, trembling, from sight. After some hours, the dogs, harassed and half dead
from running in every direction, their tongues hanging out of their
mouths, leap at one another and with incredible swiftness tear one another into a thousand shreds. They do not behave this way out of
cruelty. Once, eying me glassily, my mother said to me: "When you
are in bed and you hear the baying of dogs in the countryside, hide
under the covers, do not mock their behavior; for like you, like me, like
the rest of pallid, long-faced humanity, they have an unquenchable
thirst for the infinite. I even allow you to stand at the window and observe this spectacle, which partakes of the sublime." Since then, I have
respected the wishes of the dead. Like dogs, I too feel the need of
the infinite . . . But I cannot, I cannot satisfy this need! According
to what I have been told, I am the son of man and of woman. This
surprises me . . . For I had thought better of myself! As for that,
what does it matter from whence I came? For myself, if it had been
a matter of my own will, I would have wished rather to be the son
of the female shark, whose hunger is the friend of tempests, and of
the tiger, whose cruelty is well known: I should be less malevolent.
You who look at me now, go, leave me, for I exhale a breath of poison.
No one has yet seen the green wrinkles in my forehead, nor the pro-
jecting bones of my emaciated face, like those of some enormous fish,
or the rocks that dot the seashore, or the sheer alpine heights, over
which I have often traveled when the hair on my head was a different
color. And on stormy nights, when I prowl about the habitations of
mankind, with burning eyes and hair lashed by the storm wind, solitary as a stone in the middle of the road, I cover my withered face
with a scrap of velvet that is as black as the soot that lines the inside
of chimneys: it would not do for eyes to witness the ugliness which

the Supreme Being laid upon me with a smile of mighty hate. Every morning, when the sun rises for others, dispensing joy and salutary warmth to all nature, while not one of my features moves, gazing fixedly into the shadow-filled space, crouching in the depths of my beloved cave, in a despair which intoxicates me like wine, with powerful hands I tear my breast to shreds. And yet I feel that I am not suffering from rabies! I feel that it is not I alone who suffer! I feel that I breathe! Like a condemned man who is soon to mount the scaffold, and who tries his muscles while meditating upon their fate, I stand upright upon my pallet, my eyes closed; I move my neck slowly from right to left for hours, and I do not fall down dead. At a given moment, when my neck can no longer keep turning in the same direction, and stops in order to begin to turn in the opposite direction, I suddenly see the horizon through the thick brush which covers the entrance: I see nothing! Nothing . . . but the countryside dancing in whirlwinds with the trees and long lines of birds crossing the sky. This upsets my blood and my brain . . . But who is it that is beating upon my head with an iron bar, like a hammer?

transition 7

Michel Leiris   *From the Heart to the Absolute*
"Un faisceau de raies noires légères."

A slight shock, the birth of a lizard which propagated itself with the noise of torn silk, and I found myself again lying beside a river which washed wood shavings and chips of tanned skin towards the brine of the Arctic seas.

In the caves of the earth thieves were heaping their treasures and counterfeiters were heating iron rods to mint coins bearing effigies of the dead. I no longer remembered the Ingénue, nor her deceits; I only remembered a bound, a rapid ascension and that vertiginous fall through the depth of a matrix whose indefinitely multiplied meanderings had led me to this place.

The landscape around me was desolate: no vegetation, but stone, stone and a few clouds. I noticed far away some abandoned quarries and wagons standing still. All wealth seemed to have crawled into the bowels of the earth, from which burst forth voices, sounds of brawls, and the blow of picks muted by the superimposed layers of stratifications which separated the obstinate seekers from the atmosphere. The air was heavy and impassible, not at all troubled by the caress of my lungs and I felt it on me like a glacier without moraines—this air which let no trace of its movements be marked by a bird.

The silence of the surface was hardly disturbed by a slight, very distant whir, the only perceptible vibration, to which my thought clung as to Ariadne's thread; it was the last organic ligament which held me still suspended above a mineral sleep; and I followed attentively the infinitely small variations of the sound engendered by that cord, which was sometimes lower or higher, in accordance with the very feeble modifications of the energy which animated it.

Yet after a few minutes, it seemed to me that the intensity of the humming sound was increasing, as if the object causing it were coming much nearer—and it was not long before I saw a black point emerge beyond the horizon—a point which soon became a line, and which moved following the direction of the river, a few meters above it, obeying the slightest turn made by the water. It was a bronze arrow which dragged in its wake a long white streamer on which I could read distinctly:

THE CATALAUNIC FIELDS

At the same time there approached a line of galleys manned by three ranks of rowers who followed the arrow with sails unfurled, their decks filled with armed warriors wearing shields and helmets.

Above their heads the pikes and rigging were crossed, forming a kind of net which bound the sky, while hanging from the masts, as breast-plates might hang from the spinal column, the sails showed distinctly the invisible torso of the air. I heard the cries of the maneuvering and noticed soothsayers circulating among the soldiers and explaining to them the predictions they should deduce from the dice game, while disheveled girls ran from one end of the deck to the other, the prettiest of them twirling flames and knives. All the boats were covered with oriflammes and statues of gods, and the largest of them carried a vast tent made of steel links, beneath which rested the Emperor, a thin, trembling old man who seemed bored under his purple mantle and at times raised his hand to adjust his crown while a nude young girl was huddled in front of him. He was protected by several rows of lances through which I saw the glitter of his scepter, pointed into the air in order to ward off lightning and other threats.

"All exigencies come from human blood," the centurions cried; their words punctuated by the toiling oh's of the rowers. *"An act of force: iron, fire, the future will be white with marvels."*

Mechanically I rose to watch the fleet pass by, but I noticed that my clothes were in rags and spattered with clay and seaweed. I ran away and hid behind a rock, and it was there I witnessed the landing of the Roman army and the flight of the barbarians; at that moment the arrow, which had become separated perpendicularly from the river, planted itself right on top of a little hill; the streamer, which was unnaturally long by now, had covered the entire plain and hid in the folds of its nineteen letters the rare accidents of the terrain and the diverse phases of the battle.

I saw the Catalaunic Fields stretching before me like a body of water swollen by cataclysms, and the plowed fields sharply determined the trail of the corpses whose ashes were being carried in closed urns to the catacombs. Strange mirage, the U was scooped like an urn; the two C's, extreme ends of the ploughshare, clove the plain for many ells, unleashing the catapults; and finally the S of treason serpentined with the last barbaric hordes who were vainly attempting a surprise action, before they fell back midst the hooting of panic.

When the combat was over, the nineteen letters crumbled together and became incrusted in the ground like memorial inscriptions.

Behind the Roman lines, I noticed the Huns in flight, brandishing torches as they ran. Many wagons got stuck in the swamps along the river, whole bands of men were sucked into the earth, and when the extremity of the firebrand they had lifted as high as possible had also disappeared, the flame became detached and fluttered about in the form of a will-o'-the-wisp. Millions of fires were thus lighted, in the dying day, while the Roman dead began to blanch, in a strange putrefaction that destroyed both bone and muscles, transforming them little by little into glabrous mannikins without sex, their spherical skulls quite nude, and their sleek limbs looking as if they were made of white tights stuffed with horsehair.

These bodies were lying around me, before the lances and standards of the Romans, which were carried by motionless soldiers who differed from the dead only in that they were vertical.

When night had fallen, the corpses began to rise slowly in ranks of ten to fifteen, then started to pursue the will-o'-the-wisps, without moving their arms or legs, and floating a few meters above ground. When they had joined the fugitives, their icy breath extinguished all the flames, and soon there were left on the plain only ranks of pikes, the tent of the Emperor still glittering like a coat of mail under the lunar light, and the white mannikins who had stretched out on the memorial letters, blending with them in an identical insensibility of stone, like gravel left there for memory's sake, a short distance from the river, which continued its course towards the North.

The nineteen white letters gleamed in the darkness, immovable and as if emerged from the ground, and they seemed to have become its suddenly exteriorized skeleton. Mist rose from the river and poised above the battlefield, becoming more opaque as the night became darker, and forming scrolls as dense as those of the draining smoke arteries.

At midnight, the vapors had become massed just above the inscription and wrote in the air

$$19,$$

which was the number of white letters, set on the blackboard of night, like the first factor of a prophetic operation the consequences of which would be felt way beyond the sensorial domain, as far as the extreme point of the needle which sews for us the woof of the universe hemmed by our human lives.

The wind blew upon the two figures and made them dance one before the other, like a couple in love. The 9, being more sinuous, was the woman, offering her round loop to the 1, which leaped vertically and at times came near in order to thrust its angle into the circle.

I observed this trick for the seventh time, when the two figures became definitely fused and disappeared; then there emerged in white against the background of the night:

$$1 - 9 = 10$$

This sum having been effected in silence, an equilibrium was maintained for an instant. But my ears were suddenly lacerated by a terrible thunderstroke, accompanied by lightning of enormous proportions which divided the number 10 and swept the 1 and 9 away, while at the same time it shook the crests on the tops of the helmets, and the pikes became tufted with innumerable sparks. Then the blasted 10 was also smashed, and I saw in its place only the two figures:

$$d \text{ and } b,$$

the first green and the second blood red, color of lips and wounds, represented by a half-nude Spanish woman in a scarlet shawl, the design of which underscored the imaginary lozenge which had as summits the stain marking the confluence of her two thighs.

Like an object and its image in a mirror, the two fives took their places opposite each other, like eagles on the escutcheon of Charles the Fifth, but the five which was turned backwards dwindled rapidly and there remained only the red Spanish woman represented by the figure of the senses, of the fingers, and of mating.

The **dancing** woman was irritated, a feeling born more of the storm than the rhythmic measure of the number which had engendered it. She, therefore, rose suddenly to her proper degree, 5 (the number of all the tricks she was capable of), by drawing from her marvelously fine, smooth black stockings a pair of castanets which she raised as high as her two hands could reach in order to unchain a crackling of figures which soon crossed the rays of the rising sun.

Before the soldiers, the dancer with the lozenge then made the ground echo with her heels, her unfurled fan cut the air in five quarters of numbers and points of departure which showed me once more that total death, like that of gestures, is only a formation of angles and a change in direction. At the same time, the teeth of her steel comb marked, through canalization, the temporal divisions created by the solar rays. Part of the light was reflected on the pikes of the legionnaires, and the dancer amused herself by conjugating the movements of her fan and those of her comb in such a way as to increase as much as possible the intensity of the reflected light.

Finally, as she whirled vertiginously about, transforming the air into a vast and luminous cage which was nothing but interlaced bars, the arms and armor of the warriors grew suddenly incandescent, and the entire Roman army became enflamed. The molten metals sank into the crust of the earth, holding in dissolution the flesh and bones of the soldiers, whose fossil imprints were found many centuries later on the ingots of a white and unbreakable substance which ignorant scientists called

MARSITE,

confounding it with those concretions of the sky that sometimes burrow into the earth, having not fallen from high enough to be able to pierce it from end to end.

The storm which had upset the figures had by now attained its maximum velocity. I stood trembling behind my senses of living water, watching for the adventure which was coming with a headlong rush.

The galleys fled, giving the appearance of a flight of cranes. The sun became a revolver barrel which slowly turned around, presenting at regular intervals a body that lay like an arrow before the orifice of the cannon. A shot rang out every minute and the body, its hair streaming ahead, was about to be lost in space. The dancer disappeared at the moment when I was about to seize her, and the entire landscape was swallowed up and replaced by a gleaming maelstrom, with spirals more dense than the wood of a cross.

I was hurled into this whirlpool from which there rose from time to time a multicolored bubble that knocked against the zenith, crashed with a great fracas, and returned to the funnel in the form of mirror flashes, pocketknives, and compasses.

Along with me there turned around the polished region a dark woman, a male goat, and a bottle containing a few pieces of paper, four crystal dice, and a ball of string all plunged into the brine. Each time my position with reference to the bottle made me see a new side of one of the dice, the woman stretched her nude arms and the goat shook its beard, while a bubble came from the funnel.

The woman was the first to fall into the central pool; I was still far away when I saw her balance herself and disappear with a long cry, like a torch that goes out. The goat followed her almost at once; but he had the luck of finding one of the bubbles, which carried him off rapidly into the air; up there he became changed into a cloud which allowed him to come down without pain—in the form of a fine rain.

As for myself, I succeeded, just as my circular voyage was about to lead me to the edge of the abyss, in clutching the bottle and, moving it violently, I threw the number 12 with the dice, which assured me the protection of the zodiac. I found, in fact, within reach of my hand, an aerial girdle decorated with the twelve signs. It placed itself without aid around my loins, and drew me away from the whirlpool, carrying me outside of the zone of terrestrial attraction.

When I came back to this planet, it was on a beautiful summer night, I was metamorphosed into a thunder stone and on my face were engraved these words, which summarized everything the figure 5 and the oriflamme of The Catalaunic Fields had taught me:

"Needle
A stippled curve
here is the thread of thought
Feast of passing the Equator
—and the Camp of the Golden Sheet—
here is where the saddle wounds
the circumvolutions
in prismatic darkness."

Translated from the French by Eugene Jolas
transition 16-17

Benjamin Péret   *In a Clinch*

To wake up in the bottom of a carafe, stunned like a fly, is enough to make you kill your mother five minutes after you get out. That is what happened to me one morning, so it is not surprising that I should now have a head shaped like a dandelion and that my shoulders should sag down to my knees. During the first few minutes after I woke up, I imagined that I had always lived in the bottom of a carafe and probably I should still believe it if I had not seen a sort of bird on the other side of the carafe, knocking it peevishly with his beak. Thanks to him, the accidental and annoying features of my situation were made clear to me and I flew into a rage. I seized a dry leaf which was near me and, shoving it into my left nostril, I cried: "Is it possible that the dog is the friend of man? Is it true the snail is the enemy of the turtle?" And from the top of the carafe, a fissure of glass murmured: "Poor idiot! Enemies are not as silly as people think. They have beards and their brains are made of celluloid scrapings and potato peelings. Friends have glass heads and bite like transmission belts."

But I insisted: "Is it true that flies do not die on clock hands? Is it true that rice straw is used to make meatballs? Is it true that oranges gush out of mine shafts? Is it true that bologna is made by blind people? Is it true that quails suck ewes? Is it true that noses get lost in fortresses? Is it true that bathrooms fade away into pianos? Is it true that the expression 'put out to grass' does not signify having frozen feet? Is it true that in dark rooms the song of dreams is never heard?"

He then made a great noise like a pot falling and rebounding on a stone staircase and a small opening appeared in my prison. Mercifully for me, it did not take long in growing to the proportions of a railroad tunnel at the entrance of which appeared a small creature which resembled both a sardine and a butterfly. I was no longer alone and consequently I was in less of a hurry to leave the carafe, which I began to find quite congenial. It wouldn't have taken much to have made me ask the sardine-butterfly to live with me, which probably she would not have refused me, for she seemed very gentle and obliging. However, I did not risk making this proposition, which many would have found strange, although there is nothing more extraordinary in it than to throw a paving stone from the height of a sixth story into a street filled with a busy crowd in the hope of killing someone. But the world is such that it is more scandalous to live with a sardine-butterfly than to live alone in a carafe. And therefore I made no proposal to this charming creature. In fact, in entering the carafe, her wings fell down, her tail disappeared and also her fins, a spark followed by a small wisp of smoke escaped from her head, and I saw nothing in its place but a signpost on which was written: SCORPION, 200 KM 120. Again I fell into a violent temper and grabbing the signpost I threw it as hard as I could against my glass prison walls. To my great astonishment the signpost went through the carafe and bounced two or three times upon its outside surface before reducing it to powder. It is then that I was surprised to find myself stretched out on my back in a field of wheat. As I made a movement to get on my feet, twenty partridges flew out of my pockets where they must have been hidden for a long time—although I had not been aware of it—for they left a large number of eggs which hatched in my hand.

Having recovered from my surprise, I reflected that one field was as good as another. Not without difficulty, I succeeded in regaining the vertical position for which I was born, and threw jets of saliva to all sides, which flew with one hasty wing stroke, followed by the shots of invisible hunters. I climbed into the ditch, taking care not to crush the pretty little white moles which were taking the air and enjoying it naively. They had this pleasure rarely enough! They were so happy that, although I was a stranger to them, they could not restrain themselves from confiding their story to me. It was a very small white mole with dragon-fly wings which spoke:

STORY OF THE WHITE MOLE

Just as you see me, I was born in a box of polish. My father was a chestnut vendor and my mother a sow. How did that happen? I cannot say. My father was a tall thin man, like a flint, except that his head was easily the largest that could be imagined. He had no nose and his ears hung like the stems of the creeping vine torn off by the wind. Naturally he was stupid, that is why he was a chestnut vendor. One day, having torn off a sow's tail, he walked throughout the city of Troyes shouting: THIS IS MY BLOOD. Soon the druggists ran on his trail, then the solicitors, hardwaremen, cesspool cleaners, lacemakers, orthopedists, justices of the peace, café keepers, sacristans, herb dealers, amateur fishermen, children of pigs, and finally the clergymen. Then, seized by an intense terror, he hid the sow's tail in a box of polish which he put in a letterbox with the following address:

CLAY PIPE
at IVORY TOWER
near SCURVY (Morbihan)

And the letter went high and low. Soon it mounted an iceberg, then descended into a vat, afterwards climbed to the branch of a tree the leaves of which it devoured, which made it fall into a well where a bucket of blue glass pulled it out to put it on the right road. Finally, after a thousand vicissitudes, it arrived in a palace. To tell the truth, the palace in question looked more like a tulip which had sprung out of a decomposing skull than a well-arranged palace. In fact, the staircase was laid out like a dead snake in the hall, and the upper stories were reached by means of an arrow which one stuck through one's rump and which the ground floor shot up to the desired level. There the letter found its addressee, who paced from one end of the stairway to the other without meeting "a living soul" and asked himself in what desert without caravans nor camels, in what desert peopled only by the crackling noises of broken glasses, in what desert he dragged his melancholy feet like an asparagus which, expecting to be eaten with French dressing, is only sucked with a white sauce. The unknown was no other than CLAY PIPE, famous for his duel with the empty bottles.

It was then that I saw the light.

But perhaps it is worth while to tell of the marvelous adventures of CLAY PIPE and the empty bottles.

CLAY PIPE had always believed that virgins lived in shards of bottles. But having opened his left eye in one of them, he found he had been deceived and was quite vexed by it. Failing to find in the bottles the young virgins he was after, he resolved to raise there grandmothers suitably shriveled by a half century of usage. Is it necessary to say that his project miscarried miserably? Hardly had the grandmothers been shut up in the bottle shards when they turned into liquid and became in a short time a sort of tar like that used to repair the streets of Paris. All hope thus to obtain a generation of small-sized grandmothers was lost. But CLAY PIPE was indefatigable. Without becoming discouraged, he sowed naval officers in the bottom of the bottles and that was his finish, for naval officers do not smoke clay pipes, but debris from ships and sailors' hair, which is bad for the health of empty bottles. CLAY PIPE was not long in seeing the effect on his protégés, and he revenged himself on the naval officers, whom he reduced to the state of slugs, creatures much appreciated by empty bottles which eat a great many of them, especially in the springtime. He was, however, wrong not to hide from them the origin of their food and the bottles, which in spite of everything were much attached to the naval officers, became distinctly angry. A duel with lanterns resulted and CLAY PIPE was beaten, having swallowed only 721 lanterns while the smallest of his adversaries had devoured at least a thousand. Since that day CLAY PIPE had paced the horizontal staircase from one end to the other in the hope of finding his empty bottles again, but in vain. They had fled long ago, thanks to the springtime sprouts of geraniums which grow so frequently in the stomachs of pregnant women to bring on a premature delivery.

And the little white mole went away as she had come, like a crescent moon. I found myself alone again, desperately alone, my feet attached to a sort of sleigh which was decorated with a host of little pigs similar to the flag of the United States. This showed me that the sleigh was made of acorns and potato flour. While I reflected on the insolidity of such a vehicle, it started to move while the pigs flew away, crying:

"Lafayette I am here! . . . Over there! . . . One doesn't make omelets without breaking eggs . . . eggs . . . eggs . . . eggs . . . eggs . . . eggs . . . eggs . . . Negroes have flat feet . . . Swedes eat mussels . . ." And a thousand other things in which the word "hair" was repeated often.

Only one young pig, glowing like a new coin, stayed on the sleigh, and when it stopped near the ear of a naturalized elephant, addressed me as follows:

"I see into toolhouses of the road menders. I eat sleighs. I read Paul Bourget beginning at the end of each line. I play night-table music. I caress the fingers of brides and I keep a well-known politician in the forest of my silks. What is he, and who am I?"

But instead of replying to him, I asked:

"Did you have to stand in line?"

"Sit down, I beg of you," he replied, "I have had a little cold and now you're saved."

"I understand nothing of all this," I could not help telling him, here where cauliflowers litter the airless rooms and turn yellow when by chance the little crystal spiders happen to meet them, playing their customary game of whist in the evening in the deserted squares, in spite of the fact that they have been closed to the public for a long time. But this stupid beast wouldn't let me go away so easily, and taking me aside asked:

"Does the gentleman want to put on his dressing gown?"

Hoping to get rid of him, I replied in the same silly tone he had adopted:

"I can't find my bedroom slippers."

Again the pig asked me:

"Does the gentleman wish me to comb his hair?"

"Just part of. I can do the rest of it very well," I replied, worn out.

During more than a day, the sleigh slid rapidly between a double hedge of porcupines, who gravely contemplated our strange rig and fled as soon as we were out of sight, uttering cries so piercing that the frightened birds fell to the ground, where they remained flattened out like a piece of putty on a glass. I began to get worried, the more so since an indefinable odor floated in the air, something like the smell of artichokes and like a well-groomed head of hair. And our speed, which increased steadily! And the pig, which had become as large as a church! This animal upset me more than I could say, with his great pale face barred vertically with a sword, and a pistol tattooed on each side of an enormous nose supporting a large cane to which were attached more than fifty children's balloons. To tell the truth, these balloons, the purpose of which I did not understand, intrigued me considerably. For most of them contained a bearded man with his chest ornamented with many rusted decorations and which opened like a door, showing inside an ash can running over with enormous rats which jostled and crushed one another, drawn no doubt by some alluring rottenness.

The pig, having observed my troubles and recommencing his questions, said to me:

"What is he, and who am I?"

"No doubt the inventor of a cattle car, so-called because it serves for the transportation of playing cards and principally clubs, like clovers, which must be spread out in good season upon green fields, in order that they may acquire the qualities of suppleness and endurance which other cards do not have."

The animal let out a great burst of laughter and murmured disdainfully:

"You're joking."

Then he commenced to sing:

> On the prairie there is a lock
> a lock that I know
> It glows and rocks
> when the birds fly around
>
> On the prairie there is a camel
> a camel with no teeth
> I will make him some with a mirror
> and his humps shall be my reward

On the prairie there is a pipe
where my destiny hides
On the prairie there is an armchair
And the tribunes will be at my feet
It will be warm, it will be cold

I will raise centipedes
which I will give to the dressmakers
and I will raise chair rungs
which I will give to bicycles

For a long time he continued in this manner, which was far from reassuring to me. Suddenly, as we approached a forest which had barred the horizon for a long time, I saw the forest leave the ground and come galloping to our sides after having bowed with respect to my companion, who, at this moment, appeared to be filled with unbearable self-sufficiency. They had a long conversation of which I could grasp several words which gave me no idea of what it was about!

". . . Down there, in this pavilion . . . what can these letters mean: S.G.D.G. . . . If we should visit the naval section . . . provided that we should come safely into port . . . ," etc.

However, I guess that it had to do with me, and I had no doubt they intended to do me a bad turn, so I prepared to defend myself. I had no time for that. The forest grabbed me from behind, held me motionless in a second, then shoved my head into my stomach, glued my arms against my buttocks, and carried me away, rolling me like a barrel one pushes before one.

. . . .

And since that day I have wandered over the world.

Translated from the French
by Elliot Paul

transition 12

Raymond Roussel

from
African Impressions

Soon the sound of footsteps was heard; all eyes turned towards the left, and around the southwest corner of the esplanade a strange, pompous procession could be seen approaching.

It was headed by the emperor's thirty-six sons, grouped six deep according to size, who composed a Negro phalanx ranging in age from three to fifteen. Fogar, the eldest of them all, was in the back among the taller ones, and he carried in his arms an immense wooden cube, transformed into a playing die by a thorough whitewashing on which were painted black hollow dots. At a sign from Rao, the native in charge of the maneuvers of the parade, the children's group started to walk slowly along the side of the esplanade bordered by the Bourse.

After them, in a delightful drill figure, came the ten wives of the sovereign, graceful Ponukeleian women of great charm and beauty.

Finally the emperor Talou VII appeared, curiously gotten up as a cabaret singer, in a low-cut blue dress, with a long train in back, on which the number "472" stood out in black figures.

His Negroid face, that displayed savage energy and a certain character, contrasted with his feminine wig with its carefully waved, magnificent blond hair. He was leading by the hand his daughter Sirdah, a slender child of eighteen whose close-set eyes were veiled by a thick film. She bore on her black forehead a red birthmark that seemed to be in the form of a miniature corset with yellow darts.

Next came the Ponukeleian troops, composed of superb ebony-skinned warriors, heavily armed under their attire of plumes and amulets.

Little by little the procession followed the same direction as the children.

Passing in front of the sepulcher of the zouave, Sirdah, who undoubtedly had counted her steps, suddenly approached the tombstone, and gently pressed on it a long kiss filled with the purest tenderness. After having accomplished this pious gesture, the blind girl took her father's hand affectionately.

When they had nearly reached the far side of the esplanade, the emperor's sons, headed by Rao, turned right so as to go along the north side of the vast quadrilateral. Then, when they had reached opposite corners, they maneuvered a second time and came down towards us, while the procession, which was still being swelled at its source by numerous fresh cohorts, followed exactly in their footsteps.

Finally, the last black warriors having made their entry as the children in the front ranks reached the southern limits, Rao cleared a space around the altar, and all the newcomers gathered together in an orderly manner along the two sides, their heads turned towards the center of the square.

From every direction a crowd of Negroes, formed by the population of Ejur, had assembled behind the sycamores to take part in the charming spectacle.

On reaching the middle of the esplanade, the emperor's sons, still six deep, stopped with their faces turned towards the altar.

Rao took the monstrous die from Fogar's arms and balanced it several times so as to throw it in the air with all his might; the enormous cube, which was fifty centimeters high, whirled about, a white mass specked with black. Then, describing a well-closed curve, it rolled along the ground before it settled in one spot. In a single glance, Rao read the number *two* on the upper face and, coming towards the docile phalanx, pointed to the second row, who were the only ones to remain in their places; the rest of the group, picking up the die, ran mingling with the crowd of warriors.

Talou then slowly joined the chosen ones whom fate had just designated to serve him as pages. Shortly after, in the midst of a deep silence, the emperor started majestically towards the altar, escorted by the six privileged children, who carried the train of his robe.

After having ascended the few steps that lead to the summarily spread table, Talou ordered Rao, who was holding the heavy coronation coat in both hands, to approach. He presented it inside out, as the emperor, stooping over, slipped his head and arms into the three openings cut in the middle of the cloth. Its deep folds soon covered him all the way to the ground.

Thus attired, the monarch turned proudly towards the assembly as though to display his new costume to all eyes.

The rich, silky stuff represented a large map of Africa, on which were indicated the principal lakes, rivers, and mountains.

The pale yellow of the land contrasted sharply with the shaded blue of the sea, which extended on every side as far as the general shape of the garment demanded.

Fine silver lines in curved and harmonious zigzags streaked the surface of the Ocean, so as to evoke, through a sort of design, the continual undulating movement of the waves.

The southern half of the continent was all that could be seen between the emperor's neck and ankles.

On the western side, a black point accompanied by the name "Ejur" was to be seen near the mouth of a river that had its source in a mountainous pile, rather far towards the east.

On both sides of this vast stream of water an immense red blot represented the states belonging to the all-powerful Talou.

Flatteringly, the designer of the model had extended the limits indefinitely. Little was known, in fact, about this imposing domain which was subject to one scepter; the brilliant red, widely distributed to the north and east, extended southward as far as the terminal point, where the words "Cape of Good Hope" were spread out in large black letters.

After a while, Talou turned towards the altar; on his back, the rest of the stole showed the northern part of Africa, hanging down in the center of a similar marine frame.

Now the solemn moment was at hand.

The monarch, in a loud voice, started reading a native text traced with the aid of hieroglyphics on a sheet of parchment placed in the center of the narrow table.

It was a sort of bull through which, by virture of his religious power, Talou, who was already emperor of Ponukele, ordained himself king of Drelchkaff.

When the proclamation came to an end, the sovereign took the vase which was intended to represent the ampula, and, turning to one side, poured oil on the end of his hand, in order later to grease his forehead with his fingertips.

He forthwith put the phial back in place, and, descending the altar steps, walked to a foliage-covered couch shaded by rubber plants. Placing his foot on the corpse of Yaour, he then heaved a long sigh of joy and raised his head triumphantly, as though to humiliate the remains of the defunct king before everybody.

After this proud gesture, he gave the heavy coat, which he had promptly removed, to Rao.

Escorted by his six sons, who once more carried his train, he walked slowly in our direction, then turned towards the theater of the "Incomparables," to take his place before the crowd.

At this moment the wives of the emperor came into the center of the esplanade.

Rao soon joined them, carrying a heavy bowl which he placed on the ground in their midst.

The ten young women fell forwards around the receptacle, which was filled with a thick blackish food-substance that they ate hungrily, using their hands to carry it to their lips.

After a few moments, the entirely empty bowl was taken out by Rao, and the satiated Negresses took up their places for the *Lunn'chetuz,* a religious dance much in favor in the country and especially reserved for solemn occasions.

They started with several slow steps accompanied by supple, undulating movements.

From time to time they let out loud reports through their wide-opened mouths, which soon increased with prodigious rapidity. But instead of attempting to conceal these repugnant sounds, they forced them to ever greater brilliance, seeming to rival with each other as to the amount of noise obtained.

This general chorus, which served as musical accompaniment to the calm and gracious pavane, revealed to us the rather special virtues of the unknown substance they had just absorbed.

Little by little the dance became more lively, till it took on a fantastic character, while in one powerful crescendo the reports continued to increase in intensity and frequency.

There was a moment of impressive climax during which the harsh, deafening noises marked the rhythm for a diabolical sarabande; the feverish ballerinas, disheveled and exhausted by their terrible belching as well as by blows with the fists, pursued each other in every direction with contortions that made them seem prey to some sort of vertiginous delirium.

Then gradually everything grew calm, and after a long diminuendo the ballet ended in a group apotheosis, underlined by a final chord which was further prolonged by organ-point.

Soon the young women, still shaken by belated hiccoughing, walked slowly back to their original places.

Translated from the French by Maria Jolas

transition 12

Tristan Tzara   *from*
The Approximate Man

imperfect returns of long magic meditations
of meditations in quest of hauntings and explosions
from the extreme points of luminous longitudes
from the lofty gaze of the fatigue of snows
imperfect returns of long magic meditations
to the seasons here below
soaked in those algae swarming with transparencies
of the mantling of heteroclite eternities dragged in the mud below here
eye always new to the return to things
indefatigable return from the heights of migratory dreams
I inhabit the music in the stove where shadows bake
a tear—cold trace of a lizard—is enough—dazzling negligence
to put out in each lamp the silence that buries us in pillows of dawn
and leading the star by the leash the affluent of the world tour tempts
   the infinite with drizzling imitations
nor closes yet the star at the window of the eyes
detaches from the pontoons the clairvoyance of those phantoms whose
   chain-convulsed hands
gather the airy flight of the fluorescent prophecies of suicides
and the inexhaustible speculations of the upper studies of atmospheres
   in the leper homes in the clouds

under the dome of the talking wings who can number the grotto's darts
and the lever of the night holds in its iron hand all the heavy hair under
   lock and key
thus in your heart of cloistral leers the child keeps the balance in the
   center of its heart of sponge
in the shadow of the rude and stormy force
and despite the lunar hesitation of the seated young perspectives
in the soft fields of edelweiss where legions of honor grow wild
the shrubs tied to the goats unscrew the flashes snatched up by the mist
let the anemone face lick the steep moon stain
and let the eyebrows of bitter wool above the temple of salt
linger over attempts at blossoming made by nocturnal prows

no matter—the ostrich hearts hide the landscape's head in the sand
and the brush of sorrow keeps gliding over all flesh—be it of pearl or
of linen
and over so many more

. . . .

and whether it be the names of flowers the river banks of expressions
mingled with gold of the isles
the morals of roads the capes of grave senses
where everything is true and the garden of the hesperides is no farther
than the handshake
where languages make their dregs foam down to the last swallow
and all the final disappointments and their fire ducts
which seal the pagan repast to the silences of the rock
whether it be the prodigious usury of clamors
whether it be the funicular trains of quaking aspirations that circulate
in the herb shops of the dream
and the bamboo galleries that gravitate around the acrobatic ceremonial
of the oars
so slow is the navigation of the spirit which trusts in the solemn pledges
of melancholy
and eloquent the lantern presaging so many supple emotions to the
womb of night
to the solemn pledges of melancholy
what of it—the junk of prodigies traces the new paths
on this earth of hearts—its empire
do not close your eyes
from which come labyrinths and the elastic snares of dementia-soaked
flesh
and if you open the zephyrs to the solemn womb of melancholy
do not tremble—the garlanded circus of the pagoda handbells opens to
the peony
and the commotions have used the saddles of the orchestral cascades
so many nights have lighted their pipes by the flashing stirrup of the
mystic winds
that have taken breath at the base of your word
do not close your eyes yet awhile
to the kennel of the sun has come all of music
which the roots have pushed to the tortures of sporadic orbits
and by following the coasts and the landslides of metaphors
the eyes of the numbers are filled with the time struck in the game of
the arts
and human love petrified under the crust of disgust

which is coagulated in its iron belly by the unconsoled pallor of dry
  prisons
and fear which increases on ladders of truth
invents itself and loses itself in the eye of the young wild boar
and the chimerical tears harmonize on stills
hatred which nidificates in the memory of wine
scales off and finds itself again in the hours of frozen flint
and sorrow—calix of wrinkles—which the agricultural face of the
  immemorial day desires
and drinks—prolific season of obsequies the temples unyoked
and whether it be the sadness of the wind carried to the nickel brow
that fills the oliphant with dark loam of the lyrical passions of routed
  clans
the numbers are leveled the immensity of the instincts goes so far
to the divine fertilizer—the carrion
and whether it be the heart that goes to its lovers tryst or rancor
there will always be so many others and so many others
do not close your eyes yet awhile
nor those of the others

Translated from the French
by Eugene Jolas
transition 19-20

6. verticalist texts

Hugo Ball *Gnostic Magic*

What was understood by magic, and which were the forms of worship that were considered particularly magical? The ancient believer could imagine the connection with God only in a magical way. The entire religious service is magical. Yet, even in ancient days there seems to have existed a religion for the crowd and a religion for the initiates. The lower pictural grades of worship are accessible to everybody, but the higher spiritual grades are only known to the priests.

The mystery celebration proper consists of a sequence of inexplicably exalting procedures. An inexhaustible meaning inheres in the rites and ceremonies. Lanterns and lights in gleaming symmetry; a primitive mixture of animal and children's sounds; a music which rings in cadences that have disappeared long ago; all this shakes the soul and reminds it of its first home. The spirit is seized by a longing for first beginnings, it is submerged in the long-forgotten paradises of the over- and under-world. Strangely masked presences bear astral signs and symbols, turn in a circle, and with their motions bring the gentle image of the stellar sphere right into an earthly space. The choir leader is called "Creator," the torchbearer "Sun," the priest standing before the altar "Moon." There is even a "Writer of the Sun," whose task it is to take care of the ritual books. The inside of the temple itself is an image of heaven. Zoroaster is said to have been the first to make geometrical divisions in a cavern. They represented the various parts of heaven and the elements, and thus imitated the order of the world *in nuce*. It is generally known that there was a stairway in the Mythras mysteries with seven steps, with rooms of seven divers-colored metals (corresponding to the planetary spheres through which the soul ascends and the gods descend). The sects also cultivated architectonic and astral magic. Saint Epiphanius describes such a mystery rite: In the Coreion, at

Alexandria, the gnostic society keeps watch before the image of the Virgin during the night to the accompaniment of flutes and chants. Then, at cockcrow, they bring up a carved work from the crypta. It has five golden crosses. Chanting hymns, they carry it seven times around the image of the Virgin. The magical mysterium represents the birth of the Aeon Christ and his dance around the higher wisdom, the Hagia Sophia. It was during these and similar rites that those magic hymns which are attributed especially to Bardeison and Valentinos were sung.

Magic is thus the belief in the astral symbol. The spirit is considered irresistible if it nevertheless rises in highest concentration as light and presence. It then has the power to change man and to elevate him. Magic is also the sacerdotal application of this force. One might call it the active, the productive wisdom. It teaches detachment and the ascension to God. It reawakens the world of the blessed primal beginnings in pure light; the wonder of those spaces that lie before birth and behind death. Magic is, finally, the supernatural in all its communications. It brings about the liberation of the spirit from every chain. Thus, in the old Orient it is also redemption. It is the only worship worthy of divinity. Without the use of magic which builds the bridge with God man cannot be saved. If he wants to escape error, decline, extinction, he must strive to become a particle of the Godhead.

transition 23

Harry Crosby *Suite*

Aeronautics

A procession to the Hill of Montmartre (where stand the famous windmills) in the midst of which is a large Balloon, mounted on wheels and drawn by two donkeys. Behind comes a monkey standing on its hind legs, in clerical garb, and a donkey both of them with trousers on, and looking happy. At the back is the personification of Fire on a cloud, holding a scroll in her hand on which are depicted two Balloons. The

Balloon is in mid-air and is encircled by monkeys and donkeys waiting for the Ascent. A Blind Man leaves the scene saying, I can see nothing. The Balloon is rising from the platform, in front of which is an enormous crowd of spectators. The Balloon has ascended into the atmosphere. The Balloon moves off in a horizontal direction. The Balloon has disappeared into space. An Explosion is heard. The Balloon has Exploded. The Balloon is on the ground and Peasants are attacking it with pitchforks. Landscape with cottage and hay barn and old white timber inn with thatched roof, men seated drinking, to left a farm girl feeding pigs, wagoner with his horses at water trough. The inn stands on the banks of the river behind spreading trees. A cow is drinking. The Virgin seated by the Tree. The Virgin with the Rabbits. Saint George with the Dragon. The Circumcision in the Stable. The Betrothal of the Virgin. The Wondrous Hog. The Brood Mares. The tiled buildings of the mill are seen on the further bank of the river. In foreground to right two women washing clothes. In center soldiers firing. To left spectators with the American Flag above in various attitudes of alarm. A vixen sits on the ledge of the bank and looks towards five cubs, a sixth cub peers out of a hole in the bank. Enter the Blind Man. Enter an Aardvark. Enter a man with a knife left hand raised to his face (female figure partly nude floating in the air beside him). He is followed by a young woman plucking a fowl. Her hair is in curls she has pearls round her neck and she is wearing an ermine cloak with jewels. Enter a young peasant girl carrying basket rejecting the advances of a young man in uniform (female figure partly nude floating in the air beside him). Enter mother and child (the child has pyelitis). Enter Elsa de Brabant. Enter an Augur observing Birds. Enter a Flying Fox. Enter a Stork and a Pelican. Enter a Black Hawk. Enter a Red Swan. Enter Santa Claus with a portion of caviar. Enter Tilden. Enter Walter Hagen in a knitgrip knicker (no buckles to buckle). Enter the Tenth Plague of Egypt. Enter the Madonna of the Sleeping Cars. Enter Anna Livia Plurabelle. Enter La Mère Gérard. Enter La Vieille aux Loques. Enter La Marchande de Moutarde. Enter the Red Dress. Enter two girls, one combing her hair. Oh! Why!—I don't know about loving him very much. Enter Daniel Webster. Thank God! I—I also—am an American! Enter Christ and the Woman of Samaria. Enter the Man in the Moon. Enter Champagne Charley. Enter the Monkey in clerical garb (female figure partly nude floating in the air beside him) fur cap coat with fur cuffs reading aloud a book of common prayer. Come Holy Ghost our souls inspire. Lightning flashing in the background. Enter old red man with red helmet on his head. Enter old bearded man in a high fur cap with closed eyes. Enter an Animal of No Importance. Enter a Virgin making much of time.

Enter Renoir (female figure partly nude floating in the air beside him). If women had no breasts I would not have painted them. Enter H.D. wrapped in a palimpsest. Enter a well-dressed man in everyday attire arm in arm with a Follies Girl in a modish three-color one-piece club-striped combination travelo swim-suit. I've simply nothing to wear. Enter Prufrock in a Rock Fleece Overcoat. Enter Miss Everis. I am five months pregnant. The other day I felt a pain in my abdomen. Enter Steve Donoghue. Enter Kefalin winner of the Grand Prix. Enter an Onanist. Enter a Masochist. Enter Europe's Greatest Lover. Enter Antony and Cleopatra. Enter the Harvard Track Team. Enter Standard Oil Bearer right hand holding gloves left grasping staff of standard, so safe so sure so easy to handle. Enter Porphyria's Lover. Enter Mr. and Mrs. Lingam with an attendant behind. Enter a Jury of Annoyance. Enter Sportsman holding up a hare in his right hand. Enter a Feudal Ladye amorous to be known. Enter a Knight Errant. Enter T. Noord-ner-Quartier (halitoxio). Enter Nicolas Alfan de Ribera Marquis de Villanneva de las Torres de Dugnes d'Alcala Grand d'Espagne. Enter Lindbergh with a Lion-Tamer. Enter Vandals and Visigoths. Enter the Pancake-Woman reading aloud What Every Girl Should Know. Enter Joseph telling his Dreams. Enter Blasus de Manfre, the Water-spouter. Enter Roman Youth Swallowing Stones (burst of applause from a London whore who appears standing between a lion and a unicorn). Enter an ignorant Physician. Enter a Fair Lady in Revolt. Enter Mr. Guy Holt with a flair for civilized fiction. Enter a Magician. Enter a fawn dressed up as a Girl. Enter Queens in Hyacinth. Enter Jamaica God of Rum. Enter His Excellency Kno Sung Tao holding a jar (black idol) in both hands. Enter the Donkey Ambassador holding a lemon in both hands, very rare in this undivided state. Enter a Pederast holding a lipstick in both hands. Enter John Paul Jones supported by an officer of the law white cravat hat and sword in right hand. Enter Marie Antoinette powdered hair lace silk combination pajamas. Enter Shepherdesses pursued by Illustrious Americans. Enter Miss Atlantic Monthly. Brekete ex Kotex Kotex pursued by the Earl of Fitzdotterel's Eldest Son. I reflect with pleasure on the success with which the British undertakers have prospered this last summer. Enter the Ghost of Hamlet. Enter a Temple Boy. Enter Alpha and Omega. Enter the Soul killed by the Explosion. Enter Rimbaud. Enter Van Gogh. Enter Amon Ra. Enter the Star of the East. Enter the Youngest Princess. Enter the Queen of Peking. Enter the Moon. Enter Death stabbed in the Back. There is a Circle in the Center. Enter the Gray Princess. Enter the Cramoisy Queen. Enter the Mad Queen. Enter the Sun.

The Blind Man leaves the scene, saying, I can see nothing.

Eugene Jolas   *Vertigral*

Lucifer-hymns fill the gray dusk, and the bawdy vocabulary trumpets
into a sick hour. The crowds are passing through the tear-ploughed
acres of asphalt. The hoardings cry against the eyes. Satanic heads are
covered with tang filched from the Sargossa Sea. Dervishes whirl in
Gethsemane. It is a corrosion of pain. Une apparition descend le fleuve.
Uferlos ist die trauer der seelen. Mottled rags wail before a doomflaring
distress. The sermonizers in the cathedral of the seven last verbs siren
fear. A wasserflut growls dusterwelt. How glitterglast the deathchant
fleers! The whimpertime is here. There is steelglint in the eyes of
passers-by. The cauldron waits with sulphur-fumes. The scissors crunch.
Soon it will be blade on blade, ô frontier-dreamer, the mothers' lips will
be loud with moan. Eyes will flamemuse ruined oaks. Tankmen will
invade the solitary towers. Wird die landschaft nicht mehr singen? Wo
sind die engel die uns gnade bringen? Fieberlodernd kreiseln kinder.
Ein meteor peitscht die tuerme. We want to flee the shuttered shops
in aureole-gleam. C'est l'ascension délirante. Une musique tonne. Nous
entendons la langue des étoiles dans un bruissement de feu. Soon we
are in the planetwhorl. The spinturn of the globe is stopped. The
clouds are running amuck. Porphyry temples glitterbloom orion-souls.

transition 27

Eugene Jolas   *Seraphic Ascension*

the seven archonts hold the keys
slaves look at the distressed sky
we want to storm the gloomgates
we want to hear the gleamwords

upward we rise through the brume
the sunyears crashthunder in pain
the sunyears spheremirror music
there is a praisechant of organhymns

we flitflutter out of timejungles
we luminousrise into cloudforests
the milky way meltflickers past
a cometroar bursts in our hair

titanbirds floatwave wonderblessed
they carry fairy-tale gardens in their beaks
they carry palaces of marchpane and stala
they come from far far away

asteroidbushes flishflash in springsmiles
the zodiac whorldances a roundelay
the orion glides into a platinumpond
there is a shillerflight in etherchaos

silversyllables shimmer to our eyes
lovevowels flitter mothwings
harpwords go ringaling through space
go timenaughtwinging through the light

flamewhirling rise our hungers
we pyramid through planetdust
we are hypophets with angelic choirs
we are drunken with the hymnodies of knowing

transition 23

Eugene Jolas   *The Third Eye*

Ascension to the Tremendum

Patmos cries logos.

The abyssal faces surge up in scarlet hoods. The maslight profanes the sibilant landscape. Leprous wounds bloodtrickle slowly. All the cities shake with the fumblesteps of the pallid masses.

Marble hands and the translucent windows snare muteness. O runners! The cool bell of dying will soon grieve requiem. The fruit of chaos is rotting, and the bands of blasphemy gather their slings. Why are the spirehouses doomed by winter? Why does the desert shrill-whoom in the dreambourne?

The image of incarnate love is gone. The living water of the spirit is veiled by mist. Crowds crush the cherubic metaphors on Times Square. The age circles in the tracks of the witches. A sphinx hides behind the legend of sadness, and the eyes of the workers are broken like shards. Listen to the children cry for the madonna!

Is this the time we have been waiting for in the quakehours? The time of the masses and the time of destruction? The time of death and the time of the entranced grief? The drums beat in the disquiet nerves, and the doomsayers exorcise the dementia of flight.

Where is the paradise-ladder?

The age of the acosmic lie goes into ruins. There is a conceit of hollowed faces. We walk with a terror-bruise and twist the ire of the saint. The burn-eyes stare us out. Bluster-wry we gristle in the echoes of the daemonic river. We listen to the crucifix-moan in the dust. The enthralled glories of the homo divinans are not with us.

The substantial nouns have vanished. The vortex of thunder-verbs pants. The exile-rider has forsaken the compendium of the processional. It is raining in the forest on the frontier of the invisible. Hoodwinking parallels defeat the seraphic soul.

No ransom can release the chained longings. The steel cloaks do not hide the ulcers. The feigned cordial of our weeping does not banish the black revolt. Why do the eggs blacken in the wind, and scorpions whip the skin of the wall, when the words of the ancestors weep in the time of the moon? The morrow of the prisonman blights. A litany dirges in the torrid noon.

Is it too late, is it too late for the flight of the alone to the alone?

This is the time for silences, the time for the angelic perspectives, the time for the inviolate journey.

We shall go in search of the language of God.

The numenous hymns will rise zenith-dancing.

There will be an ecstatic byss in the tremendum.

Chimera—Words from Sleep and Half-Sleep

the jungle rack and the bass gugglebooming against the contralto and the ringaringaling and the zzzzz

and the vowels a and e and the umlaut and the incantation and the germanic deepnote and the hollow click and the jingle-laughter and the tintune and the goldwhistle and the sibiliant chest-sound

the dramarap and the clickburst

was he dead

it was a northland in a snowbrush in an icehut

and a quaverhum and a muffleplash and a long long griefmoan

a string orchestra playing Brahms and a dead bird and a book and a palagra

and an owl and a lion and the sea the whale scalesilvering in moonlight the san francisco fire the tiara

the priest the ciborium

a fishnet a severed hand a woman's face a mutilated dog a newspaper the world war illustrated by

a dead man a mask a hood a boxer's face the guillotine

a hootword

a carib word

a ghulla word

a blizzard word howlblasting into the northnight

a mallatoo and a ralla a clustra with a bloo

the claram blisters gild

a mustaroad a glirra and a freel

the bannaram the bight

an allirata cum clant glits merrinane through blay

and cloora glant the lallabline gloos roane

the riparoon

the gree

yet glitz and glast the sunglint gloots against the munkle

America Mystica

Hako venoome vovoe ase amexoveva esevistavho Maheone omotom na
Maheone omotom evistaoxzevemhon Maheone na emaheonevstavho
Maheone omotom

Und die Urwelt der Steine ist noch immer in uns the great migra-
tions have not ceased the lineaments of the starfields beflame the eyes
in the baldachin blaze of ygdrasyl

Les forêts de cactus saignent il y a une nuit boréale qui appelle les
saints pour la vengeance de Dieu and Columbus drunk with the
heavenly vision found Guanahani

Where night bedabbled divination in the festival of palms which
made lightmusic in the forests the image of the green solitude was a
liturgy and the hours tremblefell

Over the eyes of the wayfarers the fairy tales found the pilgrim-hearts
bestrewn with wonder and the foreheads shone in starwhorl when the
texts of the ancient runes began to sing

And now the quiet lamp burns hymnblue in the chronicle of the still
mind the blooms of the Columbian voyage stare into the lips of the
people from Sais and the beasts break forth

From the hidden dens into music of cascades choiring through planet-
glitter that floods the pinehills and the nettles that are bedewed with
legends

When will the vagrant hearts be resurrected by the magic verb of the
stricken Christ the duologue is faraway it is deepnight over asphalt
and acres

And the drowning man looks once more at the sky before his heart
goes out the solitude cries wishmad into the travailing errplace

The storms of metal roar against the pinnacles the towers whir in
the despairing journey the bronze men are uprooted in the corrals and
an invalid stumbles over a skull

Alle Zungen der Erde sind verwirrt die daecher grauen umgitterun-
gen ich lag vor einem blauen meer südabend brandete lohglut and
hauntshapes played on the dunes

Far away on the horizon I see the chimerical America of my mind
so many titanic rivers swirlrace beneath the roarwings of the thunder-
bird

Will the continents be one in the fantasmatic forests of the soul will
the hammerworld crash into ruins will rockefeller center starsteep into
the ether

Nun sind wir tief in not und nacht die fabeltiere rasen der wortsturm
kreist die kalten waende umzingeln mich und alle menschen fluten in
mein herz

Nun bin ich selbst die menge wir brechen auf aus der verwilderung unsers wahns wir fliehen die vereinsamung we annihilate the torment

Wir sind raketen wir sind feuerbuesche ueber asphaltstaub ein schimmerwunsch treibt langsam in die gesetze der fenster und peitscht die weltendmueden

Wir steigen wie gebete la maturation des psaumes invite la vie d'extase un oiseau chante des paroles incantatoires les délices de la tempête d'acier se meurent

Une île lointaine bruit the barley sheaves fall into golden dust we unwrap the luminous fog and look for the hidden miracles the ballads of the alien races hosanna

In the dripforest and Guatemala fearsilvers the primeval forests give up their ruined temples is that Chilam-Balam qui prophétise et tous les mythes flambent

Dans une jungle de sorcellerie the valley of the gods is sunk in the entrancement of a bleeding prayer the pyramids announce the mexican future and the hunger for the sun

Does the visionholder mask his face but motion is not lost here the proliferations of the starloom go into the world of the somnambulists und nach innen geht der weg der voelker

The frontiersmen are still with us wenn die brunnen rauschen gehen sie blutumweht ins ewige sie haben die schwermut in die gosse geworfen

The tropical syntax flutters softly y los pueblos están sueños of death the roundelays of the taverns sont balbutiées in a nostalgia for the mothers

The immigrants are also here with memories of the ice-age nomads et les ancêtres chevauchent les nuits des villes d'usine des villes qui sont possédées

Yet the soul of the Pennsylvania Dutch farmer épouse l'âme de l'ouvrier franco-américain the cheyenne tongue glides into the Montana rhythm

The horizontal world is dying we want to rise higher than the Andes higher than the empire building higher than ygdrasyl voici venir l'ère de l'Atlantide

Je vous salue inconnus pleins de grace ô vous qui rêvez un avenir de cristal que les anges vous gardent du tumulte des bêtes démoniaques qui se tapissent dans les caves pourries

The voyage goes upward veergulls drift farewells in foamrhythms we stand before the conjuration of the lonely beings who wait for the ripplechants of their redemption

The continent is incandescent with the cries of the mutilated hearts the vision of the new age of glass glisters the ships are freighted with ecstatic men and women

We hear news from ungeheuren epochen da die scheitelauegler sternsuechtig in das weltall sannen the moundbuilders are here and the skystorming aztecs

Go obsidian-swinging into the migratory march we join a skyworld without horizon we dream one tongue from Alaska to Tierra del Fuego

We dream a new race visionary with the logos of God

transition 26

Franz Werfel   *from*
A Discourse on the Religious Experience

This, the deepest human experience, embraces thousands of degrees and scales, ranging from the simplest nature rapture to the *unio mystica* of the Saint with God. It rests on the intuitive perception of a supra-sensual opposite in the sense-dim mirror of our consciousness. When, in the melting moment of the sexual act, the I and the you become one, and death moves away, we find that in the religious *extasis* death not only moves away, but is without object, there is no death. And the human I is not obliterated, but suspended. But this in the profound sense of the words *suspended, dissolved, saved, sublimated*. Here language ends, or, rather, it shies like a wild horse. It is hardly possible to describe a musical experience in words. Technical expressions like dominants, cadence, tonic, do not translate a melody. But a language translation of the deepest of all spiritual experiences is out of the question.[1]

A philosopher once said very spiritedly that there existed religiously unmusical men. He meant by that men who have as little attraction to the religious experience as others have to the musical one. I deny that there are really any a-religious people, just as I once denied that there are

---

[1] Plato confesses: "I have not written anything about this, and I shall never write about it; for it is not comprehensible like other subjects of teaching; but when a man has lived with it a long time, it suddenly rises in the soul like a light that comes from a flickering fire and soon nurtures itself from its own force." (Plato: Epist. VII.)

any hopelessly apoetical men. The truth is that for many reasons the basic values of life, for the millions, are not mined, or else are heaped over with slag.

When we view the entire revolutionary and reformatory movements of the last decades on the intellectual plane, especially the radical works in literature, we undoubtedly come to the conclusion that these alleged deeds of liberation are nothing but the passionate attempt to safeguard and bar off the nihilistic state of the time-spirit and the general state of consciousness from the metaphysical peril. The revolutionaries of psychology, literature, the sexual question, etc., are revealed on closer view as being archconservatives who defend the traditional intellectualism and its expansion with a mordant rage. They walk in the worn tracks of traditional values and their intoxication with the idea of progress is only an intoxication with the speed with which they race from one station of nihility to the other. The true fighter for liberty can today only be he who leaves those tracks. Only the immeasurable longing for the charismatic depths of life can give us the strength to destroy nihilism in us.

Translated from the German
by Eugene Jolas
transition 23

Eugene Jolas   *Pan-Romanticism in the Atomic Age*

If there exists a single unifying line traversing the entire activity of *Transition,* it might be called *pan-romanticism.* Many of the writers whose original or translated work appeared in the twenty-seven numbers of the review belonged to that heritage of visionaries which was epitomized by the continuous attempt to find a synthesis through philosophical and philological transformation. *Transition* contained elements of gothic, romantic, baroque, mystic, expressionist, Dada, surrealist, and, finally, verticalist modes of thinking. In the last phase it tried to blend these traditions into a cosmic, four-dimensional consciousness.

Most of the writers were aware that the social convulsions of the epoch could be exorcised only through psychic freedom. In this striving towards a magic idealism, some of them sought the re-definition of old terms that had become exhausted and overladen with a contradictory aura. They invented new words for the expression of newly discovered areas of the psyche. In the war against all forms of totalitarian nihilism, they strove for complete liberation of the creative mind.

James Joyce pursued a pan-romantic objective by breaking through archaic literary forms. He explored the mythic unconscious of his heroes and invented a new language of many dimensions. Ernest Hemingway is a pan-romantic in that he searches for geographical and spiritual realities which will transfigure the nostalgia for love and death. André Breton is a pan-romantic in that he has continued Gérard de Nerval's and Achim von Arnim's descent into the abyss of chimeras and liberated the imagination by applying Freud's theory of free association and automatic writing. Franz Kafka was a pan-romantic in that he recognized Kierkegaard's doctrine of existential fear as a basic emotion and presented man's tortured migration towards the light as the will to escape from the prison of existence. Dylan Thomas is a pan-romantic because of his metamorphosis of Welsh folklore, his use of the myth of man's renascence, and the wealth of his metaphor.

393

Romanticism was presented in *Transition* as early as 1928, by translations of Novalis, Jean Paul, Hölderlin and others of this epoch. The "Hymns to the Night," which I translated into English in 1929, do not sing of the bitter conflict between the finite and the infinite but grow out of a certainty of redemption, a spiritualization of the sensual, in which the real and the transcendental worlds interpenetrate. Preoccupation with the nocturnal was a characteristic of the early romantics, for whom the dream and the daydream, the fairy tale and the fable constituted sources of a future literature. To them poetry and life were identical. This may have been mere *Schwärmerei,* as the philistines insist, but it was also an attempt to demolish the dualism of spirit and nature, of the I and the non-I.

After periods of *realism* and *naturalism,* the *romantic* idea came to life again in the great *symbolist* movement of Mallarmé. It ended in the dream-monologues of Maeterlinck's plays. (Maeterlinck, it should be recalled, was the first to translate Novalis's "The Disciples at Sais" into French.) There were *neo-romantic* movements in both France and Germany in the early years of the twentieth century, but not until the explosion of the first World War did a modern form of romanticism, under the aegis of Freud and the psychoanalytical school of Zurich, foster the magical operation of the inner world again. Such *expressionists* as Franz Werfel, Georg Trakl, Carl Einstein, and others, presented a frontal attack against naturalistic materialism and made possible a revolution of the soul. They liberated both form and language and reintroduced the metaphysical and the numinous into life and art.

Dada was born in Zurich in 1915, when Hugo Ball, a German poet, Tristan Tzara, a Franco-Rumanian poet, Hans Arp, an Alsatian poet and sculptor, and Richard Huelsenbeck, a German poet, along with a few others, gathered at the Café Voltaire for readings and lectures. The wild irrationalism of their utterances expressed their insurgence against a war-mad world. Looking for a suitable appellation, Ball and Huelsenbeck chose the word *dada,* which they found quite by chance in a Franco-German dictionary. They invented sonorist verses and developed an antiliterary style in which the absurd was the quintessential element. The war ended, the movement soon reached Paris. By this time Hugo Ball had withdrawn, having returned to the quietism of his Catholic faith. With the early dadaists, language was a method of conjuration, and their poems—especially in the case of Arp's verbal phantasmagoria—became fairy tales in sound.

Surrealism, under the leadership of André Breton, continued the irrationalism of Dada, but systematized its antidoctrinary elements into a rigid dogmatism. It was based on certain romantic and post-romantic predecessors (Achim von Arnim, Lautréamont, Rimbaud) and drew heavily on Freud's discoveries. In 1924, Breton gave impetus to the movement with his "Manifeste de Surrealisme." He surrounded himself with a brilliant group of young poets and painters, among whom were Benjamin Péret, Robert Desnos, André Masson, René Crevel, Antonin Artaud, Paul Eluard, Philippe Soupault. The exploration of the dream and other tenebrous aspects of romanticism found expression in automatic writing and the famous *textes surrealistes* which Breton and Soupault inaugurated with "Champs Magnétiques."

Harking back to Novalis and Jean Paul's symbolism of the flying dream, *verticalism* revolted against the nightmare quality of its predecessors and inaugurated an attempt to liberate the human personality from the possession of nihilism. It stressed the creative urge towards a liturgical renascence by reconstructing the myth of voyage, migration, flight, and particularly ascent, in all its romantic-mystic manifestations. It sought the "marvelous of the skies" in the poetry of aeronautical flight, in the conquest of the law of gravitation, and in an aspiration towards aerial perspectives. It also developed the poetry of cosmic or sidereal flight, tried to sing of the stellar spaces, and accentuated the vision of the "third eye." In the poetry of mystic flight it sought a transcendental reality. This new poetry of ascent wanted to express its vision in a language that would make possible a hymnic vocabulary.

Paris, September 1949.

selected bibliography

ABRIL, Xavier
Peruvian.
Author of: *Descubrimiente del Alba,* etc.

AGEE, James
American, b. 1909.
Author of: *Permit Me Voyage, Let Us Now Praise Famous Men,* etc.
Film critic for *The Nation.*
Contributor to *Spearhead* and other anthologies.

ALBERTI, Rafael
Spanish.
His *Selected Poems,* with English translations by Lloyd Mallan, have appeared
in America.

ALDINGTON, RICHARD
English, b. 1892.
Author of: *Death of a Hero, The Colonel's Daughter, All Men are Enemies,
Wellington* (James Tait Black Memorial Prize, 1947), etc.
Many translations from the French.

ANDREWS, Wayne
American, b. 1913.
Author of: *The Vanderbilt Legend* and *The Battle for Chicago.*

ARP, Hans
Alsatian, b. 1887, Strasbourg.
Plastic artist and poet. Intimately connected with genesis of Dada in Zurich and
with the Paris surrealist movement.
Author of: *die wolkenpumpe; Konfiguration; Des Taches dans le Vide; 1924,
1925, 1926, 1943. Gedichte; rire de coquille,* etc.

399

ARTAUD, Antonin

French (1896-1948)

Poet and dramatist, whose early work, *Le Théâtre et son Double,* greatly influenced the contemporary French theater.

Member of the original surrealist group and founder, with Roger Vitrac, of the *Théâtre Alfred Jarry* (Paris, 1927-1931).

Author of: *L'Ombilique des Limbes, Le Théâtre de la Cruauté, Héliogabale ou l'Anarchiste Couronné,* etc.

ASTURIAS, Miguel Angel

Guatemalan.

Author of a volume of Guatemalan legends, which was translated into French by Francis de Miomandre, with a preface by Paul Valéry (1932).

BALL, Hugo

German-Swiss (1886, Pirmasens—1927, Sant' Abbondio, Ticino).

Pupil of Max Reinhardt. Founded Cabaret Voltaire, Zurich, 1916—where, with with Richard Huelsenbeck, Tristan Tzara, and Hans Arp, he initiated the Dada movement.

Author of: *Flucht aus der Zeit, Byzanthinisches Christentum,* a number of plays, etc.

BASSO, Hamilton

American, b. 1904 in New Orleans.

Author of: *Days Before Lent* (Southern Author's award, 1940), as well as of volumes of short stories and essays.

On the staff of the *New Yorker.* His most recent novel, *The Green Room,* was published in 1949.

BECKETT, Samuel

Irish, b. 1906 in Dublin.

As a result of an exchange scholarship for the *Ecole Normale Supérieure,* Paris, established residence in France in 1928, and since 1945 has written exclusively in the French language.

Author of: *Murphy* (a novel), short stories and poems in both French and English, as well as a study of Proust.

BOWLES, Paul

American, b. 1910, New York.

Poet, composer, music critic.

Composed music for *Twelfth Night, Liberty Jones,* etc.

BOYLE, Kay

American, b. 1903, St. Paul, Minn.

Poet, novelist, short story writer.

Lived in Europe from 1922-1941; spent the war years in America.

O. Henry Memorial Prize, 1945.

Author of: *Wedding Day and Other Stories; Plagued with the Nightingale; Death of a Man; Primer for Combat; 1939; Year Before Last,* etc.

BRETON, André

French, b. 1896.

Former Dadaist. Chief of French surrealist group, which he founded in 1921.

Author of: *Manifeste du Surrealisme, Nadja, Le Surrealisme et la peinture, Amour Fou, Les Vases Communicants*, etc. A volume of his poems, with translations by Edouard Roditi, *Young Cherry Trees Secured Against Hares*, has been published in America.

BROWN, Bob

American.

Contributor to *The American Mercury, International Literature, The New Quarterly*, etc.

BROWN, Harry

American, b. 1917, Portland, Maine.

Author of: *The Violent; The End of a Decade, Walk in the Sun*, etc.

Served on the *New Yorker* staff, and during World War II was associate editor of *Yank*, the official U. S. Army publication.

BURNETT, Whit

American, b. 1899, Salt Lake City.

In 1929, went to Europe, as city editor of *N. Y. Herald's* European edition in Paris. Also worked in Vienna for the *New York Sun*, and there, with Martha Foley, he founded *Story* magazine, which was later transferred to America, "discovering" such authors as William Saroyan, Richard Wright, Frederic Prokosch, and others. He is the author of *Maker of Signs* and editor of a dozen anthologies, and editor of The Story Press.

CALDWELL, Erskine

American, b. 1903, Coweta County, Georgia.

Yale Review fiction award, 1933.

Author of: *This Side of Innocence, The Sure Hand of God, Tobacco Road, God's Little Acre*, etc.

CALLAGHAN, Morley

Canadian, b. 1903, Toronto.

Author of: *Strange Fugitive, Now that April's Here, More Joy in Heaven*, etc.

CANNELL, Cathleen

Canadian, b. 1892.

American fashion correspondent in Paris between the two wars.

Former wife of the French surrealist writer, Roger Vitrac.

COLEMAN, Emily Holmes

American, b. 1903.

Poet and novelist.

Lived in Paris and England between the two wars.

COLUM, Padraic

Irish, b. 1881, Dunleary, Ireland.

Co-founder of *The Irish Review*.

Author of: *Wild Earth, The Road Round Ireland, Flower Pieces,* and many other volumes of poems, stories, plays. Has also published a number of educational volumes of myths and legends.

Has lived in America for many years.

COWLEY, Malcolm

American, b. 1898, Belsano, Pa.

Poet, novelist, essayist.

In 1921, went with an American Army Field Service Fellowship to the University of Montpellier, France. Returned to America in 1923 and has been since 1929 on the staff of *The New Republic.*

Author of: *Lost Generation, Exile's Return, Dry Season,* etc.

CRANE, Hart

American (1899, Garrettsville, Ohio—1932, suicide at sea).

Author of: *The Bridge, Faustus and Helen,* etc.

See: *Hart Crane, a Biographical and Critical Study,* by Brom Weber.

CREVEL, René

French, (1900-1935).

Member of the original surrealist group.

Author of: *Detours, Mon corps et moi, La Mort difficile, Babylone, L'Esprit contre la raison, Etes-vous fous? Le Clavecin de Diderot, Les Pieds dans le plat,* etc.

CROSBY, Caresse

American, b. 1900.

Between the wars, directed, with Harry Crosby, the Black Sun Press, Paris.

Author of *Poems for Harry Crosby.*

Has edited, since 1944, *Portfolio,* published by the Black Sun Press (Washington, then Paris).

CROSBY, Harry

American (1900, Boston—1929, New York).

Author of: *Shadows of the Sun* and several volumes of verse, including *Sleeping Together, Chariot of the Sun, Mad Queen.*

Founder, with Caresse Crosby, of the Black Sun Press.

Advisory editor of *Transition,* 1928-1929.

DESNOS, Robert

French (1900-1945; died in a German concentration camp).

Member of the original surrealist group, and contributor to the Review, *La Revolution Surrealiste.*

Author of: *La Liberté ou l'Amour, Deuil pour Deuil, Corps et Biens, Fortune.*

DEVLIN, Denis

Irish, b. 1908, Greenock, Scotland. Educated Dublin, Munich, Paris, after which he entered diplomatic service of Irish Free State.

Author of: *Poems* (with Brian Coffey), *Intercessions, Lough Derg;* translator of St. John Perse's *Rains* and *Snows.*

EBERHART, Richard

American, b. 1904 in Middle West.

In 1930 he was a member of the Cambridge, England, "Experiment" group.

Author of: *Bravery of Earth, Song and Idea, Burr Oaks, Poems, New and Selected,* etc.

ELUARD, Paul

French, b. 1895 at Saint-Denis (Seine).

Dadaist, then member of the original surrealist group. During the German occupation his poem *Liberté* received wide clandestine circulation, and he was generally considered to be one of the most important resistance writers.

Eluard has been an official member of the French Communist party since 1942.

Author of: *Defense da Savoir, Les Yeux Fertiles, Capitale de la Douleur, Donner à voir,* etc.

First presented in English by *Transition* (1927).

A volume of selections from his work, in English translation, has been published by New Directions. His *Inner Life of Pablo Picasso* has also appeared in America.

EMPSON, William

English, b. 1906.

Was the first editor of *Experiment* (Cambridge, England, 1928-29). Professor at Tokio, then at Pekin. Is now Director of Far-East broadcasts at the B.B.C.

Author of: *Seven Types of Ambiguity, Poems,* etc.

His *Collected Poems* was recently published in America.

ESSENIN, Serge

Russian (1895-1925). Born in the province of Kasmin. Died by his own hand.

"I am the son of a peasant . . . I began to write verses at an early age . . . At eighteen I left for Petrograd, where I was very hospitably received . . . I was not a member of the Communist Party, because I am much more to the 'left' than they . . ." (Autobiography, 1921).

FARGUE, Léon-Paul

French (1876-1947) Paris.

Fargue belonged to no school, but was recognized as one of the most authentic and original poets of his time. In 1927 a special number of *Les Feuilles Libres* was devoted to an appreciation of his work and personality in French letters, with tributes from Paul Claudel, James Joyce, Valéry Larbaud, Archibald MacLeish, Paul Valéry, etc.

Author of: *Tancrède, Pour la Musique, Banalité, Epaisseur, Sous la Lampe, Déjeuner de Soleil,* etc.

FEARING, Kenneth

American, b. 1902, Oak Park, Ill.

Moved to New York in 1924.

Twice recipient of Guggenheim Fellowship award.

Author of: *Collected Poems, The Dagger in the Mind, Clark Gifford's Body,* etc.

FITTS, Dudley

American, b. 1903, Boston.

Author of: *Poems, 1929-1936*

Editor of an Anthology of Contemporary Latin-American Poetry, and translator of *More Poems from the Palatine Anthology*.

FORD, Charles Henri

American.

Founder, with Parker Tyler, of *Blues* (1929) and *View* (1940-1946).

Author of: *The Garden of Disorder, The Overturned Lake, Poems for Painters,*
etc.

GEDDES, Virgil

American, b. 1897 on a Nebraska farm.

Worked as journalist in Boston, Chicago, Paris.

First play, *The Frog,* produced in Boston, 1927.

First play to be produced in New York was *The Earth Between* (1929).

In 1932, founded Brookfield Players, Brookfield, Conn.

Author of numerous plays and volumes of criticism.

GIDE, André

French, b. 1869, Paris.

Poet, novelist, essayist, critic, dramatist, André Gide has dominated several generations of French writing. Among his most famous works are: *La Porte
Etroite, L'Immoraliste, Si le Grain ne Meurt, Les Faux-Monnayeurs, Nourritures Terrestres, Les Caves du Vatican,* etc.

Co-founder of the pre-1940 *Nouvelle Revue Française.*

Nobel prize for Literature, 1947.

GILBERT, Stuart

English.

After taking an Honours degree in Classics (at Oxford) Stuart Gilbert held an
official post in Burma. On retirement he settled in Paris, where he wrote a
commentary on *Ulysses,* in the French translation of which he collaborated.
He has worked for the films, published articles on literary subjects and some
stories, and translated into English works by many eminent French authors:
André Malraux, Martin du Gard, Saint-Exupéry, and Camus among others.

GOLL, Claire and Ivan

French (Lorraine), b. at Metz.

The Golls have written poetry and novels in both German and French. Their
Love Poems, with illustrations by Marc Chagall, were published in New
York.

Claire Goll is author of *A Pearl.*

During the War, Ivan Goll edited, in New York, the bi-lingual Franco-Amer-
ican review, *Hemispheres.* He is author of *Le Mythe de la Roche Percée*
(with illustrations by Yves Tanguy), and his *Chansons Malaises,* translated
by Clark Mills, were issued by the Swallow Pamphlets.

GRAVES, Robert

English, b. 1895.

1926-27, Professor of English at Cairo University. Subsequently lived in Majorca, where, with Laura Riding, he conducted the Seizin Press.

Author of: *Poems 1914-1926; Lawrence and the Arabs; Good-bye to All That; I, Claudius* (Hawthornden and James Tait Black Memorial prizes, 1934); *Count Belisarius* (Femina Vie Heureuse prize, 1939), *The White Goddess,* etc., etc.

GREGORY, Horace

American, b. 1898, Milwaukee.

Editor of *New Letters in America.*

Professor of English at Sarah Lawrence College, Bronxville.

Author of: *Chelsea Rooming House, Chorus for Survival, Poems 1930-1940,* etc.

HEMINGWAY, Ernest

American, b. 1898, Oak Park, Ill.

1921: settled in Paris and began to write novels and short stories. Leader of what Gertrude Stein once called "the lost generation" of American writers.

Went to Spain during the Civil War as correspondent for North American Newspaper Alliance.

Author of: *The Sun Also Rises, Farewell to Arms, For Whom the Bell Tolls,* etc., etc.

HÖLDERLIN, Friedrich

German, b. 1770 in Lauffen-am-Neckar; d. 1843.

Was for a time tutor in a French family in Bordeaux, whence he returned to Germany in 1803. He then began to show signs of mental derangement, and died insane.

Author (during his first 30 years) of *Hyperion, Empedocles,* etc. His later poems were signed "Scardanelli." They were not published until after World War I, when an edition was brought out in Germany, edited by Rudolf von Delius.

HUELSENBECK, Richard

American of German origin.

Connected with the Dada movement at the time of its inception in Zurich during World War I, he introduced it thereafter to Berlin. Subsequently traveled widely in the Orient and then settled in the United States.

JARRELL, Randall

American.

One-time literary editor of *The Nation;* at present Associate Professor of English at the Women's College, Greenville, N. Carolina.

Recipient of the *Southern Review* poetry award.

Author of: *Blood for a Stranger, Little Friend, Little Friend,* etc.

Contributor to: *Partisan Review, View, The Kenyon Review, Spearhead* anthology, etc.

JEAN PAUL (Friedrich Richter)

German, b. 1763 in Bavaria; d. 1825.

Famous humorist. His early satirical works were received with little favor, and it was not until the publication of *Die Unsichtbare Loge* (a romance published in 1793) that his work attracted attention.

Author of: *Titan, Die Flegeljahre,* etc., etc.

His *Quintus Fixlein* and *Schmelzles Reise* were translated into English by Carlyle, who also devoted two essays to Richter's works.

JOLAS, Eugene

American, b. 1894 at Union Hill, N.J., of immigrant parents who took him back to their native Lorraine when he was two years old. At sixteen he returned to America, where he remained over an unbroken period of ten years. In 1921 he returned to Europe, and since this date has divided his time between the United States and France.

His international educational background gave rise quite naturally to an organic use of French, German, and English.

Served with the American forces in both wars.

Author of: *Ink, Cinema, Mots-Deluge, I have seen Monsters and Angels,* etc.

JOSEPHSON, Matthew

American, b. 1899, Brooklyn, N.Y.

Came to Paris soon after World War I, and while there acted as co-editor of *Secession.* Was associate editor of *Broom* (1922-24) and contributing editor of *Transition* (1928-29). Returned to New York around 1930.

Author of: *Zola and His Time, Jean-Jacques Rousseau, Stendhal, Victor Hugo,* etc., etc., and of numerous biographical feature articles.

JOYCE, James

Irish, b. 1882, Dublin.

In 1902 he left for Paris, from where he went to Trieste. At the outbreak of the war in 1914 he moved to Zurich; and in 1921 settled definitely in Paris.

He returned to Zurich in December, 1940, and died there after an operation, on January 13, 1941.

See: *James Joyce,* by Herbert Gorman; *James Joyce,* by Harry Levin; *James Joyce and the making of 'Ulysses,'* by Frank Budgen; *James Joyce: A Decade of Criticism* selected by Seon Givens.

Author of: *Dubliners, A Portrait of the Artist as a Young Man, Chamber Music* (poems), *Exiles* (a play), *Ulysses, Finnegans Wake.*

KAFKA, Franz

Czech, b. 1883, Prague; d. 1924, Klosterneuburg.

His work was almost unknown even in Germany during his lifetime, most of it being published posthumously.

Among the writings of Kafka now available in English are: *The Castle, The Great Wall of China, Parables, Metamorphosis.*

See the Biography of Kafka by his friend and literary executor, Dr. Max Brod; also *The Kafka Problem,* an anthology of criticism edited by Angel Flores.

KREYMBORG, Alfred

American, b. 1883, New York.

Was the first to enter a "little magazine" in the battle for a new literature, and his magazine *Glebe* was one of the first periodicals to sponsor the experimental writings of the *imagists*.

Edited: *Glebe* (1913), *Others, Broom.*

Author of: *Mushrooms, There's a Moon Tonight, Troubadour, an autobiography,* etc., etc.

LARBAUD, Valéry

French, b. 1881, Vichy.

An accomplished linguist, whose work includes numerous essays written directly in English and Spanish. He also translated many books into French. It was largely due to his efforts that James Joyce became known in France, and he personally assisted with the French translation of *Ulysses.*

As a result of a paralytic stroke, Larbaud, who lives in Vichy, has published nothing since well before the last war.

Author of: *Fermina Marquez, Enfantines, A. O. Barnabooth, Amants, heureux amants, Les Poesies d'A. O. Barnabooth, Jaune, Bleu, Blanc,* etc.

LASKER-SCHUELER, Else

German, b. around 1870 in Elberfeld.

Emigrated to Palestine.

Author of: *Das Peter-Hille-Buch, Meine Wunder* (poems), *Hebraische Balladen, Gesammelte Gedichte,* etc.

LOVING, Pierre

American, b. 1893.

Washington correspondent of the United Press.

During the between-war period, worked in Paris as journalist and critic.

Author of: *The Stick-up* (play), *Revolt in German Drama, Short Poems of Friedrich Hölderlin,* and translations from the work of Schnitzler, etc.

LYLE, Marius

Irish.

Author of *The Virgin.*

McCAIG, Norman

Scottish, b. 1910.

One of the poets of the "Scottish Renaissance" 1920-1945.

Contributor to: *Scottish Art and Letters.*

MacLEISH, Archibald

American, b. 1892, Glencoe, Ill.

Long residence in Europe.

Occupied position as Librarian of Congress; Assistant Secretary of State; also Director of OFF, then OWI, during World War II.

Author of: *Tower of Ivory, Conquistador* (Pulitzer Prize), *Selected Poems, The Fall of the City,* etc.

Translated *Exil,* by St. John Perse.

MACLEOD, Norman

American.

Was one of the founders, in 1929, of *The Morada*, which followed immediately upon his first venture of this type: a magazine entitled *jackass*, which Macleod declared he founded "to fill a gaping need and a gaping hiatus in the existing periodicals. . . ."

In 1934 he founded the *Briarcliff Quarterly*, which continues to present a representative choice of new writing.

MICHAUX, Henry

French, b. 1899 in Belgium.

Painter and poet.

Has lived chiefly in France, but has traveled widely in South America and the Orient.

Author of: *Qui je fus, Au pays de la magie, Exorcismes, Peinture*, etc.

His *Un Barbare en Asie* has been translated into English by Sylvia Beach.

MILLER, Henry

American, b. 1891, New York.

In 1930, went to Paris, where he lived for nine years. Now lives at Big Sur, California.

Author of: *Tropic of Cancer, Tropic of Capricorn, The Cosmological Eye, The Air-conditioned Nightmare, Remember to Remember*, etc.

In 1946, when charges of distributing pornographic literature were brought against his French publisher by a self-appointed Vigilance Committee, a group including André Gide, Jean-Paul Sartre, and François Mauriac was formed to defend him.

MONTGOMERY, Niall

Irish, b. 1915, Dublin.

Lives in Dublin.

Describes himself as "a commercial architect, whose work largely involves alteration of ancient licensed fabrics (pubs)," and whose "transitional ambition to design and supervise erection of Tower of Babel has been abandoned since 1941, due to shortage of essential materials."

NEAGOE, Peter

American, b. in Rumania.

Emigrated to America, where he became an American citizen. Between the wars he lived in France. In 1931 was co-editor, with Samuel Putnam, of *The New Review*, "an international notebook for the arts."

In 1932 Neagoe edited an anthology entitled *Americans Abroad*.

NIN, Anais

American, born in Paris. Daughter of Spanish composer, Joachim Nin.

Author of: *The House of Incest, Winter of Artifice, Ladders of Fire, Children of the Albatross*, etc.

Contributor to *Spearhead* and other anthologies.

NOVALIS (Friedrich Leopold, Freiherr von Hardenberg)

German (1772-1801).

Poet and novelist.

Leading member of the older Romantic school. Principal among his works, which are for the most part fragments, is the unfinished romance, *Heinrich von Ofterdingen*.

(See Carlyle's fine essay on Novalis, 1829.)

His works were first issued in two volumes, in 1802, by his friends, Ludwig Tieck and Friedrich Schlegel.

PAUL, Elliot

American, b. 1891, Malden, Mass.

Co-editor of *Transition*, 1927-28.

Novelist, one-time journalist, and Hollywood scenarist.

During the between-war period he spent some time in France and Majorca.

Author of: *Impromptu, Life and Death of a Spanish Town, The Last Time I Saw Paris*, etc.

PERET, Benjamin

French, b. 1899 at Rezé, near Nantes.

After having been a member of the Dadaist group, he was one of the original members of the surrealist group, and founded *La Revue Surrealiste*.

Took part in the Spanish Civil War.

In 1942 he went to Mexico, and only returned to France in 1948.

His *Déshonneur des Poètes*, which was directed against the more "official" resistance poets, was a source of acrid controversy.

Since his return to France he has once more been active, with André Breton, in the surrealist group.

Author of: *La Brebis Galante, Le Grand Jeu, Je ne mange pas de ce pain-la, Dernier Malheur, Derniere Chance, Main forte, Feu Centrale*.

PERSE, St. John (Alexis Léger)

French, b. 1889 on an island near Guadeloupe.

Diplomat by profession. Before World War II was French Permanent Secretary for Foreign Affairs. Now lives in Washington.

Fellow of the Library of Congress.

Author of: *Eloges, Anabase* (translated into English by T. S. Eliot), *Amitié du Prince, Exil, Pluies, Vents*, etc.

PORTER, Katherine Anne

American, b. 1894, Indian Creek, Texas. Now lives in California, after having lived much abroad and in Mexico.

Has been the recipient of important literary prizes.

Author of: *Flowering Judas, Pale Horse, Pale Rider*, etc.

READ, Herbert

English, b. 1893 in Yorkshire.

1931-33, Professor of Fine Arts at Edinburgh University.

1934-39, Editor of the *Burlington Magazine*.

Author of: *Poems, 1914-1934, English Stained Glass, Wordsworth, Annals of Innocence and Experience* (autobiography), *The Grass Roots of Art, A Coat of Many Colours* (autobiography), etc.

REVERDY, Pierre

French, b. 1889, at Narbonne.

In 1910 came to live in Paris, where he founded the review *Sic*. At that time he was associated with the group that included the painters Picasso and Gris, the poet Max Jacob, etc. For the last twenty years he has been living at Solesmes, entirely withdrawn from the literary life of Paris.

Author of: *Les Epaves du Ciel, Le Voleur de Talan, La Peau de l'Homme, Plupart du Temps, Flaque de Verre, Gant de Crin, Poemes en Prose,* etc.

REYES, Alfonso

Mexican.

Diplomatic service. Has been Mexican Ambassador to Buenos Aires, etc. He is president of the Colegio de Mexico, and has been mentioned as a candidate for the Nobel Prize.

RHYS, Keidrych

Welsh, b. 1907.

Writes both in Welsh and English.

In 1937, founded *Wales,* a quarterly review, with, in 1939, Dylan Thomas as co-editor.

Contributor to: *The Welsh Review, Poetry Folios, Poetry-Scotland,* etc.

RIBEMONT-DESSAIGNES, Georges

French, b. 1884. Belonged first to Dada, then to early surrealist group. Founder and editor of *Bifur* in Paris between the wars.

Author of: *Ugolin, Confiteor, Le Bar du Lendemain, L'Autruche aux Yeux Clos, Ariane, Les Frontieres Humaines,* etc.

RIDING, Laura

American, b. 1901, New York.

Between 1925 and 1939 lived in Europe (England, Majorca, France); then returned to the United States and now lives at New Hope, Pa.

Edited *Epilogue* (1935-1938).

Author of: *A Survey of Modernist Poetry* (with Robert Graves), *Everybody's Letters, Progress of Stories, Collected Poems,* etc.

RODITI, Eduouard

American, b. 1910, in Paris. Educated at Oxford University.

Contributor to: *The Criterion, The Adelphi, Poetry, Partisan Review,* etc.

Has been editor, with Alain Bousquet and Alexander Koval, of the German publication, *Das Lot,* which, published in Berlin, sets itself the same task as the New Writings volumes in England and the New Directions volumes in America.

Author of: *Oscar Wilde.*

ROUSSEL, Raymond
French (1877-1928).
The ironic, imaginative farces of Roussel were sympathetically regarded and commented upon by the early surrealists.
Author of: *La Doublure, Impression d'Afrique, Locus Solus,* etc.

SAGE, Robert
American.
Came to Paris after the first World War, to work as a journalist, and has remained in Paris ever since. One-time Associate Editor of *Transition.*
Official translator of *Verve* magazine and of numerous other works from the French.

SAROYAN, William
American, b. 1908, Fresno, California, of Armenian parents. Now lives in San Francisco.
1942, directed Saroyan Theater, New York.
Author of: *The Daring Young Man on the Flying Trapeze, Love Here is My Hat, The Time of Your Life* (play awarded Drama Critics' Circle Prize and [rejected] Pulitzer Prize), *Great American Goof* (ballet), etc.

SCHICKELE, René
Alsatian, b. 1883 in Oberehnheim, Alsace; d. 1940, near Nice.
Although Schickele wrote for the most part in German, he considered himself definitely an Alsatian and remained in close contact with French intellectual activity.
Author of: *Hans im Schnakenloch, Das Erbe am Rhein,* etc.

SCHWITTERS, Kurt
German, b. 1887, Hanover; d. 1947, England.
Painter, sculptor, poet. Early German Dadaist. Founded *Merz* (1919) and was a contributor to *Sturm.*
After 1935, lived chiefly in Norway, whence he fled to London on an English ship to escape the Gestapo.
Wrote in English as well as in German.
Author of: *Das Veilchen, Kathedrale, Anna Blume, Auguste Bolte,* etc.

SOUPAULT, Philippe
French, b. 1897 at Chaville, Seine-et-Oise.
Poet, novelist, journalist.
Took an active part in the Dadaist and then in the Surrealist movement.
Author of: *Les Champs Magnétiques* (with André Breton), *Georgia, Le Bar de l'Amour, Le Nègre, L'Histoire d'un Blanc, Le Grand Homme, Journal d'un Revenant, Les Dernières Nuits de Paris* (translated by William Carlos Williams as *Last Nights of Paris*).

STEIN, Gertrude
American, b. 1874, Allegheny, Pa.; d. 1946, France.
In 1903, came to live in Paris and remained there, except for occasional visits to the United States. Closely associated with the painters of the Paris School

of her epoch, Miss Stein formed a notable collection of modern paintings, and she exerted a strong influence on three generations of both writers and painters, particularly Americans.

Author of: *Making of Americans, Three Lives, Lucy Church Amiably, How to Write, Autobiography of Alice B. Toklas, Picasso,* etc., etc.

SVEVO, Italo (Ettore Schmitz)

Italian, b. 1861, Trieste; d. 1928, Trieste.

Did not begin to write till past 40.

Works published in English: *The Confessions of Zeno, As a Man Grows Older,* etc.

Correspondence between Svevo and James Joyce (who at one time gave him English lessons) was published in *Inventario* (Florence), No. 5.

SWEENEY, James Johnson

American, b. 1900, Brooklyn.

Poet and art critic.

Assistant Editor of *Transition* (1935-1938); later attached to Museum of Modern Art, New York; now assistant editor of *Partisan Review.*

Author of: *Plastic Redirection in 20th Century Painting,* and of books on Miro, Calder, Chagall, Moore, etc.

SWEENEY, John L.

American, b. 1902, Brooklyn.

Author of: *Directions in Modern Poetry* (with Elizabeth Drew), etc.

TATE, Allen

American, b. 1899 in Kentucky.

Poet and essayist.

Resident Fellow, Princeton, 1939-42. Chair of Poetry, Library of Congress, 1943-47. Editor *Sewanee Review,* 1944-46.

Served in advisory capacity on *Hound and Horn, Kenyon Review.*

Editor of: *A Southern Vanguard,* anthology.

Author of: *Mr. Pope and other Poems, Reactionary Essays, Language of Poetry, The Winter Sea, Poems 1922-1947,* etc.

THOMAS, Dylan

Welsh, b. 1914 in Carmarthenshire.

At present connected with the B.B.C.

1938, won Oscar Blumenthal Prize, offered by *Poetry* (Chicago).

Author of: *Eighteen Poems, The World I Breathe, New Poems, Portrait of the Artist as a Young Dog,* etc.

TREVELYAN, Julian Otto

English, b. 1909.

Painter and critic.

Belonged to the Cambridge, England, "Experiment" group.

TYLER, Parker

American, b. 1907, New Orleans.

Associate editor of *Blues* (1929), and *View* (1940-1946).

Author of: *Yesterday's Children, The Granite Butterfly, The Hollywood Hallucination, Magic and Myth of the Movies, Chaplin: Last of the Clowns,* etc.

TZARA, Tristan

Rumanian, b. 1896.

Writes in French.

Lived in Zurich, where he was one of the initiators of the Dada movement. After World War I, settled in Paris, where he was for some time associated with the Surrealists. Since World War II, Tzara has become officially associated with the French Communist party, and recently published a Marxist attack on surrealism, entitled: *Le Surréalisme et l'Après-Guerre.*

Author of: *Le Coeur à Gaz, Sept Manifestes Dada, Mouchoir de Nuages, Indicateur des Chemins de Coeur, L'Homme Approximatif, Grains et Issues, Une Route seul soleil, vingt-cinq-et-un poemes* (illustrated by Hans Arp, published by *Fontaine*), etc.